Hybrid Warfare
*Fighting Complex Opponents from
to the Present*

Hybrid warfare has been an integral part of the historical landscape since the ancient world, but only recently have analysts – incorrectly – categorized these conflicts as unique. Great powers throughout history have confronted opponents who used a combination of regular and irregular forces to negate the advantage of the great powers' superior conventional military strength. As this study shows, hybrid wars are labor-intensive and long-term affairs; they are difficult struggles that defy the domestic logic of opinion polls and election cycles. Hybrid wars are also the most likely conflicts of the twenty-first century; competitors may use hybrid forces to wear down America's military capabilities in extended campaigns of exhaustion. Nine historical examples of hybrid warfare, from ancient Rome to the modern world, provide readers with context by clarifying the various aspects of these conflicts and examining how great powers have dealt with them in the past.

Williamson Murray is Professor Emeritus of History at The Ohio State University. At present, he is a defense consultant and commentator on historical and military subjects in Washington, DC. He is the author of *War, Strategy, and Military Effectiveness* and *Military Adaptation in War* (both Cambridge, 2011). He is co-editor of numerous books of military and international history, including *The Shaping of Grand Strategy* (with Richard Hart Sinnreich and James Lacey, Cambridge, 2011), *The Making of Peace* (with James Lacey, Cambridge, 2008), *The Past as Prologue* (with Richard Hart Sinnreich, Cambridge, 2006), *The Dynamics of Military Revolution, 1300–2050* (with MacGregor Knox, Cambridge, 2001), *Military Innovation in the Interwar Period* (with Allan R. Millett, Cambridge, 1996), and *The Making of Strategy* (with Alvin Bernstein and MacGregor Knox, Cambridge, 1994).

Peter R. Mansoor is the General Raymond E. Mason, Jr., Chair of Military History at The Ohio State University. He assumed this position in 2008 after a 26-year career in the United States Army that culminated in his service in Iraq as the executive officer to General David Petraeus, the commanding general of Multi-National Force – Iraq. He is the author of *The GI Offensive in Europe: The Triumph of American Infantry Divisions, 1941–1945*, which was awarded the Society for Military History's distinguished book award and the Army Historical Society's distinguished book award in 2000. He also wrote a memoir titled *Baghdad at Sunrise: A Brigade Commander's War in Iraq* (2008), which was awarded the Ohioana Library Association's distinguished book award.

Hybrid Warfare

Fighting Complex Opponents from the Ancient World to the Present

Edited by

WILLIAMSON MURRAY
Professor Emeritus
The Ohio State University

PETER R. MANSOOR
The Ohio State University

CAMBRIDGE
UNIVERSITY PRESS

CAMBRIDGE UNIVERSITY PRESS
Cambridge, New York, Melbourne, Madrid, Cape Town,
Singapore, São Paulo, Delhi, Mexico City

Cambridge University Press
32 Avenue of the Americas, New York, NY 10013-2473, USA

www.cambridge.org
Information on this title: www.cambridge.org/9781107643338

© Cambridge University Press 2012

This publication is in copyright. Subject to statutory exception
and to the provisions of relevant collective licensing agreements,
no reproduction of any part may take place without the written
permission of Cambridge University Press.

First published 2012

A catalog record for this publication is available from the British Library.

Library of Congress Cataloging in Publication Data

Murray, Williamson.
Hybrid warfare : fighting complex opponents from the ancient world to the present /
Williamson Murray, Peter R. Mansoor.
    p. cm.
Includes index.
ISBN 978-1-107-02608-7 (hardback)
1. Asymmetric warfare. 2. Asymmetric warfare – History. 3. Irregular warfare –
History. 4. Military history, Modern. I. Mansoor, Peter R., 1960– II. Title.
U163.M87   2012
355.4′2–dc23   2012002139

ISBN 978-1-107-02608-7 Hardback
ISBN 978-1-107-64333-8 Paperback

Cambridge University Press has no responsibility for the persistence or accuracy of URLs
for external or third-party Internet Web sites referred to in this publication and does not
guarantee that any content on such Web sites is, or will remain, accurate or appropriate.

Contents

Figures		*page* vii
Contributors		ix
Acknowledgment		xi
1	Introduction: Hybrid Warfare in History *Peter R. Mansoor*	1
2	Conquering Germania: A Province Too Far *James Lacey*	18
3	Keeping the Irish Down and the Spanish Out: English Strategies of Submission in Ireland, 1594–1603 *Wayne E. Lee*	45
4	The American Revolution: Hybrid War in America's Past *Williamson Murray*	72
5	That Accursed Spanish War: The Peninsular War, 1807–1814 *Richard Hart Sinnreich*	104
6	The Union's Counterguerrilla War, 1861–1865 *Daniel E. Sutherland*	151
7	Fighting "this nation of liars to the very end": The German Army in the Franco-Prussian War, 1870–1871 *Marcus Jones*	171
8	Small Wars and Great Games: The British Empire and Hybrid Warfare, 1700–1970 *John Ferris*	199

9 An Unexpected Encounter with Hybrid Warfare:
    The Japanese Experience in North China, 1937–1945   225
    Noboru Yamaguchi
10 Hybrid War in Vietnam   254
    Karl Lowe
11 Conclusion: What the Past Suggests   289
    Williamson Murray

Index   309

Figures

1	Germania, AD 9–16.	*page* 25
2	Ireland, 1594–1603.	58
3	American Revolution, 1775–1783.	83
4	Peninsular War, 1807–1814.	108
5	American Civil War, 1861–1865.	153
6	Franco-Prussian War, 1870–1871.	181
7	Boer War, 1899–1902.	215
8	Second Sino-Japanese War, 1937–1945.	244
9	Vietnam War, 1965–1973.	262

Contributors

John Ferris, *University of Calgary*

Marcus Jones, *United States Naval Academy*

James Lacey, *Marine Corps University*

Wayne E. Lee, *University of North Carolina*

Karl Lowe, *Independent Scholar (Colonel, U.S. Army, Ret.)*

Peter R. Mansoor, *The Ohio State University*

Williamson Murray, Professor Emeritus, *The Ohio State University*

Richard Hart Sinnreich, *Independent Scholar*

Daniel E. Sutherland, *University of Arkansas*

Noboru Yamaguchi, *National Defense Academy of Japan (Lieutenant General, Japanese Ground Self-Defense Force, Ret.)*

Acknowledgment

The editors wish to acknowledge the generous assistance of the Mershon Center for International Security Studies at The Ohio State University, whose grant made possible the conference in May 2010 in Columbus, Ohio, from which these essays originated.

I

Introduction

Hybrid Warfare in History

Peter R. Mansoor

In his magisterial work *On War*, Prussian military philosopher Carl von Clausewitz writes, "War is more than a true chameleon that slightly adapts its characteristics to the given case."[1] He goes on to state that "war is a remarkable trinity" composed of violence and hatred, chance and probability, and political considerations – elements that play out through the interaction of people, military forces, and governments. These factors have been a part of war since the dawn of recorded history. Nevertheless, as war in the twenty-first century morphs into seemingly unfamiliar forms that combine regular and irregular forces on the same battlefields, some defense analysts have posited the emergence of a new type of war – hybrid war.

That buzz word has become fashionable among both civilian and military leaders in the Pentagon and elsewhere. However, as Clausewitz stated nearly two centuries ago, although war changes its characteristics in various circumstances, in whatever way it manifests itself, war is still war. War in the twenty-first century has been and will remain a complex phenomenon, but its essence has not and will not change. Through a careful examination of history, this study illustrates that although there is little new in hybrid war as a concept, it is a useful means of thinking about war's past, present, and future.

The lines of warfare in the twenty-first century are becoming increasingly blurred. America's security challenges include state-on-state wars, counterinsurgency conflicts, terrorism, and combinations thereof.

---

[1] Carl von Clausewitz, *On War*, ed. and trans. Michael Howard and Peter Paret (Princeton, 1976), p. 89; originally published as *Vom Kriege*, 1832.

U.S. conventional military superiority, at least for the immediate future, will force potential opponents to develop alternate means to achieve their goals and oppose American power. Increasingly, those means will include conventional as well as irregular – or hybrid – forces working in tandem.[2] Potential enemies will blend various approaches to war to fit them within their strategic cultures, historical legacies, geographic realities, and economic means. Against such enemies, technological superiority is useful but insufficient. As the wars in Iraq and Afghanistan have underlined, turning battlefield victories into long-term strategic gains also requires an understanding of history and culture, in other words "the other," as well as adequate numbers of troops with the requisite military skills and cultural savvy to secure populations and deal with the root causes of societal violence.

Hybrid warfare will be a critical challenge to the United States and its allies in the twenty-first century, a challenge openly recognized by the U.S. defense establishment.[3] To counter hybrid opponents, however, the United States and its allies must first understand the characteristics of hybrid warfare. Regrettably, the intellectual apparatus of the American military, namely the staff and war colleges, has on the whole failed to understand the future by reference not only to the distant past but to the immediate past as well. We have compiled this collection of essays, the result of a conference at the Mershon Center for International Security Studies at The Ohio State University in May 2010, because we believe that history has a great deal to say about hybrid warfare as well as other issues. The sooner not only historians but also the larger defense intellectual community examine past examples of hybrid warfare as well as present ones, the better will be the prospects for the future utilization of U.S. military power.

This collection of essays represents a first step toward examining the nature of hybrid conflicts more closely. We have defined hybrid warfare as conflict involving a combination of conventional military forces and irregulars (guerrillas, insurgents, and terrorists), which could include both state and nonstate actors, aimed at achieving a common political purpose. Irregular forces need not be centrally directed, although in many cases

---

[2] Frank G. Hoffman, "Hybrid Warfare and Challenges," *Joint Forces Quarterly* 52, First Quarter 2009, pp. 34–39; Max Boot, *War Made New: Technology, Warfare, and the Course of History 1500 to Today* (New York, 2006), pp. 472–473.

[3] "'Hybrid War' to Pull US Military in Two Directions, Flournoy Says," *Defence Talk*, May 6, 2009, accessed at http://www.defencetalk.com/hybrid-war-to-pull-us-military-18521/.

they form part of a coherent strategy used to oppose an invader or occupation force.[4] Hybrid warfare also plays out at all levels of war, from the tactical, to the operational, to the strategic. In particular, military organizations must not ignore the political framework and its narrative within which all wars occur. At the strategic level, nations might choose to support insurgent movements with conventional forces to weaken an adversary, much as the French did when they allied with the Americans in 1778 to weaken the British. At the operational level, a commander might use guerrilla forces to harass enemy lines of communication or prevent the enemy from massing forces, as General Nathanael Greene did in the Southern campaign in 1780–1781 in the American Revolution. Finally, regular and irregular forces might occasionally join tactically, as they did at the Battle of Cowpens in 1781.

"Hybrid threats," writes Frank Hoffman, "blend the lethality of state conflict with the fanatical and protracted fervor of irregular warfare."[5] Hybrid war does not change the nature of war; it merely changes the way forces engage in its conduct. However it is waged, war is war. Much as the term "combined arms" describes the tactical combination of infantry, armor, artillery, engineers, and other branches of service in battle, the term "hybrid warfare" is a useful construct to analyze conflicts involving regular and irregular forces engaged in both symmetric and asymmetric combat. Although there may be some slight differences in how our authors define the term "hybrid warfare," we have allowed them to pursue these scholarly variations because such an approach further underlines the complexity of the subject.

Despite its prominence as the latest buzz word in Washington, hybrid warfare is not new. Its historical pedigree goes back at least as far as the Peloponnesian War in the fifth century BC. During the conflict between Athens and Sparta, the Spartans recognized they needed to keep significant forces in Laconia and Messenia to prevent an uprising by the Helots, upon whose backs their agricultural and military systems rested. Athenian stratagems such as the move to build an expeditionary base at Pylos rested in part on the aim of creating the conditions for a Helot

---

[4] Some historians and analysts create a distinction between "hybrid" and "compound wars," stating that the latter involve regular and irregular forces fighting under unified strategic direction, whereas the former is a special case in which regular and irregular capabilities are fused into a single force. See Frank G. Hoffman, "Hybrid vs. Compound War," *Armed Forces Journal*, October 2009. For this study, we make no such distinction between hybrid and compound war.
[5] Hoffman, "Hybrid Threats," p. 5.

uprising, which would then add an irregular dimension to the conventional conflict. After Athenian forces fortified Pylos on the southwest coast of the Peloponnese in 425 BC, they garrisoned the outpost with Messenians of Naupactus, whose ancestors the Spartans had expelled from the area after the great Helot uprising of 464 BC. The Messenians began a series of incursions into Laconia, aided by their ability to speak the local dialect. Helots soon began to desert to Pylos, thereby creating a national emergency in Sparta. This insurgency represented a form of war for which the exceptional Spartan phalanxes were ill suited. The Athenian historian Thucydides records, "The Spartans, hitherto without experience of incursions or a warfare of the kind, finding the Helots deserting, and fearing the march of revolution in their country, began to be seriously uneasy, and in spite of their unwillingness to betray this to the Athenians began to send envoys to Athens, and tried to recover Pylos and the prisoners."[6] The mere threat of hybrid war had brought the Spartans to terms.[7]

As examples throughout history suggest, hybrid opponents form a difficult and often powerful combination. Simply put, the existence of conventional forces requires a military force to mass against them, but doing so makes logistical lifelines and contested areas vulnerable to insurgents, guerrillas, and other irregular forces. The German Army on the Eastern Front during World War II suffered continual disruptions to its lines of communication as a result of the activity of tens of thousands of Soviet partisans and other irregulars, many remnants of conventional forces bypassed during the opening phases of Operation Barbarossa. The brutality of German *Einsatzgruppen*, SS police units, and other security forces could not suppress the partisans, despite the mass murder of hundreds of thousands of Soviet citizens in attempts to do so. Moreover, because of the strength of Soviet conventional forces, the Wehrmacht could not afford to release units from the front to deal with the threat to its rear.[8]

Prime Minister Winston Churchill also recognized the power of using irregular forces to combat the Wehrmacht in conjunction with regular military operations. In July 1940, he charged a new organization, the

---

[6] *The Landmark Thucydides*, ed. Robert B. Strassler (New York, 1996), pp. 245–246.
[7] Regrettably, the Athenian assembly refused the Spartan peace overture and the war continued. Thebes eventually ended Spartan hegemony over Greece after the Battle of Leuctra (371 BC) by reestablishing the independence of Messenia, thereby freeing the Helots and devastating the Spartan economy.
[8] Leonid Grenkevich, *The Soviet Partisan Movement, 1941–1944: A Critical Historiographical Analysis* (London, 1999).

Special Operations Executive (SOE), with the mission to "set Europe ablaze."⁹ For the next several years, British agents assisted local resistance movements, British aircraft delivered arms and ammunition to partisan forces, and SOE operatives engaged in sabotage of Nazi facilities throughout Western Europe and the Balkans. In the end, Britain could not have won the war by using only a combination of strategic bombing, naval blockade, and the encouragement of revolts in Europe. Nonetheless, resistance movements provided a boost to Allied forces when they returned to Europe after D-Day, and they proved especially useful in delaying German reinforcements headed to the Normandy battlefront.¹⁰

Hybrid warfare is not just a Western phenomenon, as the Second Sino-Japanese War from 1937 to 1945 shows. Mao Tse Tung and his generals became experts on mixing regular and irregular forces to attack the enemy in both a symmetric and asymmetric manner. Indeed, Mao clearly viewed guerrilla and conventional forces as existing on the same continuum. After the Japanese surrender, his Communist forces used the techniques of hybrid warfare against their Nationalist enemies. Regular Communist divisions were very good, as they demonstrated in battle not just against the Nationalist forces of Chiang Kai-shek in China but also against U.S. forces in Korea in 1950. Nationalist forces actually outnumbered the Communists, but harassment by hundreds of thousands of guerrillas led to the dispersal of much of the Nationalist strength. Hybrid warfare enabled Mao's forces to gain superiority at critical points in China during the campaigns of 1948–1949, which ended with the ejection of the Nationalists from the mainland to Formosa (Taiwan). Communist victory in the Chinese Civil War further validated the effectiveness of hybrid warfare in the right geographic, historical, and cultural circumstances.¹¹

There are also cases in which both sides in a conflict used hybrid warfare against their adversary. Perhaps the prime example of this was the French and Indian War in North America from 1755 to 1763. Initially, the French held the edge because of their use of Indian auxiliaries and

---

⁹ Gerhard L. Weinberg, *A World at Arms: A Global History of World War II* (Cambridge, 1994), p. 150.
¹⁰ Max Hastings, *Das Reich: The March of the 2nd SS Panzer Division Through France* (New York, 1981).
¹¹ Gary J. Bjorge, "Compound Warfare in the Military Thought and Practice of Mao Zedong and the Chinese People's Liberation Army's Huai Hai Campaign (November 1948 – January 1949)," in *Compound Warfare: That Fatal Knot*, ed. Thomas M. Huber (Leavenworth, KS, 2002), pp. 169–219.

unconventional methods, but by 1759, both sides were using a combination of regular military forces, colonial militias, and native irregulars to contend for mastery of the North American continent. British adaptation to French-Canadian methods doomed France to defeat as Indian scouts, American rangers, and British light infantry took their place alongside conventional Redcoat battalions. British commanders such as James Wolfe and Jeffrey Amherst even went so far as to use light infantry and rangers to raid French-Canadian settlements, thereby wreaking havoc on morale and causing desertions as militiamen left the ranks to protect their families.[12]

The French commander, the Marquis de Montcalm, actually degraded the capabilities of his forces by shunning the type of warfare practiced so successfully by the natives and French Canadians in earlier decades. Instead, he offered the British an opportunity to engage in a conventional war in which the side with the bigger battalions held all of the advantages. No longer possessing a conceptual or tactical advantage over their opponents, the 6,000 French soldiers in Canada and the Ohio River Valley had no hope of defeating 44,000 British and Colonial soldiers and sailors arrayed against them.[13] The British seizure of Quebec in 1759 and Montreal the next year sealed the French defeat.

Western militaries have occasionally used hybrid warfare to their advantage in the modern era. The British campaign against Ottoman Turkey during World War I benefited from an uprising of Arab tribes led by Grand Sherif Hussein bin Ali and aided by the talents of Captain T. E. Lawrence ("Lawrence of Arabia"). Arab irregular forces tied down thousands of Ottoman troops through continual attacks against the Hejaz railway and on occasion defeated Turkish forces in battle. Arab guerrillas provided intelligence on Ottoman positions and disrupted Turkish supply columns. The Turks struggled to come to grips with this seemingly invisible foe. "It seemed a regular soldier might be helpless without a target," wrote Lawrence, "owning only what he sat on, and subjugating only what, by order, he could poke his rifle at."[14] By spreading Turkish forces thin across Arabia, these activities materially aided General Edmund Allenby's campaign against Turkish forces in Palestine,

---

[12] Michael D. Pearlman, "The Wars of Colonial North America, 1690–1763," in *Compound Warfare*, p. 35.

[13] Ibid., 12. For the most outstanding discussion of the conflict for North America during the Seven Years War, see Fred Anderson, *Crucible of War: The Seven Years War and the Fate of Empire in British North America, 1754–1766* (New York, 2001).

[14] T. E. Lawrence, *Seven Pillars of Wisdom* (London, 1962), p. 198.

which climaxed in the crushing British victory at Megiddo in September 1918.

Throughout history, hybrid adversaries have been willing and able to extend wars in time and space to achieve their goals over the long run. Unless great powers possess a deep commitment, time is on the side of their hybrid opponents. If the clock runs out, the side that possesses the ground wins by default. This temporal aspect has represented a major challenge to militaries engaged in conflict outside their homelands against hybrid adversaries, a point made by T. E. Lawrence when he wrote of the Arab revolt, "Final victory seemed certain, if the war lasted long enough for us to work it out."[15] Hybrid adversaries test the strategic patience of their opponents.

Despite the success of Allenby's campaign in the Middle East during World War I, hybrid war usually worked against Western military powers in the twentieth century, as the wars of colonial devolution attest. France's attempt to retain its empire after its resurrection after World War II illustrates the difficulty that Western powers have experienced in defeating hybrid adversaries willing to wait out the clock. In Indochina, the Viet Minh, under the political leadership of Ho Chi Minh, contested French control after the Japanese surrender in September 1945. Initially, French military forces outclassed their Vietnamese adversaries. For several years, Viet Minh guerrillas harassed French occupation troops, but lack of arms and ammunition limited their efforts. The victory of the Communists in the Chinese Civil War in 1949 dramatically altered the strategic balance. Chinese advisers, weapons, and training transformed the Viet Minh into a hybrid military force. With Chinese assistance, General Vo Nguyen Giap reorganized part of the Viet Minh irregular forces into five conventional infantry divisions (he would later add an artillery division to the mix). With this retooled force, the Viet Minh soon contested French control of the border region between Vietnam and China, while Viet Minh guerrillas harassed the French in the Red River Delta.[16]

The French, under the leadership of General Jean de Lattre de Tassigny, created a series of fortifications (the De Lattre Line) to shield the delta from the Viet Minh. For a time, the line held as Viet Minh divisions took heavy losses in efforts to breach the perimeter. Giap then withdrew his

---

[15] Ibid., p. 202.
[16] Bernard B. Fall, *Street Without Joy: The French Debacle in Indochina* (Harrisburg, PA, 1961).

divisions into the jungle and contested the Red River Delta by means of guerrilla operations. In an attempt to draw Viet Minh formations into a conventional battle, in 1952 the French began to deploy their formations in fortified positions beyond the De Lattre Line. French forces enjoyed some success during Operation Lorraine and the Battle of Na San (23 November to 4 December 1952), inflicting several thousand casualties on Giap's forces. He countered by expanding the war into Laos in 1953. To thwart the Viet Minh move, the new French commander, General Henri Navarre, created an air–land base at Dien Bien Phu, 175 miles west of Hanoi. Giap responded by moving several divisions to the area, where they seized the high ground surrounding the airstrip and systematically overran the French forces hilltop by hilltop. On 8 May 1954, the final French position, Strongpoint Isabelle, fell to Viet Minh forces and the remaining French forces entered captivity.[17]

The Viet Minh victory at Dien Bien Phu was a stunning blow to the French position in Indochina, but the fact is that the French still held Hanoi, the Red River Delta, and most of the southern part of Vietnam. The will of the French to continue the fight, however, had collapsed. They could not contest the Viet Minh in the battle of narratives that shaped the perceptions of the Vietnamese that this was a fight for their nation against foreign occupiers. Nor did the French create a satisfactory political alternative to the Viet Minh. The Vietnamese rejected efforts to empower the former Vietnamese Emperor Bao Dai, correctly sensing he was little more than a French puppet. Thus, when French political will collapsed, the Viet Minh emerged victorious. The best the French could do was to agree to a compromise peace that left the Viet Minh in possession of the northern part of the country, with vague promises of later nationwide elections. These never took place.

As the French experience in Indochina suggests, political will is a crucial component of hybrid warfare – as it is in all wars. Even had the French won at Dien Bien Phu, chances are that the Viet Minh would still have emerged victorious. One need look no further than Algeria, which most Frenchmen agreed in 1954 was an integral part of their country. Having learned its lessons from the Vietnam debacle, the French Army performed much better in a military sense in combating Algerian insurgents. Indeed, by the end of the decade, the Algerian insurgency was on the ropes. By then, however, the French will to continue the struggle

---

[17] Bernard B. Fall, *Hell in a Very Small Place. The Siege of Dien Bien Phu* (New York, 1966).

had evaporated. In 1962, President Charles De Gaulle granted Algeria its independence.[18]

By extending conventional war to include the people, hybrid forces amplify their otherwise limited power and extend the conflict in both time and space, thereby providing a chance to win a protracted contest of wills when they could not otherwise achieve a conventional military victory. While regular military forces conduct conventional operations against the armed forces of their opponent, irregular forces work to achieve control over the population. This dichotomy is why the French failed so disastrously in Indochina; although they could defeat Viet Minh conventional divisions in most circumstances, they could not simultaneously control the Vietnamese people. In the end, the lack of a stable indigenous partner and sufficient local forces to assist in securing and stabilizing the population doomed the French effort.

The French lost the battle of narratives with their Vietnamese and Algerian opponents. To a certain extent, all war includes a battle of narratives, namely which side possesses the moral high ground or can convince the people of the justice of its cause. By bringing the population into the conflict, hybrid warfare magnifies the importance of perceptions. Although wartime propaganda is a time-honored tradition as far back as the ancient world, modern communications systems such as the Internet, satellite television, and radio radically amplify the transmission rates of propaganda and public information. Insurgents realize that military actions are but a supplement to the information war, by which they try to sway perceptions of both their own people and the enemy's population.

As counterinsurgency expert John McCuen points out, the battle over competing narratives plays out among three audiences: the indigenous population, the home front of the great power, and the wider international community.[19] Great powers risk losing conflicts in which they fail to understand either the human terrain or the "decisive battlegrounds of public opinion at home and abroad."[20] In hybrid wars, conventional military forces conduct operations to defeat their regular opponents, while other military forces and interagency assets must work to clear areas of irregular forces, to control those areas over the long term, and to counter-organize the population in order to pacify it. Military success and the establishment of legitimacy among the population will lead to increased

---

[18] Alistair Horne, *A Savage War of Peace: Algeria, 1954–1962* (London, 1977).
[19] John J. McCuen, "Hybrid Wars," *Military Review*, March–April 2008, pp. 107–113.
[20] Ibid., p. 107.

home-front and international support, without which great powers risk defeat.[21]

Sadly, America's enemies have, more often than not, proved more adept than the United States at harnessing the power of propaganda and influencing public perceptions. The land of Madison Avenue and Wall Street has found itself consistently outmaneuvered in the media space by al Qaeda operatives working with a laptop computer and an Internet connection. In the modern information environment of instantaneous communications and 24/7 news coverage, the United States must become more adept at engaging in the battle of narratives that can determine the difference between victory and defeat. Even when military forces of a great power enjoy enormous success, as U.S. forces did in destroying the bulk of the Viet Cong during the Tet Offensive in 1968, failure to win the battle for public perception will lead to defeat. In the world of hybrid war, it is not enough to destroy the enemy's armed forces; to win, the indigenous, home-front, and international audiences must believe that the war is over. In other words, military success must lead to a commensurate political outcome as perceived by the affected populations.

As these examples have illustrated, a foreign power rarely can generate the military forces, financial wherewithal, and political commitment required to prosecute a hybrid war to an acceptable conclusion. Overlapping conflicts and interests in these wars often create "wicked problems" that cannot be solved, only managed. Historians who in retrospect posit facile solutions to these conflicts misread their complexity. In the quest for decisive outcomes, great powers all too often have succeeded only in miring themselves in quagmires.

The recent history of the wars in Afghanistan and Iraq attest to the validity of this statement. After the terrorist attacks on the World Trade Center in New York and the Pentagon in Washington, DC, on 11 September 2001, U.S. forces attacked the Taliban regime and al Qaeda terrorist bases in Afghanistan by using hybrid means. U.S. Special Forces and Central Intelligence Agency operatives teamed up with indigenous Afghan irregular forces of the Northern Alliance to battle Taliban militia. The U.S. military bolstered the war effort with heavy doses of air power and a conventional infantry unit, the 10th Mountain Division. This hybrid combination proved extremely effective at destroying Taliban formations when they stood their ground, but it was less adept at pursuing fleeing al Qaeda remnants into the mountains or in the

---

[21] Ibid., p. 111.

conduct of counterinsurgency operations since 2002. In December 2001, in a mountainous area of eastern Afghanistan known as Tora Bora, American commanders failed to deploy sufficient conventional military assets and instead relied on Afghan irregulars and air power to finish off al Qaeda. This decision doomed the mission to failure and allowed the escape of Osama bin Laden and his allies across the border into Pakistan. This was perhaps the most serious strategic and political error the United States made in the war against al Qaeda, only partially rectified by the 2011 raid that killed Osama bin Laden at a safe house in Pakistan. The insistence of Secretary of Defense Donald Rumsfeld on validating his "light footprint" approach to warfare allowed America's greatest enemy to escape to fight another day.[22]

In Iraq, too, the U.S. military has learned about hybrid war the hard way. In just three weeks of combat in March and April 2003, the U.S. military and its coalition partners destroyed the armed forces of Iraq and toppled the regime of Saddam Hussein. For President George W. Bush, Secretary of Defense Donald Rumsfeld, and all too many defense analysts, the results of the war seemed to validate their vision of high-tech armed forces capable of engaging in rapid, decisive operations to achieve quick victories in conventional warfare.[23] Advocates of defense transformation rooted that vision in the American military's experiences from the end of the Vietnam War to the Iraq War – that is, a period of barely three decades, dominated by the end of the Cold War and the unipolar moment of U.S. superiority that followed. However, in the months after the seizure of Baghdad, the United States struggled to solidify its occupation of Iraq, an effort made more difficult by a growing insurgency that destabilized large portions of the country.[24] U.S. armed forces, organized, trained, and equipped to fight conventional enemies, were unprepared to counter a growing insurgency that by 2006 had pushed Iraq over the brink of civil war.

To understand why this happened, one needs to trace the history of doctrinal development in the U.S. Army from defeat in Vietnam to the

---

[22] U.S. Senate Committee on Foreign Relations, *Tora Bora Revisited: How We Failed to Get Bin Laden and Why It Matters Today*, 111th Congress, 1st session, 30 November 2009, pp. 13–17, accessed at foreign.senate.gov/imo/media/doc/Tora_Bora_Report.pdf.
[23] United States Joint Forces Command, J9 Joint Futures Lab, "A Concept for Rapid, Decisive Operations," 9 August 2001.
[24] Tom Ricks, *Fiasco: The American Military Adventure in Iraq, 2003 to 2005* (New York, 2007); Peter R. Mansoor, *Baghdad at Sunrise: A Brigade Commander's War in Iraq* (New Haven, CT, 2008).

beginning of the Iraq War in 2003. In the wake of defeat in Vietnam, the U.S. Army entered a period during which it almost totally ignored the lessons of the counterinsurgency war it had waged during the previous decade and instead turned its attention to the high-tech, conventional war it potentially faced against the Red Army in Europe.[25] Senior officers concluded that Vietnam represented an exception to the conflicts that U.S. forces would wage in the future. Moreover, they argued that the United States should avoid such conflicts. For its part, the institutional army did its best to forget Vietnam by ridding itself of material associated with the conflict and disregarding lessons learned in waging counterinsurgency in Southeast Asia.[26]

For a time, events proved them correct. The army experienced a doctrinal renaissance in the late 1970s and 1980s, embodied first in the theory of active defense and later in the more successful concept of air–land battle. Army and marine forces fought mock conventional battles at combat training centers in California, Arkansas, Louisiana, and Germany that superbly prepared them for the realities of conventional combat. The stunning victory in the Gulf War of 1991 emboldened President George H. W. Bush to declare, "By God, we've kicked the Vietnam syndrome once and for all!"[27]

Of course, part of the Vietnam syndrome was the avoidance of counterinsurgencies, and the Gulf War did nothing to convince the American military to abandon that attitude. During the 1980s, the United States had successfully supported a counterinsurgency campaign in El Salvador with just 55 military advisers – a light footprint of Special Forces replicated in the U.S. support of the Northern Alliance in Afghanistan in 2001. The lack of activity in this realm after the Cold War convinced one strategic analyst to write in 1995 that "the insurgents of the world are sleeping."[28]

The lack of insurgent threats to national security convinced most military analysts to focus their thinking on great power confrontation and a coming revolution in military affairs, the latter a reflection of the lopsided

[25] Many U.S. Army leaders never really understood counterinsurgency warfare, even after years of conflict in Vietnam. They preferred to treat the war as a conventional military operation rather than as a hybrid conflict with multiple dimensions. See Andrew F. Krepinevich, Jr., *The Army and Vietnam* (Baltimore, MD, 1986).
[26] Conrad C. Crane, *Avoiding Vietnam: The U.S. Army's Response to Defeat in Southeast Asia* (Carlisle, PA, 2002).
[27] George C. Herring, "America and Vietnam: The Unending War," *Foreign Affairs*, Winter 1991/1992.
[28] Steven Metz, *Counterinsurgency: Strategy and the Phoenix of American Capability* (Carlisle, PA, 1995), p. 1.

victory of the United States and its allies in the Gulf War. The combination of advanced intelligence, surveillance, and reconnaissance systems and precision-guided munitions would supposedly provide the American military a decisive edge in future conventional warfare. The key, these analysts believed, was to perfect the information-precision revolution in military affairs to ensure that the United States retained a decided advantage over potential conventional adversaries. Who those potential adversaries were, however, was an open question. No other nation in the world had developed conventional capabilities even approximating those of U.S. forces, nor were they likely to do so in the foreseeable future. Concepts such as network-centric warfare, therefore, aimed at destroying mirror-imaged enemies. By the turn of the millennium, the U.S. military was well on its way to developing a system perfectly suited to fight itself.[29]

The descent of the U.S. Army and Marine Corps in Iraq between 2003 and 2006 into a morass partly of their own making convinced some to rethink the doctrinal basis for counterinsurgency operations. A number of mid-grade officers in Iraq instituted counterinsurgency tactics and procedures to guide the operations of their units, most notably Colonel H. R. McMaster in Tal Afar in 2005 and Colonel Sean MacFarland in Ramadi in 2006.[30] Under the leadership of Lieutenant General David Petraeus and Lieutenant General James Mattis, the two services produced an updated doctrinal manual for counterinsurgency warfare, Field Manual 3–24, in December 2006.[31] Despite the success of this doctrine during the surge of U.S. forces to Iraq in 2007–2008, some analysts worry that the doctrinal pendulum has swung too far away from conventional warfare and that the American military is in danger of losing critical war-fighting capabilities. Yet, the debate should not be an either–or proposition.[32] Future wars

---

[29] For proponents of network-centric warfare, see Admiral William A. Owens, *The Emerging U.S. System-of-Systems* (Washington, DC, 1996); Vice Admiral Arthur Cebrowski and John Gartska, "Network-Centric Warfare: Its Origin and Future," *Naval Institute Proceedings*, January 1998; and David S. Alberts, John Gartska, and Frederick P. Stein, *Network Centric Warfare: Developing and Leveraging Information Superiority* (Washington, DC, 1999). For some critiques, see Milan Vego, "Net-Centric Is Not Decisive," *Proceedings*, January 2003; and H. R. McMaster, "Learning from Contemporary Conflicts to Prepare for Future War," *Orbis*, Fall 2008, pp. 564–584.

[30] George Packer, "The Lesson of Tal Afar," *New Yorker*, April 10, 2006; Jim Michaels, *A Chance in Hell* (London, 2010).

[31] Field Manual 3–24, "Counterinsurgency," Department of the Army, December 2006.

[32] The either–or nature of the debate on force structure and doctrine is exemplified by John A. Nagl, "Let's Win the Wars We're In," and the response by Gian P. Gentile, "Let's Build an Army to Win All Wars," *Joint Force Quarterly* 52, First Quarter 2009, pp. 20–33.

will likely entail an increasingly vague distinction between the conventional and the irregular; indeed, these forms will meld into one, thereby creating a hybrid form of war that takes advantage of the most effective parts of conventional and irregular operations.[33]

Hybrid warfare in the twenty-first century will prove to be even more dangerous as a result of the proliferation of advanced weaponry. Irregular forces are increasingly armed with the latest weapons and technology, making them more difficult to combat. In the Iraq War, Shi'a militias used Iranian-made rockets and explosively formed projectiles to battle American forces equipped with the latest military technologies.[34] Explosively formed projectiles have proven capable of destroying the most advanced armored vehicles, such as the M1A1 tank. Other nonstate groups in the Middle East are armed with advanced anti-tank missiles, rockets, cruise missiles, and unmanned aerial vehicles. Even this aspect of hybrid warfare, however, is not new. More than a century ago in the Boer War, Boer forces used 75-mm and 155-mm Creusot guns, 120-mm Krupp mortars, 37-mm Vickers-Maxim automatic "pompom" guns, Mauser rifles, and Maxim machine guns to outclass (or at least equal) their British opponents.[35]

Informed observers should not have been surprised, then, by Hezbollah's use of advanced anti-tank missiles to destroy Merkava tanks during the Israeli invasion of southern Lebanon in 2006. Indeed, Israel's war against Hezbollah and its more successful operations against Hamas in 2008 in Gaza demonstrate some of the difficult challenges faced by conventional armed forces in combating hybrid adversaries. Responding to the kidnapping of an Israeli soldier in northern Israel on 12 July 2006, Israeli Prime Minister Ehud Olmert authorized military operations against Hezbollah targets in Lebanon. The Israeli Air Force pounded Hezbollah positions and command and control centers, but Hezbollah fighters responded by firing large numbers of rockets into northern Israel. When the Israeli Defense Forces (IDF) attacked into southern Lebanon to clear the area of Hezbollah rocket teams, they came up against well-armed and trained militia, which inflicted stinging losses against their Israeli

---

[33] Frank Hoffman, "Hybrid Threats: Reconceptualizing the Evolving Character of Modern Conflict," *Institute for National Strategic Studies Strategic Forum* 240, April 2009, pp. 5–6.

[34] Richard Esposito and Maddy Sauer, "Iranian-Made IEDs Are the Most Deadly U.S. Forces Have Seen, and Their Use Is on the Rise," ABC News online, 30 January 2007, accessed at http://blogs.abcnews.com/theblotter/2007/01/iranianmade_ied.html.

[35] Byron Farwell, *The Great Anglo-Boer War* (New York, 1976), pp. 43–45.

opponents. Hezbollah fighters used advanced weaponry such as anti-tank missiles, anti-ship cruise missiles, rockets, and unmanned aerial vehicles to counter Israeli attacks. Meanwhile, Hezbollah skillfully employed the Internet and other media for its propaganda and to build a narrative that Hezbollah fighters were standing toe to toe against the IDF and winning.

The IDF, well trained for counterinsurgency operations on the West Bank and in the Gaza Strip, was not ready for the conventional fighting it encountered south of the Litani River. Theoretical concepts such as systemic operational design, developed over the preceding decade to guide Israeli doctrinal thinking, confused more than they clarified. For its part, the Israeli Air Force's reliance on the equally opaque effects-based operations – a concept developed by the U.S. Air Force and at the time fully embraced by transformation advocates in the United States – proved ill suited to achieving Israeli goals. Precision munitions directed by high-tech sensors proved useless without adequate intelligence with which to target the enemy, as Hezbollah forces camouflaged themselves exceptionally well. High-tech Israeli forces were often unable to locate their targets, and their operations failed to break Hezbollah's will to fight. In the event, precision munitions were not an effective substitute for sufficient numbers of well-trained infantry and effective combined-arms teams. At the strategic level, Hezbollah's adroit use of information and propaganda swayed world opinion from the early days of the conflict. After three weeks, Israel, commonly understood to have the most capable conventional armed forces in the Middle East, agreed to a cease fire without having achieved its objectives.[36]

The Israeli military learned from its mistakes in Lebanon. Over the next two years, the IDF revisited its intellectual understanding of warfare and retrained its active and reserve forces to fight on both conventional and irregular battlefields. The Israelis rejected the use of effects-based operations that aimed to pound enemy targets with precision-guided munitions, while eschewing seemingly messy ground operations. Instead, the IDF sought ways to conduct combined-arms operations within the constraints of the hybrid battlefield. The Israelis also learned to compete in the realm of information warfare.

Thus, when the IDF invaded the Gaza Strip to combat Hamas fighters in January 2009 during Operation "Cast Lead," the Israeli forces

---

[36] Matt M. Matthews, *We Were Caught Unprepared: The 2006 Hezbollah-Israeli War* (Leavenworth, KS, 2008); Andrew Exum, *Hizballah at War: A Military Assessment*, Policy Focus #63 (Washington, DC, 2006).

were much better prepared to cope with hybrid challenges. They enjoyed improved intelligence and a better understanding of how the enemy would fight. Despite the profusion of mines, improvised explosive devices, tunnels, and other obstacles and fortifications, the IDF effectively used fire and maneuver to attain its objectives. It was particularly effective when fighting at night. Precision air strikes complemented but did not replace ground maneuver. Palestinian fighters attempted to replicate the success of Hezbollah militia in Lebanon and managed to fire dozens of rockets into Israel. Nevertheless, on every level, the Israelis decisively defeated Hamas in just under three weeks.[37]

As this discussion and the following essays show, as the United States military prepares for the future, it would be a serious mistake to disregard the lessons of several thousand years of recorded history. The United States cannot merely focus on the wars it wants to fight and ignore the rest, for messy small wars have a way of challenging America despite U.S. conventional military superiority.[38] Indeed, as Williamson Murray notes in the chapter on the American Revolution, the United States was birthed in a hybrid war. It is all the more astonishing, then, that some policy makers in Washington look on the wars in which America is engaged today as something new. They are not.

American military forces must possess a wide range of means to combat hybrid opponents, from conventional power to counterinsurgency and counterterrorism capabilities. Combat power in hybrid war consists of more than just the tanks, artillery, infantry, aircraft, ships, and other weapons that a military force possesses. Intelligence, civil affairs, psychological operations, and interagency civilian capabilities are necessary to fight hybrid wars. A military force cannot fight one element of the enemy while ignoring the remainder. In this regard, the U.S. Army has acknowledged the simultaneity of combat and stability operations in its most current doctrine. Doctrine writers did well to eliminate the phased approach to combat and postcombat operations, for in the real world, they blur together.[39] The problem with the phased approach in Iraq in 2003, for instance, was a nearly singular focus on combat operations at the expense of so-called Phase IV stability operations. In the future, the U.S. military needs to prepare more effectively to fight irregular adversaries from the

---

[37] Scott C. Farquhar, *Back to Basics: A Study of the Second Lebanon War and Operations CAST LEAD* (Leavenworth, KS, May 2009).

[38] Max Boot, *The Savage Wars of Peace: Small Wars and the Rise of American Power* (New York, 2002).

[39] U.S. Army Field Manual 3-0, "Operations," Department of the Army, February 2008.

beginning, not just after a period of adjustment and adaptation. As the invasion of Afghanistan in 2001 underlined, the United States should also be ready to engage in hybrid warfare when conditions allow.

As the following chapters illustrate, effective political and military leadership is essential to victory in hybrid warfare. Political leaders set national objectives, work to bolster national will, and build and keep intact international coalitions to share resource burdens. They develop and explain the strategic narrative that maintains popular support for the war effort. Above all, they must understand the nature of their opponent as well as the extent of the commitment necessary to win the war. Military leaders must adjust existing doctrine to take into account the kind of war in which their forces engage, as well as to counter enemy strengths and exploit enemy weaknesses. Senior leaders must create viable operational concepts that link strategy to tactical actions. Leaders at all levels must gather lessons learned from ongoing military operations and alter doctrine, operational concepts, and strategy to meet unexpected challenges and opportunities. In a nutshell, leadership matters.[40]

The nine case studies in this book are representative of the history of hybrid warfare from ancient times to the present. They span the ages from the Roman experience in Germania early in the first century AD, to the Nine Years' War in Ireland at the turn of the seventeenth century, to the American Revolutionary War, to Napoleon's war in Spain, to the U.S. Civil War, to the Franco-Prussian War, to the Boer War and the larger British experience with hybrid warfare over the centuries, to the Second Sino-Japanese War, and to America's hybrid struggle in the Vietnam War. This examination highlights the continuities of the historical experience; examines the changes wrought by new technology and doctrine; and analyzes the impact of geography, history, culture, religion, and other factors on hybrid warfare over the past two millennia. By shedding light on the past, we believe that this study will help as well to illuminate the future of warfare in the twenty-first century.

---

[40] For an examination of the crucial contribution of good leadership to success in counterinsurgency warfare, see Mark Moyar, *A Question of Command: Counterinsurgency from the Civil War to Iraq* (New Haven, CT, 2009).

2

Conquering Germania

A Province Too Far

James Lacey

A small German tribe rose in revolt and in immediate reaction three legions marched. Their commander, Varus, was well schooled in the Roman method of stifling insurrections: React rapidly and massively at the first sign of trouble. Following the Roman playbook, which he had implemented to good effect in the Eastern Empire, Varus led his legions through recently "pacified" Germania, demonstrating for all to behold the might of Rome.[1] The Romans knew from experience that, left to fester, uprisings grew worse and more expensive in blood and treasure the longer they delayed action. At the onset of rebellion, the preferred Roman method was a rapid march with all troops available; followed by a short, bloody, decisive engagement; and concluded with a flurry of swift trials and slow executions. Unfortunately for Varus, his opponent, Arminius, was Roman educated and trained and therefore intimately familiar with the Roman playbook.

The legions marched as if they had few concerns. Spread out over almost 10 miles, the formation became ragged. Many of the legionnaires walked unarmed among the baggage and camp followers. At no place did Varus maintain the tactical integrity of the legions. Worse, the German

---

[1] The following reconstruction is the author's own. It is based on evidence provided by ancient writers and recent archeological excavations of the Teutoburg Wald battle site. See Cassius Dio, Book 56, chapters 18–24 (style hereafter is, e.g., 56.18–24); Velleius Paterculus, Book 2, chapters 117–120 (hereafter 2.117–120); Tacitus, *The Annals*, section 1.60-62; and Florus, *Epitome of Titus Livy*, section 2.30. This reconstruction was also informed by two recent works: Adrian Murdoch, *Rome's Greatest Defeat* (London, 2006), and Peter S. Wells, *The Battle that Stopped Rome* (New York, 2003).

auxiliary force, commanded by Varus' "trusted" adviser, Arminius, had received permission to ride off and ensure the route ahead was clear of obstructions or threats. Believing that Arminius would alert him to any trouble in sufficient time to form his legions, Varus marched unprepared.

In the early morning of the second day's march, a soft rain started, which grew more intense as morning gave way to afternoon. Lashing winds and pelting rain beat against the legionnaires. Soon the soft ground turned to mud and the baggage trains slowed to a crawl. Wretched legionnaires bundled themselves against the elements and doggedly trudged forward, unmindful of everything except their own misery. As the Romans entered a narrow pass between two clumps of forests, they trusted Arminius to warn them of any danger and therefore failed to take their normal precautions as they marched into a carefully laid trap. There was to be no warning, for Arminius had already deserted the Roman cause. As the legions advanced, Arminius joined his fellow Germans in making final preparations for a battle he hoped would obliterate Roman power east of the Rhine.

Suddenly, the Romans found themselves beset by missiles from all sides. Chaos prevailed, causing the Romans to react with uncharacteristic slowness. Emboldened, German warriors edged closer, hurling ever more missiles, and overwhelmed weaker parts of the line.[2] Gradually, but inexorably, legionary discipline asserted itself and battle-hardened centurions moved to the nearest standard, gathered nearby legionnaires, drew their swords, and counterattacked. After a ferocious fight, the legionnaires repulsed the first frenzied attacks.[3] As the Germans melted back into the woods, centurions moved along the line, slowly bringing pockets of order to the chaos. Hundreds of pierced, smashed, and mutilated men were already down. Wounded horses and mules kicked in frenzied agony. The Germans had overturned the baggage carts, while panicked camp followers clung to any legionnaire who could afford them protection.

The hastily organized and conducted counterattack had not broken the Germans, but it had bought time.[4] Varus had not yet given up. He still

---

[2] Cassius Dio, 56.20.4–5.
[3] The sources do not discuss this phase of the battle. However, the author believes that it is a fair reconstruction because it is certain that the Romans repulsed the first frenzied attacks. Also, there is recorded instance of ambushed legions behaving in this manner when Caesar's army was attacked by the Nervi in 57 BC.
[4] This phase of the fight is also not mentioned in the ancient sources, but recent archeological finds indicate that there was a hard fight at the wall.

had the bulk of three veteran legions. They were shaken but recovering rapidly. At his direction, the survivors hastily constructed a fortified camp and burned the cumbersome baggage train. That night, Varus held a council of war where he decided to break camp and march west in hopes of returning to the Roman fortified base at Haltern.[5] After a sharp early morning fight, the Romans smashed open a gap in German lines and broke into open country. All day they marched as a continuing storm pelted them and the Germans harried their formation. Varus, totally unaware he was playing into Arminius' hands, doggedly led his legions forward. Eventually, the battered Romans marched into the narrow Kalkrieser-Niederweder-Senke pass. Bordered by a high hill to the south and an impenetrable bog to the north, the pass stretched for almost 4 miles and was on average only 300 feet wide.[6] Here, Arminius and the bulk of the Germans waited behind a wall built at the hill's base.

As the Romans marched through the pass, the Germans attacked again. This time, however, the legions had deployed and were ready to meet the assault. Knowing, however, that they could not defeat the Romans in a head-to-head fight, the Germans did not come straight at the Roman lines. Instead, they stayed behind a protective wall and hurled thousands of missiles in an attempt to break up the Roman formations. In several places, Roman cohorts advanced on the wall. In most cases, they were repulsed with heavy losses, but at some points legionaries were able to break through the wall, only to be cut down by the thousands of Germans waiting on the far side.[7] When Arminius judged the moment right, he unleashed his warriors on the faltering legions. In ferocious close combat, Roman losses mounted into the thousands. German losses must have been greater, but they were receiving fresh forces by the hour, while the nearest Roman help was more than 60 miles away. Against all odds and despite heavy losses and the crumbling tactical integrity of the army, the Romans somehow punched through the pass and onto open ground.

That night, the remains of the legions made camp, but they no longer had the energy to fortify it. In the morning they awoke to even worse weather and found themselves surrounded by ever-growing numbers of Germans. The gloom of the Romans deepened when it became known

---

[5] Although farther away on the Rhine, it is possible the Romans decided to march toward the larger and better defended fort at Xanten.
[6] The pass was in reality about a mile wide, but men and beasts could only move along the edges as a result of the high water table.
[7] Archeological digs show evidence of dead Romans on the German side of the wall.

that their cavalry had deserted. Despair set in when word spread that the grievously wounded Varus had committed suicide.[8] Knowing their doom was at hand, some of the legionnaires followed Varus' example, while others, following the lead of surviving senior commanders, surrendered.

In a four-day running fight, the Germans had obliterated three legions (XVII, XVIII, and XIX). Over the next days, the victors tortured Roman prisoners before hanging them or, in the case of senior commanders, burning them alive. Decapitated heads were nailed to trees or the skulls taken as souvenirs. In the succeeding weeks, German bands destroyed isolated Roman outposts and trading centers; Roman power east of the Rhine disappeared.[9] Two decades of Roman policy toward Germania lay in tattered ruins. Although Rome was slow to accept that reality, Germania would never become an imperial province. Distraught over the collapse of his policy and the irreplaceable loss of 3 of the Empire's 28 legions, Augustus went into mourning, tore at his clothes, and let his hair and beard grow. As he walked the halls of his residence, the ancient sources claim, he would often stop and hit his head against a wall, wailing, "Varus, give me back my legions."[10]

Six years later, Germanicus, at the head of a new Roman army, visited the battle site. Tacitus recorded the event:

> Varus' first camp, with its broad sweep and measured spaces for officers and eagles, advertised the labors of three legions: then a half-ruined wall and shallow ditch showed that there the now broken remnant had taken cover. In the plain between were bleaching bones, scattered or in little heaps, as the men had fallen, fleeing or standing fast. Hard by lay splintered spears and limbs of horses, while human skulls were nailed prominently on the tree-trunks. In the neighboring groves stood the savage altars at which they had slaughtered the tribunes and chief centurions. Survivors of the disaster, who had escaped the battle or their chains, told how here the legates fell, there the eagles were taken, where the first wound was dealt upon Varus,

---

[8] Varus' subordinate, Vala, had led the cavalry in a breakout. Tradition holds that this was a cowardly attempt to escape, which left the infantry exposed. However, the cavalry was more of a hindrance than a help in this fight and it is just as likely that Varus ordered them to flee in order to save something from the disaster engulfing his army. In any case, they did not make it. German horsemen ran the Roman cavalry to ground and annihilated them.

[9] Only a small force based at Aliso, near modern Haltern, commanded by Cadencies (an experienced veteran and likely the *primus pilus* – commander of a legion's first cohort – of the XIX Legion), managed to cut its way through enemy territory back to the safety of Gaul.

[10] Suetonius, *The Twelve Caesars*, trans. Robert Graves, 1957; revised, Michael Grant, 1979 (New York, 1989).

and where he found death by the suicidal stroke of his own unhappy hand. They spoke of the tribunal from which Arminius made his harangue, all the gibbets and torture-pits for the prisoners, and the arrogance with which he insulted the standards and eagles.[11]

GOALS AND OBJECTIVES

Historians attempting to ascertain the strategic framework or policy of the Empire during the reigns of Augustus and Tiberius immediately run into a major obstacle. There is no source that explains or even hints at a coherent strategy. In the absence of real evidence, historians have relied on conjecture or the expedient of claiming that the Romans had no strategy. Conjectures have led many to take Augustus at his "supposed" word, when he advised his successors to consolidate Rome's possessions and not to expand the empire beyond its current borders.[12] Whether or not Augustus actually provided such advice is still a matter of historical debate.[13] What is certain is that Augustus himself never followed such a policy.[14] One look at his *Res Gestae* makes it clear that the first emperor saw himself as a conqueror in the same mold as his uncle and adopted father, Julius Caesar.[15] Eight of the *Res Gestae*'s 35 pages deal with his conquests and military accomplishments.

In fact, some historians believe that Augustus, based on a mistaken notion of geographic distance, was intent on conquering the entire world.[16] J. C. Mann has gone as far as to claim:

> There seems little doubt that Augustus saw that the security of the empire demanded above all the conquest of Germany. The Elbe would only have formed a temporary frontier. Was the further aim to envelop the lands beyond the Danube, and even beyond the Black Sea, thus securing the vulnerable left flank for an ultimate advance into Iran? Such plans need not

[11] Tacitus, 1.60–61.
[12] Cassius Dio, Book 56.
[13] For an excellent outline of the debate, see Josiah Ober, *Historia: Zeitschrift für Alte Geschichte*, vol. 31, no. 3 (3rd Qtr. 1982), pp. 306–328.
[14] Modern historians have followed P. A. Brunt's lead, and it is now generally accepted that Cassius Dio created a fiction that Augustus was always oriented toward peaceful solutions. Dio, who was opposed to expansion, was perfectly willing to create a pacific Augustus as an exemplar for future emperors. See P. A. Brunt, *Roman Imperial Themes* (Oxford, 1990), pp. 96–109.
[15] Alison Cooley, *Res Gestae divi Augusti*, edition with introduction, translation, and commentary (Cambridge, 2009).
[16] Brunt, *Roman Imperial Themes*.

have seemed wildly unrealistic to the Rome of Augustus. At the foundation of the republic, who could have foreseen that one day Rome would control all Italy? Even with all of Italy under Roman control, who would have forecast that one day she would control the whole Mediterranean basin? It is necessary to try to imagine the state of mind of the Roman of the Augustan period. With such a history of unparalleled divine benevolence, how could he fail to conclude that it was Rome's destiny to conquer? The preamble to the Res Gestae makes the view plain.[17]

After all, if Caesar could conquer Gaul in ten years with only a fraction of Rome's resources, what could Augustus do with the wealth and might of the entire Roman world at his disposal?[18]

For Mann, the Roman frontier was an accident, drawn at the limits of Rome's ability to project power. In this interpretation, Rome did not halt its expansion as matter of policy but rather as a result of exhaustion. For the most part, the path described by Gibbon on the first page of *The History of the Decline and Fall of the Roman Empire* remains the dominant historical theme:

> The principal conquests of the Romans were achieved under the Republic: and the emperors for the most part, were satisfied with preserving those dominions which had been acquired by policy of the senate, the active emulation of the counsels, and the martial enthusiasm of the people. The first seven centuries were filled with a rapid succession of triumphs; but it was reserved for Augustus to relinquish the ambitious design of subduing the whole earth, and to introduce a spirit of moderation into pubic councils.[19]

Unfortunately, too many historians still cling to the idea that Augustus only fought wars of necessity, allowing them to overlook the simple fact that during the Roman Republic and through the early decades of the Empire, expansion and conquest were a necessity.

Although Gibbon's interpretation of Augustan policy was waning by the mid-twentieth century, particularly in regard to Germany, it received a new lease on life in Edward Luttwak's *Grand Strategy of the Roman Empire*.[20] It is accurate, if somewhat simplified, to state that Luttwak

---

[17] J. C. Mann, "Power, Force, and the Frontiers of the Empire," *The Journal of Roman Studies*, vol. 69 (1979), p. 179.
[18] C. M. Wells, *The German Policy of Augustus: An Examination of the Archaeological Evidence* (Oxford, 1972).
[19] Edward Gibbon (author) and David P. Womersley (editor), *The History of the Decline and Fall of the Roman Empire, Vol. 1* (New York, 1996), pp. 1–2.
[20] Edward Luttwak, *The Grand Strategy of the Roman Empire: From the First Century A.D. to the Third* (Baltimore, 1979).

views the Roman Empire as having hunkered down behind a series of fortified lines – the *limes* – and having been protected by client buffer states surrounding its territory.[21] Whatever truth this view may hold during the later Empire, it certainly has no validity for the early Principate. As historian Peter Wells states, "There is no trace at this period of *limes* such as developed under the Flavians. The Augustan commanders did not have a Maginot Line mentality. They were not thinking about keeping the barbarians out, but of going out themselves to conquer the barbarians."[22]

Augustus never viewed either the Rhine or the Danube as settled frontiers. It was always his intention to conquer Germany, at least as far as the Elbe. Although various interpretations of ancient writers might appear to make this arguable, the actions of Roman armies during this period make Rome's intent clear. As early as 12 BC and for several years after the Teutoburg Wald disaster, Roman armies campaigned across the Rhine and, at least until AD 9, they were building the infrastructure of empire (Figure 1). For Rome, the words of Virgil were part of the ingrained national consciousness: "*Romane, memento (hae tibi erunt artes) pacique imponere morem, parcere subiectis et debellare superbos* [Remember, Roman, you rule nations with your power (these will be your talents) and impose law and order, spare the conquered, and beat down the arrogant]."

For the Germans, strategic policy was simple. There were always a number of tribes willing to work with the Romans and even accept varying

---

[21] Although Luttwak's position has come under vitriolic attack by many historians of the period, he still has his defenders. This author is not among them. However, although I believe Luttwak is substantially correct in his analysis, there is no evidence that the defensive attitude he describes existed in the Augustan Age. Unfortunately, a thorough discussion of Roman grand strategy over the course of several centuries is beyond the scope of this chapter. For those interested in further studying this topic, the following are excellent starting points: Kimberly Kagan, "Redefining Roman Grand Strategy," *The Journal of Military History*, vol. 70 (April, 2006), pp. 333–362; J. C. Mann, "Power, Force, and the Frontiers of the Empire," *The Journal of Roman Studies*, vol. 69 (1979), pp. 175–183; and C. R. Whittaker, *Rome and its Frontiers: The Dynamics of Empire* (New York, 2004). For what the author considers a decisive destruction of Lutwak's critics, see Everett L. Wheeler, "The Methodological Limits and the Mirage of Roman Grand Strategy: Part I," *The Journal of Military History*, vol. 57, no. 1 (June 1993), pp. 7–41; and Everett L. Wheeler, "The Methodological Limits and the Mirage of Roman Grand Strategy: Part II," *The Journal of Military History*, vol. 57, no. 2 (April 1993), pp. 215–240.

[22] Wells, *The German Policy of Augustus*, p. 246.

FIGURE 1. Germania, AD 9–16.

degrees of Roman domination. For the most part, German policy, as far as most Germans understood it, was to remain free and maintain their own way of life.[23]

RESOURCES, MANPOWER, AND ECONOMIC STRENGTH

At first look, the disparity of resources between the Roman Empire and the Germans was so great that Rome's failure to make Germania a full-fledged province seems surprising. This astonishment results from two causes: the failure to calculate what percentage of Rome's total resource base was available for mobilization to support a war in a distant theater, and an enduring, but incorrect, assumption of the resources available to the Germans.

To a surprising degree, given archeological evidence to the contrary, Tacitus' commentary on German life and industry still holds among military historians:

> They do not laboriously exert themselves in planting orchards, enclosing meadows and watering gardens. Corn is the only produce required from the earth... It is well known that the nations of Germany have not cities, and that they do not even tolerate closely contiguous dwellings. Even iron is not plentiful with them... I would not, however, affirm that no vein of German soil produces gold or silver, for who has ever made a search? They care but little to possess or use them. It is productive of grain, but unfavorable to fruit-bearing trees; it is rich in flocks and herds, but these are for the most part undersized.... Their country... generally either bristles with forests or reeks with swamps.[24]

Relying on Tacitus, many historians view Germania as a country overrun by forests and swamps, devoid of industry and agriculture, and nearly empty of towns.

Decades of archeological finds within Germany make it clear that this view is wrong. As one historian notes, "The overriding impression conveyed by the excavated sites is of stable and enduring communities,

---

[23] For those interested in delving deeper into the German society and politics during this period, the following are recommended as a starting point: Malcolm Todd, *The Northern Barbarians, 100 BC–AD 300* (New York, 1987); C. R. Whittaker, *Frontiers of the Roman Empire: A Social and Economic Study* (Baltimore, MD, 1997); Thomas S. Burns, *Rome and the Barbarians* (Baltimore, MD, 2003); and Peter S. Wells, *The Barbarians Speak: How the Conquered Peoples Shaped Roman Europe* (Princeton, NJ, 2001).

[24] Tacitus, *The Agricola and Germania*, trans. A. J. Church and W. J. Brodribb (London: Macmillan, 1877), p. 87.

some occupying the same sites for many decades or even centuries, others shifting their dwellings without moving far beyond their original confines. A few, such as Wijster and the Barhorst, display a degree of planning which is comparable with that of peasant villages within the Roman Empire and which would have surprised a Roman observer."[25] This evidence should not, however, be interpreted as meaning that Germany possessed anything approaching the economic base of a typical Roman province of this period. As late as the second century, the small towns that grew up around legionary bases on the Rhine remained limited to 5,000 people. Without the moldboard plow, local agriculture could not sustain any more beyond that number.

Still, Germania was far from an unproductive wasteland. In truth, there were sizeable tracts given over to settled agriculture and a significant amount of wealth rested in large cattle herds. Moreover, Germany had raw materials that the Romans wanted and were prepared to trade for, particularly amber, which moved from the Baltic along trade routes already centuries old by the Augustan era. Rome also coveted the gold and raw iron that flowed out of Germania, in direct contradiction to Tacitus, who doubted they were present, although he qualified his statement by saying no one had looked. In short, Germania was not as advanced as Gaul, but there was sufficient economic foundation for a patient Roman administration to turn it into a profitable province – as long as the cost of acquisition was not too great. Unfortunately for Roman prospects, Germania was sufficiently rich and militarily integrated to make the cost of conquering it great indeed.

In fact, it was this wealth and integration that gave the conflict its hybrid character. In most cases, legionnaires only had to contend with limited local resistance, easily handled by small detachments. However, the German capability to mass forces and offer pitched battle made it imperative that the Romans remain ready to move up the conflict spectrum at short notice. By AD 9, the Romans may have forgotten that imperative, for as Dio states,

> Varus did not keep his legions together, as was proper in a hostile country, but distributed many of the soldiers to helpless communities, which asked for them for the alleged purpose of guarding various points, arresting robbers, or escorting provision trains.[26]

---

[25] Todd, *The Northern Barbarians*, p. 116.
[26] Cassius Dio, 56.19.

Certain that the Germans were well along the road to integration into the Roman Empire, the legions apparently lowered their guard and moved down the conflict scale. Although Varus concentrated his legions for their fateful march through the Teutoburg Wald, the annihilation of this force makes it obvious that the Romans had discounted the possibility of the Germans' massing forces for a large conventional assault on their legions.

In contrast to apparently meager German power, Rome was the greatest empire the ancient world had yet known. By any previous measure, its wealth was vast and intimidating. Still, the Roman economy was underdeveloped. Vast amounts of its wealth remained locked up in land and financial speculation rather than enlarging investments in industry and trade – the engines of sustained economic growth.[27] The cost and economic dislocations caused by the Roman civil wars (despite a rapid recovery in many areas) represented a continuing cause of financial strain throughout the reigns of Augustus and Tiberius. Moreover, continuing military operations (Spain, Arabia) and the vast Augustan building program ("I found Rome a city of bricks and left it a city of marble") exacerbated revenue shortfalls.[28] Richard Duncan-Jones lays out a number of clues found in the sources as to the seriousness of Rome's financial situation:[29]

- Both Augustus and Tiberius often stopped paying army discharge bonuses (often equal to over a dozen years' pay) due to lack of funds.
- Tiberius was slow to pay the legacies of Augustus, presented fewer shows, and built few new buildings.
- Senators criticized Tiberius for his small gifts.
- Although Tiberius reduced the sales tax by 0.5 percent when new revenues became available from Cappadocia, he simultaneously canceled a four-year reduction in military service because he could not afford to pay the discharge costs.
- The credit crisis of AD 33, which led to a generation-long depression, is indicative of the shortage of liquidity in Rome and throughout the Empire.

---

[27] See Peter Garnsey and Richard P. Saller, *The Roman Empire: Economy, Society, and Culture* (Berkley, 1987), pp. 43, 64, for an excellent discussion on Rome's failure to develop its economy to its full potential.

[28] Suetonius, Leif of Augustus 28. In Cassius Dio (56.30.3) there is a similar quote: "I found Rome of clay: I leave it to you of marble."

[29] See Richard Duncan-Jones, *Money and Government in the Roman Empire* (Cambridge, 1998).

A fair estimate for the annual fixed cost of the Roman military establishment during the early Principate is 150 million denari, a cost that increased significantly when the army engaged in active operations.[30] In the past, Rome had often been able manage or offset the fiscal burden of its wars through plunder on a grand scale. However, a protracted war in relatively undeveloped Germany represented an unrelieved drain on the imperial treasury because plunder was almost nonexistent and the Romans were never able to haul off slaves in anywhere near the numbers Caesar had obtained in Gaul. For Rome, Germany was all cost with only the hope of potential economic gain sometime in the distant future.

To cut costs, Augustus had reduced the armies of the civil war by almost two-thirds, to 28 legions (25 after the disaster at Teutoburg Wald). However, given stable frontiers throughout the rest of the Empire, Rome was able to concentrate a substantial percentage of those legions along the Rhine for service in Germania.[31] Still, it must be remembered that Roman operations in Germania were conducted at what amounted to the end of its financial tether.

GEOGRAPHY

Despite recent archeological evidence drawing a picture of a Germania that was more settled and developed than previously believed, the region remained centuries behind even Gaul on the development curve. In fact, there is little reason to deviate from Ronald Syme's comments on this subject a generation ago:[32]

> [The Germans] were unready to accept either the culture or the domination of Rome. Nor was it an easy task to penetrate and control the country, to crush the resistance and curb the spirit of the warrior tribes. The obstacles were so considerable and movement was so slow that distances were easily

---

[30] See Duncan-Jones, *Money and Government in the Roman Empire*, pp. 33–46, for an excellent discussion of Roman imperial finances. Also see M. Rostovtzeff, *The Social and Economic History of the Roman Empire*, 2nd ed., 2 vols. (London, 1957); and Mason Hammond, "Economic Stagnation in the Early Roman Empire," *The Journal of Economic History*, vol. 6 (May 1946), pp. 63–90.

[31] With the winding down of his Spanish campaigns, the end of Rome's foray into Arabia, and the establishment of a long-term peace with Parthia, Augustus created the stability required for just such a concentration toward the end of the first century BC.

[32] That Germany was richer than commonly thought helps explain its capacity to withstand repeated Roman attacks without a complete breakdown of the social and economic order. One must be careful, though, not to go too far down this line of reasoning and try to present the German economic structure as wealthier or more sophisticated than it actually was.

multiplied. The chief problem that confronts the general, how to transport and feed the army, assumed formidable proportions in Germany. Caesar in Gaul had been able to move rapidly because he found roads, bridges and food wherever he went; he had been able to bring the enemy to battle because they had towns and property to defend. In Germany the invader had to make their own roads and bring with him his own supplies.[33]

As was often the case in the ancient world, the logistics of a campaign on the far side of the Rhine was a formidable barrier to imperial expansion.

Under such conditions, a Roman army that could be easily maneuvered and maintained would be too small to conquer, whereas a larger army would prove too unwieldy and nearly impossible to sustain. Moreover, the need to create a camp and road infrastructure during the conduct of operations made Roman actions dangerously predictable. For instance, in the Augustan period, there were six legionary fortresses, or concentration points, along the Rhine.[34] Each of these fortresses lay along one of the primary invasion routes into Germania. An alert enemy would know the Roman primary route of advance by observing the concentration points. Typically, the Germans were incapable of concentrating enough force in time to halt an invading army, although they could and did make life difficult for the advancing legions. However, real trouble would arise at the end of the campaigning season. As a result of an absence of lateral communication routes, the Romans, more often than not, found themselves forced to withdraw back to their bases along the same avenue along which they had advanced.[35]

On the way out, the Romans were marching over land they had already stripped bare, while facing concentrated German forces doing their best to make any withdrawal as difficult as possible. The true reason the Germans were able to destroy Varus' army was that once it became entangled in

---

[33] Ronald Syme, *The Cambridge Ancient History: The Augustan Empire*, vol. 10 (Cambridge, 1963), p. 361.

[34] These were Vechten (Fectio), Vetera (near Xanten), Neuss (Novaesium), Mainz (Mogontiacum), Cologne (Oppidum Ubiorum), and Nijmegen (Noviomagus). The first three fortresses were built before the first Roman invasions in 12 BC; all of them had been completed before the Varian disaster in AD 9. See Wells, *The German Policy of Augustus*, p. 95.

[35] The Romans did, at times, attempt to advance and withdraw by sea, with varying degrees of success. This situation should be compared with what Caesar found in Gaul. Although Caesar was forced to disburse his legions in the winter, he was typically able to keep his legions in Gaul year-round and sustain them off the local produce. Germania during this period did not possess sufficient food surpluses to sustain permanent garrisons. Over time, the advance of Roman fortresses along the river routes made these logistical issues easier to overcome.

trouble, it had only one choice: to march to the nearest fortress along the only route available. The Germans understood that constraint from the beginning and had prepared the entire route to support their offensive actions. Varus' legions went down to defeat as a result of the predictability of their moves. Other Roman armies barely escaped the same fate on several occasions.

THE FRAMEWORK AND CONDUCT OF OPERATIONS

There is no doubt that, at least until the Varian disaster and probably for a short period thereafter, Rome's policy was to establish Germania as a Roman province, at least as far as the Elbe. To overcome the Germans' reluctance to allow themselves to be conquered, the Romans adopted an operational concept centered on periodic invasions by the legions. This policy, despite sporadic reverses, had always worked in the past. From the Roman perspective, there was no reason to think the raiding concept would not work this time as well, as long as they were patient and persistent.

In 15 BC, Augustus traveled to Gaul. He remained there for three years, overseeing preparations for the invasion of Germany, which he entrusted to his 25-year-old stepson, Drusus (brother of Tiberius).[36] By 12 BC, Augustus judged that all was ready, and the army marched. The first objective was not conquest but rather the punishment of the Sugambri, who had crossed the Rhine five years before and all but annihilated the V Legion. In an attempt to forestall their destruction and subjugation, the Sugambri launched a preemptive attack against Drusus' army. The Romans defeated the attack with heavy loss and proceeded to devastate the territory of the Sugambri, the modern state of Westphalia. Later in the year, Drusus committed his army through a specially constructed canal (the Drusus Canal) in the Arnhem-Nijmegen region.[37] He then took it over the Zuider Zee to the mouth of the Ems River. There was little fighting; this demonstration of Roman power and engineering skill overawed the natives along the North Sea. Before Drusus' army departed the area, the Chaukian, Frisian, and Batavian tribes had all entered into alliance with Rome.

---

[36] This narrative of Drusus' campaigns is drawn mostly from Cassius Dio (54.32–55.2) and Florus (2.26, 2.30), who are both accepted as reasonably reliable on this topic.

[37] This 24-kilometer canal connected the Rhine with the Zuider Zee and then with the North Sea by way of the River Vecht.

In the following year, Drusus led a second invasion from the Roman camp at Vetera. This time, he marched east along the Lippe River. Here, the Romans constructed the great fortress of Haltern, which Varus would try to reach with the remnants of his broken legions in AD 9.[38] After a further advance to the Weser River failed to bring the Germans into the open, Drusus opted to return to the Rhine. Along the way, the Romans came under heavy attack and only narrowly escaped annihilation, mainly due to the indiscipline of the attacking German forces. Dio relates that

> for the enemy harassed him [Drusus] everywhere by ambuscades, and once they shut him up in a narrow pass and all but destroyed his army; indeed, they would have annihilated them, had they not conceived a contempt for them, as if they were already captured and needed only the finishing stroke, and so come to close quarters with them in disorder. This led to their being worsted, after which they were no longer so bold, but kept up a petty annoyance of his troops from a distance, while refusing to come nearer.[39]

In this case, the discipline of the Roman legionnaires in close combat proved their salvation.

Drusus' bad luck continued in 10 BC, when his attacks against the Chatti (near today's state of Hessen) met with little success. In his final and last campaign, Drusus reached the Elbe. However, soon after this achievement, he had to return to the Rhine, probably as a result of a lack of supplies.[40] During his return march, Drusus met an accident or was stricken by disease and died before reaching the Rhine.[41]

Augustus sent Tiberius, who had been busy subduing the Pannoians and Dalmatians, to replace his fallen brother. In 8 BC and 7 BC, Tiberius waged two campaigns within Germania. Although his army marched throughout the area between the Rhine and the Elbe, Tiberius met little resistance, except from the still-troublesome Sugambri. Adopting the tried and true Roman method of creating a desert and calling it peace, Tiberius came close to exterminating the Sugambri. The Romans transported those who survived across the Rhine where they could watch the broken tribesmen more closely. After this, the overawed German tribes

---

[38] Some histories refer to this fortress as Aliso.
[39] Cassius Dio, 54.32.
[40] Dio states that Drusus was deterred by a dream, when after trying to cross the Elbe a woman of superhuman size came to him and said, "Whither, pray, art thou hastening, insatiable Drusus? It is not fated that thou shalt look upon all these lands. But depart; for the end alike of thy labors and of thy life is already at hand" (Cassius Dio, 55.1.3).
[41] Drusus may have broken his leg when he fell off his horse; it is possible that he later contracted gangrene as a result of the injury.

offered no further resistance. Tiberius departed in AD 7 to enjoy a triumph in Rome and soon thereafter retired from public life for a decade.

Swift Roman marches through Germania, as well as several successful battles, convinced Augustus and his advisors that Germania, in the words of Velleius Paterculus, had been "reduced almost to the position of a tributary province."[42] In truth, the tribes may have been intimidated, but they were hardly defeated. In fact, much of Germany east of the Rhine had yet to experience the hard hand of a Roman army. In reality, Drusus' and Tiberius' campaigns had been little more than raids. Except for the Sugambri, Roman arms had broken no tribe: The slow process of permanent subjugation had not even started.[43]

For the next ten years, the sources are irritatingly silent on events along the Rhine and within Germania. We do know that in 6 BC the Roman legate Lucius Domitius Ahenobarbus received command of Germania. Four years later, he apparently got himself and a Roman army in trouble when he attempted to relocate the troublesome Cherusci in much the same manner that Tiberius had handled the Sugambri. As a result of this fiasco, Augustus relieved Ahenobarbus of command and replaced him with Marcus Vinicium. At about this time, many of the major tribes had risen in what Velleius referred to as a "vast war."[44] Unfortunately, nothing is known of this war, but Vinicium must have at least held his own because he was awarded a triumph upon return to Rome.

In AD 4, Tiberius returned to command the Rhine legions.[45] The soldiers greeted him effusively. According to Velleius (who was present),

> Soldiers burst into joy at the sight of him, greeted him with enthusiasms, rushed with violence just to touch his hand and could not restrain themselves. 'Are you with us again great general?' 'I was with you great general in Armenia.' 'I was with you in Raetia.' 'I was rewarded by you at Vindelicia.'[46]

For the next two years, Tiberius campaigned in northern Germany. During the first year, he conquered the Canninefates, the Attuarii, and the Bructeri and subjugated the troublesome Cherusci.[47] Soon thereafter,

---

[42] Velleius Paterculus, 2.97.4.
[43] Syme, *Cambridge Ancient History*, vol. 10, p. 363.
[44] Velleius Paterculus, 2.104.2.
[45] After leaving the German legions in 6 BC, Tiberius opted to exit the political arena and retire to Rhodes. However, with the death of Augustus' grandsons, Lucius and Gaius, who were being groomed as future emperors of the Roman Empire, Tiberius was called back to duty in AD 4. From this point forward, Tiberius was Augustus' heir apparent.
[46] Velleius Paterculus, 2.104.
[47] Adrian Murdoch, *Rome's Greatest Defeat* (London, 2006), p. 43.

Tiberius had the Cherusci (the home tribe of the victor of Teutoburg Wald, Arminius, then 21 years of age) declared "friends of the Roman people." In AD 5, Tiberius launched a combined naval and land movement from the Roman camp at Anreuppen, in which several independent forces were to converge on the Elbe. The coordinated movement of large contingents aimed at intimidating those tribes that still resisted Romanization. According to Tiberius' staff officer Velleius, the assault was a great success; afterward, "Nothing remained to be conquered in Germany."[48]

From the Roman viewpoint, the only resistance still offered within the Elbe, Danube, and Rhine triangle was the Kingdom of Maroboduus, leader of the Macromanni in Bohemia. In AD 6, as part of a brilliantly conceived operation, 12 legions marched from Raetia, Germania, and Illyricum along separate routes that converged in central Bohemia. This crowning achievement in Augustan strategy was only days away from completion when Pannonia rose in a revolt that shook Rome. It took Tiberius three years and the employment of 10 legions (supported by close to 100 cohorts of auxiliaries) to crush the last embers of that rebellion. Doing so pushed the Empire to the limits of its economic and military endurance.

Throughout this period, Germania was apparently tranquil. Its new governor, Varus, had settled in without trouble and begun the long process of integrating the region into the Empire. Over the past two millennia, an impression has taken hold that Varus was a dilettante, appointed to a job for which by temperament and experience he was unsuited and a governor who held his position because of his family relation to Augustus, who was loathe to have legions under the command of anyone not part of the Julio-Claudian clan.[49] This impression is mainly a result of the image left to posterity by one of Varus' enemies, Velleius Paterculus.[50] That reputation, however, does not however hold up to close scrutiny.

Varus, breaking an old family tradition of supporting Republican ideals, may have been with Augustus at Actium and was certainly with

---

[48] Velleius Paterculus, 2.108.1.
[49] He was first married to the daughter of Augustus' most trusted advisor, Agrippa, and later to Augustus' grand-niece, Caludia Pulchra.
[50] As Velleius states, "Varus Quintilius, descended from a famous rather than a high-born family, was a man of mild character and of a quiet disposition, somewhat slow in mind as he was in body, and more accustomed to the leisure of the camp than to actual service in war. That he was no despiser of money is demonstrated by his governorship of Syria: he entered the rich province a poor man, but left it a rich man and the province poor" (Velleis Paterculus, 2.117).

him during his tour of the eastern provinces after Antony's defeat. He then passed through a number of political posts and commanded the XIX Legion in heavy fighting under Tiberius in Switzerland. In 8 BC, Augustus appointed Varus governor of Africa, where he commanded the III Augusta. This was one of the most important governorships in the Empire; it was a major source of Rome's food supply and the only Senate-ruled province in which Augustus allowed the stationing of a legion.[51] Varus' performance so impressed Augustus that he next assigned him to Syria. Here, Varus commanded four legions (III Gallica, VI Ferrata, X Fretensis, and XII Fulminata) and was responsible for keeping the Parthian Empire at bay and an always-troublesome region pacified. While governor of Syria, he led three legions to crush a major Jewish revolt in the wake of King Herod's death. It was a major operation that saw the cities of Sepphoris and Emmaus destroyed and 2,000 Jews crucified. When it was over, Judea remained relatively quiescent for nearly 70 years.[52]

Despite Velleius' comments, one must credit Varus as an able administrator and a qualified Roman general. His failure lay in his acceptance of the then-widespread notion that Tiberius had crushed German resistance and that the country was ready for transformation into a Roman province, much as Gaul had been. But the Romans had defeated the Germans, not conquered them. Florus writes, "Under the rule of Drusus they respected our manners rather than our arms. But when Drusus was dead, they began to detest the licentiousness and pride, no less than the cruelty, of Quintilius Varus."[53]

But what was the cruelty of Varus? As far as the sources support, his crime was to try to impress Roman civic order upon unruly Germans "as if he could restrain the violence of barbarians by the rods of a lictor and the voice of a crier."[54] Varus' chief crime, in German eyes, was to attempt to make Germany pay part of the cost of its own occupation. In this he was only doing what Augustus expected of every Roman governor in a "subdued" province – institute a tax. As Dio notes, "He [Varus] strove to change them more rapidly. Besides issuing orders to them as if they were

---

[51] During Augustus' reign, there were two types of provinces: those with legions that Augustus personally controlled and those settled provinces that no longer needed the permanent presence of troops to pacify or defend them. These latter provinces Augustus allowed the Senate to control.
[52] Varus' actions made enough of an impression on the Jewish people that the entire period after Herod's death is still known as "Varus' War" in the Talmud.
[53] Florus, 2.30.
[54] Florus, 2.31.

actually slaves of the Romans, he exacted money as he would from subject nations. To this they were in no mood to submit, for the leaders longed for their former ascendancy and the masses preferred their accustomed condition to foreign domination."[55] Be that as it may, the true seeds of the explosion that culminated in the "Varian disaster" germinated in what amounted to a tax revolt.

Unbeknownst to Varus, the German tribes were rallying around a compelling new leader, Arminius.[56] His ascendancy and the timing of his revolt came at a time when Rome was least prepared to act. The bulk of the Roman army focused heavily on crushing the revolt in Pannonia. Thus, Varus' three legions remained isolated in the heart of Germania, with little help of immediate succor if they found themselves in trouble. Moreover, they were deep in a territory that had not yet been prepared to support the Roman style of warfare. As one historian has pointed out, Germany needed (1) a comprehensive fort network; (2) strong points and signal towers linked by all-weather roads and bridges, with massive tree felling to reduce concealment; (3) extensive drainage and causeway building to assist movement; and (4) a strong naval presence on the internal rivers with fortified points of entry, jetties, quays arsenals, and granaries.[57] In short, the infrastructure required to support a Roman army on an extended campaign did not exist. This reality turned an initially difficult situation in the Teutoburg Wald into a hopeless one.

Despite German discontent, the problem might have remained manageable if Arminius, a charismatic leader capable of uniting the various tribes for concerted action, had not appeared on the scene. He was the son

---

[55] Cassius Dio, 56.18.3 and 56.18.4. Reading Dio, one might note that Varus was conducting what we would consider a nation-building exercise. "The Romans were holding portions of it [Germany] – not entire regions, but merely districts as happened to have been subdued... The barbarians were wintering, cities were being founded, and they were adapting to Roman ways; becoming accustomed to holding markets and meeting in peaceful assemblages." As Dio also relates, though, "They had not, however, forgotten their ancestral habits, their native manners, and their old life of independence, or the power derived from arms." Cassius Dio, 56.18.

[56] Much has been made of Varus' ignoring the warnings of Segestes, Arminius' father-in-law, that Arminius was organizing a major revolt, as well as a second warning of the planned ambush in the Teutoburg Wald. In hindsight, Varus would have been wise to heed these warnings. At the time, the truth might not have been as easy to see. Arminius was a trusted soldier, trained in Rome, and had spent many years in Roman service. Although no one doubted Segestes' loyalty to Rome, Varus was well aware that Arminius had married Segestes' daughter against his wishes and that Segestes had sworn perpetual enmity toward his son-in-law. From Varus' viewpoint, Segestes' warning was just part of a continuing family feud.

[57] Derek Williams, *Romans and Barbarians* (New York, 1998), pp. 91–92.

of the Cheruscan war chief, Segimnerus, who had early thrown in his lot with the Romans. Segimnerus sent at least two of his sons, Arminius and Flavius, to Italy to be trained as Roman soldiers.[58] While he was there, Arminius received Roman citizenship, still a rare honor at this point in Roman history, and membership in the equestrian order – the Roman petty nobility. In AD 4, Arminius assumed command of a Cheruscan force fighting as Roman auxiliaries. It is likely that he fought in the Pannonian War under Tiberius. In AD 7, at the age of 25, Arminius returned to Germany to serve as a chief aide to Varus. As Velleius relates,

> There appeared a young man of noble birth, brave in action and alert in mind, possessing an intelligence quite beyond the ordinary barbarian; he was, namely, Arminius, the son of Segimnerus, a prince of that nation, and he showed in his countenance and in his eyes the fire of the mind within. He had been associated with us constantly on campaigns and had even attained the dignity of equestrian rank. This young man made use of the negligence of the general [Varus] as an opportunity for treachery, sagaciously seeing that no one could be more quickly overpowered than the man who feared nothing, and that the most common beginning of disaster was a sense of security.[59]

Arminius' destruction of Varus' three legions erased all signs of Roman power east of the Rhine. News of the disaster caused panic in Rome and throughout the western portions of the Empire. Many expected a German invasion of Gaul and northern Italy at any moment. In its hour of distress, Rome called on its most reliable general, Tiberius. With his nephew, Germanicus, Tiberius went north and restored calm to the Rhine frontier. For the next two years, Tiberius and Germanicus conducted a number of bloody and vicious raids into Germania. These assaults never penetrated far into barbarian-held territory and were never meant to be part of a renewed war of conquest. Rather, they aimed at impressing on the Germans and the rest of the Roman world that the legions remained invincible.

Augustus' death in AD 14 sent a shock wave through the Empire. For most citizens of the Empire, Augustus had been the only ruler they had known. Would the devastation of the civil wars again occur, as various claimants to the throne vied for power? In the event, however, Tiberius assumed power with a minimum of drama. But quiet was not the rule everywhere. In southern Germany, four legions mutinied. The Rhine

---

[58] Flavius remained loyal to Rome throughout this period.
[59] Velleius Paterculus, 2.118.

legions had long been nursing a list of complaints, and while Germanicus was away in Gaul, their discontent boiled over.[60]

Germanicus, who was a favorite of the legionnaires, rushed to the scene of the revolt. Despite his popularity, the soldiers were not easily pacified. When the general theatrically drew his sword and threatened suicide if the revolt were not ended, a nearby legionnaire handed over his own sword, saying, "Use mine; it's sharper." Fearing for the safety of his family, who were residing at the legionary base, Germanicus ordered them sent to a more secure location. Although capable of cruelty that makes modern readers cringe, Roman soldiers also possessed a deep strain of sentimentality. The sight of the tearful wife of Germanicus, Agrippina, leading away the two-year-old Caligula and a pitiful party of refugees radically changed the soldiers' mood.[61] Seizing the moment, Germanicus ascended a nearby rostrum, chastised the soldiers' disloyalty, and called for the leaders of the mutiny to be brought forth and executed. This action, along with concessions to the soldiers' grievances and the dismissal of the centurions who most offended their sensibilities, ended the revolt.

Still, Germanicus considered that one of the proximate causes of the revolt had been the idleness of the legionnaires during the summer. Although the campaign season was far along, he determined to cross the Rhine and concentrate the soldiers' minds on something besides the recently ended troubles. Avoiding the well-known invasion routes, the Romans advanced unnoticed into the territory of the Marsi. Taking along only a small baggage train and moving rapidly at night, the Romans fell upon the Marsi before they could offer any defense. After the initial slaughter, Germanicus broke his legions into smaller bodies and sent them out to devastate everything for 50 miles in every direction. A Roman punitive expedition was always a bloody and destructive affair, but on this occasion, the soldiers appear to have outdone themselves. They destroyed everything within the targeted area and "neither sex nor age moved his [Germanicus'] compassion."[62]

The Marsi were too stunned to react, but all along their borders the German tribes mobilized to strike at the Romans upon their return to the

---

[60] Among the main complaints was a decree extending each legionnaire's term of service by four years, poor living conditions, pay deductions for uniforms and equipment, brutal treatment at the hands of centurions, and the need to pay bribes to centurions to avoid unpleasant duties.
[61] Adrian Goldsworthy, *In the Name of Rome: The Men Who Won the Roman Empire* (London, 2003), p. 248.
[62] Tacitus, *Annals*, 1.51.2.

Rhine. Aware that he faced resistance during the withdrawal, Germanicus marched his army in a square formation, with his baggage in the middle. As the Romans moved through a narrow defile, eerily reminiscent of the terrain in which Varus' legions had gone down to destruction, the Germans attacked. This time, the legions were unencumbered and ready to fight. The first cohorts, although under severe pressure, held against a screaming barbarian onslaught. Germanicus, after ensuring the line would hold, rode to the flank to rally the XX Legion, the focal point of the recent revolt. Arriving in their midst he exclaimed, "Wipe out the stain of mutiny. Advance! Turn your guilt into glory!"[63] The XX legion advanced at the double and smashed into the disorganized German line with a crushing impact. The Germans fell back into open ground and were massacred.

In the following two years, Germanicus led two major invasions of Germany. Twice he fought major but inconclusive battles against Arminius, and on two other occasions he nearly lost the legions entrusted to him. At one point, panicked Roman forces on the Rhine were about to destroy a bridge and leave Germanicus isolated and at the mercy of his foes. As Tacitus relates:

> Meanwhile a rumor had spread that our army was cut off, and that a furious German host was marching on Gaul. And had not Agrippina prevented the bridge over the Rhine from being destroyed, some in their cowardice would have dared that base act. A woman of heroic spirit, she assumed during those days the duties of a general, and distributed clothes or medicine among the soldiers, as they were destitute or wounded.[64]

A disaster that would have dwarfed the one suffered by Varus was only averted by Agrippina's courageous intercession.

There is no profit to be had by a minute examination of Germanicus' invasions.[65] In most ways, they were a repeat of all that had gone before. What is important is acknowledgment of the fact that on at least two occasions, Arminius was able to hold the German tribes together and lead them against six legions in a straight-up fight. Although he was not victorious in these or other set-piece engagements and suffered a clear defeat at the Battle of Idistaviso, the Romans were unable to defeat him decisively and thereby end German resistance. The Germans were proving

---

[63] Tacitus, *Annals*, 1.51.3.
[64] Tacitus, *Annals*, 1.69.1.
[65] For those interested in a more detailed treatment of Germanicus and his military career, see Goldsworthy, *In the Name of Rome*, pp. 237–262.

quite capable of moving up and down the conflict spectrum with ease: disbursing into small guerrilla bands when faced with overwhelming power and coming together to fight pitched battles when offered an opportunity to do so on relatively equal terms. Rome's inability to overcome resistance on every level was the primary reason it never absorbed Germany into the Empire.

Germanicus argued for the continuation of the campaigns into a third year. He promised Tiberius that one more climatic invasion would see German military power overthrown. As Syme states, "Tiberius was not deceived."[66] For the new emperor, the risks of future campaigns in Germania far exceeded any benefit the Empire might gain. As far as Tiberius was concerned, the Romans had satisfied honor and it was time to end a debilitating war and bring the legions home. Hence, he ordered Germanicus home to enjoy a triumph celebrating his "victory" over the barbarians. From this point onward, the wiles of diplomacy and the enticements of commerce would suffice to secure the increasingly permanent northern frontier along the Rhine and the Danube.

TACTICS, TECHNIQUES, AND PROCEDURES

The Germans

The best source for the operational and tactical methods of the Germans remains Tacitus. The following are excerpted from his *Germania*:[67]

> Few [the Germans] use swords or long lances. They carry a spear, with a narrow and short head, but so sharp and easy to wield that the same weapon serves, according to circumstances, for close or distant conflict.
>
> The horse-soldier, is satisfied with a shield and spear; the foot-soldiers also scatter showers of missiles[,] each man having several and hurling them to an immense distance.
>
> There is no display about their equipment; their shields alone are marked with very choice colors... just one or two here and there a metal or leather helmet.
>
> Their horses are remarkable neither for beauty nor for fleetness. Nor are they taught various evolutions after our fashion, but are driven straight forward, or so as to make one wheel to the right in such a compact body that none is left behind another.

---

[66] Syme, *The Cambridge Ancient History*, vol. X, p. 378.
[67] Tacitus, *Germania*. A complete copy can be found at http://www.fordham.edu/halsall/source/tacitus1.html.

On the whole, one would say that their chief strength is in their infantry, which fights along with the cavalry; admirably adapted to the action of the latter is the swiftness of certain foot-soldiers, who are picked from the entire youth of their country, and stationed in front of the line.

To give ground, provided you return to the attack, is considered prudence rather than cowardice. The bodies of their slain they carry off even in indecisive engagements. To abandon your shield is the basest of crimes; nor may a man thus disgraced be present at the sacred rites, or enter their council; many, indeed, after escaping from battle, have ended their infamy with the halter.

Their squadrons or battalions, instead of being formed by chance or by a fortuitous gathering, are composed of families and clans. Close by them, too, are those dearest to them, so that they hear the shrieks of women, the cries of infants. They are to every man the most sacred witnesses of his bravery – they are his most generous applauders.

Tradition says that armies already wavering and giving way have been rallied by women who, with earnest entreaties and bosoms laid bare, have vividly represented the horrors of captivity, which the Germans fear with such extreme dread on behalf of their women.

Tacitus continues, relating information on the warlike ardor of the Germans:

When they go into battle, it is a disgrace for the chief to be surpassed in valor, a disgrace for his followers not to equal the valor of the chief. And it is an infamy and a reproach for life to have survived the chief, and returned from the field.

The chief fights for victory; his vassals fight for their chief. If their native state sinks into the sloth of prolonged peace and repose, many of its noble youths voluntarily seek those tribes which are waging some war, both because inaction is odious to their race, and because they win renown more readily in the midst of peril, and cannot maintain a numerous following except by violence and war.

Men look to the liberality of their chief for their war-horse and their blood-stained and victorious lance. Feasts and entertainments, which, though inelegant, are plentifully furnished, are their only pay. The means of this bounty come from war and rapine. Nor are they as easily persuaded to plough the earth and to wait for the year's produce as to challenge an enemy and earn the honor of wounds. Nay, they actually think it tame and stupid to acquire by the sweat of toil what they might win by their blood.

What is the modern historian to make of this? Tacitus, while giving full credit to the bravery and warlike nature of the Germans, still views them as an undisciplined mob. Unfortunately, this impression has embedded itself within most historical perceptions of barbarian warfare. Most view the barbarians as fierce warriors given to sudden impulses of both heroism and cowardice; able to press an attack with horrifying ferocity when they perceived an advantage but likely to melt away in disorder upon the first reverse. The problem with this viewpoint is that it does not match the military realities of Germania.

Over the course of two and a half decades, German armies had annihilated one Roman army and nearly destroyed several others. Worse, despite the years of ruin and devastation inflicted by Rome on Germania, the German will to resist and the ability of the German people to defend their homeland grew until, in the early first century, they could face the battle-hardened legions of Germanicus and hold them to a draw. For Rome, holding its own in open combat was not sufficient. To conquer Germany, Rome had to win battles and win them decisively. In the early years of Rome's attempt at conquest, Drusus had been able to march at will throughout Germania; however, the primitive German infrastructure prohibited him from maintaining an army of occupation in the region on a permanent basis. Thus, at the end of each campaigning season, the Roman army departed and the German forces regrouped.

Worse, from a Roman point of view, the Germans adapted. Over time, they learned the Roman method of warfare. In some cases, such as that of Arminius himself, they learned it at the feet of the masters who had served with the Roman army. In others, they learned it in the hardest and most efficient school of all – in battle against the Romans. By the time of the Varian disaster, the Germans had a firm grasp of Roman strengths but, more important, also of Roman weaknesses and how to exploit them. If the battle of Teutoburg Wald demonstrates anything, it is that the Germans possessed a high degree of tactical skill, unit cohesion, and battlefield discipline. If they had not, Arminius would have found it impossible to control a running four-day battle against what were arguably the finest soldiers in the ancient world. Within five years, the discipline and cohesion of German armies was sufficient to allow them to face the Romans on an open field.[68]

Even as they adapted to fight the Romans, the Germans never lost sight of the fact that it was their irregular activities that made the Romans suffer the most. We know from Dio that large numbers of Roman troops were spread throughout Germania at the time of the Varian disaster. With the exception of the garrison at Haltern, none of these detachments ever returned to the Rhine.[69]

---

[68] Admittedly from behind a fortified wall.
[69] See footnote 7.

For a modern reader, one could easily interpret Varus' actions as a form of nation building. One might assume that those most skilled with working with the Germans were out among them. However, the Romans were trying to build a nation in their own image in a culture they poorly understood and that was not yet ready to give up its traditional ways in favor of adopting the ways of a different civilization.[70] The fact that the Romans had large numbers of personnel scattered among German towns and villages, and had enlisted many Germans into their own forces, in the end availed them little. Despite intelligence that all was not as it appeared, the Romans were unable to judge the mood of the people or detect what must have been a massive mobilization of German tribes in AD 9. As a result, the Germans exterminated three legions and along with them Roman hopes for a border on the Elbe.

THE ROMANS

Historians have written volumes describing the Roman military system for every area of the Empire.[71] For the purposes of this chapter, it is sufficient to understand that that Roman army was a disciplined, highly efficient killing machine. It was also slow to adapt, as well as reliant on expensive and difficult to emplace infrastructure (roads, forts, and arsenals). Although the Roman army was capable of rapid strategic movement (note the rapid assembly of eight legions and their supporting forces along the Rhine in the months after the Varian disaster), in operational terms, it moved slowly. It was an army organized to grind an opponent out of existence, not one designed for brilliant flash. Although it was capable of extraordinary accomplishments in the hands of a genius such as Julius Caesar, the army was actually designed to be effective when in the hands of the less skilled, as it often was. The practical Romans realized that military genius occurs but rarely and so designed their military institutions for success when led by the merely competent.

---

[70] It could be argued that by AD 9, the Romans had developed a firm grasp of German culture and traditions. I believe this would be to grossly exaggerate Roman willingness to do much of what we might call sociological fieldwork among those it had set out to absorb or destroy. Furthermore, by the time Varus took command, it is very likely that most of the soldiers with extensive experience dealing with and fighting the barbarians (including many of those who spoke the German language) had been drawn off to support the planned invasion of Bohemia and to help crush the revolt in Pannonia.

[71] For more information on the Roman army, see Graham Webster, *The Roman Imperial Army: Of the First and Second Centuries* (Oklahoma, 1998); Adrian Goldsworthy, *The Complete Roman Army* (London, 2003); and Brian Campbell, *The Roman Army, 31 BC–AD 337: A Sourcebook* (New York, 1994).

Could this instrument of war have won in Germania and added that territory to the Empire permanently? The answer to that question is undoubtedly yes. However, to do so would have required the application of will and resources that Rome was not willing to expend. After all, during the Augustan–Octavian civil war several decades earlier, the Empire had supported almost 60 legions, 2 mighty fleets, and huge amounts of auxiliary troops. However, supporting such great forces at the edge of the Empire was an order of magnitude more difficult logistically. If the will had existed within the Empire, the economy of which, while still debilitated, was fast recovering from the ravages of civil war, then Rome could have maintained a military effort two or three times that which it did and done so indefinitely.

In the end, though, Rome's leaders did not believe such an effort was necessary or worth the cost because the Germans were only a distant threat. By the second decade of the first century, there were only a few in Rome who remained keen on seeking battlefield glory in Germania, considering the costs and risks involved. For most, including Tiberius, absorbing Germania into the Empire was too expensive for the potential gain – a province too far.

3

Keeping the Irish Down and the Spanish Out

English Strategies of Submission in Ireland, 1594–1603

Wayne E. Lee

> Proclaim a pardon to the soldiers fled
> That in submission will return to us:
> And then, as we have ta'en the sacrament,
> We will unite the white rose and the red"
> > The Duke of Richmond,
> > after defeating Richard III at Bosworth,
> > from *Richard III* (Act V, Scene V)

In September 1601, a Spanish army landed on the south coast of Ireland, in support of the Irish rebellion sometimes named for its principal leader, the earl of Tyrone or Hugh O'Neill (the conflict is variously called O'Neill's Rebellion, Tyrone's Rebellion, or the Nine Years' War). The English had been struggling with O'Neill since 1594 and with the Gaelic Irish in general for a good deal longer. For the most part, their wars with the Irish had been with an "unconventional" enemy – one who preferred to rely on rough country, ambush, and raid, and who avoided open battle, especially open battle against the heavier English horsemen.

O'Neill, however, had begun to build a more conventional force, armed with pike and shot like his English enemies, even as he also continued to rely on other Gaelic lords who still fought in the traditional Irish way. In the terms of Mao Tse Tung's theory of protracted warfare, O'Neill had begun to create a conventional force with the ability to fight positional territorial warfare. The Spanish arrival in Ireland, with a naval capability and an artillery train, markedly increased the threat to English rule. Now the war was a hybrid one indeed: The English simultaneously faced their old guerrilla-like Gaelic adversary, O'Neill's transformed conventional force, and the most modern and formidable army in Western Europe. Furthermore, at least in theory, additional Spanish reinforcements could land anywhere on the island. English strategic calculations in this situation, however, reflected not only the desperate and complex military situation presented by a hybrid coalition enemy but also their own long history in Ireland.

BACKGROUND: THE ENGLISH IN IRELAND

The Normans had conquered most of Ireland in the twelfth century.[1] For them, conquest meant asserting political mastery over the island, importing some of their own peasants, and dominating the population of many of the towns. Their conquest was limited in the sense that the countryside remained overwhelmingly Gaelic in custom, language, and outlook. Over the ensuing centuries, the Norman elite adapted themselves to Gaelic political and social customs and continued to rule, but they increasingly governed in ways that accommodated their Gaelic neighbors and that depended on those neighbors as props to their own power.[2]

Furthermore, as the Normans became the "Anglo-Irish," many of them gradually shed their allegiance to the English crown. By 1500, this so-called Gaelicizing process had confined real royal influence to a small enclave around Dublin called the Pale and to the larger, usually loyal Anglo-Irish earldoms of Kildare, Desmond, and Ormond in the south and west (in Leinster and Munster).

---

[1] The following survey of the English in Ireland leans heavily on Steven G. Ellis, *Ireland in the Age of the Tudors, 1447–1603* (London and New York, 1998); Colm Lennon, *Sixteenth-Century Ireland*, revised ed. (Dublin, 2005); T. W. Moody, F. X. Martin, and F. J. Byrne, eds., *A New History of Ireland*, vol. III: *Early Modern Ireland, 1534–1691* (Oxford, 1976); S. J. Connolly, *Contested Island: Ireland 1460–1630* (Oxford, 2007); Ciaran Brady, *The Chief Governors: The Rise and Fall of Reform Government in Tudor Ireland, 1536–1588* (Cambridge, 1994). Dates are Old Style, with the year corrected as if it started in January and not March. (Thus, Spanish records dated in New Style show the Kinsale landing as 1 October whereas English records show 21 September).

[2] Art Cosgrove, ed., *A New History of Ireland*, vol. II: *Medieval Ireland, 1169–1534* (Oxford, 1987); R. R. Davies, *Domination and Conquest: The Experience of Ireland, Scotland and Wales, 1100–1300* (Cambridge, 1990), pp. 11, 39–40, 88; id., *The First English Empire: Power and Identities in the British Isles, 1093–1343* (Oxford, 2000), pp. 146–147, 150–153, 176–177, 179–180, 186–187; Brendan Smith, *Colonisation and Conquest in Medieval Ireland: The English in Louth, 1170–1330* (Cambridge, 1999), pp. 51, 56.

Despite this diminution of English authority, the medieval conquest left two key legacies. One was the existence of the Anglo-Irish elite, many of whom maintained their identity as Englishmen, although they often pursued local autonomy from royal interference. The other was that the conquest established a legal precedent in English minds. English kings, queens, councillors, writers, and even soldiers regularly pointed to the Norman Conquest as having established the legal right of the English to rule the Irish. Irish resistance to being "proper" and obedient subjects only proved their barbarity. In 1541, when Henry VIII reluctantly accepted the title of King of Ireland (rather than remaining the less-demanding Lord of Ireland), it merely upped the stakes; as king, he felt compelled to assert a greater level of sovereignty and control.[3] This vision of the level of obedience owed to the monarch helped drive policies throughout the Tudor era.

In many ways, much of the history of conflict in sixteenth-century Ireland derived from these two fundamental forces: the desire of lords, whether Gaelic or Anglo-Irish, to exercise traditional lordly autonomy, and the hardening English belief that any resistance in Ireland constituted resistance to the lawful monarch and therefore was rebellion.[4] The late sixteenth century added two crucial elements to this contest over the nature and extent of English sovereignty: the Reformation and England's war with Spain. Henry's break with the Catholic Church had not taken root in Ireland, and the Gaelic and Anglo-Irish population remained loyal to the Pope.

As Elizabeth's conflicts with Spain deepened, loyalty to her seemed to demand being Protestant. Indeed, in the midst of an earlier combined Gaelic and Anglo-Irish revolt in 1570, the Pope had formally excommunicated Elizabeth. James Fitzmaurice, leader of the Anglo-Irish component of that revolt, proclaimed the rebellion a "holy war." He denounced Elizabeth as a "pretensed Queen" and called for Catholic unity in Ireland; if achieved, he said, "it is certain that there is no power in this realm able to withstand our forces." Fitzmaurice, however, continued to assert his Englishness, claiming not to fight "against the crown of England, but only against the usurper thereof." He made this claim, however, while in

---

[3] Hiram Morgan, "Right Trusty Well Beloved: Queen Elizabeth and Later Lord Deputies," unpublished conference paper presented at the Elizabeth I and Ireland Conference, Storrs, CT, November 12–14, 2009; Ellis, *Ireland*, pp. 152–153.

[4] *State Papers Published Under the Authority of His Majesty's Commission, King Henry the Eighth* (London: HMSO, 1830–1834), 2:14, 2:30–31, 2:34 (hereafter *SPH*); Ellis, *Ireland*, pp. 122–123.

contact with Spain, a fact that suggests the highly charged nature of the problem.⁵ England supported the Protestant Dutch rebels in their long revolt against the Spanish, and Spain sought not only to cut off that aid but perhaps even to restore a Catholic monarch to the English throne. From Elizabeth's point of view, the Spanish threat was truly existential – and Ireland was a natural stepping stone filled with Catholics holding old grievances against English rule.⁶

In short, much of the sixteenth-century struggle between English monarchs and lords in Ireland revolved around the problem of Irish subjecthood. The Irish were subjects who, when rebels, should be allowed to submit. When they refused to submit, they merited no mercy; they could and should be "extirped." To this long and well-established legal tradition, already gaining momentum and severity by the middle of the century, was added the problem of religion as a test of loyalty and as a lever for political power. By the middle of Elizabeth's reign, publicly claiming that Elizabeth was not the rightful monarch had come to constitute high treason.⁷ In the context of a threatened Spanish alliance and then even an actual Spanish invasion, English commanders struggled to find a strategy that balanced the existential threat posed by conventional Spanish power and the legal (and military) traditions that supposedly dictated how subject-rebels were to be treated. In this sense, the war was a hybrid one for the English not only because of the tactical styles and

---

⁵ J. S. Brewer and William Bullen, eds., *Calendar of the Carew Manuscripts Preserved in the Archiepiscopal Library at Lambeth, 1515–1624* (London, 1867–1873), 1:397–399 (hereafter CCM). For his contacts with Spain, see David Edwards, "The Butler Revolt of 1569," *Irish Historical Studies* 28 (1993), pp. 247–248.

⁶ A further factor shaping the war in Ireland was English prejudice about the "barbaric" social structures and subsistence practices of the Gaelic Irish (who also had corrupted the Anglo-Irish). In this chapter, prejudice seems less important to me than calculations of how to handle the operational and strategic problems presented by a Gaelic–Spanish alliance, and so it is not dealt with here. Furthermore, it is my sense that as an explanatory factor, ethnic prejudice has been overemphasized. See Wayne E. Lee, *Barbarians and Brothers: Anglo-American Warfare, 1500–1865* (New York, in press), chaps. 1 and 2; Rory Rapple, *Martial Power and Elizabethan Political Culture: Military Men in England and Ireland, 1558–1594* (Cambridge, 2009), passim, esp. p. 202.

⁷ Guy Halsall, *Warfare and Society in the Barbarian West, 450–900* (New York, 2003), p. 18; D. Alan Orr, *Treason and the State: Law, Politics, and Ideology in the English Civil War* (Cambridge, 2002), pp. 12–13, 16–24; Penry Williams, *The Tudor Regime* (Oxford, 1979), pp. 352–359, 375–378; J. G. Bellamy, *The Tudor Law of Treason* (London, 1979). Contemporary writers on the law of nations explicitly allowed severe treatment to rebels. Geoffrey Parker, "Early Modern Europe," in Michael Howard, George J. Andreopoulos, and Mark R. Shulman, eds., *The Laws of War: Constraints on Warfare in the Western World* (New Haven, CT, 1994), p. 44.

capabilities of their opponents but also because of the differing legal standing of Irish, Anglo-Irish, and invading Spanish.

IRISH AND SPANISH GOALS AND PROBLEMS

Before turning to the specifics of the English strategic conundrum, one must consider Irish and Spanish goals. Direct sources from the Gaelic leadership are few and far between, and it is difficult to say exactly what long-range goal they sought.[8] At a minimum, they wanted to increase or preserve their autonomy as local rulers; in Hiram Morgan's estimation, the problem was that the "Gaelic lords still entertained a medieval system of overlapping sovereignties in which authority was divided between them and the queen and her representative, the lord deputy."[9] The prospect of substantial Spanish aid, in conjunction with the religious conflict, may have given a few major clan chiefs the larger vision of ousting the English entirely, but the majority of the smaller clans no doubt fought alongside their more powerful brethren believing they were pursuing what they had always pursued – the right to rule their traditional territory in the manner to which they were accustomed.

Operationally, the Irish faced several challenges. Their traditional form of war against each other had been fought in pursuit of "preys," essentially surprise raids designed to seize cattle or other portable booty and then return home. Fortified tower houses protected the chief's family from such surprise, and the chief maintained a small, standing force of troops to respond quickly to raids by housing them on his subordinate "churls," or peasants. This kind of warfare emphasized speed and mobility, especially in the upland meadows where cattle were pastured seasonally. Except for the now-long-resident Scottish mercenaries known as *galloglaich*, Gaelic Irish fighters were lightly equipped and lightly armored – even to the extent that Irish horsemen did not use stirrups and therefore could not charge with a lance in the manner of continental European sixteenth-century cavalry. Occasionally, they fought open battles with each other when confronting or pursuing a preying raid, but it was not the aim of

---

[8] Hiram Morgan provides the best account of Gaelic motives at the start of the war, arguing convincingly that O'Neill sought to maintain a lordly role in ruling his traditional homeland, and when denied the ability to do so as a largely autonomous nominal servant of England, he sought such a status through Spanish agency. *Tyrone's Rebellion: The Outbreak of the Nine Years War in Tudor Ireland* (Woodbridge, 1993), passim, esp. pp. 215–221.
[9] Ibid., p. 219.

their normal form of warfare. Faced with heavier English cavalry, and by the 1570s at the latest, with pike and shot formations of infantry as well, the Irish avoided facing their English enemies in open battle, instead relying on their natural mobility and an undeveloped countryside to attack English columns by surprise, and to interrupt supplies destined for isolated garrisons.[10]

Crucially, in offensive war directed against English territorial control, the Irish lacked an artillery train – a capability the Spanish could provide.[11] To fight alongside a Spanish force, however, required O'Neill to prepare a more modern force capable of fighting in open battle. In the years preceding his open break with England, he reorganized his local support system to expand the number of troops he kept on hand; he trained them to fight as pike and shot (often using English captains to do so); and then, in the first few years of his eponymous rebellion, he inflicted several serious defeats on the English by using a combination of traditional and modern tactics.[12]

Beyond a lack of artillery, the Irish faced a number of other problems. Their own population was divided. In the long history of Irish and

---

[10] One disastrous exception of an open battle with the English occurred in 1579 at Monasternenagh. Thomas Morsch, "The Battle at Monasternenagh, 1579," *Irish Sword* 23 (2002–2003), pp. 305–314. For Gaelic warfare, see Bruce P. Lenman, *England's Colonial Wars 1550–1688: Conflicts, Empire and National Identity* (Harlow, UK, 2001), pp. 53–54; K. W. Nicholls, *Gaelic and Gaelicized Ireland in the Middle Ages*, 2nd ed. (Dublin, 2003); Seán O. Domhnaill, "Warfare in Sixteenth-Century Ireland," *Irish Historical Studies* 5 (1946), pp. 29–54; Cyril Falls, *Elizabeth's Irish Wars* (London, 1950); Katharine Simms, "Warfare in the Medieval Gaelic Lordships," *Irish Sword* 12 (1975–1976), pp. 98–109; G. A. Hayes-McCoy, "Strategy and Tactics in Irish Warfare, 1593–1601," *Irish Historical Studies* 2 (1940), pp. 255–279; G. A. Hayes-McCoy, "The Army of Ulster, 1593–1601," *Irish Sword* 1 (1949–1953), pp. 105–117; Hiram Morgan, ed., "A Booke of Questions and Answers Concerning the Warrs or Rebellions of the Kingdome of Irelande [Nicholas Dawtrey, ca. 1597]," *Analecta Hibernia* 36 (1995), pp. 90–97.

[11] The Anglo-Irish earls of Kildare, as Lords Deputy early in the sixteenth century, controlled the English royal artillery in Ireland and occasionally used it for their own purposes, including rebellion. The Gaelic Irish acquired some guns through capture or from Scotland. Paul M. Kerrigan, *Castles and Fortifications in Ireland, 1485–1945* (Cork, 1995), pp. 19, 24. There is no evidence, however, for a proper Gaelic siege train within the sixteenth century.

[12] Morgan, *Tyrone's Rebellion*, pp. 182–183; G. A. Hayes-McCoy, *Irish Battles* (London, 1969), pp. 108–110. To some extent, Hugh O'Donnell had also begun to reform his forces, but the vast majority of Gaelic lords continued to fight with their traditional troops and in the traditional style. For O'Donnell, see Darren McGettigan, "Gaelic Military Organisation and the Nine Years' War – The Army of Red Hugh O'Donnell," *Irish Sword* 24 (2004–2005), pp. 398–410.

Anglo-Irish rebellions, Irishmen had always fought on both sides. O'Neill's rebellion came the closest to achieving a kind of Gaelic unity in revolt, but the English proved adept at exploiting traditional Gaelic rivalries. Those rivalries, in addition to providing native troops, intelligence, and logistical support, also allowed the English to recruit Irish light infantrymen, or kern, as an answer to the asymmetry of their heavier forces. The kern, as much as the English despised them, were seen as indispensable in pursuing the Irish into the bogs and in securing English march routes.[13] Furthermore, it was unlikely that the Spanish would send vast numbers of troops and, indeed, the number of Spaniards who eventually landed at Kinsale was particularly disappointing. Finally, Ireland was simply too close to England. Elizabeth remained fiercely determined to hold Ireland, not only for its own sake but also because of the threat that a Spanish-controlled Ireland posed to England. The political will in England to reinforce English control existed, and the geography meant that those reinforcements were relatively easy to deliver (numerous failures and shipwrecks notwithstanding).

The Spanish had a different and not always harmonious set of goals and problems. In 1598, Philip III ascended the Spanish throne, and he reenergized not just the war in the Netherlands but also the idea of Ireland as a diversionary theater of operations. In addition to Ireland, he more or less simultaneously dispatched major Spanish armies to Algiers and Ostend, laying siege to the latter from June 1601 to September 1604. It was there that Spanish priorities lay, and it was there they bled their treasury dry (the monarchy stopped payments in 1607). Although as late as the 1580s the Spanish may have conceived of Ireland as a stepping stone to England, by 1600 it was probably seen more as a diversion, with aid to O'Neill's rebellion keeping thousands of English troops occupied away from the main theater of war.[14]

---

[13] Local recruiting, including of *galloglaich*, also made it easier to expand the English army in time of crisis. See Wayne E. Lee, "Subjects, Clients, Allies or Mercenaries? The British Use of Irish and Indian Military Power, 1500–1815," in H.V. Bowen, Elizabeth Mancke, and John G. Reid, eds., *Britain's Oceanic Empire: Projecting Imperium in the Atlantic and Indian Ocean Worlds, ca. 1550–1800* (Cambridge, forthcoming); id., "Using the Natives Against the Natives: Indigenes as 'Counterinsurgents' in the British Atlantic, 1500–1800," *Defence Studies* 10.1 (2010), pp. 88–105.

[14] Óscar Recio Morales, "Spanish Army Attitudes to the Irish at Kinsale," in Hiram Morgan, ed., *The Battle of Kinsale* (Wicklow, 2004), p. 92. Mountjoy assumed that the Spanish intended to invade England, after recruiting in Ireland. Fynes Moryson, *An Itinerary: Containing His Ten Years Travell*, 4 vols. (Glasgow, 1907–1908), 2:456, 2:460–461, and 3:65–68.

Operationally, the Spanish had the nominal advantage of being able to land at any point on the Irish coast. In fact, however, wind patterns, the hope for further reinforcements from Spain, and the availability of good harbors all suggested a landing on the south coast, much to the dismay of their Gaelic allies, whose strength lay to the north. To be sure, the Spanish also appear to have been unaware that George Carew had recently suppressed the local lords, who had been in rebellion in the south (in Munster).[15] They had hoped to find local allies ready to hand while they awaited the approach of O'Neill and his chief fellow rebel, Hugh O'Donnell. As seaborne invaders, the Spanish were unable to bring large numbers of horses with them; they pleaded with their allies to gather horses for their use, even though Irish horses were considerably smaller than typical European warhorses. Perhaps worst of all for the likely success of the mission, Spanish soldiers and leaders had substantial doubts about the quality of the men they were going to aid – doubts their experience at Kinsale only seemed to reinforce.[16]

STRATEGIES OF SUBMISSION?

A proper assessment of English strategies in response to the expanded complexity of the war, once the Spanish arrived in 1601, requires an examination of English policy and hopes for their rule in Ireland. In many ways, the long history of English "government" in Ireland proceeded along lines unintended by Elizabeth or her advisors – policy was often hijacked by individual profit-seeking English administrators and garrison captains. In the context of the emergency of 1601, however, we must examine royal policy and the strategic plans of the primary English commanders on the island, namely Robert Devereux, the Earl of Essex, in 1599, and then Charles Blount, Lord Mountjoy, from 1600, as well as the military advice offered by veteran captains and commanders.[17]

The ultimate goal of the English crown was to assert sovereignty and maintain a profitable order in Ireland. The definition of the former could be modified as long as the latter was forthcoming – local lords (whether

---

[15] *Calendar of State Papers, Ireland*, 11:84 (hereafter *CSPI*); Falls, *Elizabeth's Irish Wars*, pp. 292–293.
[16] Morales, "Spanish Army Attitudes," passim.
[17] The phrase "all politics are local" applies with particular force here, and this historical shortcut of focusing on royal policy and the English commanders is a dangerous one. Nevertheless, it was royal policy from 1594 to 1603 that set force levels, and all the main English commanders were constantly under Elizabeth's eye.

Gaelic, Anglo-Irish, or even English) could retain significant local autonomy provided they kept the peace and contributed to the royal coffers. In this context, it is worth considering what "conquest" and a "profitable order" meant in the pre-industrial world. John Landers has argued that pre-industrial economies were fundamentally "organic" in the sense that energy and wealth derived from controlling and tapping the production of organic goods: crops, timber, and livestock.[18] Although sixteenth-century Europeans were discovering forms of wealth accumulation based on controlling strategic points such as mines, ports, and international trading nexuses, the traditional vision of wealth as derived from controlling fields and the farmers on them continued to inform English strategy. Conquest thus involved the extension of coercive authority over agriculturally viable land, a process most effective and predictable when one was asserting control over settled inhabitants working existing farms and pastures. In this context, the English resented Irish seasonal movement or "booleying" of cattle, not just for cultural reasons but also because it was resistant to ordered conquest.

Given this quality of pre-industrial organic economies, and given late medieval social and political relations, late medieval commanders normally imagined two basic methods of conquest: decapitation and submission. Both had a long history in Ireland.

Decapitation, as described by Robert Bartlett in *The Making of Europe*, essentially assumed that the land came with labor. With the local elite eliminated, the local labor force remained – perhaps reorganized, perhaps further subordinated, but not killed or driven off, and only partially supplanted by imported labor.[19] Submission, on the other hand, especially in the context of a nominally civil war, assumed that the submitting lord would then exercise his own local power in a way that promoted order, while redirecting some surplus to the royal center. Landers has argued that feudal social relations made this process of submission simple; the submitted "lords" could relatively easily be absorbed

---

[18] John Landers, *The Field and the Forge: Population, Production, and Power in the Pre-Industrial West* (New York, 2003), pp. 202–249.

[19] Robert Bartlett, *The Making of Europe: Conquest, Colonization and Cultural Change, 950–1350* (Princeton, NJ, 1993); pp. 56, 204–211, 306–308. See also Brendan Smith, *Colonisation and Conquest in Medieval Ireland: The English in Louth, 1170–1330* (Cambridge, 1999); R. R. Davies, *Domination and Conquest: The Experience of Ireland, Scotland and Wales, 1100–1300* (Cambridge, 1990), pp. 3, 6, 30, 47–56, 56–58; R. R. Davies, *The First English Empire: Power and Identities in the British Isles, 1093–1343* (Oxford, 2000), pp. 111–112.

into a new hierarchy, provided the submission did not compromise their standing with their followers.[20]

The English in sixteenth-century Ireland had long used both of these strategies, with a strong emphasis on submission – in part because submission fit within a conception of Ireland not as foreign territory being newly conquered but rather as already part of the English royal dominion. The Norman Conquest had established the right and then, after 1541, the Irish were legally subjects of the English king – at least in English eyes. Submission was not only cheaper but easier to harmonize with English law. To be sure, examples would have to be made (through processes of both civil and martial law) and, from an English perspective, some rebels proved "incorrigible," but submission, rather than the destruction of the population or even the expensive destruction of an enemy, was the normal goal of military operations.[21]

This distinction between submission and "extirpation" was explicitly discussed in royal circles as early as 1540. In that year, the Lord Deputy and the Council of Ireland advised Henry that

> to enterprise the whole extirpation and total destruction of all the Irishmen of the land, it would be a marvelous expensive charge, and great difficulty;... [And] we have not heard or read in any chronicle, that at such conquests the whole inhabitants of the land have been utterly extirped and banished. Wherefore we think the easiest way and least charge were to take such as have not heinously offended to a reasonable submission and to prosecute the principals with all rigor and extremity.[22]

---

[20] Landers, *Field and Forge*, p. 245; Rapple, *Martial Power*, pp. 203–204. This fits in with Morgan's description of a medieval "divided sovereignty" discussed earlier.

[21] The ideology of submission and incorporation was most clearly reflected in Henry VIII's "surrender and regrant" program, which nominally applied only to the largest clan chiefs (under this program, a Gaelic chief "surrendered" his Gaelic title and his claim to clan land, and then received the land back as a royal grant, with an English noble title and the rights of an English lord over the land and its tenants). The concept, however, infused military operations at every level, and that is the focus here. For the regrant program, see Lennon, *Sixteenth-Century Ireland*, pp. 152–164; Canny, *Elizabethan Conquest*, p. 33; Ciaran Brady, "England's Defence and Ireland's Reform: The Dilemma of the Irish Viceroys, 1541–1641," in Brendan Bradshaw and J. S. Morrill, eds., *The British Problem, c. 1534–1707: State Formation in the Atlantic Archipelago* (New York, 1996), p. 95; David Edwards, "Collaboration without Anglicisation: The MacGiollapadraig Lordship and Tudor Reform," in Patrick J. Duffy, David Edwards, and Elizabeth FitzPatrick, eds., *Gaelic Ireland, c. 1250–c. 1650* (Dublin, 2001), pp. 77–97. Morgan argues that it was partly the increasing intransigence of English definitions of sovereignty that led to O'Neill's revolt. *Tyrone's Rebellion*, p. 219.

[22] *SPH*, 3:176–177 (language modernized).

Militarily, this is best understood as a recommendation to pursue submission with limited decapitation; this is not that different from the advice Lieutenant General Sir Graeme Lamb offered to Lieutenant General David Petraeus in Iraq in 2007 to divide the reconcilable elements of the Iraqi insurgency from the irreconcilable ones.[23]

What does this mean operationally? For English military men, the main problem seemed to be the elusiveness of Irishmen. As one planner rather hyperbolically complained in 1599, it was "madness" to pursue such

> naked rogues in woods and bogs, whom hounds can scarce follow, and much less men. Their ordinary food is a kind of grass. Neither clothes nor houses, generally, do they care for. With this their savage life are they able to wear out any army that seeketh to conquer them. It is no more possible to defeat them at once, than to destroy so many wolves and foxes.[24]

Unable to catch Irish forces, for much of the century the English in Ireland turned to another medieval military option, seeking to achieve submission through pressure by devastation – what an earlier era called a *chevauchée*. Repeated campaigns into the countryside of stubborn lords undermined their image, drained their income, and made it difficult to either raise or hire troops.[25] In one sense, this was a hearts-and-minds approach, but it was not the persuasion through gentility of modern counterinsurgency but rather an attack on lordship. A lord's duty was to protect his people, and failure to do so undermined his legitimacy.

Lord Deputy Henry Sidney's 1569 campaign to suppress the Butler and Desmond Fitzgerald revolt provides an example. Sidney designed his campaign of that year to use an army to pressure by devastation with the ultimate goal of achieving submission. To be sure, Sidney had relatively few troops and therefore only limited options. The paper strength of the mobile English army in Ireland in March 1569 consisted of 231 foot, 449 horsemen, and 225 kern (lightly armed Irish mercenary allies), with

---

[23] Mark Urban, *Task Force Black* (London, 2010), p. 186; "General Petraeus Stays Focused in Iraq," *Telegraph*, March 23, 2008 (accessed May 28, 2010 at http://www.telegraph.co.uk/news/worldnews/1582583/General-David-Petraeus-stays-focused-in-Iraq.html).

[24] *CSPI*, 8:363. This author, writing in 1599, did not recommend *chevauchées* but rather progressive forts, as subsequently discussed here. His description of the problem of Irish elusiveness, however, is a standard one, if a bit over the top.

[25] "Introduction," in Andrew Ayton and J. L. Price, eds., *The Medieval Military Revolution* (New York, 1998), pp. 7–8, and the citations there; Clifford J. Rogers, "By Fire and Sword: *Bellum Hostile* and 'Civilians' in the Hundred Years' War," in Mark Grimsley and Clifford J. Rogers, eds., *Civilians in the Path of War* (Lincoln, 2002), pp. 33–78.

a further couple hundred men scattered in tiny garrisons or serving in the royal artillery.[26] In short, Sidney had little choice but to parade through the countryside, taking on rebel garrisons or armies where he could find them, and defending the more important towns. Sidney departed Dublin with barely 600 men; intelligence on his enemies suggested they heavily outnumbered him.[27]

Sidney moved to protect the commercial town of Kilkenny, and he then besieged and captured three small defended castles. As for devastation, the tactic was assumed: Speaking of the White Knight's country, he said only, "I therefore passed in effect through all his countrey burning all the corne that was gathered and spoiling the rest, I rased one of his castells[,] burnt and spoiled all his other houses."[28]

This kind of pressure by devastation was not *intended* to kill the local population. The tactic of devastation in most sixteenth-century contexts was logistical and psychological – it eroded a lord's ability to control or influence his clients and thus wield military force. People suffered as soldiers went about their business and looked after their own needs, but the soldiers did not kill civilians as a matter of policy. The strategy worked relatively quickly on the Butler rebels; they submitted within a few months. Sidney accepted their submission, along with many others, and extended them a pardon.[29]

Sidney's campaign was one of many in Ireland fundamentally designed to achieve (re)submission to royal authority. There were others prior to 1590 perhaps more famous and a great deal more violent, but this strategic conception best reflects royal hopes for a managed and profitable order in Ireland.[30] From the English perspective, O'Neill's rebellion began in much the same way and escalated not only as a local threat to English

---

[26] State Papers 63/27/56, National Archives, UK (hereafter SP); 340 men had just been left to garrison Carrickfergus.

[27] "A Breviate of the gettinge of Ireland and the Decaye of the Same," Harleian Ms. 35, 210r–216r, British Library (undated, but from near this period); *CCM*, 1:393–394; SP 63/25/86 (ii); Edwards, "Butler Revolt," p. 234; *CSPI*, 1:414; Canny, *Elizabethan Conquest*, p. 142.

[28] The details of Sidney's 1569 summer campaign and the incident at Clonmel come from three different journals: Ciaran Brady, ed., *A Viceroy's Vindication? Sir Henry Sidney's Memoir of Service in Ireland, 1556–78* (Cork, Ireland, 2002), pp. 62–69; SP 63/29/70; and Ms. 660, ff. 78–91, Trinity College, Dublin.

[29] *CCM*, 1:401.

[30] The violent expropriations conducted by Sir Humphrey Gilbert and the first earl of Essex in the 1570s and 1580s were in many ways a result of private enterprise colonizing efforts. Their fundamental strategic vision differed. See Lee, *Barbarians and Brothers*, end of chap. 1 and beginning of chap. 2.

control, but also, in combination with Spanish help, potentially a threat to England itself. In those circumstances, it proved difficult to sustain a *strategy* of submission. The operational techniques, however, continued to rely on devastation, but the strategic goal of those raids began to shift over time to more outright destruction of the population.

O'NEILL'S REBELLION

What proved to be the last great rebellion of the century commenced in a series of fits and starts from 1593 to 1594, and it continued in a pattern of uncertainty through 1598.[31] In part, it was the pattern of alternating rebellion with submission that generated that uncertainty. Hugh O'Neill in particular oscillated back and forth, cleverly using truces and protestations of loyalty alternating with brisk victories to keep the English from invading his heartland in Ulster. Ulster had long remained the region least subject to English control. O'Neill reformed his military system in response to the English challenge and laid the foundations for an island-wide anti-English coalition aided by direct Spanish intervention.

During this period, the English suffered from unexpected changes of leadership and a vacillating military policy that sought merely to gain access to the interior of Ulster. The Irish victories at Clontibret (1595) and Yellow Ford (1598), combined with the increasing threat of Spanish intervention, eventually led Queen Elizabeth to make a major commitment of troops and to send the Earl of Essex to take command (Figure 2). Observers assumed that the combination of one of England's most famous generals – a man with the social status necessary to bend recalcitrant servitors to his will – along with the promise of 16,000 foot, 1,300 horse, and 2,000 monthly reinforcements, would make short work of the rebellion.[32]

---

[31] The literature on this war is extensive. Falls, *Elizabeth's Irish Wars*, is still useful. Key recent statements are Morgan, *Tyrone's Rebellion*; John McGurk, *Elizabethan Conquest of Ireland: The 1590s Crisis* (Manchester, UK, 1997); several essays in Hiram Morgan, ed., *The Battle of Kinsale* (Bray, Ireland, 2004); and David Edwards, Padraig Lenihan, and Clodagh Tait, eds., *The Age of Atrocity: Violence and Political Conflict in Early Modern Ireland* (Dublin, 2007). Lenman, *England's Colonial Wars*, provides a fine short summary.

[32] English peacetime forces in Ireland were often astonishingly small, regularly dipping as low as 1,000 men or fewer, although they expanded during the periodic rebellions. At the outbreak of O'Neill's rebellion in 1593, the English forces numbered only 1,500 men – slightly larger than the royal garrisons at the beginning of the sixteenth century but still smaller than some of the private retinues in both Gaelic and Anglo-Irish lordships. Ciaran Brady, "The Captains' Games: Army and Society in Elizabethan Ireland," in

FIGURE 2. Ireland, 1594–1603.

Elizabeth certainly assumed that Essex and this new, larger army would be sufficient to the task. Her policy in 1599 as she dispatched Essex (as well as her instructions to Mountjoy in 1600 even after Essex's failure) made her expectations clear. She tried to strike a classic balance between a promise of severity to obstinate rebels with a pledge of mercy to those who submitted. Her public proclamation in March 1599 accompanying Essex's army warned the "unnatural rebels" that her "long patience" was running out, and that obedience needed to be restored, something "which by the Laws of God and Nature is due unto us." Thus, she justified *terror*, or in her words "extraordinary Force." But she also protested no intent of "utter extirpation and rooting out of that Nation.... Our actions tending onely to reduce a number of unnaturall and barbarous Rebels, and to roote out the Capitall heads of the most notorious Traitours." She concluded by assuring a "gracious disposition to those that shall deserve mercie."[33] Even after Essex's massive failure and flight to England in 1599, her instructions to Mountjoy in 1600 reiterated this intent to seek submissions, although with pledges (i.e., hostages), and preferably after "blood service" – the latter meaning that submitted lords would have to kill or bring in their former compatriots to receive a full pardon. As for O'Neill himself, she instructed Mountjoy to allow him to submit also but to keep that particular option secret.[34]

How did military men in Ireland imagine translating a policy of balanced terror and mercy into strategy and operations? Interestingly, royal military instructions had begun to reflect the reams of advice prepared and submitted by junior officers and servitors – "captains" in the

---

Thomas Bartlett and Keith Jeffery, eds., *A Military History of Ireland* (Cambridge, 1996), pp. 144–146. For other tabulations of English armies in Ireland, see Steven G. Ellis, "The Tudors and the Origins of the Modern Irish State: A Standing Army," in *A Military History of Ireland*, pp. 120, 132; *SPH* 3:343, 433; Steven G. Ellis, *Ireland in the Age of the Tudors, 1447–1603* (London, 1998), pp. 24, 26, 67, 90, 95, 139, 145; Mark Charles Fissel, *English Warfare, 1511–1641* (London, 2001), pp. 207–210; John S. Nolan, "The Militarization of the Elizabethan State," *Journal of Military History* 58 (1994), p. 418.

[33] Humfrey Dyson, *A Booke Containing All Such Proclamations as were Published during the Raigne of the Late Queene Elizabeth*, Short Title Catalogue 7758.3 (London, 1618), pp. 361–362 (hereafter STC). She instructed Essex to allow O'Neill to submit, but only "upon simple and single submission"; his life could be granted to him provided he submitted appropriately humbly, and gave security for his future loyalty. *CCM*, 3:295. There is an important distinction between a "penitent submission" and a negotiated one. O'Neill, in particular, regularly triggered Elizabeth's ire when she believed his submissions were not in fact penitent. The issue, though important, and deeply tied to the monarch's sense of his or her honor, lies outside the scope of this essay.

[34] *CSPI*, 8:440–447.

parlance of the day, nobles or aspiring noblemen who commanded 100 to 300 men, many with long experience in Ireland. They had been calling for this level of commitment for some time, and many of them had clear visions of victory and how to accomplish it.

In previous rebellions such as that battled by Sidney in 1569, the traditional approach had been a summer campaign of devastation, combined with a wide dispersal of small defensive garrisons in more or less "friendly" territory to protect it against incursions. A new strategic consensus emerged in the late 1590s, called by some contemporaries a "mixed war" strategy, and appearing especially in the writings of 1598 to early 1600 of Captains Thomas Lee, Nicholas Dawtrey, Humfrey Willis, Carlile, John Baynard, Henry Brouncker, and Thomas Reade.[35] It was this consensus that most closely informed Elizabeth's instructions to Essex and then to Mountjoy. These captains criticized the cost and ineffectiveness of predictable and vulnerable campaign armies. Instead, they advocated the establishment of a ring of forts around and penetrating into Ulster. English garrisons in closely spaced forts inside O'Neill's country could actively patrol and devastate the country (including during the winter) and thereby squeeze O'Neill's ability to maintain his forces in the field. In one sense, the captains' advice responded to the problem of booleying and extracting resources from a too-mobile organic economy.[36] With such a chain or net of garrisons, "Tyrone and his followers will be so penned up that they will not know where to look for the pasturage of their cows and other cattle, which are their life, and without which they are not able to keep wars."[37]

---

[35] There were different areas of emphasis in their various plans, but this summary conveys their commonalities and major points. Lee: Captain Thomas Lee, "A Brief Declaration of the Government of Ireland," in *Desiderata Curiosa Hibernica or a Select Collection of State Papers; Consisting of Royal Instructions, Directions, Dispatches, and Letters. To Which Are Added, Some Historical Tracts. The Whole Illustrating... the Political Systems of... Ireland,... Faithfully Transcribed From Their Originals, or Authentick Copies* (Dublin, 1772), 1:87–150; [Thomas Lee], "The Discoverye & Recoverye," Sloane Ms. 1818, British Library; Hiram Morgan, "Tom Lee: The Posing Peacemaker," in Brendan Bradshaw, Andrew Hadfield, and Willy Maley, eds., *Representing Ireland: Literature and the Origins of Conflict, 1534–1660* (Cambridge, 1993), pp. 132–165. Dawtrey: John Dawtrey, *The Falstaff Saga: Being the Life and Opinions of Captain Nicholas Dawtrey* (London, 1927), pp. 190–200; Willis: *CSPI*, 8:327–329; Carlile: *CSPI*, 8:329–331; Baynard: *CSPI*, 8:347–352; Brouncker: *CSPI*, 7:36–38; Reade: *CSPI*, 7:449–452.

[36] I should say that even the veteran captains did not seem to understand the extent to which Ulster depended heavily on traditional agriculture; deputies from Sidney to Mountjoy were surprised at the extent of cultivation in Ulster.

[37] *CSPI*, 8:329–331.

The different plans suggested slightly varying locations for these forts, but the general outlines were similar. Thomas Lee's plan was the most developed and is exemplary in its broad outlines. He recommended major provisions bases at Carlingford, Newry, and Kells, which would then support a series of forts extending from Newry to Armagh and on to the key crossing of the Blackwater River at Charlemont, and then westward via Monaghan and Cloones to connect to the Lough Erne. Once those forts were established, the English could mount the long-hoped-for and essential amphibious operations to the Lough Foyle and to Ballyshannon, which would simultaneously surround O'Neill, split Ulster in two, and seal Hugh O'Donnell (O'Neill's chief ally, based in northwest Ulster) out of Connaught.

All the captains agreed that the garrisons should be aggressive – these were not to be the old defensive forts intended to protect settled land around them. Lee was particularly specific:

> For it is not the holding of the forces together in gross, nor walking up & down the country, nor living idle in the best towns of the English pale that will affect it. The garrisons should be placed near bordering upon the enemy, ... so to stirring in the night rather than in the day, to enter into the rebels' fastnesses; for it is the night service (well spied and guided) which must end the wars of Ireland, and not fighting with them in the daytime by fits.[38]

Aggressive offensive action, then, was preferable to sitting back and waiting for the rebels to strike at times and places of their choosing.

Even within this aggressive operational style, however, the captains' strategic intent remained to prod O'Neill's adherents into submission. As Captain Nicholas Dawtrey suggested, once a garrison was in place, a proclamation should be made that "such as are in rebellion against her Majestie and that are willing to cum in, and live as dutifull subjectes ... shalbe received to mercy and be pardoned." The forts were intended to "da[u]nt them" and make "every man to seeke means how he may make his owne peace," although, again, certain incorrigible rebels were to be killed. After all, Dawtrey argued, "It is more glorious to reforme a wicked people than to slay them all."[39]

Even Captain Henry Docwra, who led the amphibious landing to the Lough Foyle and who then pushed a chain of garrisons in between O'Donnell's land and O'Neill's, and who is usually (and rightly)

---

[38] [Lee], "The Discoverye & Recoverye" f. 75v. For clarity, this quote has been modernized and tightly paraphrased in a few places.
[39] Morgan, "Booke of Questions," pp. 100, 123, 111.

associated with some of the most violent aspects of the final conquest of Ulster, made a point of recommending land and protection for the Gaelic lords who helped him, *even at the cost of land for himself*. He argued that the Irish should not feel driven to such extremities that they would never yield.[40] A modern analyst might call this a form of population-centric counterinsurgency, although it was hardly without its harder edges, and there were far more failures to protect the Gaelic population than there were successes. Nevertheless, there was plenty of evidence that military men in Ireland saw the loyalty of the countryside as worth cultivating, even if only as a process of dividing and conquering. Captain Charles Montague's complaint in 1597 illustrates both the desire to cultivate submissions and the conflicting impulses that undermined the process. He had taken in some former rebels, given them his protection, and even taken them into the Queen's service, whereupon they were attacked by another English captain, even as English soldiers actively tried to protect them.[41]

In short, as Elizabeth's public policy promised to balance terror *and* mercy, captains wrote strategy recommendations with submission in mind as the ultimate objective. Many of those recommendations worked their way into royal pronouncements or strategic plans (especially those of Mountjoy). Actual practice sometimes followed these outlines, and sometimes it did not. Like any monarch, Elizabeth could only rely on her agents, and they in turn on their soldiers. Both groups had their own vision of the proper use of force. Montague's complaint was of a relatively isolated example, but even major operations might ignore royal instructions. Essex's campaign in 1599, for example, ignored the queen's instructions to focus on O'Neill in Ulster, and instead he chose to "shake and sway all the branches" in Munster. In this, he violated his instructions, forgot his own declaration that "by God, I will beat Tyrone in the field," and ignored much of the advice he had received about how to win the war.[42]

Essex seemed to take to heart the idea of balancing terror and mercy. Operationally, he did almost exactly what Sidney had done 30 years previously: He ran a campaign of devastation, initiated a few sieges, took a few castles, and then accepted submissions and issued pardons. On

---

[40] *CSPI*, 10:191.
[41] *CSPI*, 7:102.
[42] *CSPI*, 8:16 (shake and sway quote); T. W. Moody et al., eds., *A New History of Ireland*: vol. III (Oxford, 1976), p. 127 (By God quote).

the one hand, Essex granted local military commanders a wide range of martial-law powers that opened the door for extensive hurried executions, often intended to enrich the captain exercising the law.[43] On the other hand, he pardoned some 1,140 individuals. Some of the pardons covered the whole households of a major figure, who had submitted. James Fitzpiers's pardon, for example, encompassed 281 other names.[44]

If one can count Essex as relatively generous in allowing submissions and granting pardons, other captains interpreted the policy somewhat differently. Consider the operations of one Captain Flower, campaigning in Munster in 1600. Ordered, per Elizabethan policy, "to march into Carberry, there to burn and spoil all such as was revolted from their loyalty, if they would not come in, and put in sufficient pledges for their subjection," Flower interpreted his instructions broadly. After a skirmish or two, and the burning of some rebel castles, towns, and surrounding country, he then marched into the neighboring country where his troops "burned all those parts, and had the killing of many of their churls and poor people, [we left them not one grain of corn] within ten miles of our way,... and took a prey of 500 cows, which I caused to be drowned and killed."[45] Either no one submitted in all this march or Flower simply never bothered to ask.

To be fair, many commentators had begun to doubt the meaning and reliability of submission. Hatreds were building, and English commanders were not short of stories that led them to question the long-term value of accepting a submission and granting a pardon – even when guaranteed by hostages.[46] In the same month as Flower's march, Sir Francis Stafford reported that the garrison at Maryborough had been approached by a local man who offered to lead them to a store of desperately needed corn. The would-be guide left his wife and child in the fort as a pledge

---

[43] *The Irish Fiants of the Tudor Sovereigns*, vol. 3 (Dublin, 1994), pp. 6281, 6282, 6285, 6288, 6290, 6291, 6307, 6319, 6337, and 6342.

[44] I discuss Essex's campaign in greater detail in *Barbarians and Brothers*, chap. 2. For the pardons, see *Irish Fiants*, pp. 6280, 6284, 6294, 6302, 6303, 6305, 6309, 6312, 6314, 6315, 6323, 6329, and 6338. For use of martial law, see Edwards, "Beyond Reform"; Edwards, "Spenser's View and Martial Law," pp. 152–153.

[45] *CSPI*, 9:116–117.

[46] For concerns (not always restricted to this period) about the authenticity of submissions, see "Certain Principall matters concerning the state of Ireland collected briefly oute of primary wryters and offered after some opynions anno 1600," Ms. 3319, National Library of Ireland, Dublin; Lee, "A Brief Declaration," 1:111–112; [Lee], "The Discoverye & Recoverye," f. 51r; Morgan, "A Booke of Questions," p. 112; Barnabe Rich, *Allarme to England*, STC 20979 (London, 1578), d.ii; *CSPI*, 8:45–51.

of his good faith. He then led 20 soldiers straight into an ambush, which killed all the soldiers, and thus sacrificed his wife and child to English revenge. Stafford was stupefied by this willingness to self-sacrifice for the sake of killing a mere 20 soldiers.[47] Henry Docwra related with similar amazement the Irish captain who had long served on English behalf – a man who had delivered up 20 spies, preyed 2,000 cows, and killed some 200 Irishmen with his own hand. That same man changed sides without notice, and he and his men massacred the English company with which he was serving as garrison at Newtown, all apparently without having made a prior arrangement with Hugh O'Neill. The befuddled Docwra could only conclude that it arose "out of the mere disposition of a perfidious nature, delighted in the very quality of evil, he was moved thereunto by a sudden and mere instigation of the devill."[48]

This sort of experience, as well as the more or less constant personal profit seeking by many English captains, began to infect more than just the decisions of local commanders. English operations began to take a harder edge, even if Elizabethan policy retained a lip service about protecting Irish subjects. That shift occurred both progressively from the sort of experience described by Docwra and Stafford, and as a result of two key events: the failure of Essex's 1599 campaign and the growing certainty of a Spanish landing, realized at Kinsale in September 1601. Essex had arrived in Ireland with great fanfare and many thousands of troops. His army was organized on a scale never before seen in Ireland. When he made virtually no impression whatsoever on the depth or breadth of the rebellion, and worse, when he appeared in a private parley to collude with O'Neill himself, Essex fled back to England to restore his reputation with Elizabeth. He failed to impress her and, desperate, he soon launched a coup that led to his execution.

In terms of policy and strategy in Ireland, however, his failure abetted frustrations. It seemed beyond belief that such a large army, at such enormous cost, had accomplished so little, and even had produced yet another truce with an unrepentant O'Neill. Elizabeth excoriated Essex for his paltry successes, noting that the taking of Cahir Castle "from a rabble of rogues, with such force as you had, and with the help of the cannon, which was always able in Ireland to make his passage where it pleased," was hardly worth boasting about.[49] That winter (1599–1600),

---

[47] *CSPI*, 9:95–96.
[48] *CSPI*, 11.92–93.
[49] *CSPI*, 8:98.

O'Neill moved his army south out of Ulster, deep into Munster, where he attracted ever more followers, and addressed himself to King Philip III of Spain as "Your Majesty's most faithful subject."[50]

This sense of disappointment, cost, and the rising threat of Spanish intervention led to a new burst of strategic advice, much of it more radical than in the past.[51] These new strategic recommendations bore the marks of desperation, as well as a profound doubt about the wisdom of taking submissions and issuing pardons. In the end, the Gaelic population would bear the brunt of the new strategy. This new round of captains' advice began by repeating the strategic consensus – again recommending locations for placing aggressive garrisons in O'Neill's country. But some also began to incorporate a more radical vocabulary – a vocabulary that had existed in the past but not in such extreme forms. First, they insisted on refusing to accept submissions without blood service. Mountjoy followed this advice: As his and Carew's campaigns took effect that summer and fall of 1600, many rebels came in seeking pardons, but Mountjoy insisted on blood service before accepting them as loyal subjects.[52] Second, critically, some of the writers expanded the meaning of devastation to include the intention to generate widespread famine, famine that would not just directly force concentrated armies to withdraw from the field but that also would destroy the productive population of the organic economy and thus indirectly undermine the rebels' ability to fight.[53]

In the spring of 1600, the English finally enacted the new strategic consensus, as well as the beginnings of a strategy of famine. Even at this stage, however, especially prior to the Spanish landing, some limits on destructiveness and violence remained. Henry Docwra made the long-planned landing in O'Neill's rear at Lough Foyle; Arthur Chichester took charge on Ulster's eastern flank around the old English base at Knockfergus; the new English overall commander, Lord Mountjoy, pursued O'Neill back into Ulster and then made his first move to the Blackwater River to

---

[50] Admittedly, O'Neill was asking only for a donation for a Catholic college, but the implication of subject status, in a letter captured and copied by the English, must have been striking confirmation of English fears. CSPI, 8:337–338.

[51] Brady, Carey, and McGurk separately discuss this shift in strategy, although it is only fair to note that strategies of starvation had been used and suggested in the past. The scale and deliberateness of its execution after 1600, however, was new. Brady, "The Captains' Games," p. 158; Vincent Carey, "'What pen can paint or tears atone?': Mountjoy's Scorched Earth Campaign," pp. 205–216; McGurk, "The Pacification of Ulster, 1600–3," in Edwards et al., eds., Age of Atrocity, pp. 121, 128.

[52] Moryson, Itinerary, 2:271.

[53] CSPI, 8:45–51; CSPI, 7:383–386; CSPI, 8:365–370; CSPI, 9:147–148, 194–198.

provide a diversion for the Lough Foyle landing; and George Carew began pacification operations in Munster.

Carew was generally successful in quieting Munster during summer and fall 1600, and his assessment at the end of the next summer, just prior to the Spanish arrival, provides a clear snapshot into the ongoing debate over starvation versus submission. Writing to Elizabeth's chief advisor in early August 1601, he disagreed with those who had accused him of not being harsh enough:

> Whereas it is distilled by some that I did not pursue the war to its extremity, and that if I had done so all those who are now hollow hearted would have been starved, let me say that I do not agree. It may be that churls and women might have fallen into that misery, but in the Earl of Desmond's rebellion [1579–1583] we found by experience that the swordsman was not (notwithstanding that great famine, the like whereof no former age hath seen) pinched to starving, as the churls were; neither is it possible to starve them as long as the other parts of the kingdom hath meat.

He admitted that perhaps he could have temporarily forced out armed rebels through "burning and spoiling" (i.e., a direct strategy of devastation), but they would soon return. "Whereby I may conclude that no man can make a continued peace in Ireland but on utter extirpation of that nation, which I am sure was never harboured in her Majesty's heart nor yet advised by any of her Council." He concluded that his method for ending the war quickly, through submission, had been best.[54]

As Carew also foresaw, however, a Spanish invasion would change the game. He prepared to defend Cork against an invasion, but he predicted that "if any of her Majesty's walled cities be taken, all will be lost and a general revolt ensue."[55] It was that fear that led Mountjoy and his lieutenants Docwra and Chichester in the north to begin a more extreme form of campaigning. That same month (August 1601), Mountjoy described his plans for Ulster. In accordance with the new strategic consensus, he would maintain his garrisons within Ulster through the winter as part of a spoiling war, deliberately directed at the loyalties of the people who would suffer. He believed it would undermine the people's hope of the Spaniards and their love for O'Neill. To achieve that result, he would "cut corn and burn houses even in their fastness."

---

[54] CSPI, 11:5–6. For the extent to which he took submissions, see Moryson, Itinerary, 2:376–377.
[55] CSPI, 11:5.

Furthermore, destroying corn would leave the Irish rebels "no other means to keep their bonnaghts, which are their hired soldiers."[56] This was not just devastation as a direct strategy to force the withdrawal of troops from a particular region; it was an indirect strategy, aimed at the wider productive population, which would affect the armed rebels' ability to remain in the field at all.

KINSALE

Carew's observation about "her Majesty's walled towns" and his fear for Cork is central to understanding the hybrid threat presented by the Spanish. Over the preceding 50 years or so, England had slowly and painfully (re)built administrative control over most of the south and west of Ireland, and to some extent even in Connacht. Rebellions repeatedly flared up, but rarely had they threatened the walled cities – those were truly English in administration, orientation, and, to a lesser extent, ethnicity. Irish rebels, and even Anglo-Irish rebels, had never had the staying capacity or the artillery to change that fundamental truth.[57] Ulster lacked cities, and in many ways remained a terra incognita to Englishmen.[58] The fighting there, and elsewhere against Gaelic rebels, was a form of guerilla war, although O'Neill's reforms had allowed him to fight a somewhat more "positional" form of war as he tried to defend the heartland of his territory. Thus far, he had been successful, and he had devastated the new English "plantations" in Munster in 1598 and again in 1599–1600 (although not the older walled cities). By late summer 1601, however, English armies on the edges of Ulster surrounded O'Neill. Then, on 21 September, roughly 3,700 Spaniards landed on Ireland's south coast at Kinsale.[59]

---

[56] *CSPI*, 11:7–11.

[57] There were exceptions. Athenry was taken twice (1574 and 1596), Kilmallock in 1570, and Youghal in 1579. Regarding the latter, however, it was taken by the rebel Anglo-Irish earl of Desmond by a sudden night assault during low tide and after having lulled the town into believing he would do nothing. Kerrigan, *Castles and Fortifications*, p. 41; SP 63/70/15; SP 63/70/20.

[58] Surviving sixteenth-century maps of Ireland continued to represent the interior of Ulster as something of a forested unknown even as late as 1587 and 1599. See esp. Ms. 1209/2, "Irelande," c. 1587, Trinity College Dublin; and Baptista Boazio's 1599 map found as Figure 4 in Bernhard Klein, "Partial Views: Shakespeare and the Map of Ireland," *Early Modern Literary Studies* 4.2 (1998), pp. 1–20.

[59] The invasion force was supposed to be larger, but storms had divided the fleet.

The Spanish arrival immediately transformed the war and both sides' priorities.[60] For the English, all attention turned to the Spanish force. Kinsale was an isolated beachhead, but Cork was not far away, and from there it was a short hop to other English walled cities and the commercial and administrative beating heart of Munster. The English could not be sure how many more Spanish ships and reinforcements were on the way; they needed to contain the Spanish landing before the revolt widened. Carew, after all, had only recently pacified Munster in the wake of O'Neill's march into the region in 1598 (and again in 1599–1600). Many of the lords in that region later legitimately claimed to have revolted under direct pressure from O'Neill, and if those submitted lords were not secured, or as Mountjoy put it, "if we doe not defend them from Tirone, [they] must and will returne unto him."[61] As Mountjoy rushed his main army to contain the Spanish, he pulled in garrisons from all directions to join him in a field army capable of laying siege to the Spanish at Kinsale. The Spanish were the key; minor garrisons around Ulster no longer mattered. As Mountjoy wrote to London, "if wee beat them [the Spanish], let it not trouble you, though you heare all Ireland doth revolt, for (by the grace of God) you shall have them all returne presently with halters about their necks; if we doe not, all providence [care] bestowed on any other place is vaine."[62]

O'Neill and O'Donnell needed to join their Spanish allies, ironically to rescue them and thereby preserve the possibility of the Spaniards' widening their intervention beyond the pathetic few landed at Kinsale (650 more troops landed shortly later at Castlehaven, just to the west, and a very few more were distributed to other southwestern coastal castles). O'Neill and O'Donnell, supported by the Munster lord Donal Cam O'Sullivan Beare, quickly marched to relieve the Spanish from the English siege.

---

[60] The events surrounding the Kinsale campaign have been described in many books. The most authoritative recent work, one that most fully incorporates material from the Spanish archives, consists of the essays in Morgan, *The Battle of Kinsale*, esp. Morgan, "Disaster at Kinsale." Older versions are in Falls, *Elizabeth's Irish Wars*; Hayes-McCoy, *Irish Battles*; John J. Silke, *Kinsale: The Spanish Intervention in Ireland at the End of the Elizabethan Wars* (New York, 1970); R. B. Wernham, *The Return of the Armadas: The Last Years of the Elizabethan War Against Spain, 1595–1603* (Oxford, 1994); Darren McGettigan, *Red Hugh O'Donnell and the Nine Years War* (Dublin, 2005).

[61] Moryson, *Itinerary*, 2:454–5, 459 (quote). By 2 October, Mountjoy believed that he needed to sustain the winter war in Ulster in addition to concentrating on Kinsale. *Ibid.* 2:460–1.

[62] Moryson, *Itinerary*, 2:454.

The withdrawal of English garrisons to join Mountjoy's army made the Gaels' exit from Ulster easy, and Carew's effort to intercept O'Donnell's converging column failed in the face of greater Irish mobility. Suddenly, Mountjoy found himself outnumbered and positioned between two enemy armies. Ironically, the onset of a hybrid war had required Mountjoy to concentrate his forces, but doing so created a difficult logistical problem even in settled southwestern Ireland. And now, as the besieger had become the besieged, his army was in danger of starving or evaporating from disease, desertion, and the defection of Irish troops within his own ranks.

The ensuing siege, Irish–Spanish negotiations, and eventual attack by the combined Irish army on the English position suffered all the complexities of multiple ethnicities fighting a coalition war with different strategic expectations and different levels of training and capability. Those details proved crucial to the English victory, but they need not detain us here. In brief, fearing the continued deterioration of the besieged Spanish force, O'Neill precipitously launched an attack before it was necessary. His night-approach march generated confusion and in the ensuing battle, the English army took full advantage of their superior horsemen to utterly rout the Irish army. O'Neill and O'Donnell fled (the latter all the way to Spain), and the Spanish shortly thereafter capitulated in a surrender agreement that allowed them to return home.

In hindsight, it is clear that the "hybrid" part of the war was now over. The Spanish would not return, but that truth was not clear to English commanders dealing with continued resistance. Indeed, in the wake of Kinsale, Carew's first priority was to root out the tiny Spanish forces left behind in small castles farther south and west. Fifteen months of hard fighting were required in Munster and Ulster, and throughout that period the English feared the return of the Spanish.[63] In one sense, Kinsale therefore represented an interruption to the pattern of warfare that Mountjoy had initiated the previous spring and to which he now returned, but with perhaps an even less patient approach to the rebels or the local Gaelic population. When Mountjoy again moved into Ulster, he now removed the submitted productive population south of the Blackwater River. As always with such removals, many simply starved or were killed in the process. It was during this last 15 months of campaigning that the truly horrifying portrayals of starvation and destruction for which the war is

---

[63] Carey, "What pen can paint," p. 208; contra Wernham, *Return of the Armadas*, pp. 391–392.

now famous emerged.⁶⁴ Nevertheless, in April 1602, Mountjoy continued to advocate for a strategy of submission:

> Your lordships seem to doubt the expediency of admitting Irishmen to pardon and receiving their submission, thinking that they only remain loyal so long as the sword is heavy on them.... We cannot deny... that rebellious persons pretend loyalty not from zeal but from an impious dissimulation to shift off their present danger. But it would, as we now stand, cost the Queen too much to pull down rebellions by force only.... If we receive instructions to cease giving of pardons and protections, and to end this rebellion by force only, we shall do so; but we must tell you that such a policy is calculated to prolong the war to a great length and will involve great expense.⁶⁵

In the end, although perhaps cold comfort to the starving countryside, the war ended when Gaelic lord after Gaelic lord *submitted*, including finally even O'Neill, who was restored to his English earldom.

CONCLUSION

England's wartime strategies derived from the English view of Ireland as a component kingdom of a composite monarchy. That legal status helped drive the preference for strategies of submission. English wars in Ireland have often been portrayed as precursors to Atlantic colonization, and as such they supposedly proceeded without concern for the local population; indeed, that they approached genocide.⁶⁶ There were certainly some major figures who sought such a result as a way of "clearing" the land for personal profit and colonization.⁶⁷ But military figures in Ireland – men who served a royal master seeking an ordered, profitable sovereignty – sought the submission and incorporation of people as subjects. When those subjects rebelled, long-established legal beliefs opened the door to extreme measures, even if they were not the preferred solutions. Unfortunately, geography and certain structural aspects of Irish society – particularly the mobility of a labor force that could move its

---

⁶⁴ This is the subject of Carey, "What pen can paint."
⁶⁵ *CSPI*, 11:378–379.
⁶⁶ Ben Kiernan recounts a standard version of this argument in *Blood and Soil: A World History of Genocide and Extermination from Sparta to Darfur* (New Haven, CT, 2007), pp. 169–212 (esp. pp. 210–211).
⁶⁷ This historiographical tendency is neatly summarized by Ken MacMillan's claim that during this period of English expansion, "the English were always more interested in the possession and exploitation of land than the subjugation and conversion of native peoples." Ken MacMillan, *Sovereignty and Possession in the English New World: The Legal Foundations of Empire, 1576–1640* (Cambridge, 2006), p. 9.

chief product (cattle) around – conspired to make the normal conquest processes of elite removal or submission and the acquisition of indigenous peasant labor more difficult, perhaps even impossible.[68]

Strategies of decapitation and pressure by devastation saw the laboring population as a group whose loyalty first had to be forcibly driven from their former masters, whereupon their allegiance to their new masters was simply assumed. Allegiance did not need to be won through kind treatment, although English planners assumed that the long-term benefits of English law would in time become clear to the local people. When the population refused to transfer their allegiance, and when their resources and their armed forces proved too mobile, frustration mounted. These challenges combined with cultural differences to justify extreme solutions to the military problem of rebellion. All too often, extreme solutions served some men's personal ambitions as well. When the war became a hybrid one after the Spanish invasion, the potential for Spanish conventional forces to encourage further rebellion and form a beachhead for reinforcements demanded that the English collect virtually every resource against them. In the end, the famine campaigns of 1601–1603 were in part accidents of technique, in part deliberate methods as a response to the perceived failure of the submission strategy, and in part the result of fear of the potent hybrid threat represented by a Gaelic–Spanish alliance. As both Carew and Mountjoy recognized immediately, the Irish rebellion only became insurmountable if combined with Spanish conventional power. They therefore turned all of their resources first to destroying the Spanish, after which they assumed they could eventually handle the Irish rebels. To preserve English sovereignty, the Irish had to be kept down – whatever the cost – and the Spanish out.

[68] Cf. the "metropolitan" program of incorporation for Native Americans described in Michael Leroy Oberg, *Dominion and Civility: English Imperialism and Native America, 1585–1685* (Ithaca, 1999).

4

The American Revolution

Hybrid War in America's Past

Williamson Murray

The small scale of our maps has deceived us ... We have undertaken a war against farmers and farmhouses scattered throughout a wild waste of [a] continent and shall soon hear of our General being obliged to garrison woods, to scale mountains, to wait for boats and pontoons at rivers, and to have his convoys and escorts as large as armies. These, and a thousand such difficulties, will rise on us at the next stage of the war. I say the next stage, because we have hitherto spent one campaign, and some millions, in losing one landing place on Boston, and, at the charge of seven millions and a second campaign, we have replaced it with two other landing-places at Rhode Island and New York ... Something more is required, than the mere mechanical business of fighting, in composing revolts and bringing back things to their former order.

A citizen of London upon hearing about the defeats at Trenton and Princeton.[1]

This chapter addresses the peculiar framework within which the combatants in the Revolutionary War operated, particularly the British. There are innumerable lessons this conflict should suggest to the modern analyst, the most important of which is the obvious one of "know your enemy."[2] One might think, given the extensive experience the British had garnered in the major wars they had waged on the North American continent, that they would have possessed not only a general knowledge of their colonial opponent but also a finely tuned appreciation of his strengths

---

[1] Citizen of London quoted in Robert M. Ketchum, *The Winter Soldiers, The Battles for Trenton and Princeton* (New York, 1973), p. 327.
[2] This is a reality that can prove difficult even when one speaks the same language and shares a common heritage.

and weaknesses – after all, they had used the colonies as a base for their assault on French Canada in three major conflicts: Queen Anne's War (the War of Spanish Succession, 1702–1712), the War of Austrian Succession (1745–1750), and the Seven Years' War (the French and Indian War, 1756–1763). Thus, the British should have been ideally positioned to fulfill that ironic proposition that Clausewitz advances in Book VIII of *On War* that "[n]o one starts a war – or rather, no one in his senses ought to do so – without first being clear in his mind what he intends to achieve by that war and how he intends to conduct it."[3] On the first proposition, Lord North's ministry was crystal clear: British military operations aimed at bringing the colonists to heal and rendering them obedient in a fashion that no self-respecting, upper-class citizen of Great Britain would have tolerated. On the second, however, other than a self-fulfilling belief that all they had to do was show up, the British had not the slightest clue as to the kind of war they confronted.

Crucial to any understanding of the success of the American colonists is an understanding of the framework within which the war was fought and how the war on the North American continent influenced the larger global arena. Thus, let us begin with an examination of the war the British and the Americans had waged to drive the French from North America.[4] We then turn to the initial difficulties the British faced in the Lexington–Concord confrontation and the campaigns of 1776–1777, which made the British defeat inevitable.[5] Those two years presented the British with the problem of first projecting their military power across the Atlantic and into a hostile theater and then conducting military operations on the basis of political assumptions that had no connection to the realities on the ground.

THE WAR FOR NORTH AMERICA: 1756–1763

In the French and Indian War (the Seven Years' War to Europeans), a conflict far removed from the shores of Europe in 1756, the British and

---

[3] Carl von Clausewitz, *On War*, trans. and ed. by Michael Howard and Peter Paret (Princeton, NJ, 1976), p. 579.
[4] This essay has been heavily influenced by the work of Fred Anderson in dealing with this period. For the French and Indian War, see particularly his brilliant *Crucible of War, The Seven Years' War and the Fate of Empire in British North America, 1754–1766* (New York, 2000).
[5] In the words of the foremost historian of the British side of the Revolutionary War, "The defeat at Saratoga is the clearest turning point of the war. It marked the beginning of a general war waged throughout the world." Piers Mackesy, *The War for America, 1775–1783* (Lincoln, NB, 1992), p. 147.

the American colonists initially found themselves substantially inferior tactically to their enemies in the primeval wilderness of North America. In effect, to defeat the French in North America, the British had to achieve a number of goals. First, they needed to dominate the North Atlantic sea lines of communications to the extent possible in the age of sail. Even given the supremacy of the Royal Navy, that task was not a given. It took the Royal Navy two years to gain a general ascendancy at sea. Second, the British had to establish general superiority on the ground over the French in order to batter their way into Canada. The first two avenues of approach – to attack the great fortress of Louisbourg and move up the St. Lawrence River to take Quebec City – were open to direct assault by sea. But the other avenue, from Albany north to Lake Champlain and then into Canada, required considerable logistic and military support from the colonies – New England and New York in particular.

In examining both the French and Indian War and the American Revolution, the historian is struck by the logistical difficulties the British faced in projecting power from the British Isles across the Atlantic. One historian has calculated the time that it took 63 dispatches from Lord Germain, the Revolutionary War's director in London, to reach Major General Henry Clinton, the commander in New York, between May 1778 and February 1781: 6 took less than two months; 12 took two months; 28 took two to three months; 11 took three to four months; 4 took four to five months; and 2 took five to seven months.[6] Those figures suggest the much greater difficulties of moving men, equipment, horses, and ammunition across the Atlantic than simply a dispatch. Moreover, in the Revolutionary War, the need to ship a substantial portion of the sustenance for British troops from the British Isles further complicated logistics.

During the Seven Years' War, the major political issue lay in the willingness of the colonists to support the assault from the south against Montreal with militia and supplies. New England and New York were crucial in three respects: first, in providing militia to handle the danger of unconventional French and Indian forces; second, in mobilizing the labor required to haul supplies through the wilderness north and west of Albany; and third, in providing the supplies and foodstuffs required to support the campaign through to its terminus in Montreal. The architect of that effort was one of the great strategists in history: William Pitt.

In the first two years of the Seven Years' War, British and colonial military operations met failure, defeats exacerbated by political squabbling

[6] Ibid., p. 73.

between British governors and colonial legislatures.[7] More often than not, the latter proved recalcitrant and unwilling to provide the support the Royal authorities and British military believed necessary. British commanders, especially Lord Loudoun, displayed an arrogance and contempt for the locals that drove colonial leaders to distraction. The colonies raised short-term units from the militia, and those units were to serve for specific periods of time. The recalcitrance of colonial legislatures to provide more was partly the result of the fact that with a primitive, subsistence-based economy and limited ability to borrow, the colonies found it difficult to support the war, no matter how much they might desire to rid the continent of the French.

What went for the individual colony also went for the farmers, who made up the bulk of the colonial population. They lacked the excess labor to leave their farms for sustained periods of time, unless colonial governments or the British were willing to pay for their services. Thus, service represented a contract between the individual and his colonial state government. For British officers, such an approach to military service was nonsensical, but they soon discovered that without militia support they were not going to beat the French. A major difference between the Seven Years' War and the Revolutionary War is that in the latter case there would be no financial resources, on which the mobilization of colonial manpower in the Seven Years' War had depended.

In effect, there were two different systems of discipline at work in the British Army and the colonial militia, both in the Western tradition. The British example derived from the seventeenth-century military revolution that had reintroduced Roman organizational discipline into European armies.[8] In contrast, the modicum of discipline in the colonial militia was similar to that of the hoplites in the Greek polis, which depended on familial and societal relationships rather than the brutality of Roman-European professional armies.[9] Fred Anderson has caught the nature of

---

[7] Actual fighting on the frontier had begun two years earlier with George Washington's dismal failure in attempting to take Fort Duquesne.

[8] For a discussion of this, see, among others, William H. McNeill, *The Pursuit of Power, Technology, Armed Force, and Society since A.D. 1000* (Chicago, 1982), pp. 125–129; Hans Delbrück, *The History of the Art of War*, vol. 4: *The Dawn of Modern Warfare* (Lincoln, NB, 1984), p. 154.

[9] For a clear discussion of the makeup and relationship between officer and other ranks as well as the composition of the whole, see particularly Fred Anderson, *A People's Army, Massachusetts Soldiers and Society in the Seven Years' War* (Chapel Hill, NC, 1984), pp. 39–48.

colonial discipline in the Seven Years' War, and his comments are equally applicable to what was to come:

> We can understand the apparently erratic behavior of provincial armies in the field only by first recognizing that intense personal loyalties and expectations of reciprocity between men and officers suffused the process by which these [colonial] armies were created... Rather than a uniform hierarchy of officers and men, a provincial army was in fact a confederation of tiny war bands, bound together less by the formal relations of command than by an organic network of kinship and personal loyalties.[10]

It is not surprising then that there would be considerable friction, bordering on mutual incomprehension, between British military leaders and the colonists: "The treatment that the [colonial soldiers] received from the likes of Abercromby and Loudoun nonetheless made it emphatically clear the [British] army's leaders regarded them at best as 'an Obstinate and Ungovernable People, utterly Unaquainted with the Nature of Subordination,' and at worst as 'the dirtiest most contemptible cowardly dogs that you can conceive.'"[11] More accurately, General Richard Montgomery, a former captain in the British Army, who had immigrated to America in 1772 and led the expedition against the British in Canada in 1775, noted that "the [American] privates are all generals" but then added that they "carry the spirit of freedom into the field, and think for themselves."[12]

By the end of 1757, Loudoun's contemptuous treatment of the colonial legislatures almost precipitated a complete breakdown in relations. But before the confrontation could reach its culminating point, Pitt's hand reached out from London. Now the leading minister of George II, he had sent a series of dispatches to British commanders and colonial legislatures. Pitt's brilliance lay not only in his ability to balance the allocation of Britain's military and financial resources among a variety of theaters, including support for Britain's ally on the European continent, Frederick the Great of Prussia, but also in his recognition of what made the colonial leaders and population tick. Unlike Loudoun and other senior officers who believed they were in North America to command the colonists (while the latter were there to obey), Pitt understood the colonists

---

[10] Ibid., p. 48.
[11] Anderson, *Crucible of War*, p. 288.
[12] Montgomery would die leading the assault on Quebec City in the fall of that year. Don Higginbotham, *The War of American Independence: Military Attitudes, Policies, and Practice, 1763–1789* (Boston, 1983), p. 111.

needed to be treated as allies, truculent and irascible at times, but allies nonetheless.

On the morning of 10 March 1758, Loudoun and the Massachusetts legislature had reached such an impasse that it seemed likely the colony would vote neither men nor supplies for the proposed summer campaign. But at that moment, two dispatches from Pitt arrived, the first of which ordered Loudoun to return home. The second not only made colonial officers the superiors of lower-ranking British officers but also made clear that His Majesty George II's government would bear the costs of equipping, supplying, and paying for the troops that the colony was asked to raise.[13] A delighted Massachusetts legislature, which had been on the brink of refusing to raise 2,128 militia soldiers, did a volte-face and unanimously agreed to enlist 7,000 militia as its contribution to the war effort. The other colonies followed in quick succession at what appeared to them the completely unexpected change in British policy.[14]

From the Seven Years' War in North America emerged a number of factors that influenced the Revolutionary War, which are only clear in retrospect. The first was the most obvious, but it was the one least appreciated in London by those who instigated and then ran the war: the king, Lord North, and most of the members of the House of Commons. America was an enormous place, the occupation of which would require huge numbers of troops, especially if the British Army were unable to break the colonials in open combat. Second, if the British could not control substantial portions of the countryside, they were going to have to depend for supplies on a lifeline across the Atlantic. Third, given the size of the theater, the control of substantial portions of the countryside would depend on the support of the indigenous population.

Finally, one might note that the experiences of the war against the French distorted the perceptions of those who were to wage the next conflict. Senior British aristocratic officers shared a general contempt for the colonists and believed them incapable of making good soldiers no matter what the circumstances. That assumption imposed a heavy price on the British ability to estimate the capabilities of their opponents. But it also helps explain why they were never able to draw significant

---

[13] One of the major points of antagonism at the beginning of the French and Indian War lay in the fact that any British officer was considered to possess a higher rank than the highest-ranking American officer.

[14] Anderson, *Crucible of War*, pp. 225–227.

military strength from the loyalists. Simply put, most senior officers were as contemptuous of the loyalists as they were of the rebels. Thus, it made little sense to waste the effort in training up Tory regiments, when in their view the British Army was going to win the war on its own. When it was finally clear to the British that they could not win without training the locals, it was too late, as was to be the case with the French in Indo-China and the Americans in South Vietnam.

On the American side, there was both incomprehension of and contempt for the ruthless and, in the colonial view, "murderous" discipline the British Army inflicted on its enlisted ranks. Moreover, the colonials had observed the French and the Indians inflict major defeats on the British, most notably Braddock on the Monongahela in 1756 and Abercromby at Ticonderoga in 1758. That impression of British vulnerability would not be forgotten 12 years later when the Revolutionary War began. Even more important, the French and Indian War provided a wonderful education for a generation of military leaders who would fight the War of Independence. Some, such as George Washington and John Stark, had extensive experience; others, such as Benedict Arnold, only had minimal exposure to military life but some experience in soldiering nonetheless.

Stark is a particularly interesting figure. In the French and Indian War, he served as a leading lieutenant in Major Robert Rogers' Rangers, the most effective unit the colonists produced during the conflict.[15] Partially as a result of his prickly personality and partially as a result of the politics of the Continental Congress, Stark would not rise to high command in the Revolution, but he would have a spectacular career leading militia units. His performance at Bunker Hill, Trenton, Bennington, and Saratoga as a middle-level leader would mark him as one of the truly outstanding combat commanders of the war.[16] All in all, the war against the French provided an extensive leavening for the colonists in soldiering. From the first shots fired at Concord and Lexington, that experience would make

---

[15] Richard M. Ketchum, *Saratoga, Turning Point of America's Revolutionary War* (New York, 1997), p. 286.

[16] Stark was not only an outstanding combat commander but a moral man as well. Captured by the Indians before the French and Indian War, in the middle of running the gauntlet he had grabbed the club from a brave and beat his attacker. The Indians, always impressed by bravery, made him a member of the tribe. Returning from captivity, he joined the Rangers at the beginning of the French and Indian War but refused to participate in a raid against the tribe that had once captured him and made him a member.

the colonial militia far more lethal than simply a collection of ragtag farmers.

THE STRATEGIC AND POLITICAL FRAMEWORK OF THE REVOLUTION

Inevitably, political and military leaders embark on war with a set of assumptions, many of which prove faulty. As Michael Howard has suggested, what matters is how quickly they adapt those faulty assumptions to the reality of the conflict on which they have embarked.[17] The most basic British assumption was that the Americans lacked the stuff out of which one could shape soldiers, much less an effective army.[18] As one officer commented in 1774, he could take 1,000 grenadiers to North America and that would be sufficient to "geld all the males, partly by force and partly by a little coaxing."[19] Thus, most British officers believed the confrontation with the colonies would simply be a matter of showing up and administering a good solid dose of the bayonet. Nevertheless, the mere showing up of substantial military forces proved to be a nightmare, as Lord Germain discovered in his attempts to coordinate the initial move of forces across the Atlantic.[20]

But perhaps even more damaging to British prospects was the belief that only a small, radical minority was challenging British rule and that the solid majority would quickly rally to the crown once substantial British forces had arrived. As General Sir William Howe noted in early 1775, "I may safely assert that the insurgents are very few in comparison with the whole of the people."[21] Nevertheless, the British general in Boston, Major General Thomas Gage, had warned in fall 1774 that the Americans would fight and that even with major reinforcements, it would take one to two years of serious fighting to subdue New England.[22]

---

[17] Michael Howard, "The Use and Abuse of Military History," *Journal of the Royal United Services Institution*, February 1962.
[18] There has been a long tradition of British military leaders' underestimating the fighting qualities of Americans. In early 1942, Sir John Dill noted in a message to the chief of the imperial general staff, Field Marshal Alan Brooke, that "Never have I seen a country so utterly unprepared for war and so soft." Quoted by Eliot A. Cohen, "Churchill and Coalition Strategy," in Paul Kennedy, ed., *Grand Strategies in War and Peace* (New Haven, CT, 1991).
[19] Quoted in Anderson, *A People's Army*, p. 195.
[20] Mackesy is particularly good in his description of the difficulties the British encountered. See Mackesy, *The War for America*, pp. 62–78.
[21] Ibid., p. 36.
[22] Higginbotham, *The War of American Independence*, p. 50.

Nothing makes clearer the government in London's removal from the reality in the colonies than the instructions dispatched to Gage in early 1775: He should merely arrest the political leaders of Massachusetts and the troubles would end. As to Gage's earlier warning that such a strike might set off a war, Lord Dartmouth's missive noted that "it will surely be better that the Conflict should be brought on, upon such ground, than in a Riper state of Rebellion." In the same dispatch, Dartmouth reported that the government could not send the 20,000 reinforcements Gage had requested to meet the possibility of a major conflict.[23]

In fact, while Lord North's government was doing everything it could politically to court a confrontation with the colonists, it did little to prepare Britain's military forces for the war. When the crisis erupted, the government had to hire large numbers of German mercenaries to bolster its ground forces for the war in North America. During the conflict, Brunswick, Hesse-Cassel, and a number of smaller principalities provided nearly 30,000 soldiers, or more than 30 percent of Britain's effort to subdue the colonists.[24] Frederick the Great expressed his contempt for the enterprise by charging a cattle tax on the mercenaries who crossed his territory en route to North America.[25]

The corollary to the assumption that it would be an easy war was that British forces would have little difficulty in foraging. In other words, the British believed the situation in terms of logistics would mirror the support the colonies had rendered their forces throughout the French and Indian War. But even in the early days of the conflict, supplies turned out to be a major problem. Over the winter of 1775–1776, out of 40 transports dispatched from Britain, only 8 arrived safely in Boston; the others were either lost to American privateers or carried to the West Indies by prevailing winds.[26] The extent to which the British would have to rely on the transport of supplies from Britain rather than on foraging is suggested by the following figures: Over the course of 1776, the British transported 1,800,000 pounds of beef; 7,000,000 pounds of pork; 10,000,000 pounds

---

[23] Robert Middlekauff, *The Glorious Cause, The American Revolution, 1763–1789* (Oxford, 1982), p. 266.

[24] Michael Stephenson, *Patriot Battles, How the War of Independence Was Fought* (New York, 2007), pp. 49–50.

[25] The American Revolutionaries would mount a considerable campaign to persuade the Hessians and their German counterparts to desert. For the most part, it seems to have worked best on the Hessians after they had been captured. Higginbotham, *The War of American Independence*, p. 133.

[26] Ketchum, *The Winter Soldiers*, p. 189.

of flour; and 1,700,000 pounds of oatmeal and rice to the forces in North America.[27] These totals reflected the colonial militia's ability to control the countryside. The militia not only made it difficult for farmers to move food stuffs to areas under British control, but they also hindered British and Tory foraging parties from actively gathering up food and fodder, the latter being especially worrisome because the British could not ship it across the Atlantic due to its bulk. Thus, the value of the militia was much greater than simply that of a military force confronting British regulars in battle.[28]

Finally, one should note that no one was really in charge of British political or military strategy throughout the Revolution (in contrast to the key years of the Seven Years' War, when Pitt's firm grip had managed the global projection of British forces). Lord Germain, who had received the position of Secretary of State for America in late 1775, was generally in charge of the war. However, his position remained clouded by his performance at the Battle of Minden during the Seven Years' War, which had caused him to be court martialed and then dismissed from the army.[29] Moreover, while he was a leading hawk, he possessed little understanding of the complexities of the war, the political realities of the colonies, or the enormity of the North American theater. As he commented shortly after news of Bunker Hill had reached the British Isles, "One decisive blow on land is absolutely necessary. After that the whole will depend on the diligence and activities of the officers of the navy."[30]

Without specific guidance from London, British commanders in America simply waged their own individual wars. Moreover, the British never managed to decide whether they were waging a war to break the will of the colonists by a ruthless targeting of civilians as well as those in arms

---

[27] The strain that this effort placed on the British is suggested by a dispatch sent from London to Admiral Howe in April 1776: "The immense quantity of Tonnage employed and wanted, have drained this country of ships... The Distress for Want of Transports is so great that it would be of the utmost Benefit... if it should be possible for you to spare some of your largest Ships and return them home to be employed as Victuallers." Stephenson, *Patriot Battles*, pp. 116–117.

[28] In this respect, see particularly Mark V. Kwasny, *Washington's Partisan War, 1775–1783* (Kent, OH, 1996).

[29] At the Battle of Minden, Lord Germain, then Lord Sackville, had been commander of the cavalry of the right wing and had been slow to bring his command up when ordered to charge. Thus, he had allowed the French to escape. He was "scathing rebuked," court martialed, and then came close to being executed. Whatever the merits of the issue, the odor of cowardice remained to plague his career. For Germain's background, see Piers Mackesy, *The Coward of Minden, The Affair of Lord George Sackville* (London, 1972).

[30] Quoted in Mackesy, *The War for North America*, p. 46.

or whether they were engaged in a careful campaign to win the colonists back to their proper state of allegiance. George III and his prime minister, Lord North, supported the former, whereas the commanders in North America, particularly the Howe brothers, tended to favor the latter.

THE OPENING CLASHES

It is crucial, of course, to understand the kind of war in which one finds oneself. The opening skirmishes of the conflict should have provided the British a significant warning as to the nature of the coming conflict. In some respects, Gage's move on Lexington and Concord was similar to the French moves against Hoa Binh down Route 6 in late 1951 and against Phu Doan up Route 2 in late 1952. In both cases, the French easily reached their objectives without serious losses, but thereafter as their withdrawal picked up speed, they suffered increasingly heavy casualties as the Viet Minh rapidly gathered strength and launched raids, as well as major attacks, against French forces.[31] Similarly, Gage's raiding force had little difficulty in reaching its targets in Concord, but when time came to return to Boston, the British found clouds of Minutemen appearing at every turn of the road (Figure 3).

Fortunately for the British, the expedition's commander had requested a support force when it had become apparent early in the advance of his troops toward Lexington that the colonials had been forewarned and were gathering in strength. Otherwise, the colonial militia might well have destroyed the entire force that had marched on Concord. As it was, the relief force under General Lord Percy met the troops retreating from Concord at Lexington. The enthusiasm of the Americans, as well as their lack of marksmanship, is suggested by the fact that the Minutemen expended approximately 75,000 rounds to kill or wound 273 British soldiers.[32]

Although badly knocked about in its retreat, the combined British force of approximately 2,000 soldiers fought its way back to Charlestown, but just barely. In effect, the Concord–Lexington debacle indicated that only a British *army* could survive in the environment of a committed American militia force, most of which possessed at least a minimum of preparation for fighting, if not for soldiering. The conditions of North

---

[31] For a discussion of these battles, see particularly Bernard B. Fall, *Street Without Joy, The French Debacle in Indochina* (Mechanicsburg, PA, 1961), pp. 47–51 and 77–106.
[32] Stephenson, *Patriot Battles*, p. 14.

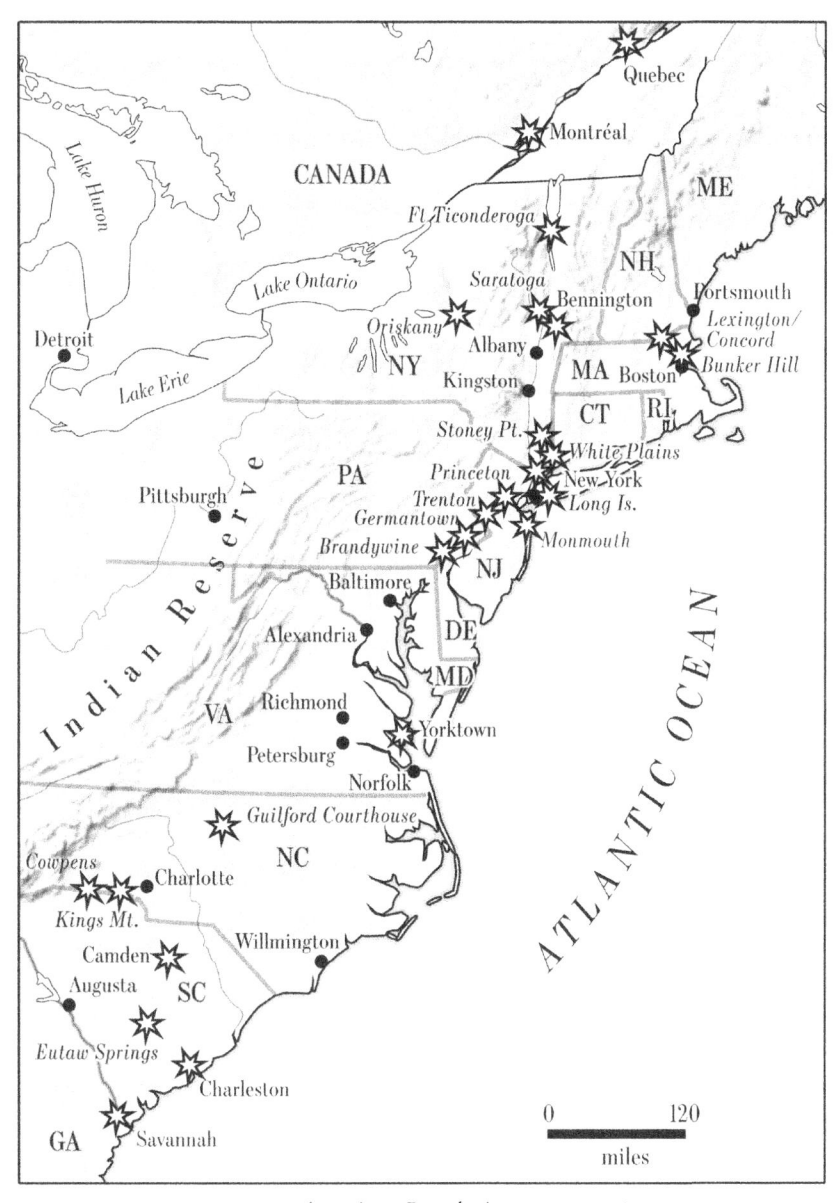

FIGURE 3. American Revolution, 1775–1783.

American topography only exacerbated the difficulties that British task forces, whether on raids or foraging expeditions, faced in standing up to substantial numbers of colonial militia fighting on their own ground. Lord Percy, a particularly perceptive British officer, noted the following about what British leaders should have learned from the retreat:

> Whoever looks upon them [the American militia] as an irregular mob will find himself much mistaken. They have men amongst them who know very well what they are about, having been employed as Rangers against the Indians and Canadians, and this country being very much covered with wood and hilly is very advantageous for their method of fighting....
>
> You may depend upon it, that as the rebels have now had time to prepare, they are determined to go through with it, nor will the insurrection here turn out so despicable as it is perhaps imagined at home. For my part I never believed, I confess, that they would have attacked the King's troops or have had the perseverance I found in them yesterday.[33]

British leaders in London would have done well to listen to Percy's counsel.

As Percy noted, the Americans possessed an important jelling factor in the experienced soldiers who had fought 15 years before at the side of the British regulars against the French. It was not so much that those men provided the basis for a regular army, although many of the senior officers among the Continental regiments had experience in the last war; rather, the essential point is that the experienced veterans of the French and Indian War at all levels provided a brace for the militia units in the early campaigns.

The British followed the rebuff of the move against Concord and Lexington with a disastrous attack on Bunker Hill. Here, they attacked into the teeth of prepared defenses – defenses that reflected the experience of colonial militia leaders in the French and Indian War. The assault was a disaster of the first order. Of the 2,250 British soldiers engaged, 1,054 (92 of them officers) were casualties, while 226 were killed.[34] General Gage, soon to return home, admitted that the seemingly ill-trained militia had displayed "a conduct and spirit against us, they had never shown against the French, and everyone has judged them from their former appearance and behavior."[35] What Gage missed is the fact that the militia would have

---

[33] George F. Scheer and Hugh F. Rankin, *Rebels and Redcoats, The American Revolution Through the Eyes of Those Who Fought and Lived It* (New York, 1957), pp. 43–44.
[34] Ibid., p. 63.
[35] Quoted in Macksey, *The War for North America*, p. 30.

proven just as capable under similar circumstances against the French, but they had never had the opportunity.

Bunker Hill underlined the importance of veterans from the French and Indian War to the colonists' effort. The overall commander of the operation, Major General Israel Putnam, had been a member of Rogers' Rangers and had risen to regimental command by the end of the conflict. Likewise, John Stark played a crucial role in bringing his 1st New Hampshire Regiment over to Breed's Hill and holding the far left of the line with great distinction. As his soldiers crossed the narrow neck connecting the town of Charleston to Breed's and Bunker's Hills under fire from British ships in the Harbor, the lead company commander hurried the men along. He later recalled that Stark "fixed his eye on me and observed with great composure, 'Dearborn, one fresh man in action is worth ten fatigued men.'"[36] But Stark was more than a disciplinarian. He held his soldiers steady and concealed behind the makeshift fortifications they had hurriedly constructed and then at almost point-blank range ordered them to rise. At 50 yards, they blew away a substantial number of the attacking Royal Welch Fusiliers.[37]

George Washington, who arrived in Cambridge shortly after Bunker Hill, and other colonial leaders recognized that whatever the success of the militia thus far in the conflict, the colonists were going to need regular forces, given the fact that militia soldiers would consistently confront the pull of farms and employment. John Adams succinctly put it this way: "We must learn to use other weapons than the pick and the spade. Our armies must be disciplined and learn to fight."[38] And therein lay the crux of the difficulty, for regular armed forces require pay and logistical support that can only come from some form of governmental taxation – which was a difficult sell in the colonies. In the harsh conditions of war, patriotism and commitment to the cause is thin gruel indeed.

The fact that the Americans were able to assemble regular forces (called Continentals, albeit admittedly ill-trained and ill-equipped by European standards) in relatively quick order underlines the commitment to the cause of substantial numbers of the population. Nevertheless, the lack of a sustainable base of taxation, even in kind, would present Washington with an extraordinarily difficult situation not only in raising a regular army but also in keeping it together. The Continentals represented the

---

[36] Quoted in Stephenson, *Patriot Battles*, p. 94.
[37] Middlekauf, *The Glorious Cause*, p. 290.
[38] Macksey, *The War for North America*, p. 30.

element that allows the Revolutionary War to fall within the framework of what has now been termed *hybrid war*. The mixture of "regular" units and militia in the field as well as in terms of population control would present the British with an impossible challenge.

THE 1776 CAMPAIGN

If the British were to have any chance of defeating the colonists, they were going to have to break their will with the military power they deployed from Europe in 1776. However, the debacles around Boston, as well as the fact that the population throughout New England appeared to be thoroughly incorrigible, led the British to change their strategy. In a strategic sense, further strikes out of Boston into the New England countryside would have led nowhere. Moreover, although substantial reinforcements were due to arrive in North America, in no fashion would they be sufficient to hold Boston *and* mount a major campaign to "liberate" another portion of the colonies that the British believed were dominated, unlike New England, by only a small group of radicals.[39] Having failed at Bunker Hill to overawe the fractious and truculent New Englanders, General William Howe now decided to try New York. Thus, Boston could not be held.

The withdrawal from Boston presented the British with a conundrum they never properly solved. The basic assumption of their political strategy was a belief that the population of the colonies wished to remain loyal to the king but had been intimidated by a ruthless, radical fringe. To withdraw from Boston because of military necessity was to put at risk those who had remained because of loyalty to the crown. An observer caught the resulting desperation of the loyalists, who had believed that the British Army would protect them:

> We were told that the Tories were thunder-struck when orders were issued for evacuating the town, after being hundred times assured, that such reinforcements would be sent, as to enable the king's troops to ravage the countryside at pleasure.... Many of them, it is said considered themselves as undone.... One or more of them, it is reported, have been left to end their lives by the unnatural act of suicide.[40]

---

[39] At no time during the conflict do the British, either in North America or in Britain, seem to have examined the issue of controlling the countryside. The assumption seems to have been this: Show up in the colonies with a substantial number of troops and things will then sort themselves out.

[40] Quoted in Stephenson, *Patriot Battles*, p. 60.

Thus began the great trek of so many Americans to what were to become the eastern provinces of Canada – refugees forced to leave everything they owned and who were to receive little thanks or support from a British government they had so loyally supported and which had begun the conflict so lightheartedly.

New York offered a number of important advantages over New England. First, in a political sense, a substantial portion of its population appeared to be Tory in sympathy – at least, that was what reports from the Royal Governor indicated. However, the reality was that at best, barely one-third of politically active Americans were Tories, while two-thirds of the politically active supported the Revolution.[41] The same appeared to be the case with the populace in New Jersey. Second, the seizure of New York would open up access to the Hudson River. Control of that important waterway appeared to position the British to cut the colonies in half and isolate the fractious New Englanders from the other colonies – or so the British believed. In many ways, the Hudson's strategic position was analogous to that of the Mississippi River in the American Civil War; the geography of the Hudson highlands possessing a similar position to that of Vicksburg blocking the Mississippi. However, the success of the Hudson River strategy would have depended on stationing garrisons sufficiently strong to defend themselves against sudden attacks by militia forces erupting from New England and on the loyalists being able to provide warning and control over much of the countryside. In the end, it was the allure of the supposedly friendly population that drew Howe to New York.

Ironically, the British may well have lost the campaign to enlist loyalist support throughout southern Connecticut, New York, and New Jersey before they even reached the area.[42] They were not the only ones who recognized there were substantial numbers of loyalists there. Consequently, the colonial militia took substantial steps in 1775, before the British fleet and transports arrived in New York Harbor, to disarm and intimidate potential loyalists and break up threatening gatherings of armed Tories before they became a threat. In October 1775, the militia broke up a gathering of loyalists near Peekskill. The following January, General Philip Schuyler led several thousand militia against a group of Highland Scots in

---

[41] Don Higginbotham presents an excellent examination of the popular temper in the colonies. See Higginbotham, *The War of American Independence*, pp. 133–137.

[42] This is not to suggest that they were larger in numbers than those who were supporting the patriot side. The results of the local struggles throughout the area speak for themselves.

Tryon County and, after disarming them, took six hostages as assurance for their continued good behavior. Meanwhile, the New York militia, supported by the New Jersey militia, broke up and disarmed a gathering of 600 loyalists on Long Island.[43]

These were the larger actions that stamped out the manifestations of support for the crown. But there were undoubtedly innumerable other activities throughout the colonies that terrorized those whose actions or political beliefs aroused the suspicion of those supporting the patriot cause. One of these measures was tar and feathering, which one enthusiastic rebel described in the following terms:

> First strip a person naked, then heat the Tar until it is thin, pour it on the naked flesh, or rub it over with a Tar Brush, *quantum sufficit*. After which, sprinkle decently with the Tar, whilst it is yet warm, as many feathers as will stick to it. Then hold a lighted Candle to the Feathers, and try to set it all of Fire; if it will burn so much the better.[44]

One surmises that only a few such proceedings were needed to encourage the vast majority of Tories to keep their political loyalties hidden.

Considering the ruthlessness with which the American revolutionaries were willing to handle those whom they suspected of wavering or disloyalty, it is not surprising that so many in Boston and then New Jersey and upstate New York were eager to fly to the protection of British troops. Thus, the militia provided a means for the colonists to maintain population and resource control over those areas where large British forces were absent. When the British moved on, as they invariably did, the militia simply flowed back into the area to reestablish control, eliminate loyalist militia, and drive out those who had been too obvious in their support of the British.[45]

The major campaign of late summer and fall 1776 proved a disaster for the Americans, whose military forces still relied almost entirely on the militia. The militia was simply incapable of standing in the open against a major British army in the field and, unlike Gage the year before, Howe was leading a force consisting of 32,000 British regulars and Hessian mercenaries. In Brooklyn, the British smashed Washington's forces and

---

[43] Higginbotham, *The War of American Independence*, p. 274.
[44] Quoted in Stephenson, *Patriot Battles*, p. 59. If the Revolutionary War failed to turn into a full-blown civil war, this was largely due to British restraint and the general weakness of the Loyalists.
[45] Mark Kwasney's *Washington's Partisan War* is an outstanding examination of the contribution the militia was to make in this regard to the winning of the Revolution.

inflicted 2,000 casualties for barely 200 of their own. Defeats on Manhattan, Westchester, and on the Jersey side of the Hudson followed hard on the heels of the Brooklyn catastrophe. Throughout the fighting around New York, the militia displayed little disposition to stand and fight, while the massive numbers of soldiers the British now deployed gave the militia few, if any, opportunities to utilize the forests and terrain of the area to their advantage. Moreover, the militia seemed even less able to hold the forts to the north of New York into which Washington and his commanders deployed them. These defeats underlined the fact that colonial militia could stand up to British and Hessian regulars only under special circumstances. By December, the British had hustled Washington out of New Jersey, across the Delaware, and into Pennsylvania with the remnants of his badly beaten Continentals and those few militia units willing to stick it out. All in all, the campaign to defend New York, its harbor, and its environs had been a shambles, revealing the Americans to be the rank amateurs in the art of regular warfare.

For the British, it appeared their assumptions about the Middle Colonies were correct. First in Long Island and then in New York, substantial numbers of Tories rallied to swear loyalty to the crown. Some had even been willing to join nascent loyalist units that began to spring up under British sponsorship. As the British chased the remnants of Washington through central New Jersey, the same pattern appeared to be repeating itself. So confident were the British of victory that on 30 November 1776, Admiral Richard Howe issued a proclamation that offered full pardon to all those who had joined the rebellion if they took an oath of allegiance to George III within the next 60 days.[46] Large numbers of the fence sitters in New Jersey and those who had been "summer soldiers" came in from the cold to swear that allegiance. Among these was Richard Stockton, the only signer of the Declaration of Independence to renege among those who had risked everything on 4 July 1776.[47]

The subtext of Howe's proclamation was that the British were in a position to protect those who swore the oath not only against those who remained in rebellion but against the depredations of British and Hessian soldiers as well. And therein lay the rub, because if the "Lobsterbacks" showed little disposition to respect the property of the colonists, whom

---

[46] Significantly, the oath was to be sworn to the king and not to Parliament, which caused considerable embarrassment to the government once news of Howe's action reached London.
[47] Ketchum, *The Winter Soldiers*, pp. 158–162.

most regarded with justifiable suspicion, the Hessians displayed even less inclination, in whose case the incomprehension of a different language exacerbated the difficulties of the relations between soldier and civilian. Moreover, the British advance out of New York into Westchester and then south into and across New Jersey pushed the British to the limits of their supply system, while loyalists flocking to New York for protection from rebel militia placed considerable strain on supplies in the city.

From the British point of view, the campaign of 1776 closed down when they reached the Delaware. Howe now spread his forces out in a series of relatively small garrisons at Trenton, Bordentown, and Burlington and farther back from the river at Princeton and Pennington. One of the reasons for the deployment of relatively small units so far forward was Howe's desire to protect the loyalists in the Jerseys as well as those who had foresworn the Revolution to swear allegiance to the crown.[48] More substantial forces, as well as most of the supply depots, lay in the central part of the state at New Brunswick. In effect, the cordon was to serve two purposes. First, it was to allow the British and Hessians to rest in winter quarters after their efforts in a campaign that had begun with the landing on Staten Island in August and continued until December. Second, it was to provide protection for the substantial portions of New Jersey that British operations had supposedly returned to the crown.

What now followed underlines why the British Army was incapable of winning the war. To begin with, the British and especially the Hessian troops had been none too tender in their foraging expeditions throughout New Jersey. It mattered not a whit to most whether a farmer had a piece of paper announcing that he had accepted the king's pardon – a pardon that only a few of the German officers could read and understand. The Germans looted the countryside to their hearts' content; after all, that was in the best traditions of Continental warfare. In addition to the normal activities by occupying troops that do little to encourage the support of local populations, there were a number of rapes and other abuses of the population.[49] General Sir Henry Clinton, upon hearing what was occurring in New Jersey, remarked that "unless we would refrain from plundering, we had no business to take up wider quarters in a district we wished to preserve loyal."[50]

[48] Higginbotham, *The War of American Independence*, p. 164.
[49] Of course, the colonists delightedly spun tales of the depredations of British and German soldiery, real and imagined.
[50] For a discussion of the treatment of the local population by the British and Germans, see Ketchum, *The Winter Soldiers*, pp. 229–233.

Not surprisingly, the result throughout December 1776 was an increasing number of guerrilla raids that hit British and Hessian foraging parties and assassinated isolated messengers. To get a simple letter from Trenton to his superiors at Princeton, Colonel Rall had to send along a guard of 50 soldiers to protect his messenger.[51] Militia units reformed in areas that were not occupied, which was virtually most of the state. Perhaps most important, intelligence dried up. The result was that the British and Germans were blind as to what was actually occurring in the countryside. Without intelligence, each of the small garrisons spread out along the Delaware and in the west-central portions of the state was vulnerable because none of these garrisons was in a position to be reinforced quickly.

Washington's strikes at Trenton and Princeton that destroyed isolated Hessian and British garrisons are well enough known not to need recapitulation. But it is important to note several factors in these battles. John Stark once again made his appearance at Trenton in driving his Continentals into the Hessian flank and breaking up one of the few stands the Germans were able to make that day.[52] In picking off the garrison at Trenton (with nearly three full regiments of Hessians in the bag), Washington restored the political viability of the rebellion. The defeat that he administered the British at Princeton one week later again emphasized that the British were not in a position to maintain small garrisons at isolated points against a rebellion able to mass its small regular force of highly motivated Continentals along with militia.

Militarily, Washington's success was sufficient to drive the British out of most of New Jersey. It added momentum to the partisan war that was gobbling up British wagon trains and messengers throughout the Jerseys, which forced the British to increase the number of troops detailed to cover each movement. When the British left, they turned the countryside back to the Jersey militia, which promptly carried out the equivalent of today's ethnic cleansing. On 25 June 1777, Howe pulled the last of his troops back from the Jerseys, in effect turning the colony back to those who supported the cause of independence. In the tracks of Howe came the dispirited loyalists, who had relied on British promises in the fall that their soldiers would protect the Tories, and who now had to abandon their wealth and lands to share the fate of their loyalist brethren in Boston.

[51] Middlekauff, *The Glorious Cause*, p. 358.
[52] Ibid., pp. 261–262.

Mark Kwasny sums up nicely the overall impact of the cooperation between Washington's army and the militia:

> The militia clearly had a decided impact on American fortunes in 1776–77. The numbers that participated in the counteroffensive help explain how the Americans were able to force the British to evacuate much of the New Jersey conquest. Washington and his small band of Continentals were critical to the success of the operations, but so was the militia. Washington did not recover so much ground with three thousand Continentals huddled along the Delaware River; he did so with that army, the supporting militia of Delaware, Pennsylvania, and New Jersey, the militia forces in northern New Jersey, and those in New York on both sides of the Hudson River. With possibly seventeen thousand [American] soldiers operating on an arc from the Delaware River to Westchester County, the British retreat into a few fortified posts along the coast becomes more understandable.[53]

Simply put, the British could take ground, but they found it difficult to hold territory against their hybrid opponents.

PHILADELPHIA AND SARATOGA

From the British point of view, the campaign of 1777 is difficult to explain. Having achieved relatively little in strategic and political terms for the immense effort and resources expended in 1776, the plans for 1777 have a peculiarly disjointed character. Certainly no one in London appears to have attempted to perform a serious strategic reassessment of goals, the nature of the enemy, or the operational and strategic objectives for the upcoming year. Lord Germain, supposedly in charge of the war's strategic direction, abdicated his responsibilities to the generals.[54] He allowed Major General "Gentleman Johnny" Burgoyne to persuade him in discussions taking place in London of the advantages of a major effort from Canada aimed at driving to Albany and creating the strategic circumstances that would allow the British to dominate the Hudson and split the colonies in two. Burgoyne does appear to have believed that he would receive support from Howe. Nevertheless, he displayed every confidence that he could reach Albany on his own. Underlining his overconfidence was the fact that he actually appears to have believed that after taking Fort Ticonderoga, he could march on the Connecticut River and down that avenue through Massachusetts into Connecticut. Moreover,

---

[53] Kwasny, *Washington's Partisan War*, p. 109.
[54] Here, the charges of cowardice at Minden, which the opposition in Parliament was delighted to impute continuously, must have played a role.

the directions Germain provided Major General Guy Carleton in Canada failed to direct him to support Burgoyne's offensive.

Meanwhile, in New York, Howe spent much of the winter in serious partying rather than in serious thinking. He was to dawdle in New York until high summer before he set off by boat to launch his attack on Philadelphia by moving up the Chesapeake instead of up the Delaware. The lateness of his move allowed Washington to dispatch a number of units, including Morgan's riflemen, to the northern front. The choice of the Chesapeake made sense because American forts had closed off the Delaware. What is more open to question was Howe's choice of a sea route rather than a march across New Jersey. The refusal to march overland against the American capital speaks volumes about British fears concerning the ability of the militia to harry the march of even a major British army. Moreover, such a march would have left the British open to logistical difficulties the farther they moved away from the main supply base in New York. Guerrilla raids launched by Jersey militia would only have served to exacerbate the problems of supply, as the troubles of maintaining the supply system in January 1777 had underlined.

In the end, Howe's strategy boiled down to a belief that if his army could win a decisive victory over Washington's Continentals, the war would be over. He made clear to Germain that he might at best provide "a corps to act defensively upon the lower part of the Hudson River [to] facilitate, in some degree, the approach of the Army from Canada."[55] Because Washington would probably move to protect the capital and the heart of the rebellion, Howe aimed his army at Philadelphia. Mixed in with that hope was the search for that mythical land where large numbers of loyalists would come out of the closet to assume control of the occupied territory. Moreover, because Pennsylvania was a land of rich farms, its loyalist population could, Howe believed, support the army until the rebellion collapsed.[56] What is astonishing is the fact that Burgoyne's operations from Canada appear not to have entered into Howe's calculations at all, or at least only to the extent that General Sir Henry Clinton in New York *might* move up the Hudson, if he were to receive timely reinforcements from Britain.

Burgoyne's march south from Canada represented armchair generalship at its worst. For those in London examining the prospects for the campaign, in particular Germain and Burgoyne, it seemed an easy

---

[55] Quoted in Ketchum, *Saratoga*, p. 262.
[56] Middlekauff, *The Glorious Cause*, p. 368.

movement of the pointer up the Richelieu River from Montreal, south along Lake Champlain and Lake George, and then a short march to the Hudson and junction with forces moving north from New York. Significantly, neither Burgoyne nor Germain, the two officers who planned this jaunt, had experienced the depths of the North American wilderness, both having served in Germany during the Seven Years' War.[57] By the time Burgoyne began his march up the Richelieu, he knew that he was going to receive minimal help from Howe. In Canada, Major General Sir Guy Carleton, whom Burgoyne had managed to replace in charge of the invasion of New York by deft political maneuvers in London, provided the support the interloper required, at least up to the letter of his orders. But Carleton also found his hands tied by Germain's order that he was not to diminish the forces that he had been assigned to protect Canada.

As Burgoyne began his march, he issued a pompous proclamation announcing that his army was marching south to liberate the colonists in his path from the "unnatural rebellion" that aimed no less than "the compleated System of Tyranny." But if the colonists were not willing to greet their liberators properly, then

> I have but to give stretch to the Indian forces under my direction, and they amount to thousands, to overtake the hardened enemies of Great Britain and America. I consider them the same wherever they might lurk... The Messengers of Justice and of Wrath await them in the field; and devastation, famine and every concomitant horror that a reluctant but indispensable prosecution of military duty must occasion, will bar the way to their return.[58]

It is difficult to see how Burgoyne could have added anything to his message that would have further enraged the colonists lying in his path or sparked their resistance to a greater degree. In retrospect, one should not forget that he was marching directly into the area that had provided the greatest support during the French and Indian War for the drive into Canada. Thus, there would be large numbers not only of leaders but also of experienced militiamen to buck up the younger men who had not yet experienced combat.

Burgoyne's campaign began brilliantly. His troops moved smoothly down Lake Champlain and then took Fort Ticonderoga. The pursuit of its

---

[57] Burgoyne, of course, had been at Boston and observed the Breed's Hill disaster, but his experiences of walking around Boston were hardly sufficient to provide a sense of the distances and terrain of America.

[58] Ibid., p. 372.

ragged, ill-prepared defenders took the British all the way to Skenesboro, when the last Americans skedaddled to the south. The question then was whether to continue driving south to the Hudson or to backtrack to Lake George and use the waterway to approach the Hudson. The latter course would have placed the British closer to the river, but Burgoyne claimed after the defeat that he had been afraid to retreat to the northern shores of Lake George for fear of adversely affecting the morale of his soldiers. It is more likely that he was simply ignorant of what American woodsmen were going to do to the primitive trail that led from Skenesboro to Fort Edward on the Hudson. The march south was a nightmare, as the British and their Indian and Tory allies hacked their way through a morass of fallen timber and wrecked bridges. Burgoyne then had to wait to bring up 30 days of supplies for his forward magazine at Fort Edward.[59]

Meanwhile, the colonial militia, badly beaten at Ticonderoga and driven south in humiliating fashion, had time to reconstitute itself as more and more units came in from as far away as New Hampshire and eastern Massachusetts. Speeding up the gathering of militia was the outrage and fear that resulted from the murder of Jane McCrea, ironically the fiancée of a Tory officer in Burgoyne's army. That, of course, did not stop the colonial propaganda machine from plastering news of the atrocious, murderous behavior of Britain's Indian allies all over the colonies. In three weeks, the news had reached the *Virginia Gazette*.[60] Burgoyne then added to his own gathering troubles by trying to bring European standards to the way the Indians fought. Although he eventually backed off, he initially demanded that the Indian brave responsible for McCrea's death be hanged. But his lectures that the Indians had to stop their normal practices of what the Europeans regarded as savagery when on the war path met stony silence. Not surprisingly, most of the Indians disappeared during the first two weeks of August, returning to Canada with their loot and captives.

On 3 August, Burgoyne received a missive from Howe that undercut his assumptions: "My intention is for Pennsylvania, where I expect to meet Washington, but if he goes to the northward contrary to my expectations, and you can keep him at bay, be assured that I shall soon be after him to relieve you."[61] Apparently, that tepid assurance of support was not

---

[59] Mackesy, *The War for North America*, pp. 132–133.
[60] The incident and its impact are discussed extensively in Ketchum, *Saratoga*, pp. 274–277.
[61] Ibid., p. 283.

enough to dampen Burgoyne's optimism. He determined to send out a strike force from Fort Edward to Bennington. Its objective, as Burgoyne informed the commander of his Germans, Friedrich Alfred Baron von Riedesel, was fivefold: to evaluate the "affections of the countryside, to disconcert the councils of the enemy, to mount [his] dragoons, to complete [the force of Tories], and to obtain large supplies of cattle, horses, and carriages."[62] The force was to advance to Rockingham almost on the Connecticut River and then move south to Brattleboro and finally to swing over to Albany to meet Burgoyne and the main army – a distance of over 200 miles through the middle of the Green Mountains.

It was a ludicrous operation, designed by a general ignorant of the conditions of the theater, the nature of the enemy, and his own precarious position. Riedesel objected that the expedition was being asked both to forage and fight and that the force was certainly not strong enough to accomplish the latter. But Burgoyne would hear none of it, and so the expedition set off. Piers Mackesy describes the slapdash nature of the effort:

> The commander [whom Burgoyne] chose was a brave German dragoon called Colonel Baum, who qualified for marching through a country of mixed friends and foes by speaking no English. His force was remarkable. He had 50 picked British marksmen and 100 German grenadiers and light infantry; 300 Tories, Canadians, and Indians; to preserve secrecy, a German band; to speed the column, 170 dismounted German dragoons in search of horses, marching in their huge top boots and spurs and trailing their sabers. They were reinforced on the march by 50 Brunswick Jäger and 90 local Tories.[63]

One can hardly imagine a force more ill designed to tackle the mission it was assigned.

A funny thing happened to this ill-matched force that had never before worked together just before it reached Bennington. It ran into John Stark, leading a brigade of New Hampshire militia. How had Stark arrived at this point? The answer is that, then as today, the politics of Congress did not always have the best interest of the country at heart. After his sterling service in the campaigns of 1775 and 1776 at Bunker Hill, Brooklyn, New Jersey, Trenton, and Princeton, one might think that he would have been promoted to brigadier general by the Continental Congress. He was not, so Stark had gone home in high dudgeon.

[62] Quoted in Ibid., 293.
[63] Mackesy, *The War for America*, p. 134.

Nonetheless, confronted by the threat from Canada and pleas from his own state legislature, Stark agreed to raise and lead the state's militia against the British. Stark had his orders written by the legislature in such a fashion that he was to cooperate with anyone he chose to, but he was not responsible to anyone except the colony of New Hampshire. Thus, Stark was independent of both Congress and the colonial army. By this point, his reputation was such that New Hampshire's male population responded to the call-up with enormous enthusiasm – 1,500 men answering the call in one week.[64] The colony's militia not only contained large numbers of veterans who had served in the French and Indian War but also an even larger group who had served with Stark in 1775 and 1776.

By the time that Stark and his men reached Bennington, the town was already swelling with militia from other New England states. The colonists and Baum's force ran into each other on 15 August in the rain, which squelched any immediate chance of battle. The German commander was worried enough to send back for reinforcements, and Burgoyne sent another contingent of Germans, this time Brunswickers, including grenadiers, perhaps the slowest-moving troops in the British force. They were under the command of Lieutenant Colonel Heinrich Breymann, who had never gotten along with Baum. The weather cleared on 16 August, and Stark struck before the two German forces could unite. That morning, the New Hampshire commander gave his men a short address, memorable for its concluding sentence: "There are the redcoats and they are ours, or Molly Stark sleeps a widow tonight."[65] In mid-afternoon, with an advantage in numbers, Stark attacked Baum's force and pinned the German dragoons down in their redoubt, while two other forces attacked the flanks. After savage fighting, the Germans and their supporting units collapsed. In the act of pursuing Baum's collapsing force, the Americans ran into Breymann's relief force and, after close combat, sent them fleeing down the road back to the main British encampment. By this point, the Americans were too exhausted to pursue.

Stark and his men had dealt the British-led army a devastating defeat. At the Battle of Bennington, the colonial militia, under superb leadership, had morphed into a force closely enough resembling an army to defeat two forces of regular, highly trained soldiers. Admittedly, the terrain had served them well, but for the fourth time in the conflict, a relatively substantial brigade-sized detachment of regular British or German troops

---

[64] Sheer and Rankin, *Rebels and Redcoats*, p. 261.
[65] Quoted in Ketchum, *Saratoga*, p. 305.

had run into the buzz saw of enthusiastic amateurs, who possessed a leavening of experienced soldiers and the advantage of terrain, surprise, and weather.

Burgoyne was in desperate trouble. A more competent commander would have recognized the indications that he had underestimated the difficulties of his task and the extent of the opposition. He would have pulled back toward the upper reaches of Lake Champlain and even to Fort Ticonderoga. Such a move would have confronted the Americans with major logistical difficulties. Moreover, Burgoyne's force had already been substantially diminished by the regiments that he had had to leave behind to garrison Forts Ticonderoga and George, and the losses incurred in Baum's expedition represented nearly 20 percent of his strength. It was also apparent that American militia numbers were swelling, and the colonists' success at Bennington had served to fuel American enthusiasm. By late August, Major General Horatio Gates, the new commander of the northern theater, could count more than 9,000 militia and Continentals at his disposal.[66] Nevertheless, ever the gambler, Burgoyne decided to fight it out. After all, to retreat would destroy his military reputation and end his military career.

On 19 September, Burgoyne came out swinging. He aimed at holding the colonial militia with a strike from the northeast, while his main move swung around to the west to take the Americans in the flank, as the British had done so successfully on a number of occasions after Bunker Hill. But the British Army, located near Saratoga, was much smaller than the forces Howe disposed of on Long Island and in the campaign against Philadelphia. Moreover, most of the terrain was broken by ravines and streams and was heavily forested. Largely because of Benedict Arnold's urging, the Americans were ready. As the British right wing under General Simon Fraser broke out onto open ground at Freeman's Farm, they ran into Daniel Morgan's riflemen stationed along the woods on the far side of the clearing. This was not the place for volley firing, and Morgan's riflemen had a field day in picking off the British officers, attempting to establish order among their disordered troops. After both sides reinforced, the engagement grew in ferocity as the afternoon passed, but the American Continentals and militia stood, only to pull back at night. In eighteenth-century terms of military etiquette, the British were the winners because they held the ground.[67] But, in fact, the British were

---

[66] Ketchum, *Saratoga*, p. 345.
[67] For an excellent description of the battle at Freeman's farm, see ibid., pp. 350–372.

the losers. They had suffered losses in men they could not afford, and they had not managed to fight their way through to Albany. Moreover, the Americans had held them to a standoff. In effect, because Burgoyne refused to consider a retreat, the British and their German allies were trapped.

Once more, Burgoyne attempted to break the colonists in the field. On 7 October, the British moved out from their fortified camp. The odds were stacked even more heavily against them: Gates now led somewhere between 10,000 and 13,000 militia and Continentals against Burgoyne's 4,000 British and German effectives.[68] This time, not only was the British movement brought to a halt, but the American counterattack under the ferocious leadership of Benedict Arnold also drove the British back to their camp and seized the main redoubt on their right flank. Had he not been wounded, it is entirely possible the Americans would have crushed Burgoyne's entire force. By the night of 13 October, Stark and his 1,000 New Hampshire militia had closed off the final escape route up the west bank of the Hudson, putting a cap on his spectacular military career.[69] Shortly thereafter, Burgoyne surrendered. As one American militia soldier expressed the fighting power the Americans had displayed in the last two months of the campaign, "we . . . had Something more at Stake than fighting for six Pence Pr Day."[70]

It would appear that the British failure to seize the Hudson River in 1777 by a combined assault with Howe's army from New York City and Burgoyne's from Canada represented the great strategic mistake of the war. The analogy to Vicksburg springs readily to mind. But that would be to miss the very different context of the Revolutionary War. In the latter conflict, the British simply did not have the troops both to hold the Hudson and move against other areas under colonial control. In the Civil War, however, the opposite was true; the North *did* have the troops both to hold the river and continue its drives into the heart of the Confederacy. Moreover, it is doubtful whether the British could have

---

[68] Stephenson, *Patriot Battles*, p. 309.
[69] Ketchum, *Saratoga*, p. 417.
[70] Ibid., p. 369. Of course, it was a matter of leadership as well. As Piers Mackesy has pointed out, "At the very top [of British military leadership] there was petrification. While the American commanders were products of a revolutionary situation in which timid men did not rise, learning the trade of war as they practised it, with everything to lose by defeat and everything to gain by victory, [the British generals] were members of a stable political community who had arrived and could not be shaken from their perch." Mackesy, *The War for America*, p. 515.

held those isolated garrison positions. As Captain Alexander Hamilton (then an aide to General Washington) noted,

> And as to the notion of forming a junction with the northern army, and cutting off the communications between the Northern and Southern States, I apprehend it will do better in speculation than in practice. Unless the Geography of the Country is far different from anything I can conceive, to effect this would require a chain of posts and such a number at each as would never be practicable or maintainable but to an immense army. In their progress, by hanging upon their rear and seizing every opportunity of skirmishing, their Situation might be rendered unsupportably uneasy.[71]

What Hamilton understood was the fact that the colonists' ability to mobilize large numbers of militia in combination with the slightly more disciplined Continentals would have allowed them to pick off such strong points at will and, when threatened by larger forces, melt back into the vast countryside where British forces, except only the largest armies, dared to follow and then only at great risk. The defeat of even Burgoyne's seemingly large army underlined how vulnerable the British were in the depths of North America.

THE WAR IN THE SOUTH

The defeat at Saratoga should have ended the war. The American triumph brought the French into the conflict and eventually the Spanish. Unlike the Seven Years' War, the British had no continental allies to draw off French military power. Thus, the wider British Empire was now at hazard in a fashion that had not been true since 1758.[72] The sensible strategic course would have been to make peace with the colonies on whatever terms might be possible and to turn Britain's attention to protecting the remainder of its global possessions. But political leaders, no less than normal human beings, are more often than not prisoners of their illusions. Thus, having failed to find sufficient loyalist support in New England, in New York, in New Jersey, or in Pennsylvania, the British now looked for it in the southern colonies.

In early summer 1778, the British abandoned another one of their captures. General Sir Henry Clinton, Howe's replacement in Philadelphia, marched the army across the Jerseys and back to New York. Once again,

---

[71] Quoted in Higginbotham, *The War of American Independence*, p. 199.
[72] For the extent and difficulties of the global war Britain faced with the entrance of the French into the conflict in 1778, see Mackesy, *The War for America*.

the British abandoned those loyalists who had rallied to the crown. In a strategic sense, there was no choice. Given the demands of a global war, they could not hold and supply both Philadelphia and New York. Clinton confronted the unpalatable reality that not only was he not going to receive any substantial reinforcements, but his concentration in New York also was going to have to supply soldiers for Canada and the Caribbean. Not until 1779 were the British able to undertake active operations against the rebels and then not until the end of the year.

Nevertheless, the British proved unwilling to dispense with the assumptions with which they had begun the war. Thus, having failed in New England and then in New York, the Jerseys, and Pennsylvania to find that great number of loyalists who supposedly existed, they turned to the southern colonies to prove their assumptions. The southern campaign was déjà vu all over again. In late December 1779, the expedition to test the steadfastness of the southern colonies embarked from New York. Within four months, it had won a major victory at Charleston, taking General Benjamin Lincoln's 6,000 Americans prisoner. From Charleston, Lord Cornwallis won a series of victories over Continental and militia armies: the disaster at Camden, which ruined Gates' reputation, one largely built on Arnold's combat competence, was followed by the incredible victory at Guilford Courthouse, where Cornwallis' outnumbered redcoats bested the army of Nathanael Greene. But conventional victories proved incapable of controlling the countryside or the population. British forces, small as they were, could only control minimal territory, whereas everywhere else, guerrillas and the militia prevailed.

As Cornwallis departed for North Carolina and eventually Virginia to pursue the Americans as well as the British dream of finding the land where Tories could defend themselves once freed from the yoke of revolutionary tyranny, the same pattern of events that had occurred in New England, New York, the Jerseys, and Pennsylvania reappeared. In this case, a ferocious guerrilla war against the loyalists crossed the boundary into civil war and spread across the countryside of Georgia and South Carolina. The historian of the British war for America notes:

> [Cornwallis'] departure sealed the fate of South Carolina and Georgia. For though the British forces in the deep South still outnumbered Greene, they were scattered in ten garrisons to control the countryside. Greene advanced against Camden. Lord Rawdon marched out and with 800 men against 1,200 and at the age of twenty-six won the first victory of his distinguished career. But Hobkirk's Hill was no more than a costly breathing space to secure his withdrawal. Now the outlying posts fell rapidly.

Augusta surrendered and Ninety-Six was evacuated with difficulty. The British were pressed rapidly back till nothing remained of their southern conquests beyond the neighborhoods of Charleston and Savannah. These they held till the peace.[73]

Without the ability to hold ground or to energize enough support from the local population to enable them to do so with minimal British assistance, the British war effort in the American South – as with its efforts farther north – was doomed to failure.

CONCLUSION

In looking back over the past two and a half centuries, it is surprising how much the French experience in Indo-China mirrors that of the Revolutionary War from the British side. Both the British and the French were up against an opponent with deeply held ideological beliefs. Both confronted a countryside largely in the hands of those in rebellion, who possessed the ruthlessness to hold it in that state; both faced the difficulty of protecting those portions of the population willing to throw in their lot with the ruling colonial power. Both confronted the difficulties involved in projecting military power to the theater over great distances. Finally, whereas their forces were capable of winning stand-up fights in the open where the training, discipline, and organization of their military forces could dominate, when they launched smaller forces deep into the countryside, the results more often than not were disastrous.

Thus, the French assaults on Hoa Binh and Phu Doan share similarities with those of the British against Lexington and Concord and from Canada aimed at controlling the Hudson River. Finally, one might note that both the British and the French efforts ended ingloriously with the siege of forces they had launched deep into enemy-held territory: for the British at Yorktown; for the French at Dien Bien Phu. So, even with all of the technological changes that occurred between 1781 and 1954, one is left with the same outcome: independence for the side with the ragged militia, fighting at times a conventional war, but combined with guerrilla war to hold political control of the countryside; and defeat for the side with technological and conventional military superiority.

Unfortunately, history does repeat itself, but mankind seems largely unwilling to accept the comment that Thucydides made two and a half millennia ago that "it will be enough for me, however, if these words

---

[73] Mackesy, *The War for America*, p. 408.

of mine are judged useful by those who want to understand clearly the events which happened in the past and which (human nature being what it is) will at some time or other and in much the same ways, be repeated in the future."[74] Thus, mankind marches ever forward into the future sure that everything is new and thus fills body bags with dead soldiers rather than reaching back into the past for the lessons others have learned at such great cost.

---

[74] Thucydides, *History of the Peloponnesian War*, trans. by Rex Warner (London, 1954), p. 48.

5

That Accursed Spanish War
The Peninsular War, 1807–1814

Richard Hart Sinnreich

Surely, it is no exaggeration to suggest that the events of the last decade have had a profoundly sobering effect on an American military that, before 11 September 2001, had succumbed to a considerable measure of doctrinal and technological hubris. For that sobering process, several factors were responsible. But the most important contributors have been the unexpectedly prolonged, frustrating, and expensive conflicts in Iraq and Afghanistan.

Americans have encountered this problem before and the response was instructive. In the late 1970s and early 1980s, reacting to a similarly prolonged, frustrating, and expensive war in Vietnam, the U.S. military rediscovered Carl von Clausewitz. The Prussian military theorist's *On War* had long been a sort of military Rorschach test, with each new generation of disciples interpreting it in its preferred way. In the U.S. military of the 1980s, the Clausewitzian concept that exercised the most powerful attraction was the injunction that military operations should always be directed at an enemy's center of gravity, "the hub of all power and movement, on which everything depends."[1] That idea seemed to offer a way to escape the militarily and politically painful attrition that had characterized the Vietnam War and, moreover, to mesh nicely with emerging theories suggesting that if one could only employ emerging precision sensor and weapons technologies to detect, target, and destroy certain carefully selected "nodal" enemy capabilities, preferably from a

---

[1] Carl von Clausewitz, *On War*, Michael Howard and Peter Paret, eds. and trans. (Princeton, NJ, 1976), pp. 596–597.

distance, then one might thereby bring future conflicts to a rapid and decisive conclusion.

Clausewitz doubtless would have been appalled by so mechanistic an interpretation of a concept that he does not even address in detail until two-thirds of the way through *On War* and then principally to warn that one must adapt military objectives to the character of the enemy. Instead, evolving U.S. doctrine, especially in the late 1990s, strongly tended to impose a preferred system template on the enemy whether or not it fit. One result was that in Iraq in mid-2003, an unexpected and expanding insurgency followed the initial tactical success. Weeks went by before anyone in uniform was willing to acknowledge that what Defense Secretary Donald Rumsfeld had cheerfully dismissed as "post-war untidiness" was neither postwar nor merely untidy.[2] The conflict that followed, moreover, defied easy diagnosis as a system, not least because the enemy declined to be systematic or even singular. Instead, coalition commanders found themselves enmeshed in a confusing and constantly shifting contest in which combatants and noncombatants mingled routinely, progress defied measurement, and today's friends could become tomorrow's enemies. Although initially obscured by the military's preoccupation with Iraq, the same frustrating phenomenon eventually manifested itself in Afghanistan, where the forces of more than 30 different foreign contingents, Afghan soldiers and police, tribal militias, Taliban insurgents, al Qaeda terrorists, and ordinary criminals continue at this writing to collide in a messy competition for the grudging acquiescence, if not necessarily the cheerful support, of the Afghan people.

In such circumstances, attempting to apply systems engineering to what some defense analysts have begun calling "hybrid wars"[3] thus far has proved a prescription for operational frustration and strategic disappointment. And yet, historically, such multifaceted contests are anything but novel. On the contrary, even so-called conventional conflicts

---

[2] See Thomas E. Ricks, *Fiasco: The American Military Adventure in Iraq, 2003 to 2005* (New York, 2007), and Bob Woodward, *State of Denial: Bush at War, Part III* (New York, 2007). For the army's own self-critique of the immediate postinvasion period, see Donald P. Wright and Timothy R. Reese, *On Point II: Transition to the New Campaign: The United States Army in Operation Iraqi Freedom, May 2003–January 2005* (Leavenworth, KS, 2008).

[3] Frank Hoffman, "Conflict in the 21st Century: The Rise of Hybrid Wars," Potomac Institute for Policy Studies, December 2007. See also Nathan Freier, "The Defense Identity Crisis: It's a Hybrid World," *Parameters*, Autumn 2009.

often have witnessed varying degrees of irregular warfare, and many prolonged occupations have confronted some measure of popular resistance.[4] History therefore should have something to tell us about the challenges associated with fighting such many-sided contests.

One of the clearest such historical antecedents was fought on the Iberian Peninsula from 1807 to 1814. The Peninsular War tends to evoke two images: of British General Arthur Wellesley's spasmodic but ultimately successful "conventional" campaign to defeat a succession of French field armies, and of the merciless warfare waged by and against the Spanish population that contributed the word "guerrilla" to the military lexicon.[5] Like any oversimplification, both images embody a good deal of truth. The progressive defeat of their armies in the field ultimately led to the French retreat from Portugal and Spain, although the regular forces that inflicted that defeat were far from exclusively British; and just as certainly, partisan warfare together with widespread albeit by no means uniform popular hostility toward the French contributed materially to that defeat, although more often than not indirectly, and at enormous cost to the Portuguese and Spanish civil populations.

But these descriptions paint too neat a picture of a contest that its participants found much less straightforward. Neither does this chapter make any pretense at painting a comprehensive picture of the conflict. Those seeking a more complete treatment of the Peninsular War should consult Sir Charles Oman's magisterial seven-volume history or one of the excellent and more recent one-volume accounts or topically focused studies.[6]

Instead, this chapter examines the Peninsular War only to try to decipher what makes hybrid or compound wars so difficult to prosecute and

[4] Hoffman originally dismissed such contests as examples of what an earlier writer had called "compound" rather than "hybrid" wars, the distinction apparently turning on the participation of combatants simultaneously exhibiting both regular and irregular qualities, as opposed to distinguishable regular and irregular forces fighting a common enemy. He since seems to have concluded that the difference is one of degree rather than kind, a view shared by this writer. See his "Hybrid vs. Compound War" in *Armed Forces Journal International*, October 2009.

[5] Originally, the term had nothing to do with irregular warfare, instead denoting the skirmishes – little wars – preceding the engagement of larger formations. During the Peninsular War itself, the usual term for organized irregular combatants was *partidas* (partisans), although *guerrilleros* also was in wide usage by the war's end.

[6] In the former category, two recent contributions are David Gates' *The Spanish Ulcer* (Cambridge, MA, 1986) and Charles Esdaile's *The Peninsular War* (New York, 2002). In the latter category, one of the best is John Lawrence Tone's *The Fatal Knot* (Chapel Hill, NC, 1994), which examines partisan warfare in Navarre. Oman's seven-volume classic is his *History of the Peninsular War*, originally published in 1902 and reprinted in 1995.

to consider what those ingredients might suggest about the design and execution of future military campaigns in which regular forces must cope with multiple concurrent conventional and irregular challenges. To make marginally easier the task of describing so long and complicated a contest in a few pages, it treats the war as a drama, as indeed it was, albeit with a plot written, often inadvertently, by the players themselves, the development of which was extraordinarily convoluted and that resulted in a dénouement, for the Spanish and Portuguese no less than for the French and British, that few if any had foreseen when the war began.

Anyone examining history should be mindful that of three basic questions that one can ask of it – What happened? Why did it happen? So what? – the last is far and away the most difficult (and perilous) to answer. That it also is the most important, for the military practitioner at least, is this chapter's excuse for attempting to do so.

THE PENINSULAR WAR DRAMA

The Stage

The Iberian Peninsula hangs like a geographical afterthought from the southwest corner of the European continent. Topographically, the peninsula resembles a spatulate hand, with its wrist, thumb, and fingers formed by four coastal and five interior mountain ranges. Of the latter, the most important are the Pyrenees dividing Spain from France, which at the turn of the nineteenth century were traversable only by rough mountain trails or along the relatively narrow coastal belts fronting the Bay of Biscay and the Mediterranean Sea; and the Central Sierra, which cuts Spain virtually in half.

The peninsula's physical compartmentation heavily influenced and continues even today to affect its sociopolitical character, historically imposing on both Portugal and Spain (especially the latter) a degree of regional differentiation that occasionally has verged on outright separatism. For much of its early history, "The map of Spain was a palimpsest of kingdoms, principalities and provinces, many of them with islands adrift in alien territories."[7] By the turn of the nineteenth century, that differentiation was most apparent in Spain's rugged northern provinces – Catalonia, Navarre, Biscay, Asturias, and Galicia – which, much like

---

[7] Ronald Fraser, *Napoleon's Cursed War* (London, 2008), p. xv.

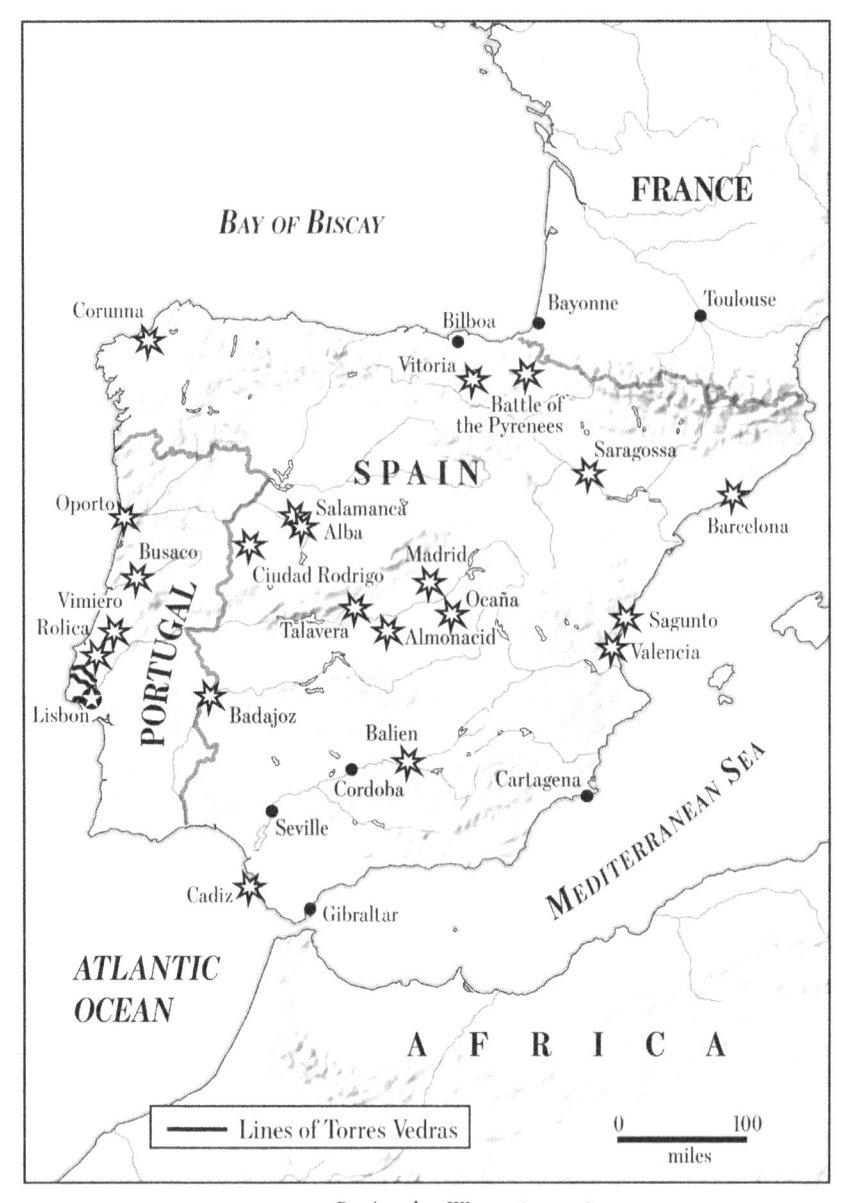

FIGURE 4. Peninsular War, 1807–1814.

modern Pakistan's northwest frontier, historically had enjoyed a considerable degree of political autonomy. As with today's conflict in South Asia, geography and its sociopolitical impact contributed materially to the character and conduct of the Peninsular War (Figure 4).

So too did the late-eighteenth-century transformation of Spain from a feudal to a modern state, a process still far from complete when Napoleon invaded Spain in 1808.[8] Effectively governed by the powerful, but venal, chief minister of a weak monarch, Spain at the turn of the nineteenth century was a sociopolitical battleground before the first French soldier set foot on its soil. In part, that aspect was also attributable to the French. As one historian put it, "The French Revolution accomplished in Spain what the American Revolution had failed to do. It provided the irritants that transformed into cancerous growths the hitherto innocuous discords brought about by the Enlightenment and economic expansion."[9]

Among those discords were regional antagonisms that pitted the provinces of the periphery against those of the center, chiefly over matters of trade and taxation; resistance by a conservative nobility, army, and clergy to mounting pressure for economic and social reform; and the growing antagonism of an increasingly dispossessed rural peasantry toward a relatively small land-owning élite. Until the turn of the century, these several rifts had been contained, in part by King Carlos III's effectiveness in centralizing power in Madrid, and in part by the positive impact of Europe's overall economic expansion during the latter half of the eighteenth century, which helped conceal the declining material value of Spain's overseas possessions. After the accession of Carlos IV in 1788, both factors weakened. Perceived tolerance of social and economic reform by the king and his widely disliked chief minister, Manuel Godoy, increasingly alienated Spanish conservatives already resentful of Carlos III's enlargement of royal power, whereas Spain's 1796 alliance with Napoleon against Britain, culminating in the destruction of the Spanish fleet at Trafalgar in October 1805, effectively severed Spain from its colonies, deprived it of what remained of those colonies' already diminished mineral wealth, and demolished its overseas trade. In turn, aggravated by a succession of poor harvests, the resulting economic decline only widened the nation's sociopolitical fissures.

Hence, when in May of 1808 the Spanish rose up against Napoleon's usurpation of the Spanish throne on behalf of his elder brother Joseph, the resentments prompting the violence that followed were anything but uniform. Although directed primarily against the French, in many cases they pitted Spaniards against each other: conservatives against reformers,

---

[8] For a detailed examination of this background, see Richard Herr's *The Eighteenth Century Revolution in Spain* (Princeton, NJ, 1958), especially his final chapter.
[9] Ibid., p. 438.

peasants against landlords, burghers against nobles, soldiers against other soldiers, and self-described "patriots" against *Afrancesados*,[10] who supported Joseph either out of genuine desire for sociopolitical reform or simply from fear of military upheaval.

For his part, just why Napoleon sought to conquer Spain in the first place remains somewhat obscure. He originally had sought alliance with Bourbon Spain (the incongruity of such a political marriage notwithstanding) to tap what he believed to be Spain's material wealth and exploit the combined power of the French and Spanish navies against Britain. But the former proved to be illusory, and the latter effectively disappeared at Trafalgar. In the process, Spain's lack of value as an ally became glaringly apparent. The potential threat presented by Spain became apparent when Godoy, just before the battle of Jena-Auerstadt and imprudently anticipating Bonaparte's defeat by the Prussians, convinced Carlos to proclaim a national mobilization with a view to sharing in the kill, only to later backpedal in terrified haste on receiving word of Napoleon's triumph. As Oman comments, "A stab in the back, even if dealt with no better weapon than the disorganized Spanish army, must have deranged all Napoleon's plans, and forced him to turn southward the reserves destined to feed the 'Grand Army.' It was clear that such a condition of affairs must never be allowed to recur."[11]

Politically, moreover, Carlos IV represented the last ruling vestige of the once pervasive Bourbon dynasty. His removal thus would complete what the Revolution of 1789 had begun, while at the same time allow Napoleon to enlarge the power of his own family, as he already had done in Holland and Italy. There can be little doubt that he considered the Spanish régime to be both politically and morally bankrupt and hence ripe for supersession.[12] Neither, given the visible dissension in Spanish society, did he apparently foresee much popular resistance to such a change. On the contrary, he was convinced, not entirely without reason, that many Spaniards would welcome more enlightened governance.

From a strategic perspective, Portugal and Spain represented unfinished business. By 1807, with conflict with Russia suspended for the moment

---

[10] The term originated during the reign of Carlos III to describe Spaniards who admired post-Enlightenment French fashions and customs. It became a term of opprobrium only after the events of May 1808. See Miguel Artola, *Los afrancesados* (Madrid, 2008).
[11] Oman, *History of the Peninsular War*, vol. 1, p. 5.
[12] And it may be, as Oman suggests, that "[h]e had against the house of the Bourbons the grudge that men always feel against those whom they have injured." Ibid., pp. 2–3.

by the Treaty of Tilsit, only Britain persisted in challenging France's European hegemony. Lacking the naval power to defeat that challenge directly, Napoleon turned to an economic embargo, his so-called Continental System, from which only Sweden and Portugal remained aloof. The former he delegated to Russia.[13] That left Portugal, into which in October 1807 he marched General Jean-Andoche Junot and 25,000 troops, having purchased via the Treaty of Fontainebleau unopposed passage through Spain by cynically promising to share Portugal with Spain (and award Godoy rulership of his own province). Fontainebleau notwithstanding, however, compelling evidence suggests that Spain itself already was in his sights, its conquest awaiting only an appropriate excuse, which familial infighting between Carlos and his son soon furnished.[14] Finally, one cannot altogether dismiss the Napoleonic ego. With Iberia in his hands, Napoleon would be effective master of Europe from the Baltic to the Mediterranean, with Egypt and the Ottoman Empire not far beyond. Megalomania thus reinforced strategy and politics, even if it did not altogether supersede them.

The Players

Between 1807 and 1814, the Iberian Peninsula witnessed uninterrupted armed conflict between and among seven distinguishable groups of combatants: the regular military forces of France, Spain, Portugal, and Britain; the latter's Royal Navy, which enjoyed virtually unchallenged dominance of peninsular waters; organized Spanish and Portuguese militias, most associated with provincial capitals and major municipalities; and a wide diversity of irregular forces ranging from Navarre's "land corsairs" to Catalonia's *somatenes* and *migueletes*. A brief description of each of these combatants suffices to illustrate the many-sided character of the Peninsular War, although a great deal more could be (and has been) written about each.

---

[13] One of the secret codicils agreed to by Napoleon and Alexander at Tilsit required that Sweden and Portugal be compelled to adhere to the embargo, if necessary by force, the former by Russia, the latter by France.

[14] Not all historians agree, some arguing that his decision to conquer Spain was largely opportunistic, hence the inadequate preparation that preceded it (see Esdaile, *The Peninsula War*, p. 36). That explanation, however, tends to be weakened by Bonaparte's expressed contempt of Spain's powers of resistance and by the secrecy and timing of French troop incursions, which clearly anticipated Carlos's dethronement and Napoleon's subsequent intervention.

The French Army. The forces committed by Napoleon to the conquest of Portugal and Spain underwent two successive metamorphoses. Initially, with the bulk of his veterans still deployed in Central Europe, the French armies that invaded the peninsula were composed largely of newly recruited and inexperienced levies. Following the humiliating collapse of those initial operations, Napoleon redeployed more than 100,000 veterans from Germany, more than doubling his peninsular commitment and significantly increasing its combat capability. It was with this enlarged force that he subsequently overran much of northern and central Spain, recaptured Madrid, and re-invaded Portugal. Convinced that the collapse of what Spanish and Portuguese resistance remained was only a matter of time, however, he then abandoned the war to Joseph and his generals, an error he would come to regret.

During the next three years, France's peninsular commitment continued to grow, at apogee reaching more than 350,000 men. Then, in June 1812, Napoleon committed nearly half a million troops to the invasion of Russia, including more than 20,000 soldiers withdrawn from Spain. The resulting disaster – fewer than 25,000 of those soldiers ever saw home again – and Napoleon's need for manpower to defend against the counterinvasion of the Sixth Coalition that followed, began to eat away even further at the Spanish commitment. The result was that from early 1812 onward, French armies in Spain declined in both number and quality. By the time Wellington crossed the Bidassoa River into France in October 1813, the forces directly opposing him consisted of fewer than 60,000 effectives.[15]

But if the number and quality of French troops varied during six years of conflict, their courage and fortitude rarely flagged and they remained dangerous adversaries to the very end.[16] Instead, more than any inherent tactical weakness, they were victims of geographical overextension coupled with mounting logistical difficulties. The latter reflected their reliance for subsistence on foraging, together with the increasingly ruthless way in which they were forced to conduct it. "The longer the war continued," notes one account, "the less effective requisitioning became. The smaller the yield, the smaller the rations issued to the French. The smaller the

---

[15] Gates, *The Spanish Ulcer*, p. 523.
[16] Allied forces investing Bayonne discovered this only a few days before Napoleon's abdication and the end of the war, when the encircled French garrison executed a well-planned sortie that inflicted more than 800 casualties on their surprised besiegers. Ibid., pp. 466–467.

rations, the more the French seized by force, thus driving more embittered and desperate men into the guerrillas."[17] In turn, guerrilla resistance merely aggravated the problem of overextension.

The Spanish Army. Like Spain's presumed wealth, its army at the turn of the century was more imposing in appearance than in fact. Manned largely by compulsion and top-heavy with superannuated officers whose only qualification was noble birth, the army had distinguished itself in neither Spain's brief 1793 war with Republican France nor in 1801's so-called War of the Oranges with Portugal. Notes Ronald Fraser, "The main enemy, Britain, was a *naval*, not a land power.... The role of Spain's regular army was conceived of as defending the colonies, *in situ* or as an ancillary of the navy."[18] By the time Spain finally awoke to Napoleon's intentions, moreover, much of what little trained strength the army possessed had been dissipated. In late 1806, furious at the incipient betrayal implied by Spain's aborted mobilization, Napoleon compelled Godoy to dispatch 14,000 of the Spanish army's best troops to Denmark to assist in the war against Sweden.[19] The following year, pursuant to Fontainebleau, Godoy agreed to deploy several more Spanish divisions into Portugal in conjunction with Junot's invasion; and although he attempted to recall them when Bonaparte's designs against Spain became obvious, scarcely half of the soldiers originally committed managed to return home successfully.

As a result of these decrements, fewer than 100,000 regular troops were available to contest Napoleon's initial invasion.[20] Raw numbers tell only part of the story, however, for the Spanish army of 1808 was not a single cohesive entity; rather, it was several separate armies under different commanders, each jealous of his authority and, after Joseph's usurpation, responsive to different and competing provincial juntas.[21] Not until the establishment of a Supreme Junta at Seville in late 1808 was there even a semblance of unified political direction. Even then, political

---

[17] Michael Glover, *The Peninsular War, 1807–1814: A Concise Military History* (London, 2001), p. 29.
[18] Fraser, *Napoleon's Cursed War*, p. xxv. Italics in original.
[19] After learning of the usurpation, the bulk of Spanish forces managed to escape back to Spain with the help of the Royal Navy.
[20] Oman, *History of the Peninsula War*, vol. 1, p. 90.
[21] At one point there were nine, a situation about which Wellington was complaining to Spanish authorities as late as December 1812. See Philip J. Haythornthwaite, *The Peninsular War* (London, 2004), p. 184.

direction was more often than not honored in the breach,[22] and not until autumn 1812, over the bitter objections of Spanish generals, were Spanish forces finally subordinated even nominally to unified military direction under Wellington.

Command difficulties apart, regular Spanish armies were rarely the tactical equals of their French adversaries. Deficient in cavalry and artillery and repeatedly forced to go into battle with ill-trained and poorly equipped recruits, the Spanish also began the struggle at least a generation behind their French and British counterparts in tactical organization and doctrine. Spanish units often maintained inadequate security, were slow to maneuver, exercised poor fire discipline, and, especially when attacked by heavy cavalry, were prone to disarticulation and collapse. Nevertheless, Spanish armies displayed astonishing resilience, managing repeatedly to rebound from what should have been decisive defeats despite horrific losses of men and materiel. "Time and again Spanish armies lost their artillery, their colours, their baggage. They suffered casualties on a scale which would have crippled a French or a British army. They never disintegrated."[23] Simply by surviving as cohesive fighting formations, they denied the French the freedom either to concentrate decisively against Wellington's Anglo-Portuguese forces or to conduct the dispersed constabulary operations needed to suppress local insurgents.

Finally, in judging the Spanish army's attitudes, and especially the less than harmonious relations of its commanders with their British counterparts throughout the war, one should bear in mind that until 1808, the two nations had been bitter enemies. In 1808, Trafalgar still rankled, Britain had seized Spanish possessions in the New World, and many Spanish generals and not a few politicians considered their new ally to be both militarily arrogant and politically untrustworthy – a viewpoint their British opposite numbers heartily reciprocated. At the soldier level, a similar albeit more basic disaffection prevailed, reflecting cultural rather than political incompatibilities.[24]

The Portuguese Army. By November 1807, when Junot's depleted and footsore French columns marched into Lisbon, Portugal's meager army

---

[22] In March 1809, for example, denied assistance by the Asturias junta after Blake's defeat at Espinosa, General La Romana simply dissolved the junta by force and took what he needed. Gates, *The Spanish Ulcer*, p. 146. See also Tone, p. 55.
[23] Glover, *The Peninsular War*, p. 52.
[24] Rory Muir, *Salamanca, 1812* (New Haven, CT, 2001), pp. 170–171.

already had largely ceased to exist, and Junot rapidly dissolved what remained.[25] Although reconstituted after the evacuation of French forces pursuant to the Cintra Convention in September 1808, Portuguese regulars played virtually no role in Sir John Moore's abortive incursion into Spain later that year; and, when a few months later the French invaded again, Portuguese General Francisco Silviera's untrained levies were easily brushed aside by Marshal Nicolas Soult's veterans – 4,000 of Silveira's troops surrendering at Chaves without firing a shot.[26] Subsequently, after losing Oporto at the cost of as many as 20,000 killed, wounded, or captured, surviving Portuguese forces recoiled on Lisbon, where Wellesley landed on 22 April 1809 with 30,000 fresh British troops.

From that moment until the final ejection of the French from Spain, Portuguese regulars effectively became adjuncts of the British Army, initially in brigade strength and then eventually as whole divisions. For this remarkable metamorphosis, they could largely credit British General William Beresford. Charged in Wellesley's absence with rebuilding the Portuguese army, Beresford made effective use of British cadres to reorganize, reequip, and retrain Portuguese units to British standards. Thanks to his efforts, by the time French Marshal André Masséna invaded Portugal in the summer of 1810, regular Portuguese units could and did take their place in the line with their British counterparts. As Wellington wrote to the Secretary of State for War on 30 September 1810, "To [Beresford] exclusively, under the Portuguese Government, is due the merit of having raised, formed, disciplined, and equipped the Portuguese army, which has now shown itself capable of engaging and defeating the enemy."[27]

The British Army. British Foreign Secretary George Canning acknowledged the central problem for the British Army in the peninsula with his warning to Lieutenant General Sir John Moore in mid-1808 that "[T]he army which has been appropriated by His Majesty to the defence of Spain and Portugal is not merely a considerable part of the dispensable force

---

[25] Portugal's court, treasury, and many of its leading citizens had been evacuated by the Royal Navy to Brazil.
[26] Gates, *The Spanish Ulcer*, p. 139.
[27] See Wellington to Liverpool, "Wellington's Dispatches, September 21st–24th, 1810," available at http://www.wtj.com/archives/Wellington.

of this country. It is, in fact, the British army."[28] From the outset of the contest with Napoleon, Britain's central strategic problem had been the dilemma of a maritime power confronting a continental adversary. So long as they maintained naval supremacy, the British could count themselves nearly immune from invasion.[29] But although defensively relatively secure, Britain with its modest volunteer army was correspondingly helpless to confront Napoleon's massive land forces offensively in the interior of a hostile continent, where British sea power could furnish neither succor nor safety.

It was in large measure the opportunity to circumvent that dilemma by using British land and naval forces to exploit and augment Portuguese and Spanish resistance on a peninsula with a lengthy and accessible coastline that convinced the British government to intervene in Iberia in the first place. Excluding Portuguese auxiliaries, however, the army with which it did so never exceeded 60,000 men. What British troops lacked in quantity, however, they made up in quality. Although modern historians tend to deprecate the traditional view that British success reflected innate tactical superiority, in particular a talent for reverse-slope defenses and a preference for deploying in line rather than column, there can be little doubt that the discipline, training, and native stubbornness of Britain's infantry units served its commanders well. In contrast, British cavalry, although audacious, was both less disciplined and less reliable, a condition that persisted as late as Waterloo, whereas British artillery, although professional and capable, never quite achieved the agility and lethality that made Napoleon's "little daughters" so effective.

Above all, however, the British Army in the peninsula was fortunate in its leadership, from noncommissioned to general officers. Especially in brigade commanders such as Maitland, Craufurd, and Byng and division commanders such as Picton and Campbell, the peninsular army enjoyed leadership the overall effectiveness of which was rare for its own time and that would be enviable in an army of any era. Wellington did his subordinates a gross disservice when, in an uncharitable and self-serving

---

[28] Gates, *The Spanish Ulcer*, pp. 114–115. Canning exaggerated – Britain committed nearly 40,000 troops to Walcheren on 30 July. Had he said "the rest of the British Army," he would have been more nearly correct.

[29] Reflecting that confidence, in 1801, Admiralty First Lord St. Vincent had dryly assured his fellow peers, "I do not say, my Lords, that the French will not come. I say only they will not come by sea." Walter Russell Mead, *God and Gold: Britain, America, and the Making of the Modern World* (New York, 2008), p. 107.

comment, he wrote in August 1810 to Colonel Torrens, military secretary at Horse Guards, "As Lord Chesterfield said of the generals of his day, 'I only hope that when the enemy reads the list of their names, he trembles as I do.'"[30]

The Royal Navy. One historian summed up the impact on the Peninsular War of Britain's maritime supremacy in a single sentence: "Without the Royal Navy, Britain's fight in the peninsula could never have been waged and certainly not with the success that was eventually achieved."[31] From the evacuation of Moore's overmatched army at Corunna in January 1809, which prefigured Dunkirk, to the siege of Bayonne in February 1814, the Royal Navy furnished the transport, resupply, and occasionally the firepower that sustained allied forces throughout the war. In addition, ranging freely along the littoral of a peninsula in which all but two of the most populous cities were situated on or only a few miles from the coast, the navy's squadrons presented a threat that tied down thousands of French troops, which were then unavailable to fight allied armies in the interior. Neither was that threat by any stretch of the imagination merely hypothetical. In March 1811, for example, the navy ferried 4,000 British troops of the besieged Cadiz garrison to Algeciras, whence, together with two Spanish divisions from Gibraltar, they marched north and surprised Marshal Claude Victor's I Corps. Combined with a sortie from the city itself, the attack inflicted nearly 3,000 French casualties and briefly broke the siege. Smaller naval actions from raids to shore bombardments kept French forces along the Atlantic and Mediterranean coasts in a constant state of alarm throughout the war.[32]

After denying the French the use of the sea, however, perhaps the Royal Navy's most significant contribution lay in its logistical support of the army. During Masséna's five-month siege of Lisbon from October 1810 to March 1811, for example, the navy fed not only Wellington's British and Portuguese soldiers but also Lisbon's civilian population, including thousands of refugees who had flooded the city during Wellington's withdrawal into his defensive positions. As a result, in an ironic reversal

---

[30] Elizabeth Longford, *Wellington: The Years of the Sword* (New York, 1969), p. 218.
[31] Gates, *The Spanish Ulcer*, pp. 28–29.
[32] For a detailed look at the maritime dimensions of the war, see Christopher D. Hall, *Wellington's Navy: Seapower and the Peninsular War 1807–1814* (Harrisburg, PA, 2004).

of the norm, the besieged enjoyed a level of subsistence far superior to that of their besiegers.

The Provincial Militias. Even before the outbreak of war, both Portugal and Spain maintained a system of organized militias. Raised and equipped largely by municipal and provincial governments, they were intended primarily to furnish local garrison security, freeing regular field forces to maneuver. During the Peninsular War, the repeated defeat of those regular forces often left the militias as the only organized defenders of threatened population centers, a task they sometimes executed with astonishing courage and self-sacrifice. At Saragossa from June to August 1808, for example, Spanish militias stiffened by a few regular units managed twice at enormous cost to frustrate French efforts to seize the city, and other militias enjoyed similar successes at various times and places throughout the war. Against French regulars in the open field, in contrast, militia units rarely could hold their ground and more often than not broke and fled.

Above all, the sheer number of Iberian militia levies, in Portugal ultimately amounting to more than 50,000 men and in Spain eventually to as many as 150,000 men, endowed them with an operational significance that neither side's leaders could ignore: French commanders because of the additional resources they had to commit to deal with local militias, and allied commanders by virtue of their contribution in relieving regular troops of the garrison responsibilities that otherwise might have diverted significant strength from their field armies.

The Irregulars. As noted earlier, the Peninsular War gave the world the word "guerrilla" and, thanks to artist Francisco Goya, novelist C. S. Forester, and film maker Stanley Kramer, the war is best known for the Spanish and Portuguese partisans who fought in it.[33] Although volumes have been written about the vicious struggle between the French army and the *guerrilleros*, much of the evidence about this struggle is anecdotal. Scholars are not even certain how many people actively participated in the irregular warfare that wracked the peninsula between 1808 and 1814.

---

[33] Goya's *Dos de Mayos* and *Tres de Mayos* depict Murat's bloody suppression of the Madrid uprising of May 1808. Forester's *Rifleman Dodd*, describing the activities of Portuguese guerrillas led by a stranded British soldier, has become something of a Special Forces breviary, while its companion novelette, *The Gun*, portraying a fictional episode of the guerrilla war in Spain, inspired Kramer's 1957 motion picture *The Pride and the Passion*.

A British effort at tabulation in early 1811 counted 111 separate partisan bands comprising some 28,000 combatants. More recently, a Spanish historian has concluded that the number of such groups may have risen to as high as 156 before declining in 1813 as the French evacuated the peninsula.[34] It does not help that both the number and strength of such groups fluctuated constantly as death, capture, moral exhaustion, and the occasional change of heart took their toll; nor that, like their modern successors, many irregulars were part timers, participating in combat operations only episodically and conditionally, whereas others were little more than the outright bandits that the French routinely accused them of being.

In the end, however, their precise numbers matter little. What matters more is that throughout a complex and expansive geography, in large segments of which men (and not a few women) were obsessed with personal honor,[35] were accustomed to bearing arms, detested outsiders, and were often fortified by religious fervor, the *guerrilleros* produced an environment in which no French soldier could feel safe unless protected by a fortified garrison or a substantial field force. Couriers, tax collectors, supply convoys, and foraging parties were favorite targets – the latter two elements eventually requiring escorts so large that they imposed a serious drain on the French army's fighting strength. Later, as partisan groups under such leaders as Merion, Diaz, and Espoz y Mina increased in size and effectiveness, they began more routinely to cooperate with the regular Spanish army, into which some were eventually incorporated.

The Plot

Considered as a drama, one can divide the Peninsular War roughly into a prologue and five acts. The latter differed significantly in duration – their

---

[34] René Chartrand, *Spanish Guerrillas in the Peninsular War, 1808–1814* (London, 2004), pp. 17–18. Fraser lists 112 groups comprising 55,531 men in 1811, falling to 60 comprising 52,265 in 1812. Fraser, *Napoleon's Cursed War*, appendix 4. None of these counts includes the Portuguese. In part, numerical uncertainty reflects the fact that irregulars were distinguished from militias less by appearance than by lack of formal regulation.

[35] Writes Chartrand, "Perhaps the most perplexing Spanish feature [for the French] was the 'Point of Honour' engrained into the character of every Spanish man and woman. This required that to maintain one's social standing any challenges to one's honour had to be met, even if this meant risking death... This fascination with the politics of pride could go as far as taking the life of an 'enemy' simply to maintain one's Point of Honour." Chartrand, *Spanish Guerrillas in the Peninsular War*, pp. 12–13. As successive invaders have discovered, much the same could be said of the Afghans.

chronological division in any case is to some extent arbitrary – but even more in character, and one can describe the latter differences with some confidence.

Prologue. The prologue began in October 1807 when, in accordance with the Treaty of Fontainebleau negotiated between Napoleon and Godoy, Junot at the head of 25,000 French troops traversed north-central Spain unopposed to invade Portugal, supported by several Spanish divisions. During the next two months, on the pretext of securing Junot's lines of communication against hypothetical (and, at the time, wholly unlikely) intervention by the British, additional French *corps d'observation* filtered into Spain's northern provinces. In February and March 1808, they occupied several vital frontier fortresses, largely without resistance.[36]

The incursion brought to a head a long-simmering rift between Carlos IV and his eldest son and heir Prince Ferdinand, who detested Godoy and had become the standard-bearer of disaffected conservative nobility, clergy, and officers. The dispute climaxed on 19 March when, threatened by a mutiny that had seized and nearly executed Godoy, the king fearfully abdicated to his son, subsequently appealing to Napoleon for assistance. Seizing an opportunity to rid himself of the Bourbons once and for all, Napoleon directed Marshal Joachim Murat with 20,000 troops to occupy Madrid. After persuading Ferdinand and Carlos to meet with him in Bayonne, Napoleon bullied them into surrendering the throne of Spain to his reluctantly acquiescent elder brother Joseph.

Furious at having a foreign monarch imposed on them, and further enraged by rumors that Murat planned to remove Ferdinand's younger siblings to France as well, on 2 May – *Dos de Mayo* – the citizens of Madrid erupted in a riot that killed or injured scores of French soldiers.[37] Aiming to quell the uprising rapidly and ruthlessly, Murat used cavalry charges and infantry volleys to scatter and slaughter the rioters. He then swept up and on the following day executed hundreds of additional

---

[36] They occupied Pamplona on 16 February, Barcelona on 29 February, San Sebastian on 5 March, and Figueras on 18 March. Only at San Sebastian did the garrison briefly resist. At Pamplona, denied access to the citadel controlling the city, the French seized it by ruse, staging a snowball fight to divert the guards. Comments Tone acidly, "The most important fortress in north-central Spain [thus fell] to a handful of French soldiers armed with snowballs." Tone, *The Fatal Knot*, pp. 43–44.

[37] Different sources report widely varying casualty counts on both sides. French General Grouchy counted 150 French casualties, only 14 fatal, and between 400 and 500 Spaniards (ibid., p. 50). Other accounts suggest much higher Spanish losses. See, e.g., Fraser, *Napoleon's Cursed War*, appendix 1.

Madrileños, many of them noncombatants. News of events in Madrid spread rapidly to the northern provinces, where, already resentful of their uninvited and badly behaving French guests, the population ignited. During the following weeks, the remainder of the country likewise descended into turmoil. French soldiers, *Afrancesados*, and innocents alike were indiscriminately murdered while partisan groups formed and insurgent juntas sprang up in nearly every province.

Act 1. These preliminaries at an end, during the first six months of the war itself, lasting from May through October of 1808, Bonaparte's confidence that Iberia would easily fall into his hands proved to be a humiliating misjudgment. In Catalonia, the French forces that had seized Barcelona quickly found themselves surrounded and virtually besieged by Catalan militia, while nearby Gerona beat off two successive French sieges. In Aragon, French attempts to capture Saragossa produced three months of bitter and bloody street fighting that ended in failure, while in Valencia, French efforts to seize the city were rebuffed at the cost of more than a thousand casualties, compelling the foiled attackers to recoil on Madrid. Worse yet, in a disaster that reverberated throughout Europe, in Andalusia two Spanish armies entrapped an entire French *corps d'armée* led by General Pierre Dupont, which resulted in the unprecedented surrender of more than 24,000 French regulars.

Together, these reverses panicked Joseph and his generals, inducing them to abandon Madrid and withdraw all French forces in Spain north of the Ebro River. To cap off this unexpected turn of events, a few weeks later, a British expeditionary force led by Lieutenant General Sir Arthur Wellesley landed north of Lisbon, defeated a French detachment under General Henri Delaborde near the village of Roliça, and then combined with Portuguese troops outside the village of Vimeiro to defeat Junot himself. A few days later, aware of Dupont's defeat at Bailén and separated from the nearest French supports by 300 miles of hostile territory, Junot surrendered on the condition that his forces be repatriated to France.[38] Thus, to Napoleon's fury, a year after it had begun, the conquest of the Iberian Peninsula, which he once had insisted the French could

---

[38] In Britain, the Cintra Convention, as it became known, which not only returned Junot and his troops to French soil aboard Royal Navy transports but also allowed them to evacuate with all their weapons and spoils, caused a public uproar, resulting in the recall of Wellesley and his superiors, Generals Sir Harry Burrard and Sir Hew Dalrymple, to face an official inquiry. All three were formally exonerated, but only Wellesley ever regained command. See Oman, *History of the Peninsula War*, vol. 1, pp. 296–300.

accomplish with only 12,000 men,[39] was in tatters. Far worse, so also was the French army's hard-won reputation for invincibility.

Act 2. The second segment of the drama began with Napoleon's redeployment of approximately 100,000 veteran soldiers from Germany, more than doubling his commitment in the Peninsula. Taking personal command of this enlarged force, in November 1808 Napoleon struck hard against Spanish armies that Bailén had rendered overconfident and that had remained virtually somnolent ever since. Dispatching Victor with 34,000 troops to destroy General Joaquin Blake's Army of Galicia, Napoleon committed 33,000 more men under Soult directly against General Francisco Castaños's Army of the Center, meanwhile sending Marshal Michel Ney with still another 20,000 soldiers to envelop the latter from the east. Helped by bickering between the Spanish commanders and interference by the newly formed Supreme Junta in Seville, the French easily routed both Spanish armies and then turned on General José Palafox's Army of Aragon, in the process investing Saragossa for the third time.[40] By 4 December 1808, Madrid once again was in Bonaparte's hands, with surviving Spanish forces broken and dispersed.

Meanwhile, unaware of the speed and extent of the Spanish collapse and misinformed regarding the strength of French forces now in Spain, Lieutenant General Sir John Moore, who had assumed command in Portugal after the recall of Wellesley and his superiors, crossed the Spanish frontier heading toward Burgos. Subsequently learning of Napoleon's advance on Madrid with the bulk of the French forces, he determined to combine with the survivors of Blake's Galicians, now commanded by General Pedro La Romana, and a smaller British force at Corunna under General Sir David Baird, to attack Soult's position near Valladolid. By thus threatening Napoleon's communications back to Bayonne, he proposed to relieve the pressure on Madrid.[41]

Instead, Moore's advance into Spain offered Napoleon a golden opportunity to entrap and destroy what amounted to the bulk of his most detested enemy's army. Accordingly, with a view to cutting the British

---

[39] Steve Douglas, "Napoleon at the Gates of Baghdad," *Executive Intelligence Review*, April 2005.

[40] This third assault proved too much for its gallant defenders. The city finally succumbed on 20 February after another bloodbath of tragic proportions.

[41] In fact, unbeknownst to Moore, Madrid's garrison already had capitulated by the time he began his advance.

off from the sea, he lost no time launching 80,000 troops to envelop what he believed to be Moore's position in the valley of the Douro River, personally driving his troops through difficult terrain and bitter weather. In the event, however, Moore was much farther north than Bonaparte believed. On learning of the strength and proximity of the French army, Moore immediately abandoned his offensive and retreated on Corunna, to which he had shifted his naval transport. Believing Moore's destruction to be inevitable, Napoleon turned the pursuit over to Soult and, after settling some political matters in Madrid, returned to Paris, relinquishing to Joseph and his generals a war that he considered already won.

With his emperor gone, Soult dutifully pursued Moore but without ever quite catching him. At last coming to grips with him outside Corunna, Soult was unable to penetrate Moore's stubborn defense. Moore thus succeeded in ensuring the safe evacuation of Britain's precious army,[42] but its departure left the French opposed in Galicia only by La Romana's few regulars and the annoying but as yet manageable partisans.[43] Thus, the end of February 1809 saw Napoleon's humiliation of the previous year effectively reversed, with Spanish armies broken and scattered, Saragossa finally taken, the British forced from Spain, Soult positioned to re-invade Portugal, and brother Joseph reseated in Madrid. Napoleon's elder sibling was confident that with this large, veteran army at his disposal, the remainder of the Iberian peninsula would soon be pacified.

Act 3. Instead, the third act proved the longest and most convoluted of the entire drama. Lasting from mid-1809 through 1811, it witnessed a sanguinary but inconclusive seesaw contest in which Frenchmen and Spaniards collided in nearly a hundred separate battles and skirmishes.[44] French and Anglo-Portuguese armies by turns invaded across, withdrew from, and then once again invaded across the Spanish–Portuguese frontier; cities such as Ciudad Rodrigo and Badajoz repeatedly changed hands; and the French found themselves threatened by Wellington, plagued by mostly ineffectual but also irrepressible Spanish armies, and enmeshed

---

[42] At the cost of his own life; he was struck down by a cannon shot in the final moments of the battle. In an unusual expression of chivalry in a war that witnessed little, Soult erected a monument on Moore's grave to the memory of his British foe. It can be visited in Corunna today, reposing in a quiet garden overlooking the bay.

[43] Spanish leaders, especially La Romana, were furious at the British Army's "desertion." Esdaile, *The Peninsula War*, pp. 151–153.

[44] Gates has done us the service of listing them, as well as assessing the winners and losers. Unsurprisingly, in 1809, the winners were mostly French. By 1812, the winners were mostly the allies. Gates, *The Spanish Ulcer*, pp. 470–474.

in a vicious insurgency that ate away at both their material and moral stamina. Regarding the guerrillas, one might apply General Sir William Napier's description of conditions in Asturias equally to all of Spain's other rebellious provinces: "The great towns," he wrote, "were overawed by fifty thousand foreign bayonets, but the peasantry commenced a war in their manner against the stragglers and the sick, and thus a hostile chain cast round the French army was completed in every link."[45]

Annoying though it was, however, in the end it was less the insurgency than the regular Spanish armies that caused French generals the most trouble throughout this period. Despite defeat after defeat, those armies simply refused to die. At Ocaña, at Alba, at Baza, at Saguntum, and in scores of lesser engagements, the French inflicted shattering defeats on Spain's regular formations, only to watch their bloodied adversaries slip away to safety in one or another of Spain's mountain fastnesses, then reappear weeks later reconstituted with fresh recruits and looking for a fight. Thereby compelled to garrison every occupied province heavily enough to defeat such sorties, French commanders repeatedly found it impossible to concentrate the strength needed to destroy Wellesley's Anglo-Portuguese forces when the two antagonists met.

The next such occasion was not long in coming. Restored to command after having been exonerated of responsibility for Cintra, Wellesley returned to Portugal in April 1809 with enough reinforcements to bring the effective strength of the British expeditionary force to 30,000 men. In addition, thanks to Beresford's training program, he could count on as many as 16,000 reconstituted Portuguese regulars. With this force, in little more than a month Wellington recaptured Oporto and threw an overextended Soult out of Portugal. Then, leaving Beresford and the bulk of his Portuguese regulars to guard the frontier, he marched 20,000 troops across the Douro River into Castile with a view to destroying Victor, who was positioned near the town of Talavera with the only significant French force between the Portuguese frontier and Madrid.

To achieve the necessary numerical superiority, however, Wellesley needed to combine forces with Spanish General Gregorio Cuesta's Army of Estremadura. Instead, Talavera was Wellington's first encounter with what would prove to be a recurring frustration. Anxious to fight Victor before he could be reinforced from Madrid, Wellesley proposed to attack on the morning of 19 July. But for five days, Cuesta refused to

---

[45] Major General Sir W. F. P. Napier, *History of the War in the Peninsula and in the South of France* (London, 1892), vol. 1, p. 23.

move, during which interval the outnumbered Victor sensibly retreated. Concerned about his overstretched logistics and certain that the French would reinforce Victor, a furious Wellesley declined to pursue Victor farther east. Cuesta set out after him alone, only to retreat headlong back to Talavera when, reinforced just as Wellesley had feared by 20,000 troops from Madrid and Toledo, Victor turned on him.

The battle that followed left the allies in possession of the field and earned Wellington his peerage, but at the cost of nearly 7,000 casualties, most of them British. In view of those losses and with his line of communication back to Lisbon threatened from the northwest by a heavily reinforced Soult, Wellington prudently withdrew back across the Tagus River. Although he remained in Spain for some additional weeks hoping for better cooperation with Cuesta, the Spanish continued to prove not merely uncooperative but also actively hostile. They abandoned Talavera, in the process surrendering British wounded to the French, and, not content with failing to furnish Wellesley earlier promised rations, attacked his foragers and threatened to sack any local villages offering to furnish them subsistence.[46]

By now disgusted with his allies, Wellington declined pleas to join them in a renewed but unrealistic offensive that ended with crushing Spanish defeats at Ocaña and Alba. Instead, he withdrew back to the frontier. There, strongly picketing the most direct routes to Lisbon and stripping the Portuguese countryside of anything that might furnish subsistence to an invading army, he set thousands of conscripted Portuguese laborers to constructing the interlocking network of fortifications stretching from the Atlantic to the Tagus River that soon would become famous as the "Lines" of Torres Vedras.

Reflecting on Talavera, one historian has written, "The campaign had ... utterly exhausted [British] forces. The importance of sound logistics in the barren peninsula had been painfully underlined, while the collapse of the strategic arrangements made by Wellington with the Spanish had weakened his soldiers' confidence."[47] As Wellington wrote to Lord Burghersh in response to criticism of his decision to retreat, "I lament as much as any man can the necessity for separating from the Spaniards, but I was compelled to go and I believe there was not an officer in the army who did not think I stayed too long."[48]

---

[46] Glover, *The Peninsular War*, p. 114.
[47] Gates, *The Spanish Ulcer*, p. 191.
[48] Glover, *The Peninsular War*, p. 115.

Both problems, of strained logistics and recalcitrant Spanish generals, would continue to plague Wellington over the next two years. The former would act like a rubber band, dragging the Anglo-Portuguese armies back each time they penetrated too far into Spain, while the refusal of Spanish generals to act in concert even with each other, let alone with the British and Portuguese, had the same repeated effect of depriving the allies of the ability to exploit tactical victories.

Meanwhile, if Talavera established the pattern of allied operations throughout the remainder of this period, Soult's subsequent failure to take Cadiz and Masséna's inability to take Lisbon similarly established the pattern of French operations. With Wellington forced from Spain and Spanish armies in northern and central Spain defeated and scattered, only Andalusia seemed to stand in the way of final French triumph in Spain, while only Wellington's grip on Lisbon preserved Britain's foothold in Portugal. The year 1810 would see the expensive frustration of French efforts to resolve both problems. In Andalusia, even as Joseph entered Seville in triumph, Soult imprudently delayed attacking Cadiz long enough for Wellington to reinforce its garrison.[49] Thereafter, protected by allied battleships and resupplied from the sea, Cadiz easily defied French investment.[50] Behind its frustrated besiegers, Spanish partisans wreaked havoc with French lines of communication. During the next two years, Andalusia would preoccupy some 60,000 French troops, two-thirds of them committed to the siege of Cadiz and the logistical and counterinsurgency operations associated with it.

Portugal proved a similar story. In July 1810, after reducing Ciudad Rodrigo at little cost,[51] Masséna advanced into Portugal with 65,000 troops. With only 52,000 soldiers of his own, nearly half of them still relatively raw Portuguese, Wellington perforce withdrew, pausing only once to administer a sharp check to the French at Bussaco on 27 September. There, misjudging the strength of Wellington's defensive position, Masséna made the mistake of attacking it frontally at a cost of more than 4,000 French casualties.

Two weeks later, on 11 October, the first French soldiers caught sight of the Lines, and for the next five months, as starvation and sickness

---

[49] Here, threatened with mob violence, it quickly dissolved in favor of a regency led by General Castaños, victor of Bailén and by the convocation of a new Cortés in March. Glover, *The Peninsular War*, p. 119; Esdaile, *The Peninsular War*, pp. 283–284.

[50] Hall, *Wellington's Navy*, pp. 146–164.

[51] The French suffered fewer than 1,200 casualties, only 180 of them fatal. Gates, *The Spanish Ulcer*, p. 227.

eroded their numbers, observing their well-fed adversaries was effectively all that they and their fellows were able to do; behind them, Portuguese *ordenanza* ambushed their foraging parties, intercepted their couriers, and murdered any French soldier incautious enough to stray far from his camp. The French, needless to say, considered such activities to be cowardly, unlawful, and contrary to the usages of war, to the point where, in September 1810, Masséna formally complained of them to Wellington. The latter's response is worth quoting at length:

> Those whom you call 'peasants without uniform, assassins, and highwaymen' are local militia, which, as I've previously had the honor to assure you, are military units commanded by officers, paid and operating subject to military laws. You seem to be insisting that those who enjoy the rights of war must wear the uniform; but you should recall that you yourself have added to the glory of the French army while commanding soldiers who had no uniform.[52]

Finally, on 5 March 1811, having accomplished precisely nothing, Masséna gave up and, after garrisoning the frontier fortresses, withdrew back into Spain. The remainder of his forces finally reached Salamanca on 11 April, the five-month exercise having cost him altogether more than 25,000 soldiers killed, captured, or lost to starvation and disease.[53]

As Masséna withdrew, Wellington advanced. The next few months witnessed several bloody but indecisive clashes between French and Anglo-Portuguese forces at Fuentes de Oñoro, Albuera, and Badajoz, but these resulted in little change in the situation of the two contending armies. Not so in the east, however, where Louis Gabriel Suchet, Napoleon's most effective peninsular general, having largely suppressed the insurgency in Aragon and reduced the Catalonian fortresses of Lerido and Tortosa, finally captured Tarragona on 28 June, destroying half of Catalonia's regular forces in the process. Four months later, after defeating Blake's Army of Valencia in a pitched battle at Saguntum on 11 October, Suchet finally succeeded in taking the city of Valencia on 8 January

---

[52] Wellington to Masséna, 24 September 1810 in "Wellington's Dispatches, September 21st–24th, 1810" (available at http://www.wtj.com/archives/Wellington), trans. by the author. At best, the response was disingenuous. Most regulated militia had withdrawn behind the Lines and those remaining behind obeyed no law but their own. But Wellington must have taken a certain malicious pleasure in drafting it.

[53] Indeed, as Glover rightly argues, the fortitude of the French soldiers throughout this purgatory rivaled that of the Spanish, and only a commander of Masséna's iron will could have held them together as long as he did. Glover, *The Peninsular War*, p. 143. One thing that helped was a virtual absence of desertion, which, in Portugal even more than in Spain, was apt to be fatal for the deserter whether or not he was caught.

1812. It was to be the high-water mark of the French conquest of Spain. Beginning in 1812, the allies would reclaim the initiative, and although there would again be setbacks, they would never wholly relinquish it.

Act 4. At the end of 1811, the operational map of Spain looked like a patchwork quilt. In addition to the former Army of Portugal confronting Wellington along the frontier, now commanded by Marshal Auguste Marmont, French armies controlled the Catalonian coast south to Tortosa, the valley of the Ebro, most of Old Castile, Santander, and Biscay, and irregular swaths of territory surrounding Madrid, Jaén, Cadiz, and Seville. The rest of Spain, harboring regular Spanish forces of varying strength, provincial militias, and countless *guerrilleros*, remained contested space through which the French moved at their peril. Merely to secure their lines of communication from Madrid back to the French border required some 70,000 French troops.[54]

By now, their partisan tormentors were beginning to operate in much more formidable arrays, some large enough to take on even regular forces with some confidence. In the early years of the struggle, such achievements had been possible only in the mountains, where irregulars could assemble, strike, and withdraw faster than French infantry could respond and pursue. In Galicia, for example, combining with La Romana's surviving regulars, partisans had virtually ejected the French from the province by the end of 1809, while in Navarre, devoid of Spanish regulars, guerrillas nevertheless succeeded in tying down 20,000 French soldiers.[55] On 27 May 1810, Francisco Espoz y Mina's Navarese destroyed a French convoy escorted by more than 1,600 men, killing or capturing 400 in the process.[56] In contrast, on the plains of León, Castile, and La Mancha, where French cavalry could operate freely, to coalesce in strength was to invite annihilation.

By 1812, however, the pressure on Joseph's widely separated armies had begun to open exploitable seams even in the central provinces. In October 1810, *El Cura* ambushed and nearly annihilated two French naval battalions in Castile. In La Mancha, Juan Blanes's *Husares Francos* gradually were able to take on even French cavalry detachments. In León, the mounted companies of Don Julian Sanchez's *Lanceros de Castilla*, cooperating closely with Wellington's forces, furnished early warning of

---

[54] Tone, *The Fatal Knot*, p. 4.
[55] Ibid., p. 82.
[56] Chartrand, *Spanish Guerrillas in the Peninsular War*, p. 8.

French movements and raided convoys and foraging parties nearly with impunity.⁵⁷ Eventually, augmented with infantry and light artillery, they were able to operate with confidence even in Castile. Finally, in Catalonia, 2,000 irregulars under Francisco Rovira managed with the assistance of the Conde de Campoverde's regulars to seize the vital fortress of Figueras. Retaking it cost Marshal MacDonald's Army of Catalonia some 4,000 men, effectively immobilizing it for months while the rest of Catalonia continued to seethe with unrest.

To a considerable extent, the escalation in partisan warfare was the fault of the French themselves. Initially, Joseph had tried hard to capitalize on *Afrancesado* and reformist sentiment in Spain, introducing programs to regularize taxation and the administration of justice, abolish monopolies, incentivize new agricultural and industrial enterprises, and establish a secular system of primary education. At the same time, with far too few French administrators to manage Spain's numerous municipalities, he made heroic efforts to co-opt Spanish élites, offering generous salaries and titles to nobles, clerics, soldiers, and bureaucrats willing to collaborate with the régime. Finally, in an effort to recapture control of the revolutionary narrative, Joseph caused gazettes to be distributed throughout the peninsula highlighting the atrocities committed by the insurgents and seeking to paint them at best as tools and hirelings of the British, and at worst as outright brigands, a charge to which the not-infrequent insurgent depredations against their own lent some credence.

For a time, especially in the interior provinces, those efforts bore fruit. They were largely undone by the French Army itself, however, whose commanders had long since internalized Napoleon's dictum that war should be made to pay for war, and over whom Joseph exerted control inversely proportional to their distance from Madrid. In addition to universally resented local exactions for billeting and subsistence, French commanders also imposed heavy monetary levies wherever they operated and confiscated goods in kind when specie was not forthcoming.⁵⁸ In many cases, this amounted to outright theft. "[R]apacity remained characteristic of French occupation until the very end... whilst Joseph's ability to do anything to remedy matters was reduced to an ever smaller compass."⁵⁹ In consequence, the longer the struggle continued, the more

---

⁵⁷ It was the capture of a French courier by insurgents, for example, that warned Wellesley of Soult's approach after Talavera. Esdaile, *The Peninsular War*, p. 276.
⁵⁸ Esdaile accuses Soult alone of robbing Andalusia of more than 1 million francs worth of art. Ibid., p. 244.
⁵⁹ Ibid., p. 245.

local support accrued to partisans who behaved with reasonable restraint toward the civil populations of the regions in which they operated.

Nevertheless, although the insurgency could bleed the French, it failed to drive them out. Had the French nothing else with which to contend, internal political fragmentation and sheer exhaustion likely would eventually have eroded both the insurgency and its popular support, especially had the French dealt with it more sensibly. Instead, what made the insurgency fatal and prevented the French from suppressing it was its connection to the concurrent war of the armies. By keeping Wellington informed while depriving his French counterparts of even routine information; by forcing the French to divert precious regulars to protect supply depots and the lines of communication connecting them to the field forces; and, above all, by forcing on French commanders geographic dispersals that precluded achieving a decisive force concentration anywhere, the partisans, increasingly in cooperation with Spanish regular forces, helped make possible the allied battlefield victories that finally forced the French from the Iberian Peninsula.

Although haphazard, regular–irregular cooperation was especially important. The two years after Bailén had not been kind to Spanish armies. Widely separated and combining poorly with each other even when they rarely managed to concentrate, Spanish forces almost invariably suffered from deficiencies in cavalry and artillery. Their initial disdain for irregulars – often as well armed as and much more mobile than regulars and with far better knowledge of the ground – deprived the Spanish armies of resources that might have helped compensate for those disadvantages. Wellington was scarcely alone after Talavera in criticizing Spain's military ineptness. Following the defeat of General Francisco Venegas's Army of La Mancha at Almonacid in August 1809, the Andalusian junta complained to the Supreme Junta in Seville that "Our generals are absolutely ignorant of how to unite their forces, totally lacking intelligence and the art of coordinating a plan of campaign.... Events have shown that we have no generals in whom [supreme] power can be safely confided."[60]

By the beginning of 1812, a few effective commanders were beginning to emerge. In Galicia, General José Santocildes, who had replaced La Romana on the latter's death, combined his 16,000 regulars with Galician partisans to besiege Benavente and Astorga, preventing the reinforcement

---

[60] Fraser, *Napoleon's Cursed War*, p. 350.

of Marmont's forces that confronted Wellington. In La Mancha, a detachment of Castaños' Army of Estremadura took Ciudad Real, although it was subsequently forced to relinquish it to a reinforced French counteroffensive. In Murcia, General Francisco Ballesteros marched 9,000 men over the mountains to attack the French at Bornos, forcing them to divert units from two different army corps to drive the Spanish back to Gibraltar. Although none of those engagements was decisive, together they and other efforts by regular Spanish armies, aided by increasingly numerous and effective partisans, compelled French commanders to engage in repeated marches and engagements that exhausted their troops, inflicted a steady stream of casualties, and, most important, deprived French forces confronting Wellington of reinforcements they soon would desperately need.

Napoleon could not rescue the situation. Early in 1812, he robbed Joseph of more than 20,000 veterans for use in his forthcoming invasion of Russia.[61] Between those withdrawals and losses to battle and disease, French strength on the peninsula dropped during the year from more than 300,000 to barely 200,000 soldiers, half of which, Glover points out, "could play no part in resisting Wellington's advance unless vast tracts of eastern Spain were abandoned to the guerrillas."[62]

By spring 1812, the French began to feel the effect of this reduction in strength in a savage struggle with Wellington's forces for possession of two key Spanish fortresses on the Portuguese border. Halfway down the frontier, Ciudad Rodrigo sat astride the route from the Portuguese coast through Salamanca, Valladolid, and Burgos to the headwaters of the Ebro, and thence to Bayonne. A little over 100 miles farther south as the crow flies, Badajoz controlled the shortest route between Lisbon and Madrid. By virtue of their locations on these main avenues north and south of Spain's Central Sierra, control of both fortresses was vital to an army invading in either direction – one to support its own advance and the other to protect against a counteroffensive by the enemy.

By the end of March, Anglo-Portuguese forces had secured both bastions, albeit not without pain. Ciudad Rodrigo cost the allies 1,300 casualties, including two general officers. Badajoz was even more expensive. Nor were costs limited to the combatants: In both cases, once through

---

[61] The exact number is disputed. Glover counts redeployments of 27,000 – Glover, *The Peninsular War*, p. 190 fn.; Esdaile only 25,000 – Esdaile, *The Peninsular War*, p. 370. Either figure would have been a body blow to the already overstretched French.

[62] Glover, *The Peninsular War*, p. 190.

the defenses, assaulting troops got out of hand, and Spanish civilians, whom their liberators should have embraced, instead found themselves subjected to atrocities as horrific as any inflicted by the French. Nevertheless, by the beginning of summer, the two vital doors to central Spain were in Wellington's hands.

Accordingly, having managed by a daring raid at Almaraz to fix Soult's forces southeast of Badajoz and assisted by the diversionary Spanish actions, on 13 June, Wellington crossed the Agueda River with 52,000 troops and headed for Salamanca, where Marmont awaited with nearly the same number. The battle that followed on 22 July erupted almost by accident. Neither commander believed that he enjoyed a sufficient numerical advantage to risk a pitched battle. When, however, Marmont unwisely attempted to pursue what he incorrectly perceived to be the allies' retreat, he inadvertently opened a gap between his right and left wings. Wellington quickly capitalized on the French error. Attacking into the gap, allied forces destroyed the isolated French left wing and then turned on the right. With Marmont badly wounded, the French broke. Only the timely arrival of nightfall, together with allied forces nearly as confused in victory as the French in defeat, enabled the latter to escape unmolested to Alba, having suffered 13,000 casualties to Wellington's 4,800. The following day, after a sharp rearguard action at Garcia-Hernandez, the battered Army of Portugal retreated north across the Douro.[63] Three weeks later, on 12 August, the allies triumphantly entered Madrid, from which Joseph had withdrawn to Valencia and Suchet's protection.

If one can argue that the war of armies had a distinguishable turning point, it probably was Salamanca. Fought between two more or less evenly matched opponents, neither enjoying an insuperable terrain advantage, Salamanca was a body blow to French prestige. "The myth of French invincibility, tarnished at Bailén, was shattered at Salamanca."[64] Perhaps as important, the lopsided victory resuscitated British domestic support for the war that Wellington's earlier retreat into Portugal had badly shaken. After Salamanca, his grip on the conduct of peninsular operations would never again be seriously challenged.[65]

---

[63] One of the few cases on record in which unsupported cavalry, in this case the King's German Legion, managed to shatter an infantry square. Esdaile, *The Peninsular War*, p. 397.

[64] Glover, *The Peninsular War*, p. 222.

[65] Not an inconsequential achievement, given that only two months earlier, a cabinet crisis had seriously threatened Wellington's recall and Britain's abandonment of the peninsula altogether.

But although Salamanca and the liberation of Madrid enhanced Wellington's reputation and solidified his authority, the resulting operational situation confronted him with a major problem. In the north, the former Army of Portugal, now commanded by General Joseph Souham, had by no means been destroyed. Meanwhile, Joseph once again ordered Soult to abandon Andalusia and instead join in attacking the allies from the south.[66] Were northern and southern French forces to coordinate successfully, Wellington would find himself assailed simultaneously by superior forces on both flanks. He could evade the dilemma only if, by securing the crucial route through Burgos, the allies could bottle up the Army of Portugal in the valley of the Ebro. Furthermore, he needed either the Spanish to keep Soult occupied or the autumn rains to swell the Tagus sufficiently to minimize the number of potential crossings that had to be defended against an advance from the south.

None of those conditions transpired. Although the French evacuated the city of Burgos without a pitched battle, the fortress garrison left behind stubbornly refused to be dislodged, and after suffering nearly 2,000 casualties, Wellington called off efforts to reduce the city. Meanwhile, enraged by the Cortés's offer of supreme command to Wellington,[67] Ballesteros mutinously refused orders to distract Soult.[68] In early October, after an acrimonious meeting with Joseph, Soult finally agreed to join d'Erlon's Army of the Center in attacking north with a combined force of 61,000 men with a view to cutting Wellington off from Portugal. The Tagus remained unfortunately fordable; with his forces north and south of Madrid separated by nearly 150 miles, Wellington dared delay no longer. On 21 October, he began withdrawing from the north, followed not long afterward by the similar withdrawal of General Rowland Hill's covering force on the Tagus. Although neither withdrawal was completed without a few tense moments, the allies successfully avoided entrapment. Even so, pausing only briefly at Madrid, Joseph pressed the pursuit. Two weeks later, after halting momentarily at Salamanca, where the French

---

[66] An order that Soult, still committed to seizing Cadiz, initially arrogantly refused to obey. Glover, *The Peninsular War*, p. 208.

[67] Formed after the dissolution of the Supreme Junta on its withdrawal from Seville to Cadiz, the Cortés offered Wellington overall command of Spanish armies on 22 September, an offer that, qualified as it was with numerous restrictions and certain to infuriate many if not most Spanish generals, did not fill him with joy. Esdaile, *The Peninsular War*, pp. 408–409.

[68] His insubordination led to his relief but too late to influence events on the Tagus. Gates, *The Spanish Ulcer*, pp. 371–372.

unaccountably declined to attack, the allies were back at Ciudad Rodrigo, from which they had begun their offensive so optimistically only five months earlier.

During all of this activity, of course, the key question was where were the Spanish regulars? Despite the changes in command arrangements noted earlier, Spanish armies remained reluctant (and, in some cases, simply unable) to operate in accordance with a unified plan of campaign. Ballesteros was far from the only Spanish commander resentful of Wellington's appointment to supreme allied command, hedged as it was, and the geographical dispersal of Spain's regular forces would have made concerted action difficult in any case.

But if Spanish regulars failed to prevent the French concentration that forced Wellington back to the Spanish frontier, Spanish irregulars were not slow to exploit the territorial vacuum resulting from it. During the allies' retreat and afterward, while the main armies went into winter quarters, partisan forces under such leaders as Sanchez, Mina, and *El Empecinado* enjoyed freedom of action in Navarre, northern Aragon, and Andalusia, while at the opposite corners of the peninsula, in Galicia and Catalonia, their counterparts in conjunction with Spanish regulars made life increasingly miserable for the occupying forces.[69] Napoleon's angry but ill-considered reaction to these operations would help convince Wellington to invade Spain for the third time, this time to stay.

Act 5. On 22 December 1812, Lord Liverpool jubilantly informed Wellington that "the most formidable army ever collected by Bonaparte has been substantially destroyed." "Under these circumstances," he added, "the question naturally arises whether he will leave the French army in Spain.... The only efficient French army at the present moment in existence is that under Soult: and whatever it may cost Bonaparte to abandon Spain, I think he will prefer that alternative to the loss of Germany."[70]

Britain's prime minister underestimated Napoleon's stubbornness, ingenuity, and ego. The first made it unthinkable that he would voluntarily surrender what he had invested so much to acquire, abandoning his brother in the process. The second enabled him to rebuild his shattered *Grande Armée* with astonishing speed without reducing his peninsular

---

[69] Catalonia additionally benefited from Napoleon's unwise decision of January 1812 to annex the province outright to France. Fraser, *Napoleon's Cursed War*, p. 446.

[70] Gates, *The Spanish Ulcer*, p. 376.

troop commitment below 200,000.⁷¹ The last convinced him that even this diminished force still could bring Spain if not the entire peninsula to heel if properly managed. For their part, the allies after Salamanca had been forced to relearn the lesson of Talavera. As Wellington acknowledged, "It is obvious that we cannot expect to save the Peninsula by military efforts unless we can bring forward the Spaniards in some shape or other."⁷²

Accordingly, in a letter to Spain's acting minister of war on 4 December 1812, Wellington demanded fundamental changes in the terms of his appointment as supreme allied commander, including exclusive control over communications with Spanish commanders, reduction in the number of Spanish field armies, authority over military promotions and appointments, the right to purge or reassign unsuitable officers, and military authority, in the persons of Spanish army captains-general, over provincial and local governments. His demands produced an uproar even among those in the Cortés who had urged his appointment, and he finally had to threaten to resign in order to obtain agreement to most (although not all) of what he demanded.⁷³

Moreover, agreement was one thing, execution another. During the next five months, his efforts to enforce the new arrangements encountered one obstacle after another, from continuing resistance by Spanish commanders to repeated political interference by the Cortés itself. In March 1813, for example, the latter appointed one of its own former regents to be captain-general of Cadiz and, not content with that, authorized him to raise and command a new Andalusian "Army of Reserve," all without reference to Wellington.

Notwithstanding these irritations, with the arrival of spring, Wellington once more took the offensive, impelled in part by Napoleon's disastrous response to events in the north. In April 1813, furious at the increasing depredations of Mina and his fellow partisans in Navarre and Aragon and convinced that Wellington lacked the numerical superiority to mount a renewed offensive campaign, the emperor directed Joseph to reassign a significant portion of the Army of Portugal to the harried Army of the North, leaving his hapless brother with fewer than 40,000 troops in

---

[71] Within weeks, he once more was marching east, and in August he trounced the combined Austrian, Russian, and Prussian armies near Dresden. It would be his last victory on German soil.
[72] Esdaile, *The Peninsular War*, p. 421.
[73] Ibid., pp. 423–425.

central Spain to face an allied army reinforced during the winter to more than 80,000 men, most of them from the increasingly capable Portuguese army.[74] The winter, moreover, had seen more than just an increase in Wellington's numbers. His troops' health, training, and logistics all had improved. As he reported to the Secretary of State for War on 11 May, "I shall never be stronger or more efficient than I am now."[75]

Accordingly, on 22 May 1813, Wellington divided his force into two unequal columns and sent the smaller under General Rowland Hill up the old road through Salamanca to fix Joseph's attention, while the larger under General Sir Thomas Graham sliced northeast, bridging the Douro and Esla Rivers and flanking Joseph's lead elements. Rejoining Hill at Toro, the main column was joined as well by 20,000 Spanish regulars of Spanish General Pedro Giron's Fourth Army. Joseph, finding himself facing not the 30,000-odd allied troops Napoleon had so cavalierly dismissed but instead nearly 100,000 well-trained soldiers, quickly retreated from Valladolid to Burgos. There, augmented by still another 5,000 Spanish troops, Wellington once again enveloped the French from the north and the latter once again withdrew until, on 21 June, fearing to be hustled out of Spain altogether and having concentrated two of his armies and what could be spared from a third, Joseph finally stood to fight outside Vitoria.

The battle that followed was not as tactically decisive as it might have been. The allies failed to sever Joseph's line of retreat, which allowed the bulk of his forces to escape to the foothills of the Pyrenees after suffering 8,000 casualties to the allies' 5,000. But Vitoria's operational and strategic ramifications were profound. Operationally, heroic efforts to hold the forward edge of the Pyrenees by Soult, whom Napoleon at last appointed commander-in-chief of all French forces,[76] proved futile. Unable to relieve allied pressure on Pamplona and San Sebastian, which between them controlled the principal northern roads into France, Soult's forces in the north had no choice but to withdraw behind the Pyrenees. By 2 August, the French Army was back inside its own borders for the first time in five years. It now made little sense for Suchet to attempt to retain his own overextended and isolated position in Valencia. By the end

---

[74] Overextended, plagued by insurgents and Murcia's regular Spanish forces, and further diverted by an abortive Anglo-Sicilian attack on Tarragona, Suchet and his Army of Valencia were in no position to assist.
[75] Gates, *The Spanish Ulcer*, p. 383.
[76] Joseph, who had accepted the throne of Spain with reluctance in the first place, was packed off into retirement, in which he apparently was a good deal happier.

of the year, he too had evacuated all but the small corner of Catalonia immediately adjacent to France.

Vitoria's strategic impact was, if anything, even more significant than its operational results. Advised of Wellington's victory on 3 July, the British government wasted no time passing the news on to other European governments. On 12 August, Austria joined the Sixth Coalition and declared war on France. Two months later, at Leipzig, the combined armies of Russia, Prussia, Austria, and Sweden decisively defeated Napoleon. In Spain, meanwhile, Wellington's forces, having finally captured San Sebastian, crossed the Bidassoa River onto French soil. Pamplona held out until the end of the month and Barcelona even longer,[77] and allied operations in southern France continued until April 1814. But for all practical purposes, the end of 1813 also saw the end of Napoleon's accursed Spanish war.[78]

Curtain Call

In an interview early in 2010, retired British Lieutenant General Sir Graeme Lamb, charged with coordinating Afghan reconciliation and reintegration for NATO, reportedly commented that "Clausewitz was right, but he didn't finish his sentence: If war is an extension of politics, then to politics it must return."[79] On 14 March 1814, Ferdinand VII, *Fernando el Deseado*,[80] crossed back into Spain at the frontier bridge near Biscara to the cheers of his subjects.[81] He returned to a Spain that six years of war had virtually bankrupted and the sociopolitical landscape of which had fundamentally altered. Even while fighting Napoleon, "Patriot" Spain had adopted many of his reforms, including a constitution sharply limiting the power of the monarch and nobility.[82] More important, the war and especially the insurgency had thrust into power a group of leaders who, in prewar Spain, never would have been allowed near it.

---

[77] It would not be surrendered to Spain until after Napoleon's abdication on 6 April 1814.
[78] The last major battle was fought at Toulouse on 10 April 1814.
[79] David Ignatius, "Ending Wars Through Sit-Downs," *The Washington Post*, Sunday, 4 April 2010, p. 15.
[80] He was "The Desired One," although not for all, and for many others, not for long. His father never returned to Spain.
[81] His early return resulted from an agreement by Napoleon to restore him to the throne in return for a separate peace, which Ferdinand unsurprisingly disavowed the moment he was back on Spanish soil. Gates, *The Spanish Ulcer*, p. 451.
[82] And even, albeit to a lesser extent, the power of the Catholic Church.

Encouraged by conservative and clerical opponents of reform, to which in any case he himself was anything but well disposed, Ferdinand lost little time reversing them. On 4 May, he abolished the Constitution of 1812 on the grounds that the Cortés that had adopted it had been seated without his approval. A week later, he arrested the liberal leaders responsible for its adoption. During the next six years, he ruled as an autocrat, changing advisers repeatedly. Finally, in 1820, his arbitrary behavior prompted an internal revolt aimed at restoring the constitution. Ferdinand himself was briefly imprisoned at Cadiz, only to be rescued, ironically, by the French army, which in 1823 invaded Spain once again, this time to restore rather than remove a Bourbon monarchy and as the agent of the other major continental powers. That task having been accomplished, the French were compelled to watch in disgust as Ferdinand revenged himself by executing thousands of his own people.[83] Hence, for Spain, the principal legacy of what the Spanish called the War of Liberation was a bitter conflict between liberals and conservatives that would continue to divide the nation for the rest of the century and into the next.[84]

In Portugal as well, war led ultimately to revolution. At the request of the Portuguese, Beresford stayed on as commander of the army, but Prince John, acknowledged as king after the death of his mother, refused to return from Brazil until 1821, by which time a nonviolent revolution had produced a constitutional government that, as in Spain, radically curtailed the power of the monarchy. As in Spain, however, Portugal's reactionaries remained undaunted. John's death in 1826 produced a succession crisis. Its resolution triggered a civil war that lasted until 1834, when the constitution finally was restored.

For Britain, victory in the peninsula and its undoubted contribution to Napoleon's defeat helped guarantee her a seat at the table when the major continental powers assembled in Vienna to settle the arrangement of post-Napoleonic Europe. Wellington, meanwhile, went on to complete his military resumé by defeating the Little Corporal himself at Waterloo on 18 June 1815. In the end, the ten years framed by Trafalgar and Waterloo would leave Britain the world's preeminent power for the remainder of the nineteenth century.

---

[83] Including two of the best-known partisan leaders, *El Empecinado* and Juan Diaz Porlier. Fraser, *Napoleon's Cursed War*, p. 482.

[84] Esdaile, *The Peninsula War*, pp. 506–507; also see Fraser, *Napoleon's Cursed War*, pp. 482–484.

As for France, what Napoleon called his "Spanish ulcer" cannot be said to have brought him down. Absorbing as it was for the other participants, and as expensive for the French themselves, for Napoleon it always was a sideshow. His fate would be decided, as indeed it eventually was, in Central Europe. But there can be no doubt that his ill-conceived and worse-managed attempt to conquer Iberia hastened that reckoning, consumed his military resources, destroyed his generals' reputation (and eventually their loyalty), and ate away at the nation's stamina.

Suchet, perhaps the best of Napoleon's peninsular generals, may have offered the final word on Napoleon's accursed Spanish war. He wrote in memoirs published after his death in 1826:

> It will readily be admitted that a country so peculiarly adapted to a defensive warfare, inhabited as it is, by men no less remarkable for their active and sober habits than for their courage and intelligence, can with difficulty be conquered. Various nations have successively invaded it. History exhibits them seizing upon Spain after long and sanguinary wars, establishing their dominion on various points, without being able wholly to subdue the Spaniards, and defeated at last, or driven out as much by the constancy of the inhabitants as by the usual inconstancy of fortune.[85]

FIGHTING HYBRID WAR

So much, in abbreviated form, for the Peninsular War drama of 1807–1814. Even in so heavily compressed an account, however, some of the challenges associated with fighting hybrid wars are difficult to miss, affecting as they did all of the combatants. If a single quality characterized the war, it was the sheer complexity resulting from its multiplicity of contending combatants, whose interests and objectives even when nominally allied tended to diverge sharply, and whose relationships, as a result, were likely to be fragile at best and at worst dangerously volatile.

All parties in the Peninsular War were slow to recognize and accommodate that complexity, and the French never managed to do so – a failure manifested in both large and small ways. On the one hand, in the broadest sense, Napoleon never really troubled to capitalize on Spain's reformist leanings or the Spaniards' lingering resentment against Britain; and by the time that his hapless brother attempted to do so, the French already

---

[85] Louis-Gabriel Suchet, *Memoirs of the War in Spain*, available at http://www.wtj.com/archives/suchet/sucheto2a.htm.

had made themselves universally unpopular. On the other hand, neither did the French systematically seek to exploit the widespread counter-revolutionary sentiment of either the landed nobility or the higher Spanish clergy. Either approach – and both could have succeeded at different times and places notwithstanding their intrinsic incompatibility – might have bought them the indigenous support that they so desperately needed.

Similarly, few French commanders made any effort to understand, still less to exploit, the potential afforded by prewar tensions between the central and exterior provinces and between the provinces and Madrid. "Even in Galicia, where the uprising seemed nearly unanimous to the French, the insurgency received little help from the bourgeoisie and almost none from ecclesiastics and nobles."[86] There was even more scope for attracting popular support in remote and semiautonomous provinces such as Navarre. Instead, in Navarre as elsewhere, taxation policies along with the predatory behavior of the French Army systematically alienated even those who might otherwise have acquiesced to a French-dominated national government.[87]

The allies were more fortunate. As one commentator puts it, perhaps too starkly, "Though the British, Spaniards, and Portuguese hated one another, in the end they hated Napoleon still more."[88] Although "the enemy of my enemy is my friend" may furnish a rationale for military partnership, it does not ensure its smooth operation. Especially between British and Spanish military and political authorities, tensions persisted throughout the war and contributed not a little to prolonging it. It did not help that neither army's leaders fully appreciated the challenges confronting their opposite numbers. To Wellington, for example, the Spanish army's deficiencies were traceable directly to flaws in the national character. As he commented acidly after Talavera, "They [the Spanish] are really children in the art of war, and I cannot say they do anything as it ought to be done, with the exception of running away, and assembling again in a state of nature."[89] For their part, Spanish commanders considered their British counterparts overbearing, impatient, and wholly unwilling to recognize the difficulties with which they themselves were burdened. For example, their repeated failure to satisfy British subsistence requirements more often than not reflected the inability of Spanish armies

---

[86] Tone, *The Fatal Knot*, p. 54.
[87] Ibid., p. 147.
[88] Esdaile, *The Peninsular War*, p. 482.
[89] *Dispatches*, August 1809, in George Henry Francis, *Maxims and Opinions of Field-Marshal His Grace The Duke Of Wellington* (London, 1845), Project Gutenberg EBook.

to feed even their own troops, let alone those of their more demanding allies.[90]

In the end, of course, the conflict's complexity worked mostly against the French and in favor of the allies. But it did so less because of any intrinsic allied wisdom than because, needing ultimately to stamp out fires that their enemies had only to keep alight, the French failed to find the means to deprive them of fuel. Instead, French military and civil behavior alike merely fanned the flames of Spanish and Portuguese resistance, paradoxically nurturing in both countries the very sense of nationhood that their own leaders had failed to create but one increasingly hostile to French interests.

J. F. C. Fuller once remarked that all the principles of war could be subsumed under the principle of economy of force.[91] Another way of saying the same thing is to argue that, absent a coherent design that establishes and enforces priorities linked clearly to the strategic aim, military operations risk being piecemealed and hence unlikely to achieve benefits commensurate with their costs.

During the Peninsular War, achieving operational coherence was a challenge for both sides, but especially for the French. As a result, from the outset, and with only a single brief interruption, Napoleon's central operational problem was overextension. That the problem was in many respects self-inflicted is beside the point. Even had the French Army behaved faultlessly toward the indigenous population, it still would have found itself compelled to conduct concurrent combat, constabulary, and sustainment operations across an extensive and topographically difficult geography and against a multiplicity of adversaries. At best, those conditions would have complicated the achievement of operational coherence. In the event, French treatment of the civil populations among which they operated merely aggravated the complication, while overstretching the resources needed to cope with it.

As we have seen, in part French behavior reflected Napoleon's approach to sustaining his armies. As Oman put it, "One of the cardinal blunders of Napoleon's whole scheme for the conquest of the Peninsula was that he persisted in treating it as if it were German or Italian soil,

---

[90] As Wellington's quartermaster-general George Murray commented not altogether facetiously at one point, "Historians will say that the British army ... carried on war in Spain & Portugal until they had eaten all the beef and mutton in the country, and were then compelled to withdraw." Longford, p. 305.

[91] J. F. C. Fuller, *The Foundations of the Science of War*, available at http://cgsc.leavenworth.army.mil/carl/ resources/csi.

capable of supporting an army on the march."[92] That error had several unhappy results. For starters, because no significant garrison could feed itself for long from local resources, any troop concentration meant committing a significant share of its strength to foraging. Even had that effort been pursued with far more restraint than the French displayed, its adverse impact on already marginal local economies had the inevitable effect of incentivizing the insurgency. In turn, the insurgency compelled the French to divert still more troops to protect their foraging effort. That the French army was able to subsist as well as it did for as long as it did was possible only because, as Wellington himself admitted, the French soldier was willing and able to live far more austerely in the field than his British counterpart.[93]

Quite apart from sustainment, however, Napoleon repeatedly refused to acknowledge the imbalance between the resources he was prepared to commit to the peninsula and the scale of the task they confronted. Instead, even before invading Russia, contemptuous of the Spanish and Portuguese, and even of the British on land, Napoleon insisted on treating the conquest of the peninsula as a trivial military problem – a disdain only reinforced by his own brilliantly successful and apparently decisive operations during the winter of 1808–1809. In consequence, Napoleon neither made any effort to sequence operations in a way that would permit the progressive stabilization of the areas controlled by French armies nor encouraged his subordinates to do so. Instead, until nearly the end of the war, he essentially ignored the need for operational coherence and the unity of command essential to producing it. On the contrary, he ensured, by his constant interference and refusal to discipline his generals, that brother Joseph would be no more successful in achieving it.

For the allies as well, although for different reasons, achieving operational coherence was a persistent problem. For the Spanish, disunity in the field reflected both similar political disunity and the self-indulgence of Spanish commanders who too often viewed cooperation even with each other as tantamount to subordination. Preexisting tensions between the exterior and central provinces and between both and Madrid, which translated into similar tensions among provincial juntas and between them and the Central Junta,[94] further contributed to the fragmentation of Spanish effort, as did the problem of sustaining field armies in provinces

---

[92] Oman, *History of the Peninsular War*, vol. 1, p. 87.
[93] Gates, *The Spanish Ulcer*, p. 33.
[94] Esdaile, *The Peninsular War*, pp. 116–117 and 165–166.

far from wealthy before the war and only further impoverished by it. Ironically, however, it was in part the very fragmentation of the Spanish effort that frustrated the French, for in their reluctance and inability to concentrate their efforts, the Spanish also avoided presenting the French a single assailable military target.[95] The strategic ambiguity, thus inadvertently created, merely aggravated the persistent French failure to develop a coherent operational design.

For the Anglo-Portuguese forces, the problem of focus was more a matter of how to capitalize on French mistakes and compensate for Spanish weaknesses than the result of any intrinsic operational defect. As Napier rightly noted, "A general's capacity is sometimes more taxed to profit from a victory than to gain one," and that was the root of Wellington's challenge until 1813.[96] Logistically, Wellington was unable to rely on the Spanish to sustain him and he could therefore advance no further than his own lines of communication could stretch. Not until French control of Spain's northern coastline was broken could Wellington relax his grip on his base at Lisbon. The prerequisite for decisive offensive operations thus was achievement of theater-wide superiority sufficient not only to defeat the main enemy army but also to prevent any other significant French force from threatening to sever his communications.

In the end, therefore, as Wellington acknowledged, allied success depended on the success of Spanish forces, both regular and irregular, in tying down so many French soldiers in the exterior provinces – Galicia, Navarre, Catalonia, and Valencia – that Joseph's central armies were thrown on their own resources. It was Wellington's achievement to preserve the support of his army, his allies, and his own government long enough to make that possible. As Napier notes, "Wellington's system of warfare [visualized] the gradual liberation of Spain by the Anglo-Portuguese army ... by nature he was inclined to daring operations – but such efforts, however glorious, could not be adopted by a commander who feared even the loss of a brigade lest the government he served should put an end to the war. Neither was it suitable to the state of his relations with the Portuguese and Spaniards."[97]

---

[95] By affording the Spanish government a protected base from which to continue to claim sovereignty, Cadiz to some extent represented a political center of gravity, whence the prolonged French effort to reduce it. Absent any real ability to contest British sea control, however, such an effort had little or no chance of success. Instead, it merely consumed military resources that would better have been employed elsewhere.
[96] Napier, *History of the War in the Peninsula and in the South of France*, vol. 5, p. 252.
[97] Ibid., p. 251.

It should be apparent from the preceding discussion that in hybrid war, coherence and complexity are in some degree intrinsically at odds. The former urges consistent intention, commonality of effort, and limited subordinate freedom of action. The latter urges nearly the opposite: objectives adapted to time, locale, and circumstance; tolerance of significant case-by-case differences in means and method; and the maximum delegation of subordinate discretion.

With the debatable exception of the two months in the winter of 1808–1809 during which Napoleon managed operations personally, the French never succeeded in reconciling these competing requirements. Efforts by Joseph to impose operational consistency and unity of effort on his nominal military subordinates were repeatedly frustrated by their mutual jealousies and his brother's unpredictable interference. With the notable exception of Suchet, French commanders never accepted that the irregulars constituted a strategic challenge in their own right. Nor, for that matter, did Napoleon himself concede that the partisan problem deserved a coherent operational response. "Though he took the 'brigand' threat seriously enough," Fraser argues, "he never came to believe in the guerrillas' fighting capabilities."[98] Not until late 1812 did Napoleon finally acknowledge that in the provinces nearest the French frontier, at least, those capabilities no longer could be ignored; and when he finally paid attention to the problem, his belated solution merely opened the door to Wellington's final offensive.

For their part, left for better or worse to their own devices, French commanders largely failed to capitalize on their freedom of action by adapting their methods to local conditions. Instead, their arrogance, indifference, and not infrequent venality alienated even local populations that they might reasonably have won over.[99] Their cavalier disdain of operational coherence thus purchased no advantage in managing complexity.

The allies also suffered from this intrinsic tension but increasingly less as time went on. In the war of the armies, coherence accrued in stages: initially limited to the Anglo-Portuguese partnership, thereafter expanded to episodic but increasingly productive cooperation between Spanish regular forces and partisans, then eventually, although scarcely smoothly, to execution of a more or less unified campaign under the direction of a

---

[98] Fraser, *Napoleon's Cursed War*, p. 423.
[99] Not excluding their troops. "This war in Spain," read a French graffito, "means death for the men, ruin for the officers, and a fortune for the generals." Esdaile, *The Peninsula War*, p. 275.

single commander. Meanwhile, for the irregulars themselves, complexity was both sword and shield. The very local and provincial differences that the French stubbornly refused to acknowledge enabled partisan leaders such as Espos y Mina, Villacampa, and *El Empecinado* to exploit local resentments to recruit irregular combatants and to sustain them in the field.[100]

Finally, the sheer scale of the contest presented an ends–means dilemma that burdened both sides but which the French, compelled not merely to defeat hostile armies but also to control vast swaths of territory, never successfully resolved. Unwilling to acknowledge the extent of the latter challenge, Napoleon never even considered sequencing the campaign in a way that would have permitted solidifying control of one region before taking on the next. For the French, therefore, all local successes tended to be fleeting. As one of Soult's officers lamented concerning the march through Galicia, it resembled "the progress of a ship on the high seas: she cleaves the waves, but they close behind her, and in a few moments all trace of her passage has disappeared."[101] For this predicament Napoleon could thank the irregulars and, to a lesser extent, the Spanish army. But rather than compensate by increasing his generals' resources or curtailing their territorial responsibilities, he chose instead to diminish the one while enlarging the other. Eventually, the occupation strangled the French army in Spain. As Joseph's chief of staff noted pointedly in his memoirs, "If only instead of 'hold all you have, and conquer the rest bit by bit,' we had been told that we might evacuate some provinces and concentrate the troops, there would have been much good in the instructions."[102]

For the British – limited institutionally rather than by overambition – the ability to reconcile means with ends resided from the outset in building up the strength of the Portuguese and Spanish armies and in developing their capacity and willingness to support each other. Beresford began the task with the Portuguese and was so successful that Wellington was moved after Badajoz to declare them nearly the equal of his British troops.[103] He himself was less successful with the Spanish, who continued

---

[100] That does not mean that all irregulars were welcomed by local populations. Some were brigands nearly as detested as the French and who imposed similar deprivations and exactions. French commanders' failure to recognize and exploit the distinction merely compounded their problems.
[101] Oman, *History of the Peninsula War*, vol. II, p. 251.
[102] Marshal Jean-Baptiste Jourdan, *Memoires Militaires*, quoted in Gates, *The Spanish Ulcer*, p. 309.
[103] *Dispatches*, 3 May 1812, in George Henry Francis, *Maxims*.

to resist proposals for army reform virtually to the end of the war. However, after 1811, the allies enjoyed the advantage of largely being able to choose their fights. By the Battle of Vitoria, not only Wellington but also several of his subordinates were successfully combining operations with their Spanish counterparts.[104]

"Between 1808 and 1814," writes John Lawrence Tone, "the French apparently destroyed the guerrilla movement in Navarre four times, only to see it reborn with greater strength than before."[105] As Americans have had to relearn more than once, no aspect of hybrid war is more difficult than defining and measuring success. Even where it is possible to diagnose clearly the relationship between military effort and strategic result, combatants habitually tend to conceal such assessments, instead preferring, for domestic purposes if no other, to minimize their losses and exaggerate their successes. Thus, writing of the challenge of assessing progress during the Vietnam War, the authors of *The Pentagon Papers* commented:

> In its efforts to show progress, some members of the Administration were continually interpreting statistics and events in the most favorable light possible, and its critics – particularly the press – were interpreting the same events in the most unfavorable light possible. Since events in Vietnam were usually open to at least two different interpretations, the gap between the Administration and its critics over the basic question of How Are We Doing? grew steadily.[106]

Hence, measuring progress in war is an arcane enterprise at best, and at worst a charade that can undermine military operations as severely as, and far more insidiously than, a lost battle.

The measurement problem is especially acute in hybrid war, where the criteria underwriting estimates of progress are likely to differ according to the varying objectives of the participants. Certainly that was true of the Peninsular War, in which each combatant had a demonstrably different definition of success. For most Portuguese, ejection of the French and restoration of Portugal's displaced monarchy were sufficient reason to fight, to which the hatred engendered by French behavior during their several occupations merely contributed. In Spain, in contrast, in which the war merely ripped apart an already strained social and political fabric,

---

[104] In a few cases, such as Sir John Murray's abortive attempt on Tarragona in June 1813, they did this less than successfully.
[105] Tone, *The Fatal Knot*, p. 146.
[106] *The Pentagon Papers*, vol. 2, ch. 6.

objectives were much less consensual and hence the definition of progress much less straightforward. As late as 1812, there still were a considerable number of Spaniards who had tied themselves for one reason or another to Joseph and whose fortunes would be imperiled by a French defeat, whether resulting in restoration of the *status quo ante bellum* or in the establishment of a reformed regime dominated by Spanish nationalists. Perhaps more important, establishment of the Cadiz Cortés by no means resolved the regional jealousies that had existed even before the war. Given centuries of mutual antagonism, the British and Portuguese were only slightly more welcome than the French, and that cooperation could be expected to evaporate (as indeed it did) the moment the imperative need for it diminished.

For France and Britain, the strategic objectives were relatively straightforward. Napoleon wanted a quiet Spain and Portugal firmly under his control and a continent closed to British forces and goods.[107] The British wanted Napoleon off the peninsula as a prelude to removing his baleful influence from Europe altogether. For both, the Iberian Peninsula was merely one theater of a much larger war, in the same way that Vietnam was for the United States against what Americans at the time considered to be a monolithic communist enemy.

But a crucial difference characterized French and British objectives, making the assessment of progress far more difficult for the former than for the latter. The British had no particular interest in remaking the societies of the nations with which they were allied, beyond ensuring that they stayed in the fight and contributed to it. Apart from Wellington's efforts to rationalize Spanish command arrangements, efforts prompted by purely military concerns, the British largely avoided interference in Portuguese and Spanish politics. In contrast, not content merely to exercise strategic control of the peninsula, an objective he might have achieved much more cheaply by leaving a compliant Ferdinand on the throne of Spain, Napoleon insisted on conferring the presumed sociopolitical benefits of Napoleonic France on a country that he believed to be ripe for such enlightenment. Even had the Spanish universally desired such change, however, which was far from the case, few Spaniards were prepared to accept it at bayonet point. Indeed, as Wellington commented perceptively in 1809, "I declare that if I were in Buonaparte's situation, I should leave the English and the Cortes to settle Spain in the best manner they could;

---

[107] He wanted more than that, of course, including a Britain at minimum resigned to his domination of Europe, but that objective was not limited to the Iberian Peninsula.

and I should entertain very little doubt but that in a very short space of time Spain must fall into the hands of France."[108] Meanwhile, from an operational perspective, Napoleon's insistence on confusing strategic with sociopolitical objectives at once complicated his military challenge and contributed not a little to the consistent failure of his commanders to recognize and deal with the intensity and tenacity of the antagonisms their operations unleashed.

When one searches for asymmetries among the combatants in the Peninsular War, many of today's commonly cited candidates disappear. For example, no significant technological disparities distinguished the combatants. Even the irregulars, armed as they eventually were either directly by allied armies or with arms captured from the French, used essentially the same weapons and equipment as regular combatants. Regulars, militia, and irregulars clearly differed in tactical proficiency and discipline, both among themselves and from each other, but such disparities tended to narrow the longer the war went on.

Logistically, the French clearly were disadvantaged in lacking an organic system of replenishment, which compelled them to rely on local procurement for subsistence. However, there were regions in which that need not have been a problem had the French been more careful about the means used to obtain it.[109] In any case, Spanish armies frequently had the same problem. As for the Anglo-Portuguese, as noted several times, their dependence on external resupply engendered its own logistical problems. From an operational standpoint, therefore, the belligerents confronted different but equally burdensome logistical challenges.

Finally, both sides suffered from command-and-control deficiencies. On the French side, Napoleon's repeated interference merely aggravated Joseph's persistent inability to exert effective authority over his self-willed generals. On the allied side, cultural differences together with Spanish politics had essentially the same effect of obstructing the execution of a unified chain of command even after supreme authority nominally had been vested in Wellington. In principle, therefore, the problems should have canceled each other out.

That they did not was a reflection of what may have been the most important asymmetry between the French and their adversaries. In a nutshell, for the allies, identifying the French center of gravity was not all that difficult. From a strategic perspective, it was lodged in the mind

---

[108] *Dispatches*, 22 September 1809, in George Henry Francis, *Maxims*.
[109] Tone, *The Fatal Knot*, pp. 182–183.

and resolve of a single man, and from an operational perspective, in the regular armies through which he exerted his will. For all the depredations inflicted on the French by the partisans, in the end only the decisive defeat of his armies could shake Napoleon's determination. Achieving that defeat certainly was no small task, and it is not clear that anyone but Wellington could have accomplished it. Niether does it take anything away from that accomplishment to acknowledge that, without the Spanish and Portuguese armies even more than the contributions of the irregulars, it simply could not have been done.

For the French, in contrast, locating the enemy's center of gravity was far more problematic. For if one thing is clear from the history of the Peninsular War, it is that a belligerent confronting a hybrid threat does not have the luxury of choosing which piece of it to fight. All the elements of allied combat power – Spanish armies, militias and partisans, Wellington's Anglo-Portuguese forces, and even the Royal Navy – interacted with one another. The synergy among all of these forces was the allies' vital source of strength.

The French failure to recognize the nature of their enemies was perhaps their most serious error. The reality is that deprived of the ability to concentrate on one problem at a time, the belligerent seeking to defeat a hybrid threat has only two alternatives: increase the number of forces committed to the conflict, directly or by finding allies; or reduce the demand for them, either by stripping away some part of the other side's capability or by sequencing operations to limit the ground that friendly forces must control at any given time, accepting the consequent prolongation of the conflict.

In the Peninsular War, Napoleon largely ignored both alternatives by diverting rather than increasing his troop strength just as the need for it was becoming most acute; by declining to meter the territorial responsibilities with which that diminishing strength would have to contend; and, above all, by failing to attempt in any systematic way to exploit the potential divisions among his several enemies. Whether or not any of these options or all of them in combination would have succeeded is unknowable. In their absence, however, only a failure of will on the part of his adversaries could produce success; and, from 1811 onward, all the evidence should have discounted any such expectation. As he himself later acknowledged, Napoleon's refusal to read and heed that evidence must be counted among his most serious strategic failures.

In the end, it is hard not to conclude from an examination of the Peninsular War that the best approach to hybrid war is to avoid fighting one in the first place. Failing that, however, the earlier that political and military leaders recognize the hybrid character of the contest and frame operations to reconcile and accommodate its competing demands, the less likely that they will find themselves, like the Emperor of the French, enmeshed in a frustrating dilemma the more bitter for having been self-inflicted.

6

The Union's Counterguerrilla War, 1861–1865

Daniel E. Sutherland

The Federals should have seen it coming. No sooner had the 6th Massachusetts Infantry arrived in Baltimore, Maryland, on 19 April 1861, than local pro-Confederates attacked the regiment. The New Englanders were en route to Washington, DC, to help defend the capital, when rebel sympathizers began throwing stones, bricks, and bottles at them. Some brandished pistols and muskets. The soldiers fired a volley over the heads of the rioters. When that failed to intimidate them, the soldiers fired directly into crowd. The regiment escaped, but not before 4 soldiers and 12 citizens had died, with 36 soldiers and 49 citizens wounded. They were the first casualties of the American Civil War.[1]

The mayor of Baltimore and the governor of Maryland denounced the attackers as a "mob," but they may have just as accurately described them as urban guerrillas. In the days and weeks that followed, the countryside around Baltimore came alive with gangs of armed men who ripped up railroad tracks, cut telegraph lines, stole livestock, and took opportunities to ambush Union army patrols and pickets. By summer, rebel irregulars had sprung into action across the entire upper South, from Missouri to Virginia. They would not relent until after the surrender of the Confederate armies, four years later. By that time, rebel guerrillas had operated in every southern state.

None of it had been planned. If the Federals were surprised by this response to invasion, so too were Confederate leaders, civil as well as

---

[1] Daniel E. Sutherland, *A Savage Conflict: The Decisive Role of Guerrillas in the American Civil War* (Chapel Hill, NC, 2009), pp. 1–6, describes this episode and its aftermath.

military. This was very much an uprising by the people, without prompting or encouragement from the government. Yet, in retrospect, it was hardly surprising. It would, after all, take many weeks before Confederates could recruit, arm, and drill armies sufficiently to take the field. Even then, the armies would be unable to stop Union invasions or to protect rebel sympathizers in the upper South. Missouri and Maryland, for example, were slave states that Union troops occupied before Confederate sympathizers could effectively mount secession movements within their borders. It was impossible to rush Confederate troops into such places without being accused of invasion. Even more delicate was the situation in Kentucky, which had proclaimed "neutrality" in the war. Neither the United States nor Confederate States dared move into that state until September 1861.

In this ambiguous situation, the rebels relied on a combination of local militia, home guards, and independent guerrilla bands not only to halt the Federals but also to defend themselves against their Unionists neighbors (Figure 5). Indeed, the single most important fact necessary to understand the guerrilla conflict is that it was not purely military in nature. It remained at heart a struggle to secure individual communities, whether against invading armies or disagreeable neighbors. Irregulars fought for and against both sides in this war, albeit with rebel guerrillas being more numerous. People spoke not so much of preserving the Union or winning Confederate independence as they did of "home protection." Julian Bates, a son of Abraham Lincoln's attorney general, informed his father from Missouri in July 1861, "There will be hard fighting in Mo, [but] not between the soldiers, & in many of the Counties there will be ugly neighborhood feuds, which may long outlast the general war." The senior Bates, at once seeing the potential dangers, warned the state's pro-Union provisional governor, "If things be allowed to go on in Mo as they are now, we shall soon have a social war all over the State."[2]

Not that rebel guerrillas ignored the Federal army. Although they never openly confronted large bodies of Union troops, Confederate guerrillas worried and hounded them ceaselessly. By September 1861 in Missouri, another son of Edward Bates declared that these annoying "robbers, spies, and assassins" ought to be "summarily shot by thousands." In the last ten days of 1861 alone, without a single Confederate soldier in the

---

[2] Julian Bates to Edward Bates, 15 July 1861, Bates Family Papers, Missouri Historical Society, St. Louis; Edward Bates to Hamilton R. Gamble, 16 July 1861, Hamilton R. Gamble Family Papers, Missouri Historical Society, St. Louis.

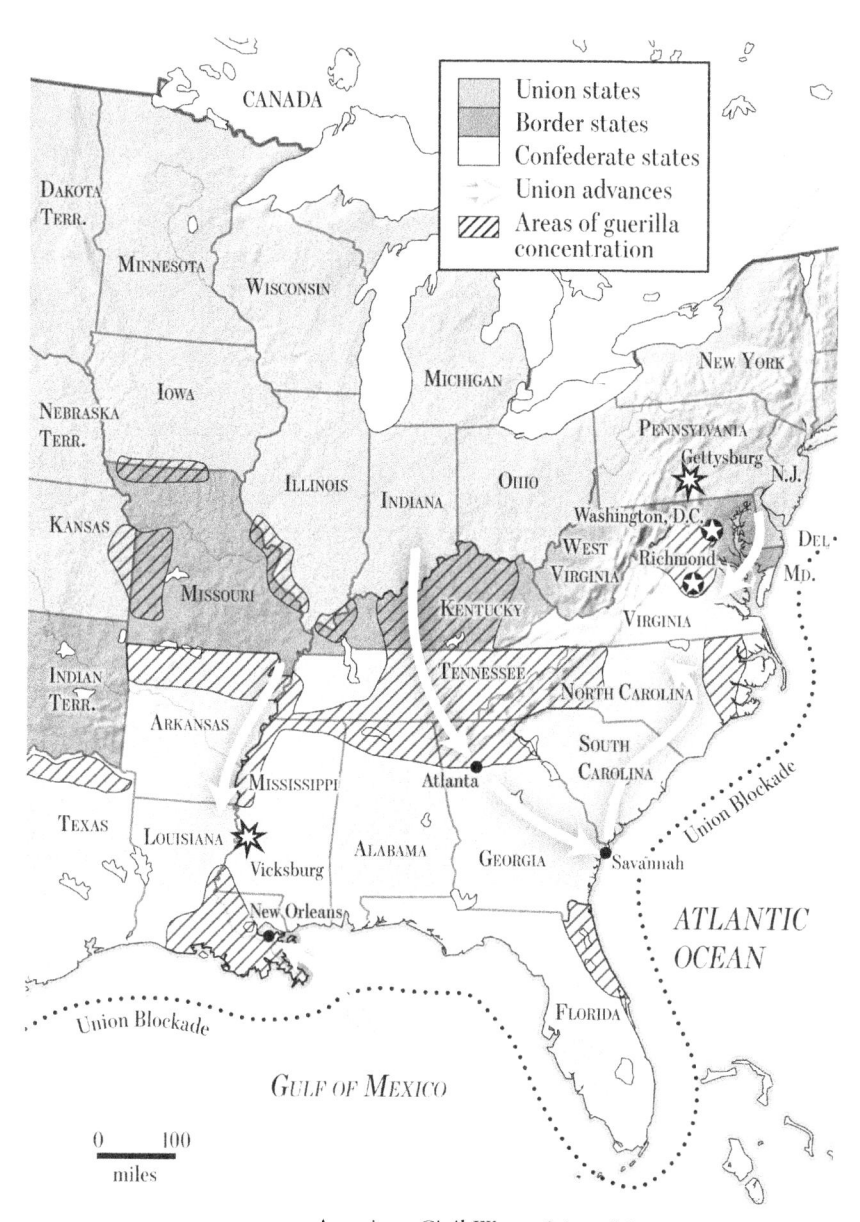

FIGURE 5. American Civil War, 1861–1865.

state, Union authorities in Missouri estimated that attacks on railroads and bridges had destroyed $150,000 worth of property.³

The same dynamics held true east of the Mississippi River. In Virginia, Edmund Ruffin, one of the South's most vocal fire-eaters, had encouraged guerrilla warfare from the earliest days of the war. By June, he could gleefully report that guerrilla fighting had well and fairly begun in his state near Alexandria and Hampton. "Some of our people, acting alone, or in small parties, & at their own discretion, have crept upon & shot many of the sentinels & scouts. It is only necessary for the people generally to resort to these means to overcome any invading army, even if we were greatly inferior to it in regular military force." At approximately the same time, rebels in Tennessee echoed Ruffin's advice. "If the people are armed and have powder, balls and caps in their houses, ready for use," insisted one man, "they will rise en masse and the whole country will be filled with armed men to repel the enemy at every point."⁴

Union commanders in the field responded slowly, in ad hoc fashion, to such warfare. No policies, no rules, no guidelines existed to deal with the menace. Guerrillas presented an entirely different problem than the one faced by Union commanders dealing with Confederate armies. At no point did the guerrillas appear to act in concert with conventional forces. Large bands operated, as in Missouri, where no rebel armies existed, and even when conventional rebel forces were in their vicinity, the irregulars seemed to operate entirely independently. Union officers reported fights with vaguely defined "hostile organizations," "marauders," "mounted rebels," "bands of armed secessionists," "irregular forces," and "rebel hordes." What was more, the rebels followed none of the recognized rules of "civilized warfare," operating, as one of the Bates boys had said, like "robbers, spies, and assassins."⁵

The first Union field commander to respond was Major General George B. McClellan. Responsible for securing the rugged, mountainous region of northwestern Virginia, ferocious guerrilla resistance greeted McClellan

---

³ Emphasis in the original; Barton Bates to Edward Bates, 8 September 1861, Bates Family Papers; U. S. War Department, *War of the Rebellion: Official Records of the Union and Confederates Armies*, 128 vols. (Washington, DC, 1880–1901), ser. 2, vol. 1, p. 247, and, for a variety of reports on guerrilla activity, pp. 251–280. Cited hereafter as *ORA*.

⁴ Emphasis in the original; William K. Scarborough, ed., *The Diary of Edmund Ruffin*, 3 vols. (Baton Rouge, LA, 1972–1989), vol. 2, p. 52; John S. Daniel, Jr., "Special Warfare in Middle Tennessee and Surrounding Areas, 1861–62" (M.A. thesis, Univ. of Tennessee, 1971), pp. 35–37, 40–43, 52–53; *Memphis Daily Appeal*, 13, 19 June 1861.

⁵ *ORA*, ser. 1, vol. 3, pp. 130–131, 135, 159, 163, 166, 422, 432, 438–439, 449, 473, 499–496.

long before conventional rebel forces appeared in the region. He had also witnessed the upheaval caused by the local war between Secessionists and Unionists. To bring both under control, he announced on 23 June 1861 that his forces would treat "marauding parties" according to the "severest rules of military law." A few weeks later, with McClellan's departure for Washington to serve as commanding general of all Union armies, his successor in western Virginia, Brigadier General William S. Rosecrans, upped the ante. Citizens must take "prompt and vigorous action to put a stop to neighborhood and private wars," he insisted, and so "prevent the country from being desolated by plunder and violence, whether committed in the name of secessionism or Unionism." Anyone failing to join in the effort to suppress this "species of warfare" would be treated as "accessories to the crime."[6]

This last bit of the McClellan–Rosecrans response is worth emphasizing. The generals understood the independent nature of guerrilla actions and that the unconventional foe operated, as the saying went, "on his own hook." More than that, they recognized that Union forces could effectively counter this unconventional foe – coming as it did from the local community, operating primarily to protect that community, and being shielded and maintained by the people of the community – only by holding noncombatants responsible for the actions of their guerrilla defenders. This created a potentially explosive situation for the Union army, especially for conservative commanders such as McClellan and Rosecrans, who believed in a nonpunitive approach to the war. Indeed, if one could argue that the U.S. government began the war with any clear strategic policy, it was that its troops should treat noncombatants in a conciliatory spirit. Certainly, President Lincoln believed that the latent Unionism among southerners was so strong that it only required a show of goodwill by invading armies to generate a backlash against the rebel government and so promptly end the rebellion. Rebel guerrillas had wrecked that plan by the end of the first summer of the war.[7]

---

[6] Ethan A. Rafuse, *McClellan's War: The Failure of Moderation in the Struggle for the Union* (Bloomington, IN, 2005), p. 111; Kenneth Noe, "Exterminating Savages: The Union Army and Mountain Guerrillas in Southern West Virginia, 1861–1862," in Kenneth Noe and Shannon H. Wilson, eds., *The Civil War in Appalachia* (Knoxville, TN, 2004), pp. 107–109; *ORA*, ser. 1, vol. 2, pp. 195–196, vol. 5, pp. 575–577.

[7] Mark Grimsley, *The Hard Hand of War: Union Military Policy Toward Southern Civilians 1861–1865* (Cambridge, 1995), pp. 1–6, suggests, although not necessarily convincingly, a measured progression in Union policy from "conciliation" through "pragmatism" and finally to "a hard war" policy.

Equally worrisome signs of things to come appeared on the other end of the border, in Missouri. Conciliation in that state never stood a chance. In July, Major General John Pope, commanding troops in northern Missouri, announced even more proscriptive actions against guerrillas than those taken by McClellan and Rosecrans. He held all citizens living along the North Missouri Railroad, the army's lifeline in his region, responsible for "wanton destruction" of its bridges, culverts, and tracks. Residents within a five-mile radius of guerrilla "outrages" would pay a "levy of money or property sufficient to cover the whole damage." A week later, Pope toughened and extended his orders to all of northern Missouri. He now held citizens responsible for the "peace and quietude" of their communities. He was tired of trying to keep "lawless marauders" at bay, he explained, and the labor of "hunting out these guerrilla parties" was "demoralizing" his men. If he must send troops on fruitless expeditions into the mountains and bush, their commanders would quarter and provision them at the expense of the inhabitants.[8]

Almost inevitably, Pope's punitive measures became even more oppressive when applied by some overzealous officers and men. Some local commanders went beyond monetary penalties to hold guerrillas and their supporters "individually responsible, both in persons and property, for any outrage...committed on Union men." Civilians complained of unwarranted retaliation. People in one county had been arrested "without cause," their homes "opened and searched, for no good reason." Federal troops had stolen livestock, foodstuffs, and personal items, and they had raped black women.[9]

A few weeks later, at the end of August, Major General John C. Fremont, arriving in Missouri to command the entire state, went beyond even Pope's stern measures. Issuing a sweeping policy of martial law in this Union state, he announced his intention to eliminate the "bands of murderers and marauders" whose "daily-increasing crimes and outrages" were "driving off the inhabitants" of Missouri. Anyone taking up arms against the United States would be court-martialed, he announced; people found guilty would be shot. The property of people taking up arms would be confiscated and their slaves freed. People guilty of sabotaging

---

[8] Peter Cozzens, *General John Pope: A Life for the Nation* (Urbana, IL, 2000), pp. 36–40; ORA, ser. 1, vol. 3, pp. 134, 403–404, 415–418, 421–424, 427, 456–457; ser. 2, vol. 1, pp. 185–194, 196–203, 206–208, 210–213.

[9] ORA, ser. 1, vol. 3, pp. 133, 458–459; ser. 2, vol. 1, pp. 204–206, 214–215, 218–219; Charles Gibson to Hamilton R. Gamble, 8 August 1861, Robert N. Smith to Gamble, 12 August 1861, Gamble Papers.

railroads, bridges, or telegraphs would "suffer the extreme penalty of the law."[10]

Lincoln, when informed of Fremont's policy, forced the general to modify the emancipation policy but allowed the other orders to stand. Nonetheless, the President's response betrayed a wide gap between his understanding of how the war should be conducted and the thinking of his commanders in the field. He had opposed Fremont's policies, and rightly so, primarily because he feared they would elicit retaliatory measures by the rebels. Nevertheless, Lincoln let those orders stand because he believed such drastic actions would rarely be required. When he replaced Fremont in November 1861 with Major General David Hunter, the president told "Black Dave" that the guerrilla threat in Missouri was all but over. "Doubtless local uprisings will for a time continue to occur," he advised, "but these can be met by detachments and local forces of our own, and will ere long tire of themselves."[11]

Major General Henry W. Halleck knew better, and when he replaced Hunter as department commander within the week, he established antiguerrilla policies that would become a Union template for the remainder of the war. In December, he made all rebel guerrillas liable to capital punishment, to be tried not as soldiers but as criminals. If found guilty, they would be shot. This directive had no effect, as guerrillas continued to burn bridges, destroy railroads, and cut telegraph lines. Halleck then dispensed with the niceties of arrests and trials. "These men are guilty of the highest crime known to the code of war," he declared. "Any one caught in the act will be immediately shot." By the time Lincoln summoned Halleck to Washington in July 1862 to replace McClellan as commanding general of the armies, even the president seemed to understand the nature of the war.[12]

The Confederate government had also caught on by then, and it tried to respond, both to the violent, uncontrolled actions of rebel guerrillas and to the "stringent orders" of Union generals such as Halleck. President

---

[10] *ORA*, ser. 1, vol. 3, pp. 466–467.
[11] Ibid., ser. 1, vol. 3, pp. 469, 477–478, 485, 553–554, 561–562, 565, 693; Louis S. Gerteis, *Civil War St. Louis* (Lawrence, KS, 2001), pp. 149–152; Daniel E. Sutherland, "Abraham Lincoln and the Guerrillas," *Prologue*, Spring 2010, pp. 18–19.
[12] John Marszalek, *Commander of All Lincoln's Armies: A Life of General Henry W. Halleck* (Cambridge, MA, 2004), pp. 110–111; Gerteis, *Civil War St. Louis*, pp. 172–176; W. Wayne Smith, "An Experiment in Counterinsurgency: The Assessment of Confederate Sympathizers in Missouri," *Journal of Southern History* 35, August 1969, pp. 363–368; Clay Mountcastle, *Punitive War: Confederate Guerrillas and Union Reprisals* (Lawrence, KS, 2009), pp. 34–39; *ORA*, ser. 2, vol. 1, pp. 233–235, 237, 240–243.

Jefferson Davis and his state governors had permitted, even welcomed, partisan warfare on the border because it proved useful in thwarting Union invasion and occupation. However, not many months had passed before Richmond also appreciated the difficulties of an unchecked and uncoordinated guerrilla war. In June 1861, Davis directed that no guerrilla companies could be accepted into service, if the term "guerrilla" implied "independent operations." Early the next year, Secretary of State Judah P. Benjamin stated flatly, "Guerrilla companies are not recognized as part of the military organization of the Confederate States." Yet, by that time, the guerrilla war was in full swing and the politicians, whatever their desire, could not simply forbid it. Not only was the guerilla war thriving, but more and more Confederate citizens also were demanding its expansion. The best the government could do was to contain the guerrilla war, try to control guerrillas, and attempt to counter the embarrassing Union accusations of barbarism.[13]

The solution, enacted in April 1862, was the Partisan Ranger Act, which permitted the recruitment of guerrillas but insisted that they operate according to strict rules. District military commanders would decide when, where, and to what extent such partisan rangers would be used. There would be no "independent" fighting. "The object of this rule," the War Department reminded commanders in the field, "is both to restrict the number of such Corps within the actual wants of the service, and to ensure the selection of suitable persons for such commissions." Similarly, a new Confederate secretary of war, George W. Randolph, cautioned, "The Partizan [sic] service is considered as subordinate to the general service.... To have two independent armies, conducting two independent systems of warfare in the same field, would lead to inevitable confusion and disaster." The name "partisan," of course, was an appeal to southern pride and patriotism. Southern irregulars of the American Revolution, such as Francis Marion and Thomas Sumter, had been called partisans. Thus, Confederate government hoped the romantic name would help popularize their new, limited, and disciplined guerrilla corps.[14]

---

[13] Lynda L. Crist et al., eds., *The Papers of Jefferson Davis*, 12 vols. (Baton Rouge, LA, 1971–2008), vol. VII, p. 201; *ORA*, ser. 4, vol. 1, p. 1008.

[14] Daniel E. Sutherland, "Guerrilla Warfare, Democracy, and the Fate of the Confederacy," *Journal of Southern History* 68, May 2002, pp. 281–283; George W. Randolph to R. J. Breckenridge, 29 April 1862; R. G. H. Kean to Thomas Brooks, 2 May 1862; Randolph to R. J. Johnson, 6 May 1862; A. T. Bledsoe to James W. Greene, 19 May 1862; Bledsoe to Richard S. Ewell, 30 April 1862; Randolph to Ivermont Ward, 15 May 1862; Letters Sent by Confederate Secretary of War, War Department Collection of Confederate Records, Record Group 109 (M522), National Archives.

Far from working as the government had hoped, the Confederates wound up with an even more confusing and less disciplined guerrilla network. Davis got his partisans, but thousands of rebel guerrillas refused to play his game. One of the main attractions of guerrilla operations for many was the independence of action the government wished to deny them. "Most of these men," as an Arkansas guerrilla observed, "preferred the free but more hazardous life of an independent soldier or scout, to the more irksome duties of the regularly organized forces of the Confederate Army." Not only that, but the new regulations required that partisan rangers operate wherever the government assigned them. More than likely, that would be nowhere near their homes and communities, which, of course, had been the other principal attraction of guerrilla service. As things turned out, local independent guerrillas became even less likely than before to cooperate with local Confederate commanders for fear of being forced into regular service.[15]

As the war dragged on, the reputation and record of partisan rangers for operating effectively with the army in a nineteenth-century version of hybrid warfare remained spotty at best. Most partisan companies, battalions, and occasionally regiments tended to be as ill-disciplined and unreliable as their independent brethren, untold numbers of whom continued to operate outside the partisan system. In Tennessee, Colonel Robert V. Richardson organized the 1st Tennessee Partisan Rangers in November 1862. He gave the Union army in the western part of that state fits, but worked in conjunction only with independent guerrilla bands – never with the Confederate army. He also made local Unionists as much his target as he did the Union army, extorting money from them, plundering their property, and committing violence against them. These were precisely the sorts of activities the Confederate government wished to quash. When Richardson then began to funnel men taken under the conscription act into his own command rather than sending them into the conventional army, the War Department revoked his commission.[16]

---

[15] T. Lindsey Baker, ed., *Confederate Guerrilla: The Civil War Memoir of Joseph Bailey* (Fayetteville, AK), pp. 39–40; H. T. Harrison to Leroy Pope Walker, 19 April 1861; Thomas F. Fisher to Walker, 1 May 1861; I. W. Garrott to Walker, 5 June 1861; T. L. Faulkner to Walker, 26 June 1861; Letters Sent by Confederate Secretary of War; George T. Maddox, *Hard Trials and Tribulations of an Old Confederate Soldier*, ed. by Richard R. Norton and J. Troy Massey (Springfield, MO, 1997), pp. 11–12.

[16] Robert V. Richardson to John C. Pemberton, 26 April 1863; Richardson proclamations of 25 January, 5 February 1863; Letters Received by Confederate Secretary of War; *ORA*, ser. 1, vol. 24, pt. 2, pp. 423–426; pt. 3, pp. 111, 176–178, 654, 658, 696–697, 757.

In Louisiana, partisan rangers initially saved the state from complete collapse after the surrender of New Orleans. With nearly all Confederate troops in the state siphoned off into Mississippi, including the last Confederate general officer in Louisiana, Governor Thomas O. Moore authorized the raising of 50 partisan companies in May and June 1862. The War Department complained that Moore had "greatly over done" the partisan program, but the rangers held things together until Major General Richard Taylor arrived in August to reorganize the state's defenses. However, well aware of the attitude in Richmond and being greeted with a slate of complaints about the behavior of the rangers, Taylor rejected all new applications for partisan service and integrated most of the existing companies into the conventional army.[17]

In Mississippi, Colonel William C. Falkner, great-grandfather of the future novelist, sometimes coordinated the actions of his partisan regiment with Major Generals Earl Van Dorn and Sterling Price, but Price worried about the reputation of Falkner's men for playing rough with Unionists. Some Confederate citizens complained that the rangers only did enough to antagonize Union troops, but that when the Federals retaliated, Falkner's men were nowhere to be seen. They were "notoriously more cunning than brave," complained one newspaper. Like Richardson, Falkner violated the conscription law by using it to increase the strength of his own regiment. When ordered to place his men in conventional service, he resigned his commission.[18]

One of the most fruitful experiments in hybrid warfare for the Confederates came in Virginia, where Colonel John S. Mosby became the poster boy for partisan operations, or nearly so. Mosby worked as a

---

[17] Barnes F. Lathrop, "The Lafourche District in 1861–1862: A Problem in Local Defense," *Louisiana History* 1, Spring 1960, pp. 99–129, and "The Lafourche District in 1862: Militia and Partisan Rangers," *Louisiana History* 1, Summer 1960, pp. 230–244; Samuel C. Hyde, Jr., *Pistols and Politics: The Dilemma of Democracy in Louisiana's Florida Parishes, 1810–1899* (Baton Rouge, LA, 1996), pp. 110–116; ORA, ser. 1, vol. 6, pp. 653–654, 885–890; vol. 15, pp. 124–126, 508–509, 567, 740–741, 747–749, 767–769, 773–774, 824; vol. 53, pp. 805–807, 813–814; Thomas O. Moore to Jefferson Davis, 3 June 1862; George W. Randolph to Moore, 3 July 1862; Letters Received by Executive, 1860–1863, Records of Louisiana Government, 1850–1863, War Department Collection of Confederate Records, Record Group 109, National Archives.

[18] Andrew Brown, "The First Mississippi Partisan Rangers, C.S.A.," *Civil War History* 1, December 1955, pp. 371–399; Albert Castel, *General Stirling Price and the Civil War in the West* (Baton Rouge, LA, 1968), pp. 95–96, 128–134; *Memphis Daily Appeal*, 25 August 1862; ORA, ser. 1, vol. 17, pt. 2, pp. 668–669; J. P. Tehul to John J. Pettus, 26 October 1862, John J. Pettus Papers, Mississippi Department of Archives and History, Jackson.

"scout" for Major General James E. B. Stuart in the early part of war, not receiving his partisan commission until March 1863. Stuart urged him to avoid calling himself a ranger. The name, Stuart said, was "in bad repute." Still, before the year was out, even Lieutenant General Robert E. Lee, who distrusted the whole partisan–guerrilla network, found himself impressed by Mosby's work. The problem, however, was that even when operating in conjunction with conventional troops, rebel partisans and guerrillas were still regarded as renegades by the Federals, who continued to retaliate against the citizenry for their actions. At one point, early in his career, the people of one county petitioned Mosby to "discontinue" his brand of warfare. To their dismay, Mosby "unhesitatingly refused to comply." As he explained to them, "My attacks on scouts, patrols, & pickets, which have provoked this threat, are sanctioned both by the customs of war & the practice of the enemy."[19]

By their retaliation, the Federals admitted the effectiveness of partisan and guerrilla operations. In Mississippi, for example, where Falkner and scores of independent guerrilla bands flourished, Major General Gordon Granger, commanding Union cavalry in the state, complained in August 1862 about the "infernal guerrilla system." Make no mistake, he warned his superiors, "It is bound soon to waste our entire army away for no equivalent. We must push every man, woman, and child before us or put every man to death found in our line." In Arkansas, Major General Samuel R. Curtis, having broken up the only rebel army in Arkansas at the battle of Pea Ridge, in March 1862, had thought he would easily capture the state capital at Little Rock. Instead, a resurgent rebel force, the bulk of it composed initially by rebel partisans and guerrillas, smothered his army. Curtis had to bypass his objective and seek safety at the Mississippi River town of Helena in July 1862. It would be another 14 months before the Federals captured Little Rock.[20]

---

[19] James A. Ramage, *Gray Ghost: The Life of Col. John Singleton Mosby* (Lexington, KY, 1999), pp. 46–57, 73; Jeffry D. Wert, *Mosby's Rangers* (New York, 1990), pp. 73–76; James E. B. Stuart to John S. Mosby, 25 March 1863, John S. Mosby Papers, Library of Congress.

[20] *Memphis Daily Appeal*, 1 September 1862; ORA, ser. 1, vol. 17, pt. 1, pp. 39–40; William L. Shea, "1862: 'A Continual Thunder,'" in Mark K. Christ, ed., *Rugged and Sublime: The Civil War in Arkansas* (Fayetteville, AK, 1994), pp. 41–42; ORA, ser. 1, vol. 13, pp. 35, 393, 396; Thomas A. Belser, Jr., "Military Operations in Missouri and Arkansas, 1861–1865," Ph.D. dissertation, Vanderbilt University, 1958, pp. 362–374, 398–403; Diane Neal and Thomas W. Kremm, *Lion in the South: General Thomas C. Hindman* (Macon, GA, 1993), pp. 128, 134; Edwin C. Bearss, "The White River Expedition, June 10–July 15, 1862," *Arkansas Historical Quarterly* 21, Winter 1962, pp. 305–362.

The ultimate measure of how effective the guerrilla war had become, especially when combined with conventional cavalry raids, came in October 1862. Major General Don Carlos Buell, having failed to capture Chattanooga, was relieved as commander of the Department of the Ohio. Not only that, but the government ordered a military commission to investigate his handling of the department. The so-called Buell Commission ran for nearly six months and revealed the large role that rebel guerrillas, in conjunction with rebel cavalry, had played in frustrating Buell's operations. They had repeatedly cut his supply lines, which had required him to deploy so many men in his rear that his advance was weakened.[21]

Seeing that it could not rely on retaliation alone to end the guerrilla menace, the Union army used more practical measures to protect its supply and communication lines and to root out rebel irregulars. Networks of stockades and blockhouses along railroad lines became the most visible symbol of this new approach. Most often positioned at bridge crossings, the most vulnerable points on the rail lines, the blockhouses generally held an entire company and the stockades up to two companies. An army engineer in the Department of the Cumberland estimated that more than 150 blockhouses had been constructed along seven railroads (totaling more than 700 miles of track) between 1862 and 1864 in Kentucky and Tennessee. This is not to say that these fortifications solved the problem. Rebel cavalry and guerrillas enjoyed plenty of successes against even this elaborate system, but without the blockhouses, the situation would have been much worse.[22]

"Special operations" became another alternative for the Union army. Networks of spies, scouts, and paid informants infiltrated communities to discern rebel intentions and break up guerrilla bands. Major General Grenville Dodge, under the command of Major General Ulysses S. Grant, directed one of the most successful early operations. Based at Corinth, Mississippi, Dodge selected his operatives, assigned their missions, and distributed payments. Between November 1862 and August 1863, he

---

[21] Stephen D. Engle, *Don Carlos Buell: Most Promising of All* (Chapel Hill, NC, 1999), pp. 247–249, 326–336; ORA, ser. 1, vol. 16, pt. 1, pp. 8–9, 12–13, 31–37, 40, 59–60, 254–258, 628.

[22] Robert R. Mackey, *The Uncivil War: Irregular Warfare in the Upper South, 1861–1865* (Norman, OK, 2004), pp. 105–106, 134–137, 142, 154, 168–172; "Use of Blockhouses During the Civil War," pp. 1–3, Box 38, vol. 87, file 7, Grenville M. Dodge Papers, Iowa Historical Library and Archives, Iowa City; W. E. Merrill, "Block-Houses for Railroad Defense in the Department of the Cumberland," *Military Order of the Loyal Legion of the United States* (1888), pp. 416–421; ORA, ser. 1, vol. 23, pt. 1, pp. 148–150; pt. 2, pp. 33, 155, 157.

paid scores of agents in Tennessee, Mississippi, Alabama, and Georgia the staggering sum (at the time) of $21,000 for information. Those of his agents who were not drawn from the army were southern Unionists. One of Dodge's staff officers considered the system an essential part of the army's anti-guerrilla campaign.[23]

More directly, the army assigned regiments of "guerrilla hunters" to track and destroy guerrilla bands. Many of these regiments, like the agents on special service, were drawn from the southern Unionist population. Whenever possible, these regiments were also assigned to the regions from which the men had been recruited. Thus, they knew the local terrain, the most likely rendezvous points of their foes, and the sympathies of the citizenry. Equally, and perhaps most important, these men, far more than Union volunteers from the North, were absolutely determined to destroy the rebel guerrilla system. Their own families had often suffered at the hands of guerrillas, and they themselves had had to flee their homes to escape violence or conscription. Returning now as well-armed, well-mounted Union soldiers, they were the closest thing the Federals had to partisan rangers.

One of these Unionist regiments was the 5th Tennessee Cavalry. Commanded by Colonel William B. Stokes, his men had a fearsome reputation. They did not pursue guerrillas exclusively, but they were good at it. They were supposed to capture their prey and return them to be tried by military commissions. More often, they executed Confederate guerrillas on the spot. Neither did they spare the families of known guerrillas or suspicious-looking "citizens." If unable to catch the men they pursued, they contented themselves with burning the homes of suspected guerrillas.[24]

Union forces used slightly different methods to combat rebel guerrillas who endangered military and civilian river traffic. Guerrillas were a problem along virtually all southern rivers, but especially in the west,

---

[23] William B. Feis, *Grant's Secret Service: The Intelligence War from Belmont to Appomattox* (Lincoln, NB, 2002), pp. 123–130, 166–167; Receipts, and E. D. Coe to Brother James, 12 April 1863, Box 63, vol. 148, Dodge Papers; Mildred Throne, ed., "A Commissary in the Union Army: Letters of C. C. Carpenter," *Iowa Journal of History and Politics* 53, January 1955, pp. 64, 70–71. For the adventures of one of Dodge's scouts, see Thomas D. Cockrell and Michael B. Ballard, eds., *Chickasaw: A Mississippi Scout for the Union: The Civil War Memoir of Levi H. Naron as Recounted by R. W. Surby* (Baton Rouge, LA, 2005).

[24] Thomas A. Wiggenton et al., *Tennesseans in the Civil War*, 2 vols. (Nashville, TN, 1964), vol. I, pp. 329–333; Amanda McDowell Diary, July 24–25, 1863, Curtis McDowell Papers, Tennessee State Library and Archives, Nashville.

where the security of the Ohio, Mississippi, Tennessee, and Cumberland rivers and their tributaries was essential to the Union advance. Most dramatically, these methods often resulted in the destruction of entire towns known to harbor river guerrillas. Rear Admiral David G. Farragut was appalled by the situation on the lower Mississippi River in spring 1862. "The elements of destruction to the Navy in this river are beyond anything I ever encountered," he reported to the secretary of the navy, "and if the same degree of destruction continues the whole Navy will be destroyed in twelve months." He ordered his gunboats to shell river banks where guerrillas had fired on his men, even in the vicinity of towns and villages. When warnings to stop firing on river traffic from the Louisiana town of Donaldsonville (located midway between New Orleans and Baton Rouge) had no effect, Farragut's warships and a landing party of marines partially destroyed it.[25]

Rear Admiral David D. Porter issued similar orders when he took command of the Mississippi Squadron in autumn 1862, as did lesser-ranking flotilla commanders on other rivers. Lieutenant Le Roy Fitch, operating under Porter, destroyed settlements, confiscated property, and imposed financial assessments when either naval or commercial craft were attacked by rebel guerrillas. In March 1863, he burned and destroyed stores and houses at Betsy Town, a notorious rendezvous spot for guerrillas on the Cumberland. He did similar work on the Tennessee River, where he confiscated livestock, provisions, and cotton and torched plantations known to be "guerrilla haunts." Swinging back to the Cumberland, he began the month of April by burning the town of Palmyra. "Not one house left," he reported to Porter. "A very bad hole," he explained. "Best to get rid of it and teach the rebels a lesson."[26]

The ultimate, although far from successful, Union solution to these problems was the Mississippi Marine Brigade. Recruited in late 1862 and early 1863, this "special" unit was more a legion than a brigade, a self-sufficient body that included infantry, cavalry, and artillery. Transported on converted civilian packet boats, they became a mobile force that could move quickly in strength to any trouble spot along the river. Although

---

[25] Lathrop, "Lafourche District in 1861–62," pp. 118–125; U.S. Navy Department, *Official Records of the Union and Confederate Navies in the War of the Rebellion*, 35 vols. (Washington, DC, 1894–1927), ser. 1, vol. 18, pp. 516, 520–521, 534; vol. 19, p. 191 (cited hereafter as *ORN*); Hyde, *Pistols and Politics*, pp. 114–116; Barnes F. Lathrop, "The Lafourche District in 1862: Confederate Revival," *Louisiana History* 1, Fall 1960, pp. 301–302; Mountcastle, *Punitive War*, pp. 70–72.

[26] *ORN*, ser. 1, vol. 23, pp. 316–318; vol. 24, pp. 39, 59, 62–65, 71–72, 75, 84, 86–87; vol. 25, pp. 159–160.

the brigade did not operate exclusively against guerrillas, rebel irregulars became its most frequent and elusive opponents. Like other components of both army and navy, when unable to corner the guerrillas, the brigade retaliated against the civilian population by burning towns and mills and confiscating cotton and livestock.[27]

A less tangible, if no less real, consequence of the guerrilla war was the psychological stress it placed on soldiers and sailors. Union commanders often spoke about the ill effects of guerrilla warfare on the "morale" of their men, and the men themselves often mentioned the problem. Even troops who never engaged in battle but who spent the war guarding railroads and sniping at guerrillas felt the strain. "We have been learning our full share of the realities of this conflict," reported a Pennsylvania soldier from western Virginia in summer 1861, "rendered more terable [sic] in this section than in any other from the savage and brutal mode in which it is waged by our enemies... who carry on a war more baborous [sic] than any waged by the savages who once inhabited this same country."[28]

The pressure grew as the months and years rolled by. "We are kept almost constantly in suspense," revealed a railroad guard in Tennessee in September 1862, "not knowing when or where they may make a strike." Small detachments of troops felt vulnerable at every hour of the day and night. "We were scattered in small squads," one railroad guard explained to his sister, "where guerrilla bands were thick as hail and the citizens would aid them against us at any moment." The "irregular" nature of the guerrilla contest most oppressed Sergeant Eugene Marshall of the 5th Iowa Cavalry. Marshall contended with guerrillas in Kentucky, Tennessee, and Alabama over a period of two years, but the contest never grew easier. "It is getting to be any thing but pleasant to scout or do picket duty in this country," he reported in May 1863. In September he reported, "Tennessee is not quiet it is & will be for some time full of Guerrillas & to this war I see no speedy end." It was almost a relief to Marshall when in September 1864 his regiment deployed to the Dakota Territory to

---

[27] Chester G. Hearn, *Ellet's Brigade: The Strangest Outfit of All* (Baton Rouge, LA, 2000), esp. pp. 74–79, 151–184.

[28] John B. Pendleton to wife, 7 July 1861, Pendleton Family Papers, Virginia Historical Society, Richmond; Ruth C. Carter, ed., *For Honor, Glory, and Union: The Mexican and Civil War Letters of Brigadier General William Haines Lytle* (Lexington, KY, 1999), pp. 78–79; W. M. McKinney to cousin, 25 July 1861 (No. 858), Roy Bird Cook Collection; West Virginia Regional History Collection, West Virginia University Libraries, Charleston; Charles R. Williams, ed., *Diary and Letters of Rutherford Birchard Hayes*, 5 vols. (Columbus, OH, 1922–1926), vol. 2, p. 64; Evelyn Benson, comp., *With the Army of West Virginia, 1861–1864: Reminiscences and Letters of Lt. James Abraham* (Lancaster, PA, 1974), p. 65.

deal with the Sioux uprising. He gave his opinion of this new opponent in a letter to his sister: "A white man can beat them all the time.... The Guerrillas of the south are far more formidable."[29]

Not until mid-1863 did the Federals attempt to devise anything like a uniform policy for dealing with rebel irregulars, and even that policy was not uniformly implemented. The policy became known as the Lieber Code. It originated with Halleck. Concerned about the legality of the precedents he had set in Missouri, Halleck turned for advice to German-born Dr. Francis Lieber, who taught history and political philosophy at Columbia College in New York. Lieber responded within weeks with as essay entitled "Guerrilla Parties Considered with Reference to the Laws and Usages of War." He defined nearly a dozen types of irregular warfare. Irregulars, he said, should be punished with the "utmost rigor of the military law," although he allowed that "partisans," if captured "in fair fight and open warfare," might be treated as soldiers rather than as "guerrillamen."[30]

In August 1863, Lieber followed up these specific recommendations concerning guerrillas with a more broadly applicable code of military conduct to provide guidelines for the treatment of noncombatants. That code, too, largely endorsed Halleck's precedents. "Military necessity" was the code's operative principle, and although Lieber emphasized that soldiers on both sides should treat combatants and noncombatants with compassion, his edicts defended the use of retaliation "to obtain great ends of state" and to battle "against wrong." Nations waging war in a "noble cause," he said, must base their actions on "principles of justice, faith, and honor," but "the more vigorously" they pursued such wars, "the better... for humanity."[31]

---

[29] Lorna Lutes Sylvester, ed., "Gone for a Soldier: The Civil War Letters of Charles Harding Cox," *Indiana Magazine of History* 68, March 1972, pp. 42, 48, 51; Eugene Marshall Diaries, May 25, 1863, September 10, 1863, November 6–8, 22, 1863, Eugene Marshall Papers, Perkins Library, Duke University, Durham, NC; Eugene Marshall to sister, November 4–9, 15, 1863; September 20, 1864, Marshall Papers.

[30] Daniel E. Sutherland, "Abraham Lincoln, John Pope, and the Origins of Total War," *Journal of Military History* 56, October 1992, pp. 584–585; Grimsley, *Hard Hand of War*, p. 148; *ORA*, ser. 3, vol. 2, pp. 301–309. See also Francis Lieber, *The Miscellaneous Writings of Francis Lieber*, 2 vols. (Philadelphia, PA, 1888), vol. 2, pp. 277–292.

[31] Francis Lieber to Henry W. Halleck, November 13, 1862, Francis Lieber Papers, South Caroliniana Library, University of South Carolina, Columbia; U.S. Adjutant General, *General Orders Affecting the Volunteer Force: 1863* (Washington, DC, 1864), pp. 64–87; *ORA*, ser. 3, vol. 3, pp. 148–164; Grimsley, *Hard Hand of War*, pp. 149–151; Marszalek, *Commander of All Lincoln's Armies*, pp. 167–168; Burrus M. Carnahan, "Lincoln, Lieber and the Law of War: The Origins and Limits of the Principle of Military Necessity," *American Journal of International Law* 92, April 1998, pp. 213–231.

The problem was to implement the new guidelines, an effort that does not seem to have met with success. It is rare, in all the correspondence and reports of Union commanders in the field, to find any reference to either set of Lieber guidelines. Most officers and men had long since determined how best to deal with rebel guerrillas. Lieber himself admitted that the section of his code concerning guerrillas, in particular, must necessarily be "much diminished by the fact that the soldier generally decides these cases for himself." Beyond that reality, the sometimes confusing and contradictory legal dicta would have struck many men as naive, issued, as they were, in the same month that William Clarke Quantrill's band murdered 140 men and boys in Lawrence, Kansas, while also torching and looting much of the town.[32]

Among Union field commanders, Major General William T. Sherman may have best understood the nature of the guerrilla war and how to deal with it. Not surprisingly, he endorsed retaliation. In September 1862, Sherman, convinced the town of Randolph (25 miles north of Memphis) harbored a gang of river guerrillas, ordered it destroyed. "It is no use tolerating such acts as firing on steamboats," he explained matter-of-factly. "Punishments must be speedy, sure, and exemplary." He held that opinion throughout the war and taught subordinates to see its wisdom. Concerned as he drove toward Atlanta in summer 1864 that the Union commander in Kentucky, Major General Stephen Burbridge, was not doing enough to safeguard his supply line against guerrillas, Sherman issued directives on how to deal with the rebels. Guerrillas, he said, were "not soldiers but wild beasts unknown to the usages of war." Burbridge must arrest any man or woman suspected of encouraging or harboring them. "Clear out the guerrillas, root, and branch, and banish vagabonds that, under the pretense of being Confederates, commit murder and highway robbery," he urged. Sherman repeated his orders to district commanders in Tennessee, who did his bidding.[33]

But as severe as Sherman sometimes seemed to be, he also saw at least one inherent danger in this guerrilla war for the Confederates. While still

---

[32] Marszalek, *Commander of All Lincoln's Armies*, pp. 178–179, 218; ORA, ser. 3, vol. 2, p. 307; Allan Nevins, ed., *A Diary of Battle: The Personal Journals of Colonel Charles S. Wainwright, 1861–1865* (New York, 1962), p. 184; Thomas Goodrich, *Bloody Dawn: The Story of the Lawrence Massacre* (Kent, OH, 1991).

[33] Brooks D. Simpson and Jean V. Berlin, eds., *Sherman's Civil War: Selected Correspondence of William T. Sherman, 1860–1865* (Chapel Hill, NC, 1999), pp. 305–310; ORA, ser. 1, vol. 17, pt. 1, pp. 144–145; pt. 2, pp. 235–236, 261, 279–281, 285, 287–289, 860; vol. 32, pt. 2, p. 486; vol. 39, pt. 2, pp. 19, 135–136, 146–167, 153–154, 174, 198, 208, 212–215, 231–232, 248–249; Michael Bradley and Milan Hal, "'Shoot If You Can by Accident,'" *North & South* 3, November 1999, pp. 33–46.

at Memphis, he reversed an order that forbade known Confederates from trading their cotton and corn for groceries and clothing in the town. He knew that many rebel citizens had become "justly indignant" because their own guerrillas and partisans, under instructions, had been burning cotton that might fall into Union hands. What better way to undermine the Confederacy, he reasoned, than to demonstrate that his army could be more compassionate than the rebel authorities? He acknowledged that some of the supplies acquired at Memphis might wind up in guerrilla hands, but he believed that most citizens, if not becoming Unionists, would eventually see the futility of the guerrilla war and welcome the protection of the Union army over that of rebel "bandits."[34]

In time, Sherman's prophecy came true, although continued Union retaliation contributed to the end result. By 1864, with no end to the war in sight, growing numbers of rebel citizens lost faith in the possibility of Confederate independence or, rather, the political goal of independence no longer seemed worth the cost. Their response grew partly, and naturally enough, from the military setbacks suffered by their conventional armies and the rising death toll of husbands, brothers, and cousins. Yet, they were equally appalled by the destruction and upheaval caused by the guerrilla war. Whether measured by the weight of punitive Union policies; retaliation by Unionist guerrillas and guerrilla hunters; or the deprivations caused by rebel guerrillas in search of horses, weapons, food, or personal gain, substantial numbers of loyal Confederates across the South yearned for peace.

"The whole country is full of robbers and murderers," moaned an Arkansas woman as early as February 1864. "Some of our citizens have been robbed and then hung off in the woods, where the family would not find them for days, others hung till almost dead and some burned nearly to death and released." Conditions had deteriorated to the point where she welcomed Union occupation, "anything for Peace and established Laws again," she noted. A partisan ranger, whose company disbanded after the surrender of Vicksburg, believed the Confederacy was a lost cause. He returned home to plant corn and mow hay when able. The rest of the time he spent dodging both Union and Confederate patrols. The guerrilla war could only worsen and prolong the suffering of the innocent, insisted a woman in Mississippi. "Everybody is down on them," she said of the partisans in her state. A North Carolinian was ready to give up if victory depended on a "protracted guerrilla war." The

[34] ORA, ser. 1, vol. 17, pt. 2, pp. 261, 273, 861.

results, he shuddered, could only "make one vast Missouri" of the entire country.[35]

The Confederate government understood the seriousness of this backlash too. In March 1864, all partisan units (except for two battalions in Virginia) were disbanded, the men ordered into the conventional army. When some suggested after the fall of Richmond that the Confederacy continue the war solely as an irregular affair, Jefferson Davis's cabinet recommended unanimously to end the fighting. Lee, who could have predicted all this would happen, offered the same advice. "A partisan war may be continued, and hostilities protracted," he admitted, but that would only cause needless suffering and devastate the country. "I see no prospect by that means," he concluded, "of achieving a separate independence."[36]

Even so, the Confederacy's guerrillas were the last rebels to concede defeat and surrender their arms. Some men feared that they would be treated as outlaws and executed as was, indeed, the fate of some of them. Others, given their independent status and therefore not obliged to surrender, saw no reason to quit fighting. John Mosby claimed that no one had ordered him to capitulate. Even when recognizing the inevitable, following the surrender of Lieutenant General Joseph E. Johnston's army in North Carolina, the Gray Ghost could not bear to "surrender." He simply told his men, "I am no longer your commander," and asked them to "disband." Enough bands persisted that Grant found it necessary in May to offer a two-week period of amnesty that guaranteed the safety of all men who came in out of the bush. Grant thought it a "cheap way to get clear of guerrillas," of which he had seen enough. He later had to extend the amnesty into June, but it largely did the trick.[37]

---

[35] Sarah Bevens Kellogg to Sister Eva, February 29, April 4, 1864, Robert R. Kellogg Papers, Ohio Historical Society, Columbus; Annette Koch to C. D. Koch, August 9, 1863, April 24, June 19, July 6, July 19, 1864; C. D. Koch to Annette Koch, August 14, 1863, February 7, April 27, 1864; Elers Koch to C. D. Koch, October 3, 1864, Christian D. Koch Family Papers, Special Collections, Louisiana State University Libraries, Baton Rouge; J. G. de Roulhac Hamilton, ed., *The Papers of Thomas Ruffin*, 4 vols. (Raleigh, NC, 1918–1920), vol. 3, p. 348.

[36] *ORA*, ser. 1, vol. 33, pp. 1082–1083, 1124, 1252–1253; ser. 4, vol. 3, p. 194, vol. 47, pt. 3, pp. 806–807, 823–824; Ramage, *Gray Ghost*, pp. 134–137; Clifford Dowdey and Louis H. Manarin, eds., *The Wartime Papers of R. E. Lee* (New York, 1961), p. 939. See also William B. Feis, "Jefferson Davis and the 'Guerrilla Option': A Reexamination," in Mark Grimsley and Brooks D. Simpson, eds., *The Collapse of the Confederacy* (Lincoln, NB, 2001), pp. 104–128.

[37] Wert, *Mosby's Rangers*, pp. 279–290; Carl B. Beamer, "Gray Ghostbusters: Eastern Theater Union Counterguerrilla Operations in the American Civil War, 1861–1865,"

In the end, the Union response to hybrid warfare succeeded, although it was by no means an easy victory. Given the reluctance of many guerrillas to lay down their arms, the Federals appear to have been more successful in intimidating rebel noncombatants than in quashing rebel irregulars. In fact, considering what happened in the years immediately after the war, when the United States faced the challenge of politically "reconstructing" the South, many ex-Confederates were not the least bit fazed by wartime Union policies. The violent responses to Reconstruction policy by the Ku Klux Klan, Knights of the White Camellia, and similar paramilitary organizations suggest that southerners still saw irregular warfare as a viable means of resistance. They did not call themselves guerrillas, or even partisans, but the inspiration for their methods was obvious.[38]

Even ex-guerrillas who acknowledged their military defeat and rejected postwar violence often took pride in the role they had played. Some of the larger bands, including the followers of Mosby and Quantrill, held reunions well into the twentieth century. Mosby, who had ignored Jeb Stuart's advice to avoid calling himself a partisan, said as late as 1899, "I never understood guerillas as a 'debasing' epithet." He still took pride in having been a "Guerilla Chief."[39]

Ph.D. dissertation, Ohio State University, 1988, pp. 256–259, 261; ORA, ser. 1, vol. 46, pt. 3, pp. 444–445, 590, 830–831, 839–841, 868–870, 897, 910, 1091, 1108, 1134, 1396; vol. 47, pt. 3, p. 303; vol. 48, pt. 2, p. 249; vol. 49, pt. 2, pp. 418–419, 557, 691, 711, 737, 885, 911, 1000, 1025–1026, 1088–1090.

[38] George C. Rable, *But There Was No Peace: The Role of Violence on the Politics of Reconstruction* (Athens, GA, 1984), pp. 1–15; Samuel C. Hyde, Jr., "Bushwhacking and Barn Burning: Civil War Operations and the Florida Parishes' Tradition of Violence," *Louisiana History* 36, Spring 1995, pp. 185–186; Victoria E. Bynum, *The Free State of Jones: Mississippi's Longest Civil War* (Chapel Hill, NC, 2001), pp. 131–144; Margaret M. Storey, *Loyalty and Loss: Alabama's Unionists in the Civil War and Reconstruction* (Baton Rouge, LA, 2004), pp. 196–231; John C. Inscoe and Gordon B. McKinney, *The Heart of Confederate Appalachia: Western North Carolina in the Civil War* (Chapel Hill, NC, 2000), pp. 266–285; Kenneth C. Barnes, *Who Killed John Clayton? Political Violence and the Emergence of the New South, 1861–1893* (Durham, NC, 1998), pp. 7–32. Also see Michael Fellman, *In the Name of God and Country: Reconsidering Terrorism in American History* (New Haven, CT, 2010), pp. 97–142, who discusses postwar southern resistance as a form of terrorism.

[39] John C. Inscoe, *Race, War, and Remembrance in the Appalachian South* (Lexington, KY, 2008), pp. 322–349; Daniel E. Sutherland, "Forgotten Soldiers: Civil War Guerrillas," *Hallowed Ground* 2, Summer 2001, pp. 20–24; Albert Castel, *William Clarke Quantrill: His Life and Times* (Norman, OK, 1999), pp. 231–232; Wert, *Mosby's Rangers*, pp. 290–295; Adele H. Mitchell, ed., *The Letters of John S. Mosby* (2nd ed., Clarksburg, VA, 1986), pp. 100, 214–215.

7

Fighting "this nation of liars to the very end"

The German Army in the Franco-Prussian War, 1870–1871[1]

Marcus Jones

> Who in 1870 ever dreamed of bread coupons, meat coupons, potato coupons, fat shortages, and other provisioning difficulties? Who could have presumed that the English would try to cordon off and starve millions of people? And who at the time had any notion that a future war would be decided in factories, would amount to a technical wrestling match? From a war of armies arose a war of peoples in the fullest sense ... the entire people, including women and children, would be subjected to the austerities of war, and the entire people would have to share in the work of meeting the gigantic requirements of the war effort.[2]
>
> "Unpolitische Zeitläufe," November 1916

Military organizations engage in hybrid warfare when, having expected and prepared to wage a particular form of war, they find themselves compelled simultaneously to wage another type.[3] One may also understand the concept as a historical fault line, along which shifting social, economic, cultural, and technological forces grate and combine in new and unanticipated ways, leading to the rise of new forms of warfare. Such concepts describe the Franco-Prussian War of 1870–1871 particularly well, but they also apply in varying degrees to almost every major war fought since the dawn of recorded history.

---

[1] The quotation is from Michael Howard, *The Franco-Prussian War: The German Invasion of France, 1870–1871* (New York, 2003), p. 436.
[2] Quoted in "Unpolitische Zeitläufe," *Westfälischer Merkur* 608, 18 November 1916 (Mittags-Ausgabe); from Christoph Nübel, *Die Mobilisierung der Kriegsgesellschaft: Propaganda und Alltag im Ersten Weltkrieg in Münster* (Münster, 2008), p. 11.
[3] Introductions to the topic include Frank G. Hoffman, "Hybrid Warfare and Challenges," *Joint Forces Quarterly* 51:1 (2009), pp. 34–39; and John J. McCuen, "Hybrid Wars," *Military Review* 88 (2008), pp. 107–113.

The war that culminated the long process of German unification incorporated institutions and ideas deeply infused with eighteenth- and early-nineteenth-century understandings of limited force and its utility; it also displayed important early indications of the factors that would prove decisive after 1914 – mass mobilization and industrial potential, force application across a spectrum of intensity, and a stronger emphasis on absolute aims and outcomes in the face of popular enthusiasms. And like most hybrid wars throughout history, the Franco-Prussian War proved conceptually frustrating to a generation of officers compelled to make sense of its intellectual inheritance.

But arguably the most important consequence of the Franco-Prussian War was the initiation of a German discourse on the nature and conduct of war that led to the formative experience of twentieth-century military history, the First World War.[4] Although the Franco-Prussian War appears historically to have been among the last of the conventional *Kabinettskriege* between nation-states, the unexpected course it took and the difficult process through which it was concluded suggested to German military leaders how drastically different future "people's wars" would be from the limited conflicts that dominated the European military history of the post-Napoleonic era: the Crimean War, the War of 1859, the Danish War of 1864, the Austro-Prussian War of 1866, the Russian–Turkish War of 1876–1878, and the Greek–Turkish War of 1896–1897, none of which were understood by the German military to have been true mass conflicts.[5] The general responsible for Prussia's stunning successes in 1866 and 1871, Helmuth von Moltke, gradually came to understand

---

[4] Daniel Pick, *War Machine: The Rationalisation of Slaughter in the Modern Age* (New Haven, CT, 1993), p. 144.

[5] Helmuth von Moltke, "über den angeblichen Kriegsrath in den Kriegen König Wilhelms I," *Gesammelte Schriften und Denkwürdigkeiten des Generalfeldmarschalls Grafen Helmuth von Moltke*, 8 vols. (Berlin, 1891–1893), p. 426; the American Civil War was perhaps the most important exception, little appreciated even by contemporaries, a point disputed by Mark E. Neely, Jr., "Was the Civil War a Total War?" and upheld by James M. McPherson, "From Limited War to Total War in America," both in Stig Förster and Jörg Nagler, eds., *On the Road to Total War: The American Civil War and the German Wars of Unification, 1861–1871* (Cambridge, 1997), pp. 29–51 and pp. 295–309; an explicit comparative analysis is in Stig Förster, "Vom Volkskrieg zum totalen Krieg? Der Amerikanische Bürgerkrieg 1861–1865, der Deutsch-Französische Krieg 1870/71 und die Anfänge moderner Kriegsführung," in Walther L. Bernecker and Volker Dotterweich, eds., *Deutschland in den internationalen Beziehungen des 19. und 20. Jahrhunderts. Festschrift für Josef Becker zum 65. Geburtstag* (München, 1996); for a sharp summation, see id., "Wie modern war der amerikanische Bürgerkrieg?," in Ute Scheneider and Lutz Raphael, eds., *Dimensionen der Moderne. Festschrift für Christoph Dipper* (Frankfurt, 2008), pp. 177–194.

that Germany would defeat European opponents in future conflicts only with the greatest difficulty. Awed and dismayed by the social complexities of warfare between modern societies, he was to advocate the diligent avoidance of war by the end of his career.

What a number of commentators perceived almost immediately was that a great paradigm shift took place with the Prussians' efficient destruction of the Imperial armies of Napoleon III and the adoption of territorial war aims. The French popular resistance that then arose ushered in a notional "hybrid moment" in warfare and marked the transition from one pattern of conflict to another.[6] The Republican authorities, who assumed power in Paris, proclaimed a *guerre à outrance*, or total war, and launched measures to mobilize the entire population and economy to raise new armies throughout the country and provoke a partisan war against German forces.

In this war, comfortable distinctions between civilians and military personnel evaporated as guerrilla bands, or *franc tireurs*, struck at German rear areas. Increasingly extreme German reprisals served only to ratchet up the intensity of the insurgency in the countryside and to drive the German general staff to distraction. But if the Franco-Prussian War was a hybrid war in an age in which conflict was generally thought to be conventional, it also typified the ancient problem of military conflict as resistant to purely military solutions and rational strategic calculation. For German officers inclined to consider the nature and conduct of warfare, the war also demonstrated that after 1871, the possibility of short, decisive wars between professional armies for limited ends was highly unlikely and that future conflicts would mobilize populations fired by national passions in support of brutal and absolute objectives.

FROM *KABINETTSKRIEG* TO *VOLKSKRIEG*

The origins of the hybrid-war transition of 1870–1871 lay in the evolutionary leap from one form of conflict to another in the early nineteenth

---

[6] The best survey remains Howard, *Franco-Prussian War*; also notable are Geoffrey Wawro, *The Franco-Prussian War: The German Conquest of France in 1870–1871* (Cambridge, 2003); and Wolfgang von Groote and Ursula von Gersdorff, eds., *Entscheidung 1870: Der Deutsche-Französische Krieg* (Stuttgart, 1970). There are several histories of the war by contemporaries soon after the fact, none as important as the official history of the Great General Staff in five volumes and four map addendums: Kriegsgeschichtliche Abteilung des Großen Generalstabes, ed., *Der deutsch-französische Krieg 1870/1*, 5 vols. (Berlin, 1874).

century.⁷ Early modern paradigms of interstate armed conflict involved comparatively small, professional armies waging limited wars on behalf of dynastic interests, led largely by officers of high social caste and insulated from broader civilian populations. The French revolutionary wars from 1792 to 1815 upended this comfortable stasis. Volunteers fired by national enthusiasms fought across the European landscape and in a wide variety of forms, including conventional armies, citizen militias, and guerrilla bands. Decisive battles of annihilation on behalf of vague ideological objectives, as well inconclusive harassing attacks, replaced the limited operational outcomes and bounded political objectives of the previous era. Noteworthy about the "total" wars in this era were the extraordinary financial, economic, and social pressures imposed on the states compelled to wage them. Few perceptive observers could fail to note that the willing and enthusiastic participation of commoners, broadly understood, had become the currency of military effectiveness and, to a lesser extent, the key ingredient in defining the political legitimacy of the state's objectives. Even fewer could take seriously the hope, fostered by the Metternichian settlement of 1815, that the prospects of total war returning to Europe were remote.

Nevertheless, in the reaction that followed the Napoleonic era, conservative statesmen tried mightily to turn back the clock and bottle up the political consequences of popular nationalism. The so-called Holy Alliance of arch-conservative European states – Prussia, Russia, and Austria – formed as a bulwark against the outbreak of further total wars, enjoyed noteworthy success until the era of German unification. What conservatives could not stanch was the transformation of the social, economic, and technological landscape on which future wars would occur. The Industrial Revolution quite simply transformed the entire framework

---

⁷ The basis for the present interpretation is the pathbreaking work of Stig Förster, "Optionen der Kriegsführung in Zeitalter des 'Volkskriegs:' Zu Helmuth von Moltkes militärisch-politischen Überlegungen nach den Erfahrungen der Einigungskriege," in Detlef Bald, ed., *Militärische Verantwortung in Staat und Gesellschaft. 175 Jahre Generalstabsausbildung in Deutschland* (Koblenz, 1986), pp. 83–107; id., "Facing 'People's War:' The Elder Moltke and Germany's Military Options after 1871," *Journal of Strategic Studies* 10 (1987), pp. 209–230; id., "General-Feldmarschall von Moltke und die kriegsgeschichtlichen Folgen des deutsch-französischen Krieges," in Philippe Levillain and Rainer Riemenschneider, eds., *La guerre de 1870–71 et ses consequences* (Bonn, 1990), pp. 86–96; and id., "Helmuth von Moltke und das Problem des industrialisierten Volkskrieges im 19. Jahrhundert," in Roland G. Foerster, ed., *Generalfeldmarschall von Moltke: Bedeutung und Wirkung* (München, 1991), pp. 103–115.

of European societies. Advances led to the ever-larger-scale production of armaments, with concomitant increases in their destructive power and reach. In a relatively short span of historical time, militaries found that it had become possible to kill more people – soldiers as well as civilians – more quickly and more consistently than ever before.[8]

Also important was the growing capacity of states to mobilize national resources, an ability facilitated by the willingness of citizens and institutions to mobilize themselves. This had much to do with the bellwethers of the liberal nineteenth century, the expansion of the public sphere and democratization of politics, processes that superseded the practical limitations of traditional regimes to compel people to contribute to the war effort. Indeed, a crucial feature of total war in the modern age has been that state power and direction alone were clearly inadequate for success. After 1871, armies understood that mobilization was a bottom-up as well as top-down process. Railways and more sophisticated communication and control networks ensured that much larger armies arrived more quickly to operational areas and were sustained more consistently, greatly enhancing their effectiveness. Military staffs gradually assumed greater responsibility for the massive technical and organizational challenges of carrying out increasingly elaborate plans. Warfare in the industrial age meant that nations and military institutions had to undertake a comprehensive reconsideration of the utility of force.

German officers and military theorists explained the transition in terms of an epochal shift from *Kabinettskriege* to *Volkskriege*, or popular war.[9] Both terms litter the writings of Helmuth von Moltke, the stalwart chief of the Great General Staff in the unification era and perceptive observer of contemporary military affairs. The term *Kabinettskriege* (literally, cabinet war) refers to the series of conflicts in the mid-nineteenth century that were

---

[8] A good survey of these broad trends in this period is Geoffrey Best, *War and Society in Revolutionary Europe, 1770–1870* (Oxford, 1986); also the essays collected in Peter H. Wilson, ed., *Warfare in Europe 1815–1914* (Aldershot, 2006).

[9] The evolution is tracked usefully in Heinz Hermert and Hansjürgen Usczeck, *Preussischdeutsche Kriege von 1864 bis 1871: militärischer Verlauf* (Berlin 1975); the terms are used here in awareness of the multiplicity of perfectly defensible alternatives, such as "people's war," "industrialized war," "citizen's war," and "modern war," among others; see Talbot Imlay, "Total War," *Journal of Strategic Studies* 30 (2007), p. 549. An otherwise excellent example of a typology that virtually omits meaningful references to Moltke's position in this evolution is Hans-Ulrich Wehler, "Der Verfall der deutschen Kriegstheorie: Vom 'Absoluten' zum 'Totalen' Krieg oder von Clausewitz zu Ludendorff," in *Krisenherde des Kaiserreichs, 1871–1918: Studien zur deutschen Sozial- und Verfassungsgeschichte* (Göttingen, 1970), pp. 85–112.

thought to evoke the limited wars of the eighteenth.[10] According to this notion, during the eighteenth century and after the conservative reaction to the French Revolution in 1815, European states fought most wars for limited strategic objectives with militaries far less taxing on their domestic population and resources than those of the French Revolutionary era.

The armies of most states of that era – that of Prussia being a notable exception – consisted of long-service professionals, institutionally partitioned from civil society and well suited to brief, episodic campaigns that presented little threat to European stability. Operations tended to affect only those populations in the immediate theater of engagement, with little impact on the civilian economy and living standards. Statesmen strove to contain national passions, the more effectively to prevent the upward creep of war aims and risks. They managed these conflicts well enough, given the limited democratic franchise of most states. In the broadest historical perspective, the conditioning attribute of this paradigm was the reinforcement of the long-standing desire of European states, after the hellish experience of the Thirty Years' War, to retain a strict monopoly on the instruments and uses of violence.[11]

The Prussian approach to conflict in the era of *Kabinettskriege* had been the product of a long-standing tradition of rapid, decisive operations that aimed to drive an opponent to the bargaining table and realize the objectives of the war before the country's grave vulnerabilities impacted the conflict. This tradition was the product of a peculiar strategic disposition. Prussia's leaders understood their country to be small, comparatively poor, and surrounded by larger and more powerful neighbors; victory in war, by extension, was thought to be possible through speed and concentration at the enemy's decisive point of weakness, well before opponents could mobilize and bring the full weight of their resources to bear.

---

[10] See the very useful definitions by Stig Förster in Stig Förster, ed., introduction to *Moltke: Vom Kabinettskrieg zum Volkskrieg: Ein Werkauswahl* (Bonn and Berlin, 1992), pp. 3–4; a rough typology of these forms can be found in Siegfried Fiedler, *Kriegswesen und Kriegsführung im Zeitalter der Kabinettskriege*, vol. 2, *Heerwesen der Neuzeit* (Koblenz, 1986); Frank Gose, "Der Kabinettskrieg," in Dietrich Beyrau, Michael Hochgeschwender, and Dieter Langewiesche, eds., *Formen des Krieges: von der Antike bis zur Gegenwart* (Paderborn, 2007), pp. 121–148; built around this distinction is the official survey series by the Militärgeschichtliches Forschungamt, Karl-Volker Neugebauer, ed., *Grundkurs deutsche Militärgeschichte*, vol. 1, *Die Zeit bis 1914*, and vol. 2, *Das Zeitalter der Weltkriege 1914 bis 1945* (München, 2006–2007).

[11] See Ekkehart Krippendorff, *Staat und Krieg: die historische Logik politischer Unvernunft* (Frankfurt a.M., 1985).

In these simple respects, this tradition was also characteristically Clausewitzian, based as it was on a stylized and strict understanding of war as an expression of the political goals of legitimate states. If such a view of war was unduly narrow, it also provided clear boundaries within which military leaders could promulgate and implement coherent operational doctrines in a technical, workmanlike fashion. This the German general staff accomplished with unerring competence and thrift. The astounding German victories at Königgratz and Sedan are considered classic examples of this long-standing German doctrine of decisive maneuver warfare, which goes occasionally by the name "annihilation" warfare as well. In its most elemental form, a strategy of annihilation breaks the enemy's will to fight by attacking and destroying his army in the field (preferably in a single climactic battle) and usually involves an envelopment of his defenses.[12] Killing every enemy soldier is not fundamental to success, the moniker notwithstanding.[13] Rather, the strategy would render the opposing force combat ineffective by cutting it off from supply or reinforcement and compelling it to surrender.

The point was to shorten major conflicts and leverage the talents of German military institutions for planning and execution while minimizing the vulnerabilities of the German war effort against wealthier, more populous opponents. The doctrine was fundamental to the culture of the Prussian, and later German, general staff after 1866. Victory led to an enhancement of the status of the officers corps well beyond merely technical competence. Indeed, Moltke's general staff won the right after the victory at Königgratz not merely to plan operations in advance but also to conduct them upon the outbreak of conflict, with obvious implications for the character and ends of the war effort. The meticulous approach of the general staff to prewar planning, its enthusiastic adoption of new technologies, and its effective bureaucracy and staff work transformed

---

[12] The literature on this strain of German strategic thought is immense. See Jehuda L. Wallach, *The Dogma of the Battle of Annihilation: The Theories of Clausewitz and Schlieffen and Their Impact on the German Conduct of Two World Wars* (Westport, CT, 1986); Antulio J. Echevarria, *After Clausewitz: German Military Thinkers Before the Great War* (Lawrence, KS, 2000); Carl-Gero von Ilsemann, "Das operative Denken des älteren Moltke," and Lothar Burchardt, "Operatives Denken und Planen von Schlieffen bis zum Beginn des Ersten Weltkrieges," both in Horst Boog, ed., *Operatives Denken und Handeln in deutschen Streitkräften im 19. und 20. Jahrhundert* (Herford, 1988).

[13] See Colmar Freiherr von der Goltz, *Kriegsführung: kurze Lehre ihrer wichtigsten Grundsätze und Formen* (Berlin, 1895).

victories in 1866 and 1871 into a reputation rarely equaled in modern military history.

PLANNING FOR THE FRENCH CAMPAIGN

As circumstances in the 1860s for a unification of the German states became more propitious, Prussian military leaders embraced the prospect of a war with France, which many had long viewed as the "eternal enemy" of any establishment of German national power and autonomy in central Europe. As far back as the Rhineland Crisis in 1831, Moltke had expressed his conviction that the realization of German national aspirations depended on a subordination of the French, a sentiment obviously well beyond the technical confines of planning and executing a campaign against the French Army.[14] In this way, the strategic prudence of the Prussian staff faltered; its increasing enthusiasm for a German nation colored its view of what was both possible and preferable in the event of war with the French.[15]

As early as 1859, Moltke began to advocate the separation from France and annexation to Prussia of the traditionally German territories of Alsace and Lorraine, a demand all but certain to transform any war into a national struggle for the French. He cloaked his reasoning in largely military concerns, arguing that no political entity in the heart of Europe could hope to survive without command of those crucial avenues of invasion from the West. But the larger context of his argument betrayed an increasing enthusiasm for a decisive and final reckoning with Napoleon's empire, a problem to which he devoted himself after 1866.[16] Before 1870, it remained doubtful to most informed observers that the Prussians could bend France, widely understood to be the preeminent continental military power, to their demands in a quick war. Were the smaller and poorer Prussian monarchy to prevail, Moltke assumed that the war would have to take place in strategic circumstances conducive to a quick and decisive campaign, much like those of 1866. Such circumstances – namely, the isolation of France diplomatically and the articulation of clear, realizable objectives – played to Germany's strengths in planning and

---

[14] Howard, *Franco-Prussian War*, p. 46.
[15] Förster, "Optionen der Kriegsführung," p. 89.
[16] See Heinz Helmert, "Der preussische Generalstab in der Vorbereitung des Krieges gegen Frankreich zwischen 1866 und 1870," in Horst Bartel and Ernst Engelberg, eds., *Die großpreußisch-militärische Reichgründung 1871: Vorausetzung und Folgen*, vol. 1 (Berlin, 1971), pp. 157–201.

command and minimized its vulnerabilities in economic depth and domestic and international political support. To Moltke's dismay, the attainment of such conditions seemed remote after 1866. In exchanges with other senior Prussian officials, he gloomily characterized war with France as unavoidable and probably unwinnable. He expressed a strong preference for seizing the initiative with an offensive strategy.[17]

As time passed, however, Moltke came to view the coming war in increasingly more optimistic terms. In a key planning memorandum of 1868–1869, which formed the basis for the subsequent invasion, Moltke expressed his sense that a quick, hard-hitting offensive would unseat Napoleon III and lead to a prompt settlement. Despite this new-found optimism, there was scant appreciation in his prewar planning that he grasped how military fortune interacted with popular will, or the likely reception in France of German strategic aims that aimed at the dissection of large eastern districts from the empire. He took for granted that the war would remain limited to hostilities between the national armies. With the technical savvy characteristic of the twentieth-century German officer corps, Moltke laid the operational framework for a brilliant campaign designed to wipe out opposing French forces but one that was ill suited to managing the circumstances that would follow and lead to a desirable peace. One might therefore have predicted that Moltke, as well as the rest of the Prussian military establishment, would find themselves shocked when Germany reopened the Pandora's box of militarized populism for the first time since 1815, this time under the circumstances of industrial warfare.[18]

THE PATH TO HYBRID WAR

When war broke out, the French chose, without a strong basis in fact, to pursue a strategy based on putative political divisions between the major states of the North German Confederation. Their basic aim was to force a settlement based on a quick "liberation" of the southern states from Prussian oppression.[19] In the end, French forces proved incapable of mounting even that limited effort, hamstrung as they were by mediocre

---

[17] Förster, "Einleitung," in *Moltke: Vom Kabinettskrieg*, pp. 20–21.
[18] Howard, *War in European History*, p. 100.
[19] Showalter moderates this view by pointing out that southern German support was uncertain until the publication of the Ems dispatch, and that even the cohesion of the North German Confederation could be seen as somewhat questionable. Dennis Showalter, *The Wars of German Unification* (London, 2004), p. 241.

leadership and poor planning; indeed, French forces failed utterly to present any serious threat to German territory or even upset the Prussian staff's operational timetables. By contrast, the Germans conducted their operations in August 1870 with stunning efficiency and effectiveness.

Based on an innovative vision of military operations, Moltke's leadership had transformed the general staff into the most capable command organization in the world at that time. Exhaustive prewar planning and exercises ensured that by 3 August, more than 320,000 German troops stood on the French border. Swift operations through the Lorraine gap led to three major French defeats in rapid succession at Weissenburg on 4 August and at Wörth and Spicheren two days later. The French managed to inflict relatively high casualties on German forces in a handful of subsequent engagements, but a Prussian offensive between Paris and the two main French field armies under Marshals Bezaine and MacMahon forced the former to retreat eastward and eventually hole up in the fortress at Metz on 3 September, where he effectively abdicated any meaningful role in the conflict's outcome (Figure 6). MacMahon, accompanied by Napoleon III and a reserve army from Châlons, attempted to come to Bezaine's aid. German forces adroitly surrounded MacMahon's army at Sedan and devastated it with artillery fire until it capitulated on 2 September, taking into captivity 104,000 French soldiers along with the Bonapartist emperor, Napoleon III.[20]

In fact, the first four weeks of the operation saw, with limited exceptions, an unprecedented succession of operational triumphs for Prussian arms, a testament to Moltke's planning and the German army's execution. The overwhelming victory at Sedan ranks among the most impressive in the military history of Prussia and Germany. Had the war conformed to the pattern of traditional *Kabinettskriege*, that battle would have led to an armistice and discussion of peace terms, culminating in a treaty of peace.[21] Indeed, the strategic circumstances for this outcome were favorable: Bismarck's adroit diplomacy had achieved the seemingly impossible task of isolating France diplomatically in a Europe fearful of Prussia after

---

[20] Showalter, *Wars of German Unification*, pp. 281–282.

[21] The conventional formula involved an armistice, a preliminary peace, and a final settlement. Eberhard Kolb, "Der Schwierige Weg zum Frieden: das Problem der Kriegsbeendigung 1870/71," *Historische Zeitschrift* 241 (1985), pp. 54 and 66; from Coleman Phillipson, *Termination of War and Treaties of Peace* (London, 1916), p. 94 ff.; the formal processes are also discussed in Paulus Andreas Hausmann, "Friedenspräliminarien in der Völkerrechtsgeschichte," *Zeitschrift für ausländisches öffentliches Recht und Völkerrecht* 25 (1965), pp. 657–692.

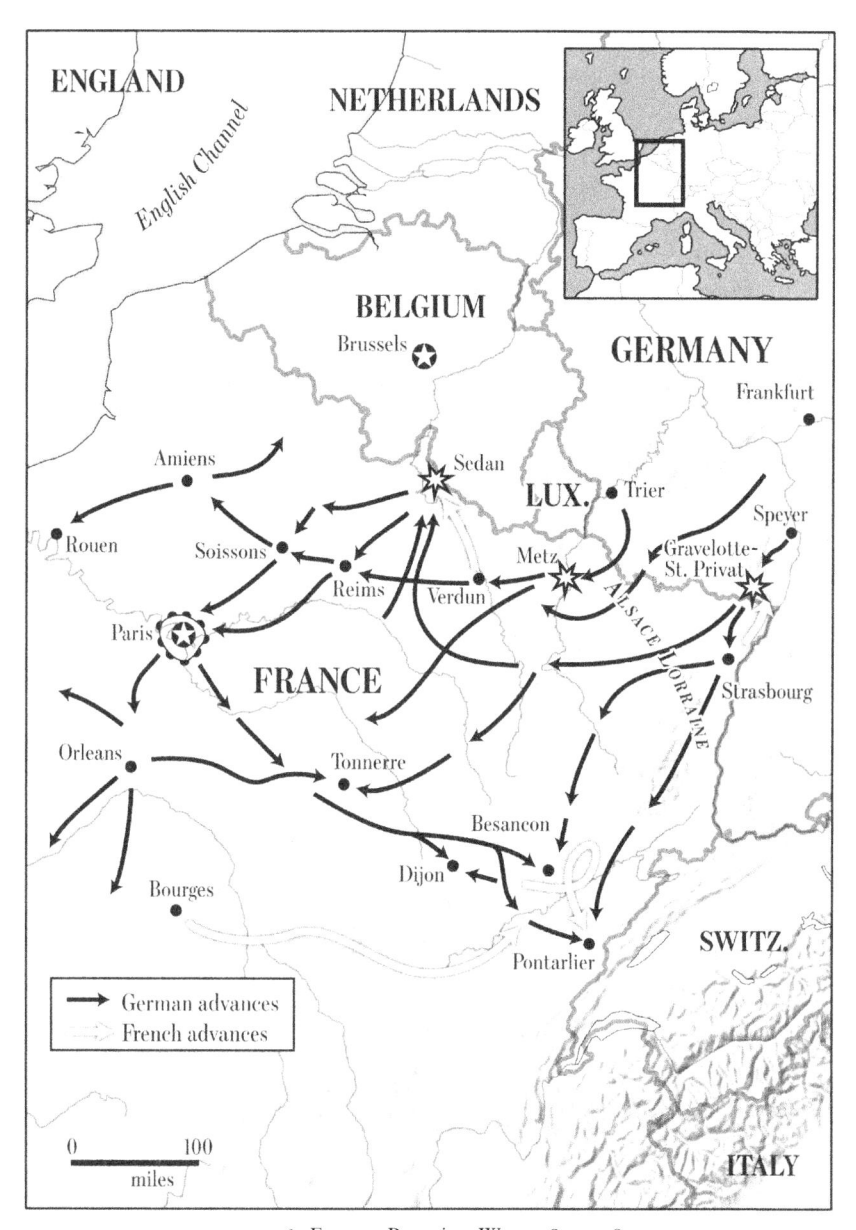

Fighting "this nation of liars to the very end" 181

FIGURE 6. Franco-Prussian War, 1870–1871.

1866, and the French themselves had squandered much international capital by declaring war on Prussia. Mobilization and operations had proceeded smoothly, with a victory at Sedan as decisive as any optimist could have hoped for in advance.

In an almost chess-like manner, Prussian forces deposed the French emperor, the rump of the defeated French army fled into the interior, and the country was stripped of the means of providing, by conventional standards, for its own security. Prussian soldiers could reasonably look forward to being home for Christmas and basking in the accolades of a job well done, conventionally understood and executed. Nevertheless, questions little appreciated in the narrow confines of prewar Prussian operational planning – of political legitimacy, domestic stability, and historical expectations and grievances – quickly pushed to the forefront of French affairs and became more fundamental for the future settlement than outcomes on the battlefield. With the fall of the emperor, liberal political factions declared a republic in Paris, scattered French forces – trained and irregular – began sniping at the German periphery, and a swelling domestic consensus in France declared German war aims as categorically unacceptable. No French authority could accept the extreme German territorial demands and entertain any hope of surviving the popular turmoil of the new republic. However, success on the battlefield had brought a heady bullishness to the Prussian leadership, resolved as it had been to play a larger role in strategic deliberations than the hated Bismarck had permitted in 1866. Thus, Prussian officers – Moltke not least among them – asserted the unconditional need to annex Alsace and Lorraine to a new German Reich.

For the Germans, political and military objectives had developed in tandem until the battle of Sedan. The aim of German military efforts had been to defeat French forces as completely and quickly as possible and so to pave the way for a diplomatic settlement consistent with Prussian terms. Bismarck's efforts to prevent the intervention of the other European powers worked until early September; they observed the defeat of Napoleon with satisfaction and the rise of a Prussian-dominated Germany with only slight unease.[22] But the speed of the Prussian victory over French forces and the sudden capture of the emperor surprised

---

[22] Eberhard Kolb, *Der Weg aus dem Krieg: Bismarcks Politik im Krieg und die Friedensanbahnung, 1870/71* (München, 1989), p. 196; Annelise Klein-Wuttig, *Politik und Kriegführung in den deutschen Einigungskriegen 1864, 1866 und 1870/71* (Berlin, 1934), p. 92.

even the optimistic observers and made Bismarck's strategic framework obsolete.

Correctly judging the popular French antipathy to the growth of German power and the depth of liberal and republican sentiments lying just beneath the surface of French politics, Bismarck grasped that a limited peace with Napoleon and a continuation of his regime was strongly preferable to any of the alternatives.[23] However, he failed to impress that understanding on the diehards of the general staff, who clung to a set of terms that included Strasbourg and Metz and the surrounding territories of Alsace, along with the greater part of Lorraine.[24] In the teeth of Moltke's staunch commitment to the two fortress towns and the jingoistic agitations of the southern German press, Bismarck had little choice but to accede to Moltke's demands. The Iron Chancellor's problem was that he was short of a constituency in France willing to accept Prussian peace terms or able to impose them domestically, "the kind of settlement which left enough on the table to deter the loser from later attempts to reverse the situation through war."[25]

News of the French defeat at Sedan and the capture of Napoleon III led to political events in Paris that quickly brought home to the Germans the implications of their victory. On 4 September, a Parisian mob disrupted a meeting of the *Corps Législatif* and joined republican delegates, led by the impulsive Leon Gambetta, in marching on the Hôtel de Ville.[26] A day later, the newly proclaimed Third Republic, with General Louis Trochu at the head of a "Government of National Defense," issued a *Proclamation au peuple français* to carry on the war against the German invader.[27] The new government faced a daunting set of tasks: to quickly bring under its control those parts of France not occupied by German forces, and to prove itself as the legitimate government of France in the midst of a

---

[23] Kolb, *Der Weg aus dem Krieg*, pp. 104–105, 195–197; Robert Giesberg, *The Treaty of Frankfort: A Study in Diplomatic History, September, 1870–September, 1873* (Philadelphia, 1966), p. 69, pp. 158–159.

[24] The best assessment of this problem is Eberhard Kolb, "Der Kriegrat zu Herny am 14. August 1870: Zur Entstehung des Annexionsentschlusses der preussischen Führungsspitze im Krieg von 1870," *Militärgeschichtliches Mitteilung* 9, 1971, pp. 5–13.

[25] Showalter, *Wars of German Unification*, p. 286.

[26] See Etienne Arago, *L'Hôtel de Ville de Paris au 4 Septembre et pendant le siege* (Paris, 1874); also Émile Andréoli, *1870–1871: Le gouvernement du 4 septembre et la commune de Paris* (Paris, 1871).

[27] Jacques Desmarest, *La defense nationale, 1870–71* (Paris, 1949); also Pierre Hoff, "Le ministère de la Guerre à Tours et à Bordeaux en 1870–1871," *Revue historique des armées* 135:2 (1979), pp. 70–85.

desperate war. The provisional government claimed nominal authority over the nation, but it specifically disclaimed any right to negotiate a peace in the absence of a popular referendum on its legitimacy. Further, it defined the minimal terms of any peace as requiring France to yield "not an inch of her soil nor a stone of her fortresses."[28]

The new government issued an order on 14 October to destroy any infrastructure of potential value to the Germans and destroy or evacuate useful materials potentially useful to the occupying army. Republican plans provided for the raising of new conventional armies in the north and west of the country, amounting to a levée en masse for able-bodied men between the ages of 21 and 40 years.[29] Crucially, the French Navy remained largely unaffected by the fighting and continued to supply the country with ample stores and munitions from abroad. It also threw substantial numbers of well-trained and equipped marines into the national resistance. Small contingents arrived from French dependencies abroad, including the Foreign Legion, previously forbidden by law from serving on French territory. The bulk of the new formations, however, came from the reserve and depot troops of the units of the now-defunct Imperial Army and by raw recruits from the agricultural hinterlands.[30] By February 1871, the Herculean efforts of the Republican government had boosted French manpower by nearly a half-million, to some 950,000 men – no small achievement for so improvisational a regime.[31] Of course, despite their impressive numbers, the new formations had grave deficiencies, particularly when measured against well-trained Prussian units. They lacked experienced officers, a sufficient number of veterans from the prewar French military to leaven the ranks, and the heavy equipment and artillery needed to conduct modern operations. Historians have also called into question the amount of actual popular support the national

---

[28] *Dépêches, circulaires, décrets, proclamations et discours Leon Gambetta*, vol. 1, J. Reinach, ed. (Paris, 1886), pp. 6 ff.; from Showalter, *Wars of German Unification*, p. 286.

[29] On French efforts to mount a national defense, see William Sermen, "French Mobilization in 1870," in Förster and Nagler, *On the Road to Total War*, pp. 283–294.

[30] See Hermann Kunz, *Die Zusammensetzung der französischen Provinzialarmeen im Kriege von 1870/71* (Berlin, 1892).

[31] Archivrat Greiner, "Der Volkskrieg in der zweiten Hälfte des Krieges 1870/71," unpublished manuscript, BA-MA, W10/50203, p. 9; cited in Robert T. Foley, *German Strategy and Path to Verdun: Erich von Falkenhayn and the Development of Attrition, 1870–1916* (Cambridge, 2005), p. 17, n. 10; on the significance of the shift to partisan warfare for the broader sweep of military history, see Dieter Langewiesche, "Zum Wandel von Krieg und Kriegslegitimation in der Neuzeit," *Journal of Modern European History* 2 (2004), pp. 5–27.

mobilization enjoyed.³² Regardless, it would take more than numbers and enthusiasm to defeat experienced German veterans.

The new authorities also called for an insurgency war, where *franc-tireurs*, or irregular formations of partisans, would launch scattered attacks on German forces and communications throughout the country.³³ Initially, such attacks were no more than a nuisance; over time, their frequency and effectiveness increased, with serious consequences for the ability of the Germans to conduct operations and supply their forces. Moltke, to his fury, eventually had to devote some 120,000 men to the task of securing communication and supply lines; partisan activity ultimately claimed the lives of some 12,000 soldiers.³⁴ Like conventional troops throughout history, German units reserved a special ire for these bands of partisans, whose tactics consisted primarily of sniping and ambushing vulnerable contingents, especially foraging parties, and occasionally killing stragglers or the wounded.³⁵ One cannot doubt that some took up the task spontaneously, but one should also not overlook the encouragement offered by Republican officials such as Léon Gambetta or the prefect of Côte d'Or, who pointed out that "[y]our fatherland does not ask you to gather in large numbers and oppose the enemy openly; it only expects that each morning three or four resolute men will leave their village and go to where nature has prepared a place suitable for hiding and for firing on Prussians without danger."³⁶

Tellingly, the effectiveness of the partisans was later discounted by French officers reflecting on the failure of the national effort. In his diary, Captain Count Maurice d'Hérisson recounted that "One would have to

---

[32] Foley, German Strategy," pp. 34–35, cites Sanford Kantor, "Exposing the Myth of the Franco-Prussian War," *War and Society* 4 (1986), pp. 13–30.

[33] See the major study by Georg Cardinal von Widdern, *Deutsch-französicher Krieg 1870/71, vol. 3, Der Krieg an den rückwärtigen Verbindungen der deutschen Heere und der Etappendienst* (Berlin, 1895), and Fritz Hoenig, *Der Volkskrieg an der Loire im Herbst 1870*, 6 vols. (Berlin, 1893–1897). Showalter, *Wars of German Unification*, p. 315, underscores the limitations on the French capacity to wage an effective partisan war; on Gambetta in the provinces, see J. P. T. Bury, *Gambetta and the National Defense* (London, 1971).

[34] Howard, *The Franco-Prussian War*, pp. 284–315.

[35] See Frank Kühlich, *Die deutschen Soldaten im Krieg von 1870/71. Eine Darstellung der Situation und der Erfahrungen der deutschen Soldaten im deutsch-französischen Krieg* (Frankfurt a.M., 1995).

[36] Thomas Rohkrämer, "Daily Life at the Front and the Concept of Total War," in Förster and Nagler, eds., *On the Road to Total War*, p. 506; from Geoffrey Best, *Humanity in Warfare: The Modern History of the International Law of Armed Conflicts* (London, 1980), p. 198.

be completely mad to believe that with the volunteer corps one could harm the masses of Prussians even a little, with franc-tireurs, with highwaymen, who they did not even bother with, and who only harmed the French farmers."[37] With historical hindsight, it seems clear that French partisans played only a marginal role in the resistance. It was only after the war that the *franc-tireurs* came to be lionized as the saviors of the military resistance and soul of the French nation, a view not necessarily reflective of their actual effectiveness.

Although popular memory exaggerated the military effects of the *franc-tireurs*, there was no doubt their activities added a troubling dimension to the war for the Prussian general staff and particularly its chief, Helmuth von Moltke. As a result, his earlier hopes for a rapid resolution to the conflict steadily hardened into a grim resolve to push operations deep into the French interior and completely quash the population's resistance to a dictated peace. As casualties mounted and his patience wore thin, Moltke came around to the view that Germany would find no peace in France until the spiteful eyes of the last French partisan were closed. Of course, in rhetoric and passion, if not intention, Moltke was far from alone. Encouraged by the advice offered by American General Philip Sheridan, who counseled the wholesale destruction of stubborn towns and villages, even Bismarck initially advocated a more savage response to the partisans.[38]

Nevertheless, the Iron Chancellor never wavered in his strategic intuition that a lengthier war threatened, through the intervention of other powers, to undo the military gains that the Prussian army had won, and that a negotiated and partial peace was preferable to the long war that unconditional surrender would necessitate. From a more practical perspective, the Prussian War Minister, Albrecht von Roon, likewise promoted a quick settlement in the belief that the embryonic German nation could not long devote so great a proportion of its manpower and economy to a bottomless campaign in the French countryside. The German system of mobilization placed the entire active levy of troops at the disposal of the general staff at the outset of a campaign; a lengthier, more intensive war necessitated the mobilization of the Prussian *Landwehr*, or regional reserve cadres. In the end, Prussian authorities mobilized some

---

[37] Graf Maurice von Hérisson, *Tagebuch eines Ordonnanz-Offiziers: Juli 1870-Februar 1871* (Augsburg, 1885), p. 58; from Manfred Messerschmidt, "The Prussian Army from Reform to War," in Förster and Nagler, *On the Road to Total War*, p. 278.
[38] Howard, *Franco-Prussian War*, pp. 380–381.

170 reserve battalions for the war in France, primarily to garrison rear areas. These forces bore the brunt of the rural insurgency.

As one might expect from unprepared conventional forces under the circumstances, the German military response to the French resistance involved no small degree of brutality and destruction, with a predictable decline in the discipline and morale of the troops, who endured partisan raids and carried out vicious reprisals. Almost nobody had foreseen these eventualities, and little had been done to prepare German forces to face them. Early in the campaign, King Wilhelm I of Prussia declared that "We are not waging war against the peaceful inhabitants of the country; rather it is the duty of every honour-loving soldier to spare private property and not to tolerate offence to the good reputation of our army even by individual examples of indiscipline."[39] French civilians were to "enjoy complete security for their person and property, as long as they do not deprive themselves of the right to my protection by hostile undertakings against the German troops."[40] The point of this idealistic nineteenth-century sensitivity for the rights and protections of civilians was a ruthless preservation of the state's monopoly on violence.

Professional German officers understood violence, in the event of war, as directed toward legitimate, state-sanctioned ends, and hence justified the use of force against civilians and property according to the principle of "military necessity."[41] Indeed, the notion that the putatively legitimate ends of war justified almost any military means, when combined with the prevailing German doctrine of rapid, decisive wars of annihilation, provided a dangerous rationalization for violence against civilians. Reflecting on the anger that irregular tactics aroused among German forces, Karl Marx sarcastically remarked, "It is a real Prussian idea that a nation commits a crime when it continues to defend itself after its regular army

---

[39] Franz Joseph Berg, *Geschichte des königl. Bayer. 4.Jäger-Bataillons*, vol. 2, *Zugleich Tagebuch des Bataillons* (Landhut, 1887), p. 336; quoted in Mark R. Stoneman, "The Bavarian Army and French Civilians in the War of 1870–1871: A Cultural Interpretation," *War in History* 8 (2001), p. 273, n. 8.

[40] Georg Hirth und Julius von Gosen, *Tagebuch des deutsch-französischen Krieges, 1870–1871: eine Sammlung der wichtigeren Quellen* (Leipzig, 1872), pp. 920–921; quoted in Stoneman, "Bavarian Army and French Civilians," p. 273, n. 9.

[41] The contemporary articulation of the concept is General Julius von Hartmann, "Militärische Notwendigkeit und Humanität," in Adolf Lasson, ed., *Prinzip und Zukunft des Völkerrechts* (Berlin, 1871); the best historical appreciation is Manfred Messerschmidt, "Völkerrecht und 'Kriegsnotwendigkeit' in der deutschen militärischen Tradition seit den Einigungskriegen," *German Studies Review* 6 (1983), pp. 237–269 and *Revue de droit penal militaire et de droit de la guerre* 22, nos. 3/4 (1983), pp. 211–241.

has lost."⁴² The rise of partisan activity underscored to Prussian military leaders the uncomfortable fact that what had begun as a limited war for discrete objectives had become a struggle against the French people, with no clear outcome in sight. The combatants had opened a "[p]andora's box of national feeling and the spirit of popular sacrifice," and there was little in the proud Prussian understanding of war that offered guidance on how to end it.⁴³

Moltke had little recourse over winter 1871 other than to pursue a more encompassing form of war and initiate a range of harsh responses to partisan activity.⁴⁴ To be sure, he continued to recognize conventional French soldiers and national guardsmen as legitimate combatants whose status warranted the customary protections afforded prisoners of war, but he specifically withheld such protections from partisans and instead declared them subject to the death penalty.⁴⁵ As Moltke exclaimed to the Prussian Crown Prince on 8 January, "We must fight this nation of liars to the very end! Then we can dictate whatever peace we like."⁴⁶ Mayors of French communities thought to be harboring *franc-tireurs* were ordered to report them or have their homes destroyed. At the least, civilians were subject to stiff fines if German forces suspected them of harboring partisans. For more serious and violent activities, Moltke advocated, in an order from November 1870, the destruction not just of individual farms but the surrounding countryside as well.

Further measures reflected even greater desperation and anger. German officers were authorized to take hostages to guarantee the safe passage of trains through dangerous areas, and French guides or spies thought to have given false information were summarily executed.⁴⁷ The steadily worsening supply situation, itself compounded by insurgent activity in the rear areas, necessitated heavy foraging and requisitions from local

---

⁴² Karl Marx, "Brief an Ludwig Kugelmann in Hannover," December 13, 1870, in Karl Marx and Friedrich Engels, *Marx-Engels-Werke*, Institut für Marxismus-Leninismus beim ZK der SED, ed., vol. 33 (Berlin, 1956–1989), p. 163; from Rohkrämer, "Daily Life at the Front and the Concept of Total War," p. 506.

⁴³ Pflanze, *Bismarck and the Development of Germany*, vol. 1, *The Period of Unification, 1815–1871* (Princeton, NJ, 1990), p. 469.

⁴⁴ See Bertram Winterhalter, "Die Behandlung der französischen Zivilbevölkerung durch die deutschen Truppen im Kriege 1870/1 (unter besonderer Berücksichtigung der Stellungnahme Bismarcks und des Generalstabs)," DPhil. thesis, University of Freiburg, Germany, 1952.

⁴⁵ Howard, *Franco-Prussian War*, p. 378.

⁴⁶ Quoted in ibid., p. 436.

⁴⁷ Isabel V. Hull, *Absolute Destruction: Military Culture and the Practices of War in Imperial Germany* (Ithaca, NY, 2005), pp. 118–119.

populations, which exacerbated tensions and provoked German reprisals in a spiraling cycle of violence. A French source recounted:

> Breaking into homes with axes, pillage, plunder, murder, and especially arson – all these atrocities continued during the whole night and following day under the orders of a disciplined organization, which places the responsibility for this as high as the Prussian government.... Long after the fighting, during the night and the following day, peaceful inhabitants, elderly people, the sick have been killed by the blows of guns and revolvers in their homes and at their doors. Some have been burned in their beds which had been set on fire; wounded people were thrown alive into the flames where they were burned to such an extent that it became impossible to recognize them.[48]

Some historians, most notably Michael Howard, have argued the German Army demonstrated remarkable restraint in the face of intentional provocations by French ultranationalists.[49] The atrocities of the Franco-Prussian War bear scant resemblance to the nightmares of the 1940s, especially on the Eastern Front. All the same, there can be little doubt that the character of the French insurgency and the German response to it inflamed hostilities and made the process of ending the war more difficult.

In Bazeilles on 1 September 1870, a company of Bavarian troops pressed into the town and were halted abruptly by well-aimed fire from French marines of the Army of Châlons. As they regrouped and began searching for tactical advantage, they realized they were taking fire from all sides, suffering numerous casualties from the crossfire. "We finally realized that the inhabitants had joined forces with the soldiers; yes, that even women took part in the battle and brazenly brandished shotguns," a Bavarian officer recalled, referring to such actions as "deceitful" and "treacherous."[50] After clearing the area, his men captured an armed civilian who had clearly been involved in the fighting. Although regulations stipulated that the Germans were to arrest and court-martial him, the Bavarians gunned him down. Friedrich Koch-Breuberg, recounting another incident involving Bavarian troops from a different unit in the

---

[48] Gustave Isambert, *Combat et Indendie de Chateaudun (18 Octobre 1870), avec Notes et Pièces Justificatives* (Paris, 1871), pp. 75–76; from Messerschmidt, "Prussian Army," p. 279.
[49] Ibid., p. 119; Howard, *Franco-Prussian War*, pp. 379–380; Stoneman, "Bavarian Army and French Civilians," pp. 290–293.
[50] Florian Kühnhauser, *Kriegserinnerungen eines Soldaten des k. bayer. Infanterie-Leib-Regiments 1870/71* (München, 1914); from Stoneman, "Bavarian Army and French Civilians," pp. 275–276.

same area, offered a rationalization for the increasingly brutal character of German actions there:

> The rage of the soldiers in Bazeilles was such, however, that everything that happened there must be excused. Those who escaped honest battle with their lives, were threatened with treacherous murder; those who fell wounded could expect that a hate filled woman or farmer would send them to kingdom come in a hideous way. The Bavarian soldiers were completely justified in seizing equally cruel countermeasures.[51]

Similar justifications led to a spiral of abuses on both sides in the conflict.

At Châteaudun, a hotbed of partisan activity, the Prussian 22nd Division fought determined and well-organized resistance in a vicious house-to-house campaign that defied any intention to uphold the civilities of nineteenth-century warfare. French national guardsmen and irregulars dug themselves into the basements and attics of homes throughout the town, while the Prussian commander, Friedrich Wilhelm von Wittich, coolly brought up heavy artillery for direct fire; the resulting carnage devastated the community and intensified the savagery of the struggle. Wittich well understood the measures required to subdue intricate defenses in a densely populated environment and did not shrink from inflicting them. Less clear was the broader impact of his decisions on French willingness to continue the war. Afterward, he leveled a fine of 400,000 francs on Châteaudun and ordered the destruction of some 200 homes. The battle there came to serve as an intellectual reference point for "German officers argu[ing] amongst themselves over the best way to handle irregular resistance in a hostile countryside," with a predictable division between those who saw the tactical utility of crushing immediate resistance and those who understood the complications this presented for the larger effort.[52] One can say that the ensuing debate is yet to be satisfactorily resolved.

The German Army was distinctly ill suited to the hybrid war that the defeat of Napoleon III and expansive war aims had thrust upon it. On a practical level, Prussia had neither the manpower nor resources to fight

---

[51] Friedrich Koch-Breuberg, *Drei Jahre in Frankreich: Errinerungen eines Truppenoffiziers aus dem Feldzug 1870–71 und der Occupation* (München, 1891), p. 80; from Messerschmidt, "Prussian Army," p. 279; Koch-Breuberg, a novelist as well as former officer, later wrote an equally interesting survey of the war: Friedrich Koch-Breuberg, *Der Deutsch-Franzosische Krieg von 1870 und 1871* (Regensburg, 1912).

[52] Showalter, *Wars of German Unification*, p. 297; the Prussian commander's account is L. von Wittich, *Aus meinem Tagebuch, 1870–71* (Cassel, 1872), pp. 93–95.

an improvised "people's war" and no prospect of securing them, to say nothing of the southern German states allied with it. On a theoretical level, the historian cannot overlook the challenge that a popular French insurgency presented to German officers with their highly developed, if ultimately dysfunctional, tradition of civil–military relations. The institutions of the Prussian military state had long been aloof from those of civil society, and they retained an active suspicion toward all forms of popular social organization and governance. Officers bred of such traditions showed little understanding of a nation resolved to avoid, through the mobilization of popular passions and national sentiment, what to them seemed the fair outcome of a stand-up fight and foregone defeat.

More important, most German officers were not amenable to the belief – axiomatic in a wide swath of French political sentiment – that sovereignty rested principally with a nation's citizenry and that actions undertaken on behalf of that citizenry, however dispersed and informal, were by definition legitimate. To them, an armed citizenry was virtually synonymous with an insurrection against the Prussian crown. As Wilhelm Deist has pointed out, "Gambetta's formation of new armies won the respect of the Prussian military, yet his actions embodied a principle that contradicted their own basic ideas... [a] people's war on the German side would first have had to be waged against the Prussian military."[53]

As it was, only Bismarck's strategic sense and his gift for bringing the king around to his view prevented the war from reaching the depths to which it might otherwise have descended. Notwithstanding Moltke's resolution to bring the *Volkskrieg* to its logical if terrifying conclusion, the nub of the conflict between the two great leaders of Germany's war effort lay in whether their forces should aim for the complete submission of all of France and thus a dictated peace or work toward the fall of Paris and a negotiated settlement. Moltke sought actively to foreclose on the latter prospect, going so far as to push for Bismarck's isolation from the Prussian king and win virtual autonomy in decision making for his general staff. Nevertheless, the king opted to circumscribe Moltke's authority by siding with Bismarck, a result that accorded with good sense but which offended Moltke's sense of the appropriate place of politics in military affairs.[54]

---

[53] Wilhelm Deist, "Remarks on the Preconditions to Waging War in Prussia-Germany, 1866–71," in Förster and Nagler, *On the Road to Total War*, p. 324.
[54] Förster, "Optionen der Kriegsführung," p. 92.

MAKING SENSE OF THE PAST[55]

Professional German military interpretations of the war reflected the peculiar strengths and weaknesses of the institutions that produced them.[56] On the one hand, German officers, in recognizing that the nature and appropriate conduct of modern warfare had shifted decisively after 1871, displayed an impressive rigor and thoroughness in their grasp of the larger strategic environment. Few professional institutions in history have achieved so high a discursive and intellectual standard in defining their identity and comprehending their environment. Contemporary military institutions would do well to derive inspiration from the intentions behind German efforts in military analysis, if not necessarily their methods.

On the other hand, German officers could not but color their assessments with undeniable cultural presumptions and a condescending view of the French national character. To be sure, many expressed a guarded appreciation of Gambetta's achievement in stimulating French popular resistance and launching a new era in the theory and practice of war. Almost all, however, discounted their appreciation with disparaging views of Gambetta's fitness for so grand a historical role. The effectiveness of France's unconventional forces brought forth fresh concerns, dormant since the Revolution, about the strategic challenges of wars based on mobilized popular nationalism and industrialism. Success in future wars seemed to belong to countries that succeeded in harnessing and directing – presumably more effectively than the French had – the immense popular energies and productivity of the modern nation-state.

German military authors generally chose not linger over the challenges such wars presented to the viability of a state such as the German *Kaiserreich*, which was, in the final analysis, a military autocracy superimposed on a modern society and economy. Nearly a half-century earlier,

---

[55] Space restricts this chapter to the reflections of Goltz and Moltke. The important work of Fritz Hoenig and Georg Cardinal von Widdern (see note 33) is surveyed capably in Foley, *German Strategy*, pp. 30–34.

[56] That the wars initiated a perceived revolution in military tactics is important but beyond the scope of this survey; see Joachim Hoffmann, "Wandlungen im Kriegsbild der preussischen Armee zur Zeit der nationalen Einigungskriege," *Militärgeschichtliche Mitteilungen* 1 (1968), pp. 5–33; id., "Die Kriegslehre des Generals von Schlichting," *Militärgeschichtliche Mitteilungen* 1 (1969), pp. 5–35; and Dennis E. Showalter, "Infantry Weapons, Infantry Tactics, and the Armies of Germany, 1849–64," *European Studies Review* 4 (1974), pp. 119–140.

Clausewitz, in particular, had cautioned against inflaming the passions of the people, which he understood to be as fickle and uncontrollable as they were boundless. To put it mildly, a core prejudice of the corporate mindset of the Prusso-German officer corps throughout the modern era has been circumspection about the wisdom and reliability of the masses. The results of the Franco-Prussian war accomplished little more than to reinforce this prejudice in German officers.

The most penetrating of the postwar analyses was *Leon Gambetta and His Armies* (1877) by Colmar von der Goltz, a brilliant and inquisitive officer who, in the course of a fascinating career, published extensively on the history and conduct of war in the industrial age.[57] Goltz set out to explore, as a warning to future military planners, the dangerous new possibilities for future warfare hinted at by Gambetta's adventures in strategic policy. He was refreshingly balanced in his assessment of French military accomplishments; in throwing an ad hoc force of some 180,000 men into the field on short notice, the French leader, Goltz argued, displayed an impressive ingenuity and understanding of French society. What more could have been done under the circumstances and in so short a time? Gambetta was able to draw on the resources and talents of a large, complex society to introduce a major roadblock onto the otherwise predictable path to peacemaking in a *Kabinettskrieg*. Future planners and statesmen would do well to consider the enormous and destructive national passions that underlay modern societies.

But there Goltz's praise ended. He denounced the obvious dictatorial streak incipient in the Republic's military crusade, seeming to suggest that the irresponsible political opportunism of leaders like Gambetta flirted with a social chaos reminiscent of the French Revolution. Goltz suggested further that Gambetta was wholly unfit for the grand historical role that

---

[57] Colmar Freiherr von der Goltz, *Léon Gambetta und seine Armeen* (Berlin, 1877); equally interesting is his fascinating discourse on the most important military theorist of the nineteenth century: id., "Karl von Clausewitz," *Velhagen & Klasings Monatshefte* 19 (May 1905), pp. 325–326; his major work on the social and political bases of contemporary war is id., *Das Volk in Waffen* (Berlin, 1883); on his remarkable career, see Hermann Teske, *Colmar, Freiherr von der Goltz: ein Kämpfer für den militärischen Fortschritt* (Göttingen, 1957); on the significance of his ideas, see Dennis Showalter, "Goltz and Bernhardi: The Institution of Originality in the Imperial German Army," *Defense and Security Analysis* 3 (1987), pp. 305–318. For a characterization of Goltz as a "professional maverick," see Antulio Echevarria, "General Staff Historian Hugo Freiherr von Freytag-Loringhoven and the Dialectics of German Military Thought," *The Journal of Military History* 60 (1996), p. 471.

his rabble-rousing presented him, and that he irresponsibly led his armies of enthusiastic volunteers to wholesale slaughter before the disciplined ranks of Prussian infantry and artillery. So untrained and undifferentiated a mass of manpower had little utility for the rapid decisive operations that the Germans considered, at the time, the hallmark of operational art. Ultimately, the French *Volkskrieg* of 1870–1871 accomplished little more than to hamstring German initiatives, delay the inevitable annihilative defeat, and complicate a straightforward political settlement.

Underlying Goltz's impressions was the German habit of infantilizing French political sentiments, reducing the popular national resistance to an irrational zeal for political posturing. One German historian has argued, moreover, that his analysis put forth a form of strategic "worst-case scenario" thinking typical of postwar German assessments of French performance in 1870–1871. This thinking consisted of "a mixture of collective memory of the *levée en masse* of 1792 – and of Napoleon's *Grand Armée* – as proof of the collective energy, and perhaps unpredictability, and therefore, danger which, for example, so greatly influenced Bismarck's image of France."[58] For Goltz, the hybrid war launched by militarized French nationalists was more a warning than a model – a terrifying instance of the kinds of entanglements and complications that Germany could anticipate in future warfare. Less obvious for Goltz were the strategic implications of that warning.

If Goltz proved particularly insightful, no appraisal of the German experience of hybrid warfare was more important than that of Helmuth von Moltke, the longtime chief of the Great General Staff and formative influence on the institutional culture and outlook of the professional officer corps. To an extent arguably greater than that of any other major writer on military affairs, Moltke wrote within the conceptual straightjacket of the nineteenth-century nation-state, and from his role atop a military establishment derived from and dependent on a traditional autocracy for the legitimacy of its ends.[59] Organized violence to Moltke – at least until the waning years of his life – was designed precisely to serve the purposes of rational statecraft. The brutal house-to-house and counterinsurgency combat of the Franco-Prussian War seemed a grotesque

---

[58] Gerd Krumeich, "The Myth of Gambetta and the 'People's War' in Germany and France, 1871–1914," in Förster and Nagler, *On the Road to Total War*, p. 642; Krumeich's sensitive interpretation of the postwar significance of the *guerre à outrance* is a critical point of departure for any treatment of it.

[59] Moltke's reflections are scattered throughout his *Geschichte des deutsch-französischen Krieges von 1870–71* (Berlin, 1891).

aberration of true warfare, a hideous monster to be avoided, or rapidly quashed:

> The days are gone by when, for dynastical ends, small armies of professional soldiers went to war to conquer a city, or a province, and then sought winter quarters or made peace. The wars of the present day call whole nations to arms... The entire financial resources of the state are appropriated to military purposes[.][60]

To professional officers like Moltke, the facilitators and practitioners of a popular resistance were beneath contempt, forcing him to contemplate a lengthy campaign in distant French provinces and pursue the complete subjugation of the French citizenry. He wrote on 18 December 1870 that he could not foresee how long such a campaign would last, as "a whole people under arms should not be underestimated."[61] But if he had a hard time brooking challenges to his view of conventional war, he was also an insightful and intelligent observer of the broad transition then underway from *Kabinettskrieg* to *Volkskrieg*, wrestled deeply with its results, and ultimately developed a notion of deterrence as the only means to avoid the catastrophe it heralded.

The adaptation of Germany's likely opponents made Moltke's efforts more difficult. The first and most obvious result of the successful German campaigns in 1866 and 1871 was a major military reform effort throughout Europe, but especially in France and Russia. All had beheld the impressive performance in the field of Prussia's superbly trained conscript infantry and recognized the importance, if they were to resist Germany's quick campaigns, of developing deep field reserves of their own. In particular, France undertook a long series of reforms to its military staff system and program of officer education, finally becoming serious after decades of neglect about the fundamentally intellectual character of senior military leadership in the modern age. More to the point, the French neither forgave nor forgot the intense humiliation of 1871, which became the cornerstone for strategic planning on both sides of the fortified frontier. Episodic tensions between Germany and Russia between 1874 and 1879 increasingly convinced Moltke of implacable Russian animosity in the east as great as that of France in the west.[62] Along with

---

[60] Helmuth Graf von Moltke, *The Franco-German War of 1870–71*, Archibald Forbes, trans. (London, 1907), p. 1; from Foley, *German Strategy*, p. 18.

[61] Moltke to Privy Councilor Scheller, 18 December 1870, in *Gesammelte Schriften und Denkwürdigkeiten des General-Feldmarschalls Grafen Helmuth von Moltke*, vol. 5 (Berlin, 1891–1893), p. 179; from Foley, *German Strategy*, p. 19.

[62] Rudolf Stadelmann, *Moltke und der Staat* (Krefeld, 1950), p. 297.

the German model, the nations of Europe took heed of the extraordinary potential of the French national resistance, and they began planning for thoroughgoing mobilizations of their own populations in future wars. "[W]ith the Franco-Prussian War, war in Europe had ceased to be a war of government against government and became one of nation against nation."[63]

In light of these factors, Moltke was deeply pessimistic by 1877 that Germany could realize conventional operational successes in another war with France as decisive as those he had accomplished in August and September of 1870, particularly if Germany had to fight Russia as well.[64] Assuming his unchanged resolve not to work more closely with German diplomats to avert crises that could lead to war, the only conceivable solution seemed to consist of defeating the opponent on one front as rapidly as possible, while temporizing with the other until Germany could throw its full weight against it. In his initial postwar planning, the rapid decision would first come in the west; by the end of the 1870s, that emphasis had shifted east. The army needed to arrive at a decision fast, he emphasized, to avoid the experience of 1870–1871 and a resurgence of popular involvement in the outcome. The greater the emphasis on avoiding a *Volkskrieg*, the greater the purely military considerations of bringing about a decisive battle and the less the consequent claim of political constraints on military planning.

The logic was both desperate and inexorable. The growing risks and dimensions of war under such circumstances motivated Moltke in his seminal essay "On Strategy" in late 1871 to assert, in contrast to the broader Clausewitzian conception that had to that point governed his thinking, that the role of politics in defining warfare had by necessity to be constrained.[65] Statesmen should steer strategic policy only at the outset and conclusion of a war. The scale and scope of armed combat, he reasoned, as well as the potential stresses of a long war, had become great enough in 1870–1871 to blur the distinction between political and military spheres of competency and highlighted the practical aspects of

---

[63] Foley, *German Strategy*, p. 35.
[64] Gerhard Ritter, *Staatskunst und Kriegshandwerk: das Problem des "Militarismus" in Deutschland*, vol. 1 (München, 1965), pp. 293 ff. Moltke shrewdly warned against this contingency in the immediate aftermath of the war with France: See his memorandum of 27 August 1871 in Ferdinand von Schmerfeld, ed., *Graf Moltke. Die deutschen Aufmarschpläne 1871–1890* (Berlin, 1929), pp. 4–14.
[65] Helmuth Graf von Moltke, "über Strategie," in *Von Kabinettskrieg zum Volkskrieg*, pp. 630–632.

military planning over the more speculative methods of diplomacy. The answer for Moltke, at least initially, was a greater role in shaping strategic affairs by the leadership of the military and a redoubled emphasis on fighting wars even more quickly and decisively. Wars were to be avoided if at all possible; failing that, they were to be prosecuted to the utmost.

What the foregoing makes clear is that, at the least, the German experience of hybrid warfare in 1870–1871 led to a reconsideration of fundamental assumptions about the nature of the future wars Germany would likely fight. More broadly, it underscores that the postwar German military, contrary to the impression fostered by generations of twentieth-century historians, was far from simpleminded in anticipating wars of maneuver and envelopment, with decisive victory the only result.[66] For decades before the Franco-Prussian War, thinkers and officers had based their planning on the constraints of the Metternichian state system and the short, sharp wars that it made possible. After the unpleasant experience of the Franco-Prussian War, Moltke cast about for ways in which Germany could prevail in lengthier, less bounded conflicts. Instead of one or two decisive battles that forced an opponent to confront the bitter calculus of decreasing returns for risk, the resources and willpower of entire peoples would be mobilized and subjected to an endurance contest. Outcomes would most probably not consist of terms dictated on the basis of unconditional surrender. Exhaustion on both sides would lead, it was thought, to ambiguous settlements without unequivocal winners and losers. If German military planners clung doggedly to the hope that a future European conflict could be won with a rapid and decisive campaign, it was less a product of confusion about this shift and more the understanding that Germany could not match the strategic depth of its opponents.[67]

For the remainder of his days, Moltke understood that Germany would defeat France in another war only with the greatest difficulty. In the event of a Franco-Russian accommodation, the likelihood diminished even further. He struggled to devise effective military alternatives to what was, in

---

[66] See, most notably, the now famous essay by Stig Förster, "Der deutsche Generlastab und die Illusion des kurzen Krieges, 1871–1914: Metakritik eines Mythos," *Militärgeschichtliche Mitteilungen* 54 (1995), pp. 61–95; reprinted in Johannes Burkhardt, Josef Becker, Stig Förster, and Günther Kronenbitter, eds., *Lange und kurze Wege in den ersten Weltkrieg: vier Augsburger Beiträge zur Kriegsursachenforschung* (München, 1996).

[67] The best and clearest expression of this revisionist interpretation of the German strategic debate is Foley, *German Strategy*.

the final analysis, an intractable problem. As the work of Stig Förster has made clear, it was not the illusion of a short war that motivated German officers before 1914 but rather the utter necessity of realizing one against all existing trends and dynamics. Historians have judged Moltke and his successors in this regard harshly, particularly after 1906, when the heightened war readiness of France and Russia drove German planners to promulgate ever more intricate and risky operational schemes to cut the Gordian knot of strategic encirclement and resource poverty.

Such criticism is warranted, at least to a point. The reduction of war to a series of intricate operational problems at the expense of a broader strategic vision of the country's interests ranks among the greatest professional malfeasances of German officers in the modern age – an impressive collection, to be sure. One prominent historian has described it in terms of "the German army's quarter century of devolution from rational actor to all-or-nothing gambler."[68] But it was also inevitable given the nightmarish strategic dilemma that faced those planners – a product itself of a larger, more systemic failure to conceive of Germany's interests and its strategic options more realistically. German officers deserve much of the blame for the cultural conceits that reinforced Germany's strategic posture before 1914, but not all of it. The basic problem of strategic culpability at the highest levels of decision making and social militarism at the lowest was strongly influenced by the high profile the German officer corps enjoyed, to be sure, but that fact should not obscure that the officer corps was not, in the end, the arbiter of Germany's fate.

---

[68] Dennis Showalter, "From Deterrence to Doomsday Machine: The German Way of War, 1890–1914," *Journal of Military History* 64 (2000), p. 710.

8

Small Wars and Great Games

The British Empire and Hybrid Warfare, 1700–1970

John Ferris

One must begin by translating between two languages – modern American and old English. The contemporary term "hybrid warfare" refers to a struggle between a conventional force, perhaps with unconventional elements, against an enemy that combines regular and irregular components, usually assumed to be guerrillas. When applied to the British imperial experience between 1700 and 1970, that term takes a broader meaning. It refers to conflicts between a regular army (usually aided by paramilitary forces) against four kinds of enemy. Ranked in order of frequency, these foes include conventional forces, ranging from phalanxes resting on spear and shield to units using European weapons and tactics; some mixture of unconventional and conventional forces; irregular forces that avoided a guerrilla strategy, because it exposed their populations to attack, but instead battled English forces on their frontiers by using conventional weapons in unconventional ways; and guerrillas who harassed conventional forces whom they allowed to occupy their villages. Hybrid warfare is one of the few areas where Britain had anything approaching a modern conception of doctrine, complete with manuals that distilled experience and guided action. The British expressed its sense through ideas such as "small wars" or "imperial policing" and linked these technical matters to political ones, especially issues of colonial policy.[1] The

---

[1] For classic views, cf. Lord Wolseley, *The Soldier's Pocket Book for Field Service* (London, 1869); Charles Calwell, *Small Wars, Their Principles and Practice* (1896); and C. W. Gwynn, *Imperial Policing* (London, 1934). The best recent studies of these matters are T. R. Moreman, "'Small Wars' and 'Imperial Policing': The British Army and the Theory and Practice of Colonial Warfare in the British Empire, 1919–1939," *The Journal of Strategic Studies* 19/4 (December 1996), pp. 105–131; and David French, "The British

British experience with hybrid warfare ranged from triumphant to incompetent. To illuminate past patterns and modern ideas, to reflect trends and variations while avoiding overgeneralization from any instance, this experience is best approached through a broad framework, combined with case studies.

These experiences stem from a context that runs like a thread across continents and centuries. European states developed armies unique on earth. Then they conquered it. From 1500 onward, they regularly fought major wars in which only the strongest survived, through a constant competition to produce armies and to improve them. State finances were honed to this end, as were administration and politics. Compromises between monarchs and nobles produced an officer corps, technically competent and politically loyal, with authority over the armies of the state. States maintained the best forces they could fund. They could become stronger simply by raising revenues and regiments. For non-European countries, conversely, to raise taxes was to create crisis, and to improve armies was to endanger the state. European polities became the most militarized and militarily effective on earth. Their armies were large, manned with specialist soldiers, dominated by heavy infantry and mobile firepower, disciplined, and slow moving, and they frequently changed tactics, weapons, and organization. They were designed for high-intensity combat or sieges and operations in territories with open terrain, large populations, and well-developed logistical infrastructure. These systems were suited only to certain environments – and not even to all of those in Europe, as Napoleonic armies found when confronting guerrillas in Spain, or Austrians discovered in their wars in the Balkans. European military systems were hard to export outside of Europe because of differences in terrain, politics, enemies, and infrastructure. To work elsewhere, the systems had to be adapted to local conditions.

This adaptation took many forms. British armies engaged in a number of strategic confrontations, roughly equal in moment, where irregular operations occurred regularly, hybrid enemies of various stripes were common, and hybridity was a way of war. In strategic terms, for Britain, hybridity meant the maintenance of forces able to manage all the

---

Army and the Empire, 1856–1956," in Greg Kennedy, ed., *Imperial Defence, The Old World Order, 1856–1956* (London, 2008), pp. 91–110. For the RAF's role in such matters, cf. note 23; and for that of the navy, cf. John Ferris, "SSTR in Perspective: The British Imperial Experience, 1815–1945," in James J. Wirtz and Jeffrey A. Larsen, eds., *Naval Peacekeeping and Humanitarian Operations, Stability from the Sea* (London, 2009), pp. 26–41.

competitions that enmeshed the empire. In operational terms, it meant the ability to recalibrate forces from one competition to another, and then to combine their strengths so to defeat any competitor. Between the middle of the eighteenth and the nineteenth centuries, the need for hybridity increasingly marked all land forces of the Crown. They evolved to fill a strategic niche across continents, combining politics, power, and technology – areas in which they had superiority over most competitors. At various times between 1700 and 1970, these elements included general-purpose forces (the British and Indian armies) and scores of specialized (regional, paramilitary, or gendarmerie) units for particular areas, such as the battalions of African soldiers with European officers that policed the empire in Africa, or the 300 members of the North West Mounted Police who secured half a continent between 1870 and 1910.

The basic units of exchange in imperial power were battalions, which were sterling but above which expertise was mixed. Only in India and England did divisions really exist and hardly ever corps. Most specialized troops were raised, cheaply, from local populations, their loyalty secured by status and salary. This burden sharing reduced the financial and human cost of empire. Particular problems were handled through a hybrid fusion of political officers, paramilitary units, and regular forces. In practice, often 12 political officers, 100 British soldiers, and 800 paramilitary personnel controlled 10 million people, with the nearest regular force lying 1,000 miles away. From 1924 to 1937, 10,000 regular personnel and 200 aircraft controlled half the Middle East; 8,000 colonial troops governed British Africa; and only 45,000 European soldiers garrisoned India.

Never had so many been ruled by so few. Most British forces, whether coastal artillery or the Khyber Rifles, were designed for use in only one arena, but some (including warships or their crews, converted to naval brigades, or aircraft) were adaptable for many of them. Except during the periods from 1914 to 1918 and 1939 to 1957, deployable forces were tiny in number, rarely reaching 10,000 soldiers for any campaign. Britain could augment these forces in times of crisis, with their power multiplied by quality and technology.

For good and ill, this system limited Britain's ability to solve problems by power and instead drove the British to search for political solutions, which matched force as a weapon in imperial strategy. Britain's sensitivity to local politics was high, even when its understanding was not. Generally, British decision makers performed well in understanding and co-opting individuals, but they were merely good in handling movements that linked elites and masses (whether open or conspiratorial). This approach led the British down a generally fruitful path. By working with local elites and interests, Britain created tolerance of and support for its presence. This approach, however, automatically created problems whenever Britain got the politics wrong. That outcome was especially true during revolutions, when allies and instruments turned suddenly and unexpectedly against it, denying the British the political and military expertise on which the system relied, as was the case with the 13 North American colonies in the 1770s, India or Palestine in the 1940s, and Arab countries afterward.

Characteristic, sometimes costly, problems emerged when forces were organized into formations or switched between competitions, from garrison to combat, or when they encountered a previously unknown difficulty. The British Empire ran on the cheap and often moved in mysterious ways. The usual rule in imperial strategy, such as the use of minimal force, stemming from the principle of minimum expense, was rejected whenever intimidation (what the ablest of Victorian soldiers, Garnet Wolseley, once called "signal chastisement") or exemplary terror seemed the better buy.[2] British leaders preferred to solve problems only when unavoidable. This approach allowed some dangers to arise without intervention and left Britain oversensitive, sometimes hostage, to the emergence of small threats, as when the army's strategic reserve was committed to Palestine during the Munich crisis or to the Canal Zone in 1953. It also increased the economy of the strategy, in terms of the allocation of resources and their effect, the specificity of the answers applied to questions, and the tendency to force solutions on problems using available, vice optimal, means.

Britain always had to balance between maintaining so much presence as to provoke local elites and too little to intimidate them. Its mechanisms to supply forces abroad for normal circumstances, such as the regimental and the Cardwell systems, were adequate.[3] The British Empire, however, never developed effective machinery to redeploy large forces from one area to another for emergencies or to mobilize for mass wars; the costs of ad hoc measures were heavy against enemies with elaborate conscription systems in the great power wars of the twentieth century. Nevertheless,

---

[2] Wolseley to War Office, Dispatch 38, 13.10.73, WO 147/27.
[3] David French, *Military Identities: The Regimental System, the British Army, and the British People, c. 1870–2000* (Oxford, 2005).

British land forces were well suited to handle the problems of empire, both normal and unique. Across the board, from 1700 to 1970, they adjusted to different competitions better than any other contemporary forces.

One can describe Western superiority over armies outside of Europe in three stages: 1750–1860, 1860–1940, and 1940 to the present. The initial roots of that superiority were in organization. Western forces had better discipline, endurance, and ability to move tactically than most non-Western foes, and they had two unique attributes – an officer corps imbued with skill and self-sacrifice, and the socket bayonet, which enabled European infantry to move instantly from fire to shock. Beyond the bayonet, technology was irrelevant: European armies frequently had no edge in firepower over non-Western forces. Until 1880, the latter sometimes adopted Western systems, while irregular or hybrid forces often stalemated European armies outside of Europe. European militaries succeeded only by altering their systems of line and volley to fit local environments, in particular by downplaying fire and emphasizing shock – by developing hybridity. British experiences illustrate these observations.[4]

THE EIGHTEENTH AND NINETEENTH CENTURIES

By 1757, British infantry proved better in battle than any other forces in India and deployed techniques of siege and storm that broke a fundamental rule in Indian warfare – that fortresses fell slowly. Hence, Britain mastered northeastern India. Wealth and administration made the British the top bidder in the market for the mercenaries of the subcontinent, a locale where logistical and economic systems could support the European system of war with unusual ease. Britain had the largest effective army in India – mostly sepoys trained on British lines, with unified command, good officers, shrewd politics, and local support – but for decades its power remained constrained. In 1757, Indian armies consisted largely of clumsy infantry and light cavalry. None had infantry of contemporary Western style. Several, however, adapted to that danger in a long struggle

---

[4] Pradeep Barua, *The State at War in South Asia* (University of Nebraska Press, 2005); Matthew Headrick, *The Tools of Empire: Technology and European Imperialism in the Nineteenth Century* (Oxford University Press, 1981); P. J. Marshall, "Western Arms in Maritime Asia in the Early Phases of Empire," *Modern Asian Studies* 14/1 (1980); David Ralston, *Importing the European Army, The Introduction of European Military Techniques and Institutions to the Extra-European World* (Chicago, 1991).

for mastery in India, which produced Britain's greatest challenges and triumphs in hybrid warfare.⁵

From 1767 to 1799, Britain fought four wars against two kings of Mysore in south India. Hyder Ali and Tipu Sultan's 20,000 disciplined but not Westernized infantry sometimes defeated secondary British contingents but always lost to the main British force. After suffering defeat, they adopted a hybrid strategy, avoiding pitched battle and holding towns while attacking British weaknesses (i.e., problems with logistics and occupation) by having their 18,000 irregular cavalry slash the supply lines of British besiegers, smash columns on the move, and raid British-controlled territories. For decades, Mysore deflected British blows long enough to force a draw in the contest for supremacy. In central India, the Mahratta Confederacy had identical success with the same strategy from 1775 to 1782. Mahrattas and Mysore also possessed and produced firearms equal to those of British forces. Britain crushed Mysore in 1799 only by concentrating all of its resources and bending politics in India to the task; through good generalship, focused on forcing decision by storming Tipu's cities; and by using allied Mahratta Horse to check Tipu's cavalry.

From 1803 to 1805, Britain deployed a similar strategy against the Mahrattas, who possessed good irregular cavalry, a Westernized army with more and better field guns than the British, and 56,000 infantryman as opposed to the Raj's 37,000. The Mahrattas failed to coordinate their cavalry and infantry in strategic terms, denying themselves the full advantages of irregular or hybrid warfare. Their leaders and their forces were divided and some were manipulated by the British, although on the whole they fought unexpectedly well. In major battles, British commanders concluded that they would lose a pounding match of firepower. Instead, they won by abandoning their plans and taking the initiative through bayonet assaults, which shattered the Mahratta regulars.⁶ Decades later, when asked to name his "best" battle, the Duke of Wellington replied "Assaye," his decisive victory against Mahrattas in 1803. The British also checked Mahratta strengths by raising 11,000 mercenary cavalry and subverting their enemy's command – especially by buying opposition battalion commanders, who mostly were European mercenaries. From

---

⁵ Randolph G. S. Cooper, *The Anglo-Mahratta Campaigns and the Contest for India: The Struggle for the Mastery of the South Asian Military Economy* (Cambridge, 2003); id., "Culture, Combat and Colonialism in Eighteenth and Nineteenth Century India," *International History Review* xxvii/3 (September 2005), pp. 534–549.

⁶ Second Duke of Wellington, *The Supplementary Despatches and Memoranda of Field Marshal Arthur Duke of Wellington* (London, 1834), vol. II, pp. 141, 354.

1817 to 1819, 120,000 Anglo-Indian soldiers crushed the Mahrattas and their irregular cavalry by using hybrid forces to master all of India outside the Punjab.

Finally, from 1845 to 1849, Britain engaged the Sikh kingdom in Punjab, which possessed 65,000 Westernized soldiers and guns to match the British. Victory rested on exploitation of political confusion within the Sikh kingdom – even so, success required the British to fight and win their two hardest battles between 1815 and 1914. In these subcontinental campaigns, Indian regular and irregular forces were good and hard to beat on their own, doubly so when combined in some hybrid fashion. Britain won only when the enemy failed to make this combination work, by forcing the enemy into engaging in decisive battles, and most important, when the British were able to manipulate Indian political divisions. British success enabled the greatest conquest of territory between 1750 and 1850.

During the eighteenth century, Britain's record was mediocre in several North American wars against an enemy with strategic hybridity: French regulars, who contained British colonies through their dominance of the inland water systems and fortification of key positions, allied with Amerindian confederacies.[7] British forces, just beginning to confront the problems of hybridity, were unprepared for such an enemy. To attack French positions by land, colonial militia of mediocre quality or regular units trained for European warfare had to advance great distances over poor roads and trackless wilderness. Thus, in 1755, General Edward Braddock's five-mile-long column crawled six miles per day on its path to destruction. Amerindians ambushed slow columns in the wilderness, isolated forts, ravaged villages, and used terror to frighten soldiers and settlers. Yet, once it employed its maritime resources to the fullest, Britain shattered this strategy through a simple means. French America was fatally vulnerable to amphibious attacks on its fortified towns, while native forces were crippled when they were not bolstered by regular European forces. Native forces could win battles but did not capitalize upon them in a strategic sense – they could not besiege forts or fight for long. British and colonial victories were more fruitful.

In later decades, British and Amerindian forces deployed strategic and operational hybridity against Americans, who returned the favor.

---

[7] W. J. Eccles, *The Canadian Frontier, 1534–1760* (Albuquerque, NM, rev. ed., 1983); Richard White, *The Middle Ground: Indians, Empires and Republics in the Great Lakes Region, 1650–1815* (Cambridge, 1991); Fred Anderson, *Crucible of Empire, The Seven Years War and the Fate of Empire in British North America, 1754–1766* (New York, 2000).

Britain's performance was poor during the American Revolutionary War because it confronted a revolution that it found hard to understand or handle.[8] Old allies and instruments turned against it. American rebels gained control over the Thirteen Colonies and their foundations for irregular and regular forces. Britain's enemies were its own local tools for war – administration and politics, working with some unity. The Americans created a new kind of battlefield, exploiting popular support while destroying any opposition and politically cleansing the loyalist population. Ideologically and organizationally, the revolutionaries created an armed citizenry that Britain found hard to contain.

Where the population remained true, as in Canada, Britain was secure, but it never could re-create loyalty once destroyed. Denied local specialists, British officers, experienced mostly in European operations, misconstrued the type of war they were fighting. They did well in deploying force to North America but were slow to recalibrate to local conditions or to handle a hybrid enemy. During the first years of the war, they won a number of victories, which yielded little control beyond the immediate battlefield. British forces never mastered counterinsurgency warfare, never found the means to sustain local allies, and failed to force their will on a hostile or neutral population (although some loyalists did create effective irregular forces, augmented by Amerindians). Meanwhile, the British edge in conventional warfare declined as the Continental Army gained experience and aid from French regular forces (which approached numerical equality with British battalions in the Thirteen Colonies). From 1778 onward, Britain's attention focused on European powers seeking to turn its danger into their opportunity. Ultimately, the British position in the Thirteen Colonies was destroyed by a classic hybrid force: a French fleet, a Franco-American army, and swarms of irregulars.

Conversely, during the War of 1812, Britain's performance in hybrid warfare was outstanding.[9] Although outnumbered heavily, British forces and commanders outclassed their counterparts in quality and recalibrated better to hybrid warfare, while their Amerindian allies matched the

---

[8] Cf. Williamson Murray, in the present volume, and the works it cites. The best account of Britain's predicament remains Piers Mackesy, *The War for America, 1775–1783* (Lincoln, NB, 1993).

[9] The War of 1812 remains an underresearched topic, and existing works are often marred by nationalism. The best of a mixed lot are Donald R. Hickey, *The War of 1812: A Forgotten Conflict* (Champaign, 1989); Charles Edward Skeene, *Citizen Soldiers in the War of 1812* (Lexington, KY, 1999); J. M. Hitsman (updated by Donald E. Graves), *The Incredible War of 1812: A Military History* (Toronto, 1999).

American forces that operated as irregulars. Britain had support from populations within its territory, ensuring political control. Its true strength in this war, however, was its enemy – American will remained divided and its military forces for the most part incompetent. The war taught Americans a lasting lesson – to attack British North America was risky and costly, although the war also enabled them to break the last resistance of eastern Amerindians to their westward expansion.

In the 1820s, Ashanti armies stalled a British expedition of a few thousand men equipped with rockets by using muskets, stockades, and natural cover to block lines of advance. Farther east, in one of Britain's greatest expeditions in Asia to date, 10,000 Anglo-Indian soldiers backed by steam-powered gunboats barely beat the Burmans. In 1873–1874, another British expedition against the Ashantis had mixed success. Even in 1882, Wolseley, the commander who opposed Egyptian forces at Tel el Kebir, described their entrenchments and firepower as formidable: "To have marched over this plateau upon the enemy's position by daylight, our troops would have had to advance over a glacis-like slope in full view of the enemy and under the fire of his well served artillery for about five miles. Such an operation would have entailed enormous losses from an enemy with men and guns well protected by entrenchments from any artillery fire we could have brought to bear upon them." Any attempt to turn this position would merely allow the enemy to withdraw to other positions. To achieve "the object I had in view, namely to grapple with the enemy at such close quarters that he should not be able to shake himself free from our clutches except by a general flight of all his army," Wolseley, like Wellington 80 years before, turned to surprise and unconventional tactics. Rather than relying on firepower, he negated it through a night attack and close assault, in which 11,000 British soldiers destroyed a force of 20,000 Egyptians for the price of 87 killed and missing.[10]

Yet another trend was on the rise. By 1840, 4,000 British soldiers and 20 warships dictated terms to China, the largest country on earth. Western military superiority increasingly grew in scale and significance. Western forces were dominant on land. European armies, their advantages in training and discipline augmented by technology, had less need to adapt their tactics to those of local forces or conditions. Britain enthusiastically applied modern technology to war.

---

[10] Wolseley War Office, Dispatch 8, 16.9.82, WO 32/6096.

From 1880 onward, it also strove to deny that technology to non-European peoples, which became a hidden element to its military superiority, as was the isolation of each theater through naval superiority and politics, and the ability to keep the dirty side of empire from public scrutiny. In East Asia, Western power was manifested through maritime and riverine forces. In Africa, quick-firing artillery, repeating rifles, and machine guns enabled tiny forces to crush native foes. African armies often were well organized, with upward of 20,000 to 30,000 regular soldiers, but they relied on spears, shields, bows, and flintlocks. The proud forces of these native states, used to fighting decisive battles, deployed their usual tactics against Western armies and were annihilated.[11] At the apex of imperialism, African and Asian states rarely could pose a threat to European forces because of the limits to the power of their regular armies and political organization.

GUERRILLAS AND IRREGULARS

Before 1945, Europeans rarely confronted guerrillas because guerrilla warfare required forces and peoples that were too weak to avoid occupation yet too strong to be defeated when occupied. That combination was uncommon during the heyday of Britain's imperial supremacy. To mobilize guerrilla campaigns from peoples with loose social organizations required a general fear by local elites and the people of a threat to their way of life, and a common ideology, often religious, to unify resistance. The two greatest, if unsuccessful, struggles against Western conquest in the nineteenth century were led by masters of guerrilla warfare supported by Sufi Muslim brotherhoods: in Algeria by Abd el-Qadir, and in Chechnya by Imam Shamyl. If overrun, few adversaries could continue the struggle. Even in the case of states where British aggression confronted popular opposition with religious institutions to channel it, as in Punjab between 1846 and 1849 and in Egypt in 1882, once Britain smashed the opposing army, there was no guerrilla resistance; instead, there was acquiescence in conquest, however sullen. To use modern jargon, insurgents rarely could move from Mao's first to third stage of guerrilla warfare, but those starting from that upper level could mount ferocious resistance, centering on battle with Western forces rather than evading them. Guerrillas became common problems for the British only in the twentieth century

---

[11] Bruce Vandervoort, *Wars of Imperial Conquest in Africa, 1830–1914* (London, 1998).

and only in occupied territories where political movements could emerge and invoke a military threat to British sovereignty.

Until then, irregular forces were more commonly used in an attempt to oppose Western invasion of tribal lands. Determined warriors sought to defeat Western armies in battle by using conventional weapons in unconventional, often innovative, ways by combining fire with terrain to create killing grounds. Maori riflemen in 1842 and Metis in 1885 used stockades and pits for cover, to bring crippling fire on attackers.[12] So, too, during the "Hut Tax" war in Sierra Leone in 1898, British flying columns had to attack one stockaded town after another, ambushed by snipers who focused on officers and porters. Britain suppressed the revolt, but this effort cost more than was needed to smash 30,000 Sokoto regulars in Nigeria during the same period. British officers disliked such enemies and hated the very idea of guerrilla war. In 1879, Wolseley heard a prediction that in a war with Britain, the Boers would adopt guerrilla tactics: "they will watch their opportunity & lay in wait for & attack small convoys, merely firing on them from behind cover & then bolting as hard as their horses will carry them." He interpreted that idea to mean "they intend becoming brigands & assassins. I can't believe this, for they have some sensible men amongst them who would warn them that such a policy would put the whole civilized world against them." Conversely, he praised enemies who fought (and died) in the open, like Zulus, describing one incident in the Ashanti war of 1873–1874 as "a hard fight that lasted all day. The enemy fought like men."[13]

Armies could defeat armed societies without a political center only through prolonged and ruthless campaigns. Britain generally achieved these aims, with partial exceptions in New Zealand and Somalia, and greater ones north of India. From 1838 to 1842, Afghans defeated 9,500 Anglo-Indian soldiers and 6,000 allies, killing half of them, largely as a result of a failure of British politics.[14] The outcome was less one-sided or costly, but equally complex, during Britain's occupation of Afghanistan from 1878 to 1881. In this instance, the enemy, although politically divided, pursued an effective hybrid strategy that combined

---

[12] James Belich, *The New Zealand Wars and the Victorian Interpretation of Racial Conflict* (Auckland, 1986).
[13] Garnet Wolseley, "South African Journal, 1879/80," entry 24.10.1879, WO 147/7; Garnet Wolseley, *Ashantee Journal*, "Ashanttee War of 1873–4," entry 31.1.74, WO 147/3.
[14] Malcolm Yapp, *Strategies of British India: Britain, Iran and Afghanistan, 1798–1850* (Oxford, 1980).

various tribal irregulars and a decent regular army; in muskets and artillery, they matched Britain in technology. This combination besieged a British brigade in Kabul during December 1879, broke another at Maiwand on 27 July 1880, and convinced Britain's leaders to alter their strategy and broker a political solution to the conflict.

Fortuitously, a solution was at hand in the form of Abdur Rahman, a leader strong enough to rule Afghanistan and smart enough not to bother British interests. Thus, Britain's military border in India came to rest on the Northwest Frontier, which was populated by large, fragmented, and warlike peoples. In 1897–1898, Pashtun snipers, often veterans of the Indian Army armed with excellent rifles, fought 59,000 British and Indian soldiers to a standstill, ambushing units and picking off officers.[15] Britain replied by finding political means to neutralize a problem that it could not solve through force, as it had done in Afghanistan.[16]

THE INDIAN MUTINY, 1857–1858

In 1857, a revolt almost broke the Raj.[17] Two matters crippled the Indian mutiny from the start. It remained confined to the Bengal Army, just one of the three British armies in India. Although the British dared not use the Bombay and Madras Armies to suppress the mutiny, they did not have to use scarce resources to oppose them as well. Although British authorities believed India was ready to explode, the mutiny imploded. The mutineers started without strategy or command apparatus and never developed either. As General Wilson, the first British commander before Delhi noted, "Luckily the enemy have no head and no method."[18] The mutineers' great hope was to spread the revolt far and fast. Instead, the mutineers rallied on Delhi and Lucknow, the prestigious capitals of the deceased Mughal Empire, and Awadh, a recently annexed kingdom in northern India from which most sepoys of the Bengal Army were recruited. They concentrated

---

[15] Tim Moreman, *The Army in India and the Development of Frontier Warfare 1847–1947* (London, 1998).

[16] John Ferris, "Invading Afghanistan, 1838–2006: Pacification and Politics," *The Journal of Military and Strategic Studies* 9/1 (Sep 2006), accessed at http://www.jmss.org/jmss/index.php/jmss/article/view/119.

[17] Rudrangshu Mukharjee, *Awadh in Revolt, 1857–58: A Study of Popular Resistance* (Delhi, 1984); Eric Stokes, *The Peasant Armed, The Indian Rebellion of 1857* (Oxford, 1986).

[18] William Coldstream (ed.), *Records of the Intelligence Department of the Government of the North-West Provinces of India during the Mutiny of 1857* (Edinburgh, 1902), p. 61.

at the center of the rebellion rather than on expanding it. The mutiny sparked many revolts but no national revolution. The mutineers instead turned for legitimacy to Mughal and Mahratta princes.

Mutineers and nobles played to religious sentiments and pursued a common front against Britain, but they failed to create one or to control the 100,000,000 people free of British rule. They made no effort to raise or rule the Indian masses. Local movements filled the vacuum. In Awadh and other areas, peasant insurgents attacked the British. Elsewhere, local groups fought each other while most regions remained quiet. This lack of unity reduced the guerrillas to a series of regional problems, which the British could crush, buy, contain, or ignore. Large armies of Indian princes stood uncertain for months and attacked British forces only after the sepoys were smashed. Britain would have lost without support from Indians. Allied Gurkha, Sikh, and Pashtun units provided half of their field forces. The mutiny was one of the few times in the existence of the empire in which British land forces overcame a revolution. They did so because the revolutionaries were divided and lacked several keys to power, the British did not lose complete control over local allies and instruments, and they found new tools to overcome the resistance to their rule.

Mutiny bred massacre. Most captured British officers and civilians were slaughtered. Few mutineers were murderers, but many paid for the sins of the few. The British, believing their rule rested on fear, killed perhaps 100 Indian civilians for every European slain. Soldiers acted spontaneously and officers tolerated or encouraged terror, which the government moved to squelch only once its rule was restored. Terror was less a tool of counterinsurgency than a substitute for it, occurring at a time when Britain had no other means to restore order. The effect was counterproductive; where it wished to make peace, instead British actions created a desert. One commander noted in late 1857, "We have established such a terror, that it is impossible to get anyone to come in."[19] While British anger toward civilians ebbed, they attempted to exterminate every mutineer – with fair success.

At various stages in 1857, upward of 100,000 sepoys were in revolt as members of princely armies or as guerillas. British resources were scant – 53,000 white troops in India or within easy reach, including local European volunteers. Seventy-five percent of them were needed to watch the Bengal and Madras Armies, to cover the peripheries of the revolt,

[19] Ibid., p. 180.

to disband Bengal Army units, and to control 300,000,000 Indians. The rest should have been used to hold the ring, wait for reinforcements, and strike with concentrated and coordinated power, but British commanders believed that quicker action was required. If they did not move fast, commanders believed, the revolt would spread; nor could they abandon civilians in isolated garrisons. Small forces immediately drove to save besieged civilians and to retake Delhi, reinforcements dribbling behind as they arrived. By July 1857, 5,000 British and allied troops stood before Delhi, held by 30,000 mutineers, while another 1,500 moved on Lucknow, against 13,000 enemies, which left just 4,000 British soldiers to garrison 25,000,000 Punjabis. In September 1857, barely 8,000 men, including 2,300 white infantry, were available to assault Delhi. Reinforcements, however, rose steadily – 30,000 British and Indian soldiers took Lucknow in March 1858.

The sepoys had large numbers but little leadership. Few mutineers had commanded 200 men in battle before; none more. Command within their forces was negotiated. Small units fought well, but the sepoys had no artillery and failed to maneuver their units tactically, and they did not establish a strategic conception for victory. They wasted their strength and lost the war. From June through July 1857, mutineers outnumbered British forces at Delhi six to one. But the sepoys failed to use their forces to crush the enemy or to cut British lines of communications. Instead, to prove its loyalty, as each body of mutineers reached Delhi, it marched before British artillery, stopped in the open, exchanged fire, and withdrew. Casualties were devastating and one-sided. British command was unimpaired and able to control new allies. Despite being thrown into ad hoc groupings, the British fought with fanaticism and overwhelming superiority in open combat. Several times on the road to Lucknow, British artillery and riflemen cut up sepoys in line as bayonet charges smashed their flanks and volunteer cavalry completed the slaughter. More effectively, soldiers of the Awadi ex-princely army used irregular tactics of snipers and ambush to force the British to abandon line and volley and launch costly assaults against strongpoints on the roads. By September 1857, mutineer losses were enormous. British losses were heavy as well, with British morale cracking and victory in assaults on towns uncertain. The first force that reached Lucknow on 25 September 1857 was so weak that it left a few reinforcements and withdrew to escort civilians to safety. On 14 September, the British attacked Delhi, shattering both its walls and the British army; 33 percent of assaulting British infantry were casualties. Discipline collapsed and men refused orders, while falling drunk against the wall. A resolute enemy could have won the battle, but instead the mutineers collapsed.

After the reconquest of Delhi, scattered mutineers fought on while princely armies raised minor revolts, but with one exception the peasant insurgency subsided. In 1858, the British advanced again on Lucknow, this time carefully, to minimize casualties from irregulars and to reestablish rule on the ground. When they took Lucknow, its garrison of 15,000 sepoys and 50,000 irregulars simply withdrew into the countryside. The British commander wrote, "the enemy is as formidable after he has been beaten as he was before." Officials estimated that 75 percent of Awadi males fought in a "general, almost universal" revolt.[20] Sepoys proved easier to defeat than guerrillas. Large in numbers, high in morale, and fighting in jungles dotted with forts, guerrillas used irregular tactics among a friendly population. Only ruthless pressure, combined with an amnesty to irregulars and a systematic effort to redress the socioeconomic causes for the rebellion in Awadh, suppressed the guerrillas. The rebels achieved a local victory. Britain won the greater prize.

THE BOER WAR, 1899–1902

The Boer War was not the greatest hybrid struggle the British Empire ever faced, if gauged simply by the enemy's quality in that sphere.[21] It did expose the largest number of personnel, 450,000 men, including volunteer units from Britain and the Dominions, to hybrid warfare. The Boer War, second only to the two world wars among imperial mobilizations, combined conventional with counterinsurgency operations. It forced the British into complex, often new, organizational problems – combining military organizations into formations to conduct combined arms operations for conventional combat, decentralizing them into smaller units for counterguerrilla operations, training large numbers of recruits, radically changing tactics, and testing the most advanced kit of the day. In matters such as command, control, communications, and intelligence; direct and indirect firepower; and combined-arms operations, the battles fought in

---

[20] S. A. A. Rizvi and M. L. Bhargava, eds., *Freedom Struggle in Uttar Pradesh*, Vol. II, *Awadh* (Lucknow, 1958), p. 353, passim.
[21] Thomas Pakenham, *The Boer War* (London, 1979), remains the classic account; cf. Bill Nasson, *The South African War, 1899–1902* (London, Arnold, 1902); Denis Judd and Keith Surridge, *The Boer War* (London, 2002); John Gooch, ed., *The Boer War, Direction, Experience and Image* (London, 2000); Peter Dennis and Jeffrey Grey, eds., *The Boer War: Army, Nation and Empire* (Canberra, 2000).

January and February 1900 were as modern as any in the 20 years before August 1914.

Although the Boer War is remembered for a mediocre British performance, in truth its enemy was little better. The Boers had the opportunity to pursue victory by means of a hybrid strategy or to use conventional forces to overrun British-controlled territory before the British could bring the weight of the Empire to bear. They achieved neither. As the war began, Boers outnumbered the British in manpower and firepower. Although launching short offensives into British territory, the Boers remained strategically passive. They defeated the initial British attacks, but even though British military and political leaders believed that a "considerable section" of the Boer population under their rule would revolt if given the chance, the Boers failed to exploit the resultant opportunities by challenging Britain's hold across South Africa (Figure 7).[22]

When reinforced British forces attacked again, the Boer army collapsed. The Boers recovered somewhat with an irregular campaign, which started well but ended rapidly, far faster than the guerrilla conflicts with the Algerians or Afghans decades before. British counterinsurgency was good; the Boer position was weak, and their command mediocre. From 1899 to 1902, Britain exported abroad more forces prepared for European warfare than it had at any time since the American Revolutionary War. Britain won the war in South Africa because the enemy's conventional forces were weak and its guerrillas vulnerable. Compared to the American Revolutionary War, the forces deployed from Europe were stronger; England retained most of its local military and political allies, instruments, and expertise, rather than losing them to a revolution. Unlike the period from 1776 to 1783, the British were able to insulate the theater from outside aid.

When the war began, the Boers attacked British forces with mixed success. At Mafeking and Kimberley, the Boers marooned 40 percent of their army in futile sieges against untrained paramilitary forces; elsewhere, they scored two minor victories and then waited. The Boer high command was politicized and incompetent. Its army used modern rifles well but, having imported 100 modern artillery pieces and European officers to train Boers in their use, failed to use them to best effect.[23] The Boers fought as they had for generations, which had advantages. They were mediocre at conventional war, finding it hard to coordinate units, let

---

[22] Lord Roberts to War Office, Dispatch 126/1, 6.2.00, WO 105/5.
[23] Ian van der Waag, "Boer Generalship and the Politics of Command," *War in History* 12/1 (2005), pp. 15–43.

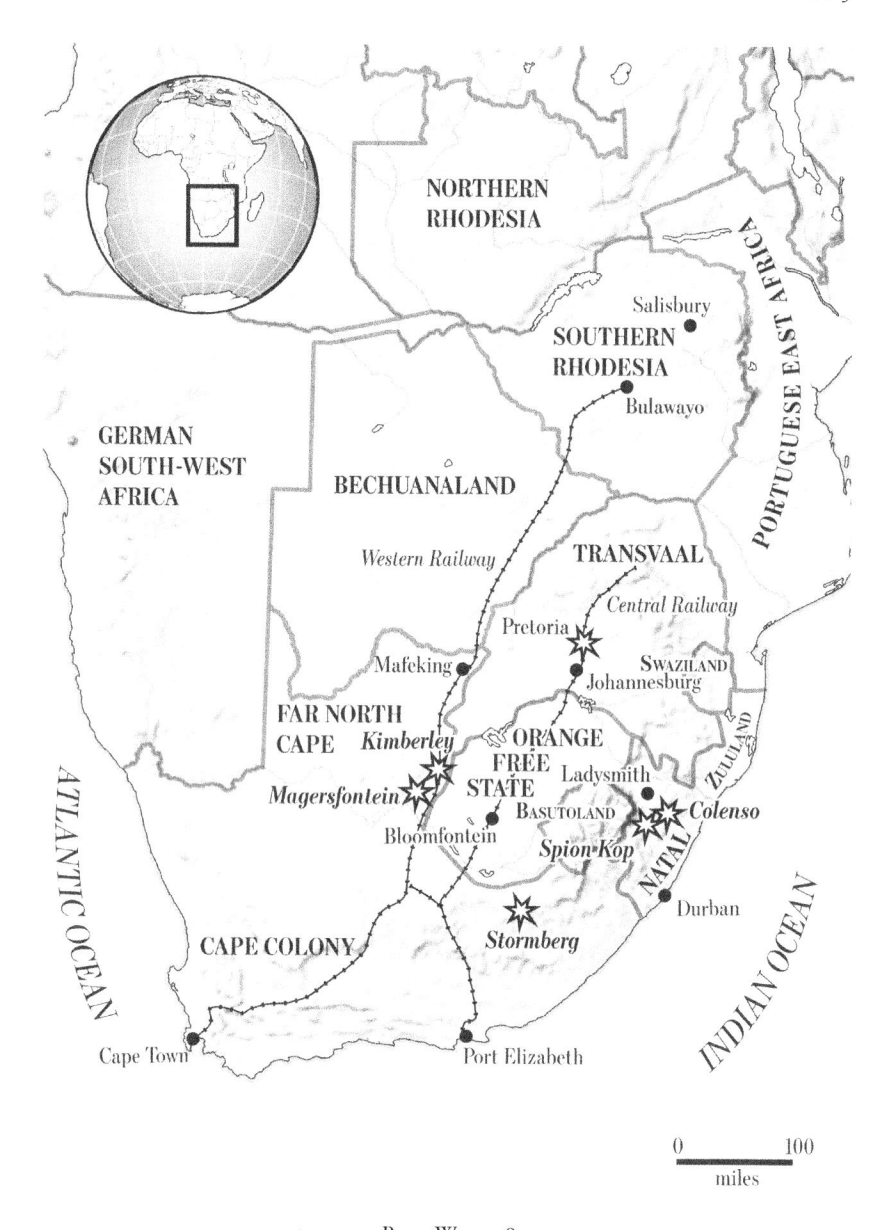

FIGURE 7. Boer War, 1899–1902.

alone formations, or to attack prepared defenses. Still, on the defense, they could put large numbers of riflemen in good (often entrenched) positions, forcing the British into attacks that required combined-arms coordination – a weak link in the British military system.

The British understood the Boer system of warfare, having been humiliated at Majuba in 1881. The Indian army understood the effect of defensive firepower, the need for dispersed order, and how to integrate fire and movement. However, the dominant experiences for forces based in Britain – attacking African phalanxes and unrealistic field maneuvers – convinced many commanders to believe that battle equaled throwing thick bodies of men straight at enemy positions, without coordination or support, under fire. General Buller, who commanded British forces in the initial debacle, had been criticized for precisely these errors during recent exercises in England.[24] These practices produced three humiliating and costly defeats during the "Black Week" from 10 to 17 December 1899.

The British recovered quickly. Capable imperial soldiers took over the forces in South Africa and beat the Boers, in large measure as a result of Boer weaknesses. Despite the ambiguous results of the war, the British implemented no systematic retraining or reappraisal of tactics: They simply doubled the army's strength to five divisions and adopted a new war plan.[25] Although the attacks of February to June 1900 were a success, the story was mixed – the British won where they were strong and the Boers weak, but they failed where the opposite was true. The real triumph was in strategy and operations. The new commanders, Lords Roberts and Kitchener, viewed the theater holistically and planned and executed operations to exploit their strengths and wreck the Boer armies. The breakthrough by one British cavalry division on 15 February 1900 and its exploitation shattered the entire Boer front in a few weeks. It also killed so many horses as to cripple units for months afterward and prevented Roberts from culminating the success with his "intention to follow them up as rapidly as possible and by taking full advantage of the shock which they have sustained to break up their organization as a fighting force."[26]

The failures were largely tactical. Formations did not cooperate well. Infantry understood the need for dispersed order and the integration of fire with movement, but the execution fell short of the understanding.

---

[24] D. M. Leeson, "Playing at War: The British Military Manoeuvres of 1898," *War in History* 15/4 (2008), pp. 432–461.

[25] For the debate on the performance of British forces in the war and their development between 1902 and 1914, cf. Stephen Badsey, "The Boer War (1899–1902) and British Cavalry Doctrine: A Re-Evaluation," *The Journal of Military History* 71 (January 2007), pp. 75–97; and Stephen M. Miller, *Lord Methuen and the British Army, Failure and Redemption in South Africa* (London, 1999).

[26] Roberts to War Office, Dispatch 126/6, 16.2.00, WO 105/6.

Untrained troops could not easily be made competent, although veterans recalibrated better. The debacle of a failed divisional assault against a smaller Boer force at Spion Kop on 23–24 January 1900 underlined the fact that battalions could not coordinate their activities nor commanders handle a complex battle, although the Boers almost cracked under the pressure and never dared such attacks themselves.[27]

The Boer state was broken but not its people. Precisely as the conventional army melted away, its fragments were reformed into guerrilla units. One day soldiers tried to hold a front; the next, they turned to irregular battle, seeking combat through hit-and-run tactics. The Boers capitalized on their strengths. The commandoes, Boer adult males, operated among a friendly population – their families – which provided supplies and intelligence. Fast-moving and straight-shooting horsemen, who knew the terrain, struck precisely against an enemy scattered across a large theater and largely ignorant of the ground. Initially, the Boers scored sensational victories, which, combined with the British practice of burning farms in retaliation for guerrilla raids, drew several thousand Boers back into battle. Guerrillas threatened British logistics and launched their only strategic offensive, an abortive effort to raise Boers under British rule by sending forces to operate among them, too late to turn the tide of the war.

However, by the usual standards of counterinsurgency war, whether measured by force ratios or length of campaign, the British recovered with remarkable speed. Problems of leadership crippled Boer operations as younger men, able but divided, replaced older generals and struggled for position. Only naïve strategists could have thought the Boer population a good base for guerrillas. Instead of being an ocean through which the fish could swim, it was a pond, like the Chinese population during the Malayan insurgency of the 1950s, easy for the ruthless to drain. Rather than adapt to the environment, Kitchener transformed it.

The British credibly reorganized their military structure in South Africa for counterinsurgency warfare. Even though their mobile columns never matched the Boers at irregular warfare, they were good enough to hound the Boers into submission. In the first year of the guerrilla campaign, Boer successes drove British commanders rapidly and ruthlessly up the ladder of escalation. They burned farms as a means first to punish specific individuals or actions and then to coerce the population. Finally, to hasten "the process of exhaustion by capture," as Kitchener called it,

---

[27] Memorandum by General Warren, undated, c. 12.1899, "The Capture and Evacuation of Spion Kop," WO 132/18.

the British conducted a wholesale destruction of the economic resources available to the foe, aiming to force the *volk* onto the veldt, to burden the guerrillas, or else into internment camps, and thereby denying supplies and intelligence to Boer forces.[28]

As a result of British incompetence and indifference, 28,000 Boer civilians (more than 10 percent of their population), along with 20,000 Africans, died in the camps. There were 50,000 British soldiers in blockhouses and another 50,000 in mobile columns that contained and harassed Boer forces, whose willingness to fight played into Kitchener's policy of attrition.[29] The Boers had no reinforcements; every man they lost was imprisoned or dead; and they could neither keep nor kill the thousands of prisoners they took or otherwise make a dent in overall British strength. During the guerrilla war, Boer strength fell from 45,000 to 20,000 men, with 30,000 more in prison camps, and 5,000 fighting in British columns. Many units focused on survival rather than war. Boer forces cracked, fearing, as their commanders agreed, that further resistance risked "the horrid probability" that "our whole nation may die out."[30] The Boers surrendered 24 months after their irregular war began, although in political terms, they gained amnesty and the chance to recover their position. Britain won everything that could be achieved through force, but it proved less successful in exploiting these gains through politics.

THE TWENTIETH CENTURY

The interwar years marked the apogee of Western control over the world, as well as the moment when that control began to fade. Initially, weapons forged for total war bolstered the power of imperial states. Spain, Italy, and the Soviet Union used poison gas to subdue guerrillas. Aircraft routinely attacked opposition, whether warriors, villages, or flocks. British authorities expected "mechanical devices" to replace manpower in imperial policing, with economy and effect, but they were inhibited with their

---

[28] Kitchener to Chamberlain, telegram, 19.6.01, PRO 30/57/19.
[29] S. B. Spies, *Methods of Barbarism? Roberts and Kitchener and Civilians in the Boer Republics, January 1900–May 1902* (Cape Town, 1977); Fransjohan Pretorius, *Scorched Earth* (Cape Town, 2001); id., *Life on Commando During the Anglo-Boer War, 1899–1902* (Cape Town, 1999); Owen Coetzer, *Fire in the Sky: The Destruction of the Orange Free State, 1899–1902* (Johannesburg, 2000); and Alexander B. Downes, "Draining the Sea by Filling the Graves: Investigating the Effectiveness of Indiscriminate Violence as a Counterinsurgency Strategy," *Civil Wars* 9/4, pp. 420–444.
[30] Christiaan de Wet, *Three Year's War* (New York, 1902), Appendix C.

use. Britain never used poison gas in its imperial wars. British authorities applied air policing less ruthlessly than they could have, because they believed this might start more hostilities than it stopped, and because their public would not tolerate indiscriminate attacks on civilians.[31]

Nonetheless, Britain used the tool ruthlessly and precisely, more so than any other power. From 1904 to 1918, Britain lost control of central Somalia to Mohammed bin Abdullah Hassan, the "Mad Mullah of Somaliland." In 1919 and 1920, Britain struck back with 800 paramilitary soldiers, thousands of tribal auxiliaries, and nine aircraft. An air strike against Hassan's encampment wounded him, killed some of his lieutenants, and scattered his flocks, which hostile tribesmen seized. He fled and died. Air power was no more important to his defeat than politics, but it was significant to a hybrid campaign. Between 1921 and 1925, Britain contained a Kurdish rebellion in Iraq through air strikes on guerrillas mounted from garrisoned airfields, supplied by mechanized forces escorted on roads by armored cars. In 1927 and 1928, armored cars and aircraft ended assaults on Iraqi tribes from raiders in Saudi Arabia. In both cases, however, these forces were responsible for only part of the victory, and their limits were notable. In 1929, air policing collapsed in Palestine during riots between Arabs and Jews, and again during the Arab revolt from 1936 to 1939.[32] Air power could not prevent revolts. When they occurred, aircraft became auxiliaries to armies.

Yet, technology and firepower are not everything in war. Britain's hold over its colonies declined from 1929, doubly so after 1945, because of changes in its capabilities and its will to deploy them. Britain's strength in great-power politics; its means to insulate colonies from each other, the world, and public opinion; and the political and diplomatic basis for its power – all of these declined. Britain lost its empire not to force or economics but rather to politics – less will at home, more opposition abroad. Attitudes inhibited actions, particularly rising doubts about the ethics of empire. Organized, sometimes mass, movements, which the British found difficult to comprehend or to defeat through force, subverted its central, political tools of control. Its enemies increasingly acquired modern weapons, raising the cost for any British use of force.

---

[31] James Corum, "The RAF in Imperial Defence, 1919–1956," in Kennedy, *Imperial Defence*, pp. 152–176; John Ferris, *The Evolution of British Strategic Policy, 1919–1926* (London, 1989); David Omissi, *Air Power and Colonial Control, 1919–1939* (Manchester, 1990).

[32] AOC Palestine to Governor, Palestine, 4.9.29, Lord Trenchard Papers, RAF Museum, Hendon, C.II/9; "Notes on Conversation with C.A.S." by S/L Slessor, 4.9.29, AIR 9/19.

More important was the impact of nationalism on native populations. Revolutions occurred across the empire, marked by rising challenges to Britain's presence and to the local leaders who cooperated with it and the loss of control over local levers of power such as police or paramilitary forces. The Indian Army shattered in Britain's hand as it enforced the partition of Punjab, the Jewish Agency subverted its rule in Palestine, and Free Officers movements turned Arab forces from auxiliaries to executioners of empire. By shaking British credibility, each revolution encouraged another, as British means and will to suppress them eroded – a process quickened as the burden and blame for empire were thrust on Britain alone.

British superiority in the strategic niche that underlay empire also declined. Although the real problem was the politics of decolonization, guerrillas were hard to fight. Compared to previous generations, they had better strategy and the means to raise military and political support through conspiratorial or mass movements, whereas Britain could not so easily escalate conflicts any longer with terror tactics or reinforcements from its crumbling empire. The British remained capable of tough actions – internment during counterinsurgencies in Kenya and Malaya may have killed tens of thousands of people – but not as often as before.[33]

Empire no longer was a simple solution to troubles abroad – it was among their chief causes. Britain's problem was not conventional armies or, unlike Jiang Jieshi in China, France in Indochina and Algeria, and the United States in Vietnam, hybrid forces, but rather guerrillas – especially urban terrorists. The latter struck precisely at key vulnerabilities in Britain's system: its reliance on small numbers of specialist officers and local allies, on tolerance by and prestige among subjects, and on walking the fine line between too much and too little presence. Urban terrorists also aimed to enrage British forces so as to provoke overreactions that would prove politically counterproductive. Britain's recalibration of forces for counterinsurgency was good, well above average, as was its performance in the practice, but the rates of success and the return on investment were below that of the previous century. From 1942 to 1954, Britain had far more soldiers abroad than ever before, with better kit, but 100,000 men could not do what 1,000 could do in earlier

---

[33] Hew Bennett, "The Other Side of the COIN: Minimum and Exemplary Force in British Army Counterinsurgency in Kenya," *Small Wars and Insurgencies* 18/4 (December 2007).

decades.[34] Its solutions remained intelligent and adaptive, but the problems became harder.

LESSONS LEARNED

Contemporary strategists often use British history, implicitly and explicitly, as a source for data or models. As with all cases of the imperial analogy, Britain's experience with hybrid warfare is so influential, but subliminal, that if one does not examine it critically, then one will misunderstand the matter as a whole. Its successes were remarkable, but they often stemmed from circumstances that one cannot possibly replicate today. The power of some of its solutions declined over time, and simplistic explanations for its rise and fall prevent useful generalizations. Hybridity was not an abstract matter. It centered on specific competitions and competitors. Britain's experiences with hybridity were not universal, but they are illuminating. They pertain to many areas where irregular or hybrid enemies might be found today. They illuminate aspects of the matter such as the role of dominance in conventional forces; how the need to prepare for hybridity and means to do so affect a military institution; the difficulties that one or one's enemy faces in creating and applying hybrid forces; and the balance sheet.

For Britain, hybridity was both a problem and a solution. Often, the solution overcame a problem that was not hybrid, as when conventional forces were recalibrated to handle irregular warfare. In strategic and operational terms, hybrid war posed unique challenges to the British. No other nation fought so many different forces and won so frequently over such a long period of time. In terms of impact on world politics, the most significant army of modern history was not the German but rather the British. No matter how easy campaigns enabled by Maxim guns might seem, British forces recalibrated tactics, weapons, and leading-edge technology well. In 1879, for instance, as British forces drove up the Khyber Pass, advanced posts of observers on mountains used heliographs to direct guns in the valleys below firing at unseen targets, in an early use of indirect fire.

After 1917, Britain led the development of aerial strike forces in counterinsurgency warfare. The favor could be reversed. Experience

---

[34] John Gallagher, *The Decline, Revival and Fall of the British Empire: The Ford Lectures and Other Essays* (Cambridge, 1982); many of the essays in Kennedy, ed., *Old World Order*, illuminate this issue.

against Mysore and Mahrattas readied Wellington for the Peninsular campaign, where no one was better prepared to flog the French than a sepoy general. Britain adapted weapons fired against it by Mahrattas into Congreve rockets, providing the red glare over Baltimore in 1814, which inspired *The Star Spangled Banner*. The Boer War provided British officers useful experience in modern tactics, especially on the defense. From 1902 to 1914, the British improved their training and coordination between arms and units to a level better than it had been for generations. Through the development of the Territorial Force, spurred by mixed experiences with volunteer units during 1900–1902, Britain came as close as its system allowed to preparing reserve elements in peacetime. These lessons were fundamental to the quality of the British Expeditionary Force in the opening months of the First World War, when despite many problems, British forces performed better than any other in Europe – a remarkable feat for an army of mercenaries, and an imperial one at that.[35] The lessons of the Boer War also aided Britain's mobilization for total war in 1915–1916, when it had to recalibrate its hybrid system to handle a total and conventional war, in which its performance was surprisingly good.

The need for recalibration made British land forces adaptable. Experience in many conflicts gave officers a unique range of expertise, although much of it was not immediately transferable. The experience with counterinsurgency from the Boer War, for example, aided only those rare officers, such as Aylmer Haldane, commander during the Iraq revolt of 1920, who engaged in such conflicts. Britain did well in raising paramilitary forces and in maintaining specialist troops, which institutionalized solutions to problems. Even so, from 1930 onward, the power of its solutions to colonial challenges eroded, for reasons similar to those that afflict Western forces operating in those areas today. Britain had no magic bullet to solve the problem in which guerrillas relied on terrorism.

British forces did well when they had already learned to play an irregular or hybrid game; they did less well when they confronted a hybrid competitor for the first time. In strategic terms, adaptability had an expense: Preparation for colonial warfare hampered the British military's ability to handle conventional, industrialized warfare. British land forces adapted so well to hybrid warfare that their greatest problem became recalibrating to conventional operations. The need to prepare forces for hybrid conflicts, to maintain specialized units abroad, and to garrison the empire

---

[35] Nikolas Gardner, *Trial by Fire: Command and The British Expeditionary Force in 1914* (Westport, CT, 2003).

sapped Britain's ability to concentrate its power and reinforced the army's tendency to decentralize down to battalions, thereby hampering preparation for high-intensity combat in Europe. The cost was notable in the period from 1939 to 1942.

One must take care in extrapolating lessons from the British historical experience with hybrid warfare. In important ways, the British approach to wars in non-Western countries was opposite to that of the United States today. Britain had strategic patience, but it was adamant that empire should pay for itself. So long as the expense, and therefore the relationship between cost and benefits, remained favorable, it could maintain stalemates for generations, as on the Northwest Frontier. In contrast, expensive and unnecessary wars always eroded British will. Britain conquered so much only because it cost so little. During the last days of the Empire, as cost–benefit assessments became bleaker, Britain's patience declined precipitously, reinforced by its increasing doubts about empire.

In recalibrating to so many environments and enemies, Britain's advantages were unified command, rational policy, greater resources, and the weakness and mistakes of its foes. The latter usually were divided and poor at strategy. They rarely possessed able conventional and guerrilla forces that comprise both halves of any hybrid force. Britain's strength stemmed less from technology than command, politics, and the quality of its units and officer corps, which outclassed virtually every enemy. Whether arrayed against Mahrattas or Boers, the primary strength of the British Army was its dominance in high-intensity battle. Often, it could force its foes into decisive battles and generally won when these occurred. Its record was less impressive against guerrillas or irregulars.

Hybrid capabilities were most useful in converting conventional forces to the exigencies of irregular war, as against fighting a hybrid foe, which really were common only in the eighteenth century. For Britain, the normal problem in hybridity was in recalibrating forces from one task to another rather than in handling two competitions at once. Failures occurred when enemy armies became organizationally effective or native peoples became politically stronger. British power, therefore, stemmed largely from matters beyond its control – the decisions of its competitors. Britain had a comparative advantage over its enemies in that it deliberately adopted a hybrid strategy. Its enemies did so only when their preferred solution failed, most often by adopting irregular strategies after their conventional forces were defeated. Britain's enemies did not prepare for hybrid warfare. This type of war was hard to execute, unless it came naturally, which occurred most easily with coalitions. That form of hybridity stemmed not from one institution with two capabilities but rather from an alliance in which various forces specialized in different practices. For Britain's enemies, politics was the biggest bar to the effective use of hybrid capabilities, which were vulnerable not just to a kinetic attack on its constituent parts but also to assaults on its political cohesion. The British did not need to read Sun Tzu to know that attacking an enemy's alliance or strategy was the best, and cheapest, path to victory.

9

An Unexpected Encounter with Hybrid Warfare

The Japanese Experience in North China, 1937–1945

Noboru Yamaguchi

On 7 July 1937, the Second Sino-Japanese War broke out at Lukouchou (the Marco Polo Bridge) with a skirmish between troops of the Chinese Nationalist XXIX Corps and the Japanese Tientsin garrison. Despite the Japanese government's policy of not expanding the conflict, a policy supported by the Imperial Army's general staff, the conflict grew into an all-out war between the two nations. Instead of declaring war, the Japanese government termed the conflict the "North China Incident," which it renamed the "China Incident" two months later as the war in the north quickly expanded to central and south China. The Japanese Army in China, consisting of two infantry brigades with some 5,600 troops in July 1937, expanded to 24 divisions with nearly 800,000 soldiers by 1939.

The eight-year-long Sino-Japanese military conflict, which finally led Japan into the Second World War, was unanticipated by its military establishment in two major respects. First, the strategic concerns of the Japanese Army were primarily a potential confrontation with the Soviets along the northern border with Manchukuo and a possible involvement in a naval war with the United States in the western Pacific. As a potential opponent, China had long been rated secondary to the Soviets and the Americans according to Japanese defense plans.[1] The name "China Incident" underlines the reluctance of the Japanese government to wage a formal war with China. Second, how the Imperial Japanese Army fought the Second Sino-Japanese War was quite different from the type of conflict

---

[1] Akira Fujiwara, *Nihon Gunji-shi (A History of the Japanese Military)*, vol. 1 (Tokyo, 1987), pp. 158–159, 216–217.

it had initially expected and prepared to fight. It was a limited, protracted war against both regular and irregular forces that was quite different from the expected short, decisive conflict. This was particularly true in the case of the Japanese military experience in north China.

There are several reasons for the gap between what Japan anticipated and what its military forces experienced. First, those officers who insisted on securing north China by force aimed at seizing a more favorable strategic position for a war against the Soviet Union. They argued that control of north China would provide security for the rear areas of the Kwantung Army in Manchukuo and its military lines of communication from mainland Japan. As Communist guerrilla forces based along the southern border of Manchukuo threatened the Kwantung Army, the command was eager to destroy those bases as well as the main body of the Communist guerrilla forces. The Japanese Foreign Ministry endorsed this position in a document entitled "On the Chinese Communist Army" issued in August 1937.[2]

Second, because of the fear of the Soviets, the Japanese government, including its military establishment, was not able to concentrate on a war with China. The Second Sino-Japanese War was neither planned nor desired by Japan. Since the Japanese Army had come face to face directly with Soviet military forces after the Manchurian Incident in 1931, the likelihood of a direct confrontation with the Soviets had increased. The Japanese Army urgently needed to build up its capabilities by modernizing its forces, particularly in aviation and mechanization. As opposed to a possible conflict with the Soviet Union, Japan's leaders expected a war with China to be neither all out nor protracted. Obviously, that assumption was flawed.

Third, the available forces were insufficient. At the beginning of the conflict, the general staff estimated that the forces available for deployment to China consisted of only 11 divisions at most, primarily because of the necessity of maintaining a deterrent posture against the Soviets.[3] However, it estimated the Chinese forces moving toward north China in summer 1937 to be 340,000 strong.[4] Accordingly, the general staff

---

[2] Ministry of Foreign Affairs of Japan, *Kokusai Jiji Kaisetsu (A Brief Explanation on Current International Situation)* (Tokyo, 1937), pp. 21–29.
[3] Japan Defense Agency, *Shina Jihen Rikugun Sakusen 1 (Army Operations During the China Incident)*, vol. 1 (Tokyo, 1975), p. 229.
[4] Japan Defense Agency, *Hokushi no Chian-sen 1 (Security Operations in North China)*, vol. 1 (Tokyo, 1968), p. 23.

concluded that Japan should keep the conflict limited and that it should withdraw reinforcements from the Home Islands as soon as possible to avoid an all-out war. The realization that it would be difficult to solve the problem of China without inflicting considerable damage on the main body of the Chinese regular (Nationalist) forces soon compromised this circumspect position.[5] Ironically, Japan's leaders assumed that it was necessary to expand the conflict to avoid total war. In other words, those advocating a limited expansion hoped to force Chinese leaders to terminate the conflict by inflicting heavy losses on Chinese military forces. Accordingly, the Japanese military launched a series of offensives in north China as well as in central China during the latter half of 1937 and early 1938. Because resources remained limited, Japanese forces never reached a level sufficient to destroy the main body of the Nationalist Chinese military forces. More important, the resources spent on the war in China were sufficient to throw the Japanese economy and society into a position as severe as if Japan had launched an all-out war.

Finally, both the Nationalists and Communists pursued a conflict that was clearly protracted, revolutionary, and to a certain extent unconventional in nature. They only had to survive by avoiding destruction in conventional campaigns and waiting until the Japanese had worn themselves out. For the Communists in particular, regular warfare between the Japanese and the Nationalists served their interests, as it weakened their main adversary and increased their domestic political influence when the Japanese won tactical and operational victories. This is not a comment made in hindsight but rather one foreseen by a strategic planner at the time. In July 1937, Major General Kanji Ishihara, who was the director of the operations department of the general staff, warned that Japan would be involved in an endless counterguerrilla war if the conflict with China expanded.

In effect, Japan would repeat what Napoleon Bonaparte had experienced in Spain after his invasion of that country.[6] As a result, the Japanese Army was never able to gain complete control over the territories it conquered. Its control was largely confined to urban areas and the lines of communication linking them, which left large areas outside its span of control. The result was a prime example of hybrid warfare, with regular and irregular warfare intermixed in a fashion that rendered Japan's

---

[5] Ibid., pp. 230–231.
[6] Japan Defense Agency, *Shina Jihen Rikugun Sakusen*, vol. 1, p. 202.

military forces almost irrelevant to the achievement of sensible political goals, which are, after all, why nations fight wars.

MISSIONS AND ORDER OF BATTLE

Prior to the outbreak of the Second Sino-Japanese War in 1937, the Japanese Army deployed the *Kita Shina Chutongun* (Army Force Stationed in North China), or simply the Tientsin garrison, the primary mission of which was to protect Japanese residents in the region as well as to prevent guerrillas from crossing into Manchukuo. The Tientsin garrison consisted of an infantry brigade of two infantry regiments supported by artillery, armor, cavalry, and other elements. The garrison's strength was approximately 5,600 soldiers, an increase of several thousand from the previous year. Although the Chinese armies in the region (which possessed some 150,000 troops) significantly outnumbered the Japanese forces, the augmentation aimed at providing the Tientsin garrison sufficient military force to achieve its political purpose.[7] After the Marco Polo Bridge Incident on 7 July 1937, the army considerably reinforced the garrison. In early September 1937, the general staff activated the North China Army with two army corps and eight combat divisions and other units assigned.[8] The mission given to the North China Army fundamentally differed from that of Tientsin garrison. The North China Army received the mission to occupy and stabilize key areas around Beijing and Tientsin and destroy enemy forces in the central part of Hopei Province. The latter mission was to break the enemy's will to continue the war. Whereas this mission remained fundamentally the same throughout the period from 1937 to 1945, the context confronting the North China Army changed substantially over time. Accordingly, its roles varied from launching major offensives against regular forces, to conducting counter-guerrilla activities involving both military and nonmilitary operations, to providing trained forces for other theaters in the effort to secure natural resources for Japan's war economy. In short, the North China Army experienced various aspects of hybrid warfare from the Marco Polo Bridge Incident to the surrender of Japan in 1945.

In the beginning, the major role of the North China Army was to secure the rear of Manchukuo, the theater where the Japanese military directly confronted Soviet forces. To accomplish this task, the Japanese

---

[7] Ibid., pp. 75–79.
[8] Ibid., p. 290.

Army initially conducted a series of conventional offensive operations against the lightly armed regular forces of the Chinese Nationalists. It also conducted protracted counterguerrilla operations, mainly against the Chinese Communists: These operations lasted until the end of the war. Because its first offensives were relatively successful in clearing Chinese regular forces from its area of responsibility, the North China Army made major efforts to battle irregular forces. In essence, north China became the rear area both for the expeditionary army in central China as well as for the Kwangtung Army deployed in Manchukuo. The former was formed in September 1939 from the main body of the Imperial Army that was locked in a conventional war against the Nationalist forces led by Chiang Kai-shek.

In the meantime, the North China Army played a key role in major offensives, but it confronted serious problems in balancing constabulary missions with its field operations. In spring 1944, the general staff decided to launch a series of large-scale offensive operations throughout China to prevent the allies from building air bases in the region within bomber range of mainland Japan. The North China Army led the first phase in Henan Province along the southern bank of the Yellow River. The main body of the North China Army, consisting of eight divisions and four brigades supported by air elements, advanced some 300 kilometers toward the west and claimed it had destroyed 60 percent of 43 nationalist divisions.[9]

Although the campaign was fairly successful, internal security in north China remained a serious issue for the army. The balance of resources allocated between offensive operations and stability operations represented a major concern for the army, which finally concentrated 67 battalions for the former mission while providing 70 battalions with four divisions and 12 brigades for the latter. This decision rested on the notion that the army should pursue conventional offensives at the expense of internal security, which, nevertheless, was essential to protect the logistical bases required by Japan's war effort. Indeed, the offensive involved most of the better equipped and trained units that were experienced in stability operations and accustomed to their assigned areas. A staff officer assigned to the North China Army's headquarters during the campaign later noted:

> At that time, Tokyo kept requesting the army to secure and send back essential resources such as iron, coal, salt, and cotton to Japan. This caused

[9] Japan Defense Agency, *Kanan no Kaisen (Henan Campaign)* (Tokyo, 1967), p. 72.

a head-on collision between administrative requirements for war resources and operational requirements necessary to carry out offensive campaigns. The Japanese military was destined to face this dilemma because the nation was extremely poor in resources.[10]

Simply put, the North China Army had more missions than it could reasonably achieve with its allocated resources.

The North China Army also became a force provider for other theaters. In the eyes of the high command, the Imperial Army's single most important theater was Manchuria, where the Kwantung Army directly faced Soviet military forces. It expected the North China Army to train and equip units prior to their deployment to Manchuria, where they would face the Red Army, one of the most highly mechanized armies in the world. As war spread to central and southern China after the Marco Polo Bridge Incident, the North China Army began to function as a force provider for other theaters in China as well. From time to time, well-equipped and highly trained divisions assigned to the North China Army reinforced offensives in other parts of China. Toward the end of World War II, after Allied offensives had pushed the Japanese military back in Southeast Asia and the Pacific, such reinforcements deployed from China to bolster island defenses.

In short, the North China Army, while continuously conducting stability operations with dispersed deployments in villages, needed to train and equip its subordinate divisions for conventional operations against three different types of major opponents: lightly armed Chinese Nationalist forces, the heavily mechanized Red Army, and the firepower-intensive U.S. Army and Marine Corps. Training, tactical organization, and equipment differed substantially from one theater to another. This complicated the army's mission as a force provider and sometimes caused confusion. A clear example of this problem occurred in 1943, when the general staff informed the North China Army that several of its divisions were to be deployed to other theaters. In May 1943, the general staff ordered the 17th, 27th, and 36th Divisions to transfer their stability responsibilities to replacement units and concentrate their troops for preparatory training before redeployment. The general staff first directed the 36th Division to train its troops in cold weather, anti-Soviet tactics in Manchukuo; six months later, it redirected the division to train for subtropical operations for a possible deployment to Southeast Asia or the South Pacific.[11]

[10] Ibid., pp. 88–89.
[11] Japan Defense Agency, *Shina Jihen Rikugun Sakusen*, vol. 1, p. 346.

As the war intensified, the requirement to provide reinforcements for other theaters became more urgent. The general staff repeatedly directed army commands in China to ensure that their units were fully prepared for any contingency. The issue of striking a balance between the need to concentrate troops for possible redeployment and the need to disperse troops for stability operations created a chronic dilemma for the North China Army. For training purposes, troops needed to be stationed together in organized units at least at battalion level. However, stability operations required that they disperse at the company, platoon, or even squad level to clear enemy guerrillas in villages and then hold the area they had pacified.

THE ORGANIZATION OF NONMILITARY ACTIVITIES

Irregular warfare in North China required a wide variety of activities conducted by paramilitary organizations. By the time of the Marco Polo Bridge Incident, the army had created special service groups in various places in China to deal with such matters. Although those organizations were officially named *Rikugun-Kikan*, which literally means army organizations, they were generally called *Tokumu-Kikan*, meaning special service groups, which functioned as secret service units.[12] Their mission was to support regular army commands by conducting political, economic, cultural, and intelligence activities that varied from group to group.

ARMY SPECIAL SERVICE GROUPS

When the Marco Polo Bridge Incident took place in July 1937, there were three major special service groups in charge of political affairs in north China: the Hopei (Beijing) group, the Tungchow group, and the Tientsin group. The general staff established smaller groups in Tsingtao, Taiyuan, Tsinan, and Changchiakou at the end of 1937. The three major groups, which functioned as executive organizations for the Japanese military establishment in China, were in charge of political and administrative affairs including preparation for establishing puppet governments in their areas of responsibility. Their activities were under the control of the chief of staff of the Tientsin garrison, which formed the basis of the North China Army.

[12] Ibid., p. 4.

Their activities, however, were neither well organized nor highly integrated under the garrison's control. There were several reasons for this lack of coherence. First, the Japanese government and the military establishment in Tokyo never reached a consensus on a single policy for Sino-Japanese relations. In particular, there was no consensus over an exit strategy except for the vague hope of settling the China issue as early as possible. Without concrete and consistent directions issued to the special service groups in China, there was no overarching strategy for their activities. Second, bureaucratic turf battles existed among the general staff in Tokyo, the Kwantung Army in Manchukuo, and the Tientsin garrison stationed near Beijing. While each possessed considerable influence, the Kwantung Army, which achieved a de facto parity with the general staff in Tokyo after the Manchurian Incident, was eager to intervene in north China because of its special interests. Although north China was out of its area of responsibility, the Kwantung Army had long insisted on securing north China as a prelude to war with the Soviets.[13] Because the Kwantung Army confronted a major threat from the north, it was regarded as the single most important command within the Imperial Army, and it had remarkable influence over decision-making processes within the Japanese military establishment. Finally, the Tientsin garrison, responsible for political affairs in north China, lacked the capabilities to plan and control such activities. Thus, each group tended to carry out its political maneuvers based on its own judgment and interests. Moreover, there was considerable intergroup rivalry in expanding spheres of influence of each of the local Chinese puppet governments.[14]

SPECIAL SERVICE SECTION OF THE NORTH CHINA ARMY

In early September 1937, when the North China Army activated, it established the special service department within the army's headquarters to assume staff responsibility for planning and controlling the political, administrative, and economic activities of the army's operations in north China. Major General Seiichiro Kita became the first chief of the section; his primary concern was to establish a puppet administration within the army's area of responsibility.[15]

---

[13] Fujiwara, *Nihon Gunji-shi*, p. 218.
[14] Lincoln Li, *The Japanese Army in North China 1937–1941: Problems of Political and Economic Control* (Tokyo, 1975), p. 49.
[15] Ibid., pp. 52–53.

From its start, the special service section became a large and strong administrative unit within the headquarters. The number and the rank structure of the staff officers assigned to it were comparable with those of the operational staff section, which was traditionally regarded as the most important part of the headquarters of higher commands. This was a reflection of the army's recognition of the importance of nonmilitary activities for counterguerrilla campaigns. As a staff organization, the section divided into four divisions: the planning division, in charge of policy and strategy; the first division, in charge of transportation, communications, postal service, and construction; the second division, in charge of economic matters; and the third division, in charge of industrial matters.[16] All of the military advisors assigned to Japanese-sponsored Chinese army units and the personnel assigned to special service groups answered to Major General Kita. As of 14 April 1938, approximately 160 military and civilian personnel, including three general officers, were formally listed on the section's organizational chart. In addition, a little more than 1,000 members of the pacification corps (see later text) had come under control of the section by early 1938.

The section played an important role in establishing the provisional government in Beijing. In its feasibility study report in October 1937, the section recommended that the new regime in Beijing should be a national government as opposed to a local administrative organization. The North China Army sent the chief of the planning division, Colonel Hiroshi Nemoto, to Tokyo to explain the reasons for this recommendation: Prominent Chinese leaders would not join to head a local government; the establishment of a local regime would provoke accusations that Japan was aiming to divide China; and a local regime would be easily overwhelmed by the Nationalist government in Nanjing.[17] With the support of the Kwantung Army, the general staff and the ministry of war accepted this recommendation in late November 1937. As a result of the work by the special service section, the provisional government was created on 14 December 1937 under Wang K'e-min, who was an able technocrat in the former Beijing government. Japanese leaders expected this regime to establish control over the puppet administrations in Beijing, Tientsin, and Tungchow.[18] Ten days later, the *Hsin-min Hui* (New People's Association) was created as a political organization favorable

---

[16] Japan Defense Agency, *Hokushi no Chian-sen*, vol. 1, pp. 42–43.
[17] Ibid., p. 44.
[18] Li, *The Japanese Army in North China*, p. 54.

to the provisional government with the support of Major General Kita.[19] The special service section also sent liaison officers to key positions in the provisional government and *Hsin-min Hui*, through whom the North China Army hoped to exercise control over political and administrative affairs. By integrating the activities of the special service groups, the liaison personnel, and the pacification corps, the North China Army's special service section became one of the most influential elements in executing Japanese policies in China. This arrangement continued until late 1938, when the China Affairs Board (*Koa-in*) and its liaison offices assumed responsibility.

THE PACIFICATION CORPS

The Kwantung Army developed the concept of the *Sembu-han* (pacification corps) in Manchuria in 1933, when it conducted an offensive operation in Jehol.[20] The idea sprang from the need of the private sector to protect the railroads in Manchuria by mobilizing the rural population for self-defense and local security. The South Manchurian Railway Company, a state-sponsored company with considerable intelligence capabilities, sent its pacification corps officers to work with army troops during military operations along the railroads. Because the corps proved to be effective in conducting battlefield propaganda and establishing local security arrangements, the Kwantung Army later decided to include the corps within its military structure.[21]

In early August 1937, a few weeks after the Marco Polo Bridge Incident, approximately 50 experienced propaganda personnel transferred to north China from the South Manchurian Railway Company to form the core of the pacification corps of the Tientsin garrison.[22] These individuals had experience in organizing Chinese civilian personnel in the countryside to secure road and railways against guerrilla attacks during the Manchurian Incident and the establishment of Manchukuo. The strength of the pacification corps increased to approximately 800 by the end of 1937, and to more than 1,000 by the end of 1938.[23] The first 50 members of the corps were divided into seven sections and deployed in the

---

[19] Japan Defense Agency, *Hokushi no Chian-sen*, vol. 1, p. 76.
[20] Li, *The Japanese Army in North China*, p. 189.
[21] Shunjiro Aoe, *Dai-Nihongun Sembu Kan* (*Japanese Army Pacification Corps Officers*) (Tokyo: Fuyo Shobo, 1970), p. 78.
[22] Li, *The Japanese Army in North China*, p. 189.
[23] Japan Defense Agency, *Hokushi no Chian-sen*, vol. 1, p. 78.

important sectors along the Beijing–Shanhaiguan Line to organize local populations to protect the railroads. As Japan's occupation expanded and the number of its members increased, the corps became involved in various other aspects of pacification. Members of the corps conducted pacification activities with army troops during operations or were stationed separately in designated villages. On entering villages with army units, corps officers were responsible for eliminating anti-Japanese posters and literature and replacing them with pro-Japanese propaganda materials. They would round up local inhabitants to give them lectures and dramatic performances praising the cause of Sino-Japanese cooperation and justifying Japan's activities in China.

The corps was initially under the control of the propaganda section of the North China Army but later transferred to the special service section in January 1938. On 22 December 1937, the North China Army issued *Gun Senkyo Chi-iki Chian Jisshi Yoryo* (*Guidelines on Maintenance of Internal Security Measures in Occupied Areas*), which outlined the corps' functions and relations with operational units and special service groups as well as general directions on internal security affairs. According to the guidelines, members of the corps would either be attached to operational units or stationed in villages by request of the respective army's subordinate commands or special service groups. The corps officers would be under the control of the operational unit when issues related to security, or were under the control of a particular special service group in charge of the area when issues dealt with politics, administration, or the economy.[24] The special service section of the North China Army was responsible for developing plans for employment of the pacification corps and for exercising overall control of its activities in its area. The guidelines also stated that recommendations and requests from subordinate commands and special service groups responsible for security and political affairs in their respective areas of responsibility were supposed to be reflected in this planning process. This arrangement continued until the corps' function was transferred to *Hsin-min Hui*, local political organizations, and the North China Railway Company in March 1940.[25]

With regard to the corps' activities, there were several basic problems. As the political arm of the North China Army, the pacification corps and the special service groups had difficulties in cooperating with one another. Whereas special service groups tended to rely on secret political

[24] Aoe, *Dai-Nihongun Sembo Kan*, p. 87.
[25] Li, *The Japanese Army in North China*, pp. 194–195.

activities, covert action, and political plotting, members of the pacification corps were inclined to be too idealistic to pursue such clandestine approaches; they also tended to lack proficiency in dealing with administrative affairs.[26] In addition to this difference in basic attitudes, the status of pacification corps officers was neither stable nor prestigious. They were not formal members of the Japanese Army but rather only temporarily employed officials, whom soldiers jokingly ranked next to army horses and carrier pigeons.[27] The special service groups, in contrast, mainly consisted of elite officers graduated from the Army War College. These differences in status and basic approach toward civil affairs caused rivalry between the two organizations and added to the difficulties involved in integrating their efforts.

Another problem resulted from the acts of Japanese nationals in China, which provoked resentment among Chinese inhabitants. Takeo Yaginuma, one of the founding members of the pacification corps in the aftermath of the Manchurian Incident, lectured young pacification corps officers that their primary role was not necessarily to pacify the Chinese people but rather to educate Japanese soldiers, officials, and merchants in China.[28] Indeed, most of military documents concerning Japanese policy on maintaining internal security in north China repeatedly emphasized the importance of discipline on the part of the Japanese to maintain decent relations with the Chinese. In recollections of former members of the pacification corps, one finds numerous cases in which the actions of Japanese nationals ruined the effort to win the hearts and minds of the rural population.[29]

THE *KOA-IN* AND ITS LIAISON OFFICES

To deal with various aspects of the problems in China, the Japanese government tried to modify the cabinet system. After a year of intensive debates, it established the *Koa-in*, or the China Affairs Board, responsible for planning and executing Japanese policies on politics, administration, economy, and culture in China. Prime Minister Fumimaro Konoye became the president of the board; the foreign, financial, navy, and war ministers received appointments as vice presidents. Lieutenant General

---

[26] Aoe, *Dai-Nihongun Sembo Kan*, pp. 84–87.
[27] Ibid.
[28] Ibid., pp. 110–111.
[29] Ibid., pp. 252, 272–273.

Heisuke Yanagawa became the board's first director and received semi-cabinet member status.

Throughout the process of establishing the China Affairs Board, intensive debates occurred over bureaucratic interests among the relevant ministries. The foreign ministry strongly opposed the board's establishment because it would diminish the ministry's sphere of influence in executing foreign policy by depriving it of its authority in diplomatic affairs. The opposition of the foreign ministry was so serious that Foreign Minister Kazushige Ugaki resigned. Nonetheless, the military establishment in Tokyo supported the creation of a ministry-level organization that would integrate the activities of the Japanese government in China. To the other ministries, it seemed that the army's position on this issue might help them regain the right to participate in the policy-formulation process on problems concerning China. As a result, the foreign ministry found itself sidelined while the other civilian ministries retained formal policy control by sacrificing the foreign officials' fiefdom.

In the meantime, the army's overseas commands also presented their positions on the establishment of the China Affairs Board and its liaison offices in China. Despite strong support from the general staff in Tokyo, the North China Army was not willing to share control over occupied territories in China with civilian elements of the government. The North China Army insisted that the responsible military commands should exercise administration of occupied areas and that a new civilian organization might confuse already established procedures for governing occupied territories.[30] Its fear of confusion and redundancy was realized when civilian liaison offices were created throughout China.

In March 1939, the new arrangement for the administration of north China was set up with liaison offices in Beijing and Changchiakou. Most staff officers assigned to the special service section of the North China Army's headquarters and special service groups found themselves transferred to the newly established liaison offices with their former jobs and additional civilian capacities. For example, Major General Seiichi Kita and Colonel Hiroshi Nemoto, who had occupied the number one and number two positions at the former special service section, became the director and the deputy director, respectively, of the liaison office in Beijing. Major General Takashi Sakai, the former chief of the special service group in Changchiakou, assumed responsibilities as director of the liaison office in the region. Other ministries also sent representatives to

[30] Japan Defense Agency, *Hokushi no Chian-sen*, vol. 1, pp. 109–110.

liaison offices in China as well as to the central office in Tokyo to protect their influence. Accordingly, the China Affairs Board, including its liaison offices in China, consisted of groups representing the different interests of various bureaucratic agencies.

The North China Army was reluctant to lose control over political and economic affairs in its area by transferring its authority to the liaison office, a nonmilitary organization. To retain influence in nonmilitary activities, the army formed a new division within its operational staff, the responsibilities of which were similar to those of the former special service section. Special service groups also remained under control of the army. As a matter of fact, the military continued to influence the activities of the China Affairs Board's liaison offices by assigning staff officers to key positions in those organizations, by restricting the board's responsibilities as much as possible, and by using the special service groups as executing agents in the field – which the board lacked and was never able to organize under its control.

The general staff in Tokyo expected to achieve two results with the board's creation. First, the board and its liaison offices would relieve the field commands of the complex aspects of political, economic, and social aspects of the war, so that they could concentrate their energy on conducting purely military operations. Second, a central organization would integrate efforts to resolve nationwide problems in China. Both of these goals were hard to accomplish. In the North China Army, the newly established board created more complicated procedures both in integrating interministry efforts and in exercising military influence on nonmilitary affairs. Despite the China Board's mission, the military remained deeply involved in political affairs. As the war intensified and substantial numbers of its units redeployed to other theaters, it became apparent that such involvement acted as a drag on the maintenance of tactical effectiveness.

In March 1943, the authority for nonmilitary affairs in China was transferred to the civilian bureaucracy of the Japanese government, a shift that aimed to relieve field armies from administrative matters so that units deployed in China could concentrate on the military aspects of the war and training for potential redeployment to other theaters, where the Allies were severely punishing Japan's forces. Directions from Tokyo noted that army forces should strictly focus on military affairs, while transferring administrative matters, including internal security, to Chinese authorities as much as possible in cooperation with organizations of the Great East Asia Affairs Ministry in China. The directions specifically ordered the abolishment of the fourth division of the North China Army's headquarters, which had replaced the former special service section in 1938 when the China Affairs Board was established. This was a serious reflection on the army's leadership, including field commanders in China. General Yasuji Okamura, commander of the North China Army (1941–1944), noted on 7 January 1943 that "To date, the Japanese side, the military in particular, has tended to be too assertive in administrative and economic aspects and to ignore Chinese positions hindering the Chinese side from exercising its own initiative.... The army should return to the basic principle as a military force."[31] The general's comment accurately reflected the concern of commanders at all levels for nonmilitary affairs. Even company-grade officers were more interested in political and economic affairs than combat efficiency. For the purpose of the war effort as a whole, the North China Army was to assume its original roles to protect rear areas and to provide forces for other theaters.

STABILITY OPERATIONS

The North China Army, using its political arm as well as its combat elements, attempted to pacify its assigned territories. While launching and participating in several conventional campaigns, the army continued to place great emphasis on counterguerrilla activities involving political, economic, and cultural means, as well as search-and-destroy operations.

On 22 December 1937, the North China Army issued *Gun Senkyo Chi-iki Chian Jisshi Yoryo* (*Guidelines on Maintenance of Internal Security Measures in Occupied Areas*). The document provided subordinate elements with guidance for conducting activities to restore and maintain security in the army's area of responsibility. By this time, the army had become aware that the major obstacles to a successful occupation were guerrilla activities and an unstable economic situation, that the local administrations run by Chinese officials were not yet ready to assume overall responsibility for the maintenance of public order, and that it needed to assist the pacification corps and special service groups in their activities along with pursuing military efforts to suppress guerrilla activities.[32]

---

[31] Japan Defense Agency, *Hokushi no Chian-sen*, vol. 2 (Tokyo: Asagumo Simbun-sha, 1971), pp. 311–312.
[32] Japan Defense Agency, *Hokushi no Chian-sen*, vol. 1, p. 53–57.

In recognition of this situation, the document outlined a basic concept of stability operations, relations among the responsibilities of subordinate organizations, and major considerations and basic procedures for conducting such operations. The following points emphasized by the directive are noteworthy to understand the nature of stability operations in the early phase of the war in north China:

1. Military stations and their lines of communication must be secured first; then these areas should be expanded. That is, first secure points, then lines of communications, and finally areas.
2. Military operations against Communist guerrilla forces, especially those attempting to destroy their bases, should have the highest priority.
3. With the exception of Communist guerrillas, surrendering insurgents must be given amnesty and provided with regular job opportunities as much as possible.
4. Local populations must be mobilized to form local police forces, self-defense troops, and railway security guards. For this purpose combat units should provide them with adequate training.
5. Since pacification activities aim to gain trust and enhance the local population's understanding of Japanese policies, the bad actions of Japanese nationals, which might cause distrust, must be strictly watched and prohibited.
6. Communist insurgents must be mopped up completely. For this purpose, counter-guerrilla operations accompanied by propaganda activities should be directed against areas under the influence of the Communists. Every possible means should be applied to separate non-Communist insurgents from Communist guerrillas. Communist insurgents based in foreign concessions in cities should be detected and eliminated by the Japanese military police or Chinese police (not Japanese field army units).
7. To enable army units to concentrate their primary efforts on defeating insurgents and protecting bases, administrative matters such as directing local governments, which are currently managed by those units, should be transferred to special services or the pacification corps as soon as possible.[33]

This document represented the first comprehensive directive on various aspects of counterinsurgency activities, and it clearly emphasized the threat of Communist guerrilla forces to stability in north China.

After the Xuzhou campaign in May and June 1938, the North China Army launched intensive counterinsurgency operations. Because a considerable portion of the forces drawn for the Xuzhou campaign came from the army's area of responsibility, relative combat power favored

---

[33] Ibid.

the Communist guerrilla forces. As a result, the Communists rapidly expanded their influence, especially in the mountainous area of Shansi.[34] The North China Army developed plans to destroy these Communist bases and restore control over these areas. On 17 July 1938, the Army issued *Gun Senkyo Chi-iki Chian Shukusei Yoko* (*Guidelines for Promotion of Internal Security in the Occupied Areas*) to guide its effort. Although this document basically followed the guidelines of the previous directive, several points are noteworthy:

1. The major objectives of stability operations are to clear Communist guerrillas from the occupied areas and to neutralize their tactics so that political, economic, and social stability can be restored. By achieving such objectives, stability operations would deteriorate the enemy's will and its hope to prolong its resistance, thus supporting the overall purpose to resolve the problems in China as soon as possible.
2. Operational units conducting mopping-up operations in villages are responsible for establishing and assisting *China Iji Kai* (local Committees for Public Safety) early in the operation. Commanders of such units should exercise control over these committees through specialists from the pacification corps or military police units. When local authorities become responsible, such responsibilities should be transferred to special service groups.
3. The army's special service groups should put the highest priority on restoring internal security when advising Chinese authorities.
4. *Tetsudo Aigo Son* ("Railway Protection Villages") should be established within a radius of ten kilometers from railroads. In order to cover the shortage of Japanese manpower, the local population of these villages should be mobilized to protect the railways.
5. Surrendering insurgents, especially those who are as well trained as regular forces, are encouraged to join the regular forces of the Chinese provincial governments. Japanese operational units should provide them with training.[35]

These guidelines, along with those previously issued, formed the basis for subsequent counterinsurgency operations in north China.

The North China Army conducted a series of aggressive activities, which included military operations and other activities, to restore public safety throughout 1939 and into 1940. These operations were well organized and by mid-1940, the North China Army was able to restore security and political stability in a considerable part of its area. Among

---

[34] Japan Defense Agency, *Snina Jihen Rikugun Sakusen*, vol. 1, p. 214.
[35] Japan Defense Agency, *Hokushi no Chian-sen*, vol. 1, pp. 214–218.

the various operational and administrative documents concerning stability operations, *Chian Shukusei Yoko* (*Guidelines on Promotion of Internal Security*), issued by the army's headquarters on 20 April 1939, was most significant in influencing internal security in north China over the following two years. This directive included a set of ideas not found in the former two documents.[36]

First, it explained the fundamental ideas and attitudes necessary for stability operations in occupied territories. While emphasizing the importance of impressing the local population with the high morale and disciplined behavior of the Japanese troops as well as the ideals of Japanese policy, it clearly underlined the importance of providing the locals with more visible benefits, such as subsidies and prizes for cooperative individuals and organizations.

Second, the directive emphasized the importance of the psychological dimensions of counterinsurgency operations. Following the articles regarding the mission statement and general guiding principles, the third article of the directive described the army's serious concerns on how to win the hearts and minds of locals. Along with the necessity of showing the strength of Japanese troops through vigorous clearing operations, the directive stated that it was essential to display the discipline of units and soldiers to win the population's trust. Inattentive and bureaucratic attitudes in conducting anti-guerrilla operations, ill-disciplined actions, and arrogant or violent behavior toward the locals were listed as absolutely forbidden to avoid a negative psychological impact on the population.

Third, the directive indicated its concern over a lack of understanding of nonmilitary factors among the field units. It noted that chiefs of staff at the division level were responsible for coordination between military and other activities of respective commands through supervision of special service groups. It particularly emphasized that chiefs of staff should understand the nature of the activities of special service groups and should treat them with sympathy so that they could maximize their performance. This stipulation undoubtedly reflected the fact that there was friction between special service groups and operational field units and that military officers in field units had difficulty with understanding the characteristics and importance of the activities of special service groups.

Fourth, the directive outlined the tactical doctrine of how divisions should disperse their troops throughout their respective areas of

---

[36] Ibid., pp. 116–130.

responsibility. It was essential for troops to remain in villages after an operation to prevent Communist guerrillas from reoccupying them. The document emphasized that dispersion of troops should not be considered as a defensive tactic but rather as an offensive one that would detect Communist activities as early as possible and enable the launching of timely counterguerrilla offensive operations.

COMBAT OPERATIONS IN NORTH CHINA

While the North China Army found itself deeply engaged in pacification activities and at the same time provided other theaters with reinforcements, the army itself conducted a series of purely military operations to secure its area of responsibility (Figure 8). These operations underlined the nature of hybrid warfare with two distinct types of operations. First, the army conducted a series of offensive operations against lightly armed Nationalist regular forces and the private armies of former warlords. It destroyed the latter almost completely in the early phase of the conflict. The second category was anti-guerrilla operations, mainly conducted against the Chinese Communist Army, whose strength continued to increase as hostilities continued.

Although the results were not decisive enough to terminate the conflict, the Japanese Army in general fought the conventional war in a skillful fashion. Following the Marco Polo Bridge Incident, the reinforced Tientsin garrison, with some 40,000 troops, launched offensive operations against the Chinese XXIX Corps of some 100,000 troops. After a few days of intensive combat, Japanese troops completely defeated the numerically superior XXIX Corps and compelled it to withdraw from the Beijing–Tientsin area. Despite their inferiority in numbers, Japanese soldiers fought successfully because they were well trained in conventional operations. Furthermore, their opponents were inferior in mobility and firepower and fought in a manner that played to Japanese strengths.

In the North China Army's area, however, major offensive campaigns sometimes worsened the situation. The retreat of the Chinese regular forces, which were willing to trade space for time, into China's vast interior lengthened the conflict and thereby endangered the overall Japanese war effort. Japan's most serious concern remained Soviet forces in Siberia, while the resources available to Japan remained limited. By late 1938, the Japanese Army had completely lost its momentum. In effect, the army had exhausted 24 divisions in China while holding 8 in Manchukuo and 1 in Korea. Only one division was left on mainland Japan as a strategic

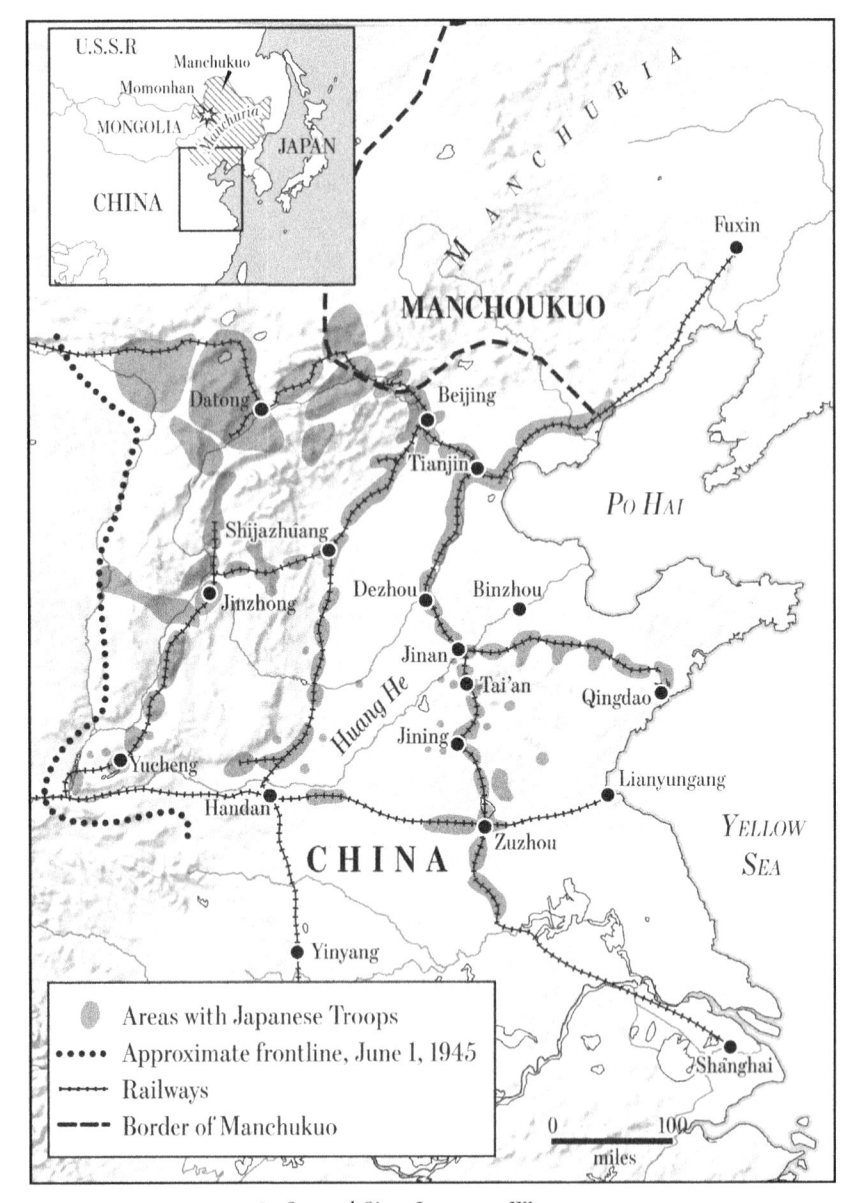

FIGURE 8. Second Sino-Japanese War, 1937–1945.

reserve.[37] Contrary to the prevailing wisdom, these offensives significantly exacerbated the difficulties the Japanese had in north China in their struggle against Communist guerrillas.

[37] Shinobu Oye, *Nihon no Sanbohonbu* (*Japan's General Staff*) (Tokyo, 1985), p. 185.

THE COMMUNIST GUERRILLA THREAT

Until 1937, a handful of warlords ruled north China. Japanese forces fighting conventional battles defeated these warlords early in the conflict. The main theater of war then moved to central and southern China, where the Japanese Army fought Chiang Kai-shek's Nationalist army. North China thereafter became a relatively unimportant theater, which enabled the Communists to expand their influence, initially in Shansi Province in July 1937.[38]

In December 1936, the Sian Incident had forced Chang Kai-shek to cease the civil war and establish cooperative arrangements with the Communists. As the Marco Polo Bridge Incident and the following Japanese invasion provoked a rise of Chinese nationalism, the cooperation between these two internal enemies had accelerated. In August 1937, the Nationalists and the Communists agreed to establish a unified front against the Japanese. The Eighth Route Army, which was reorganized from the Red Army as part of the unified front with the Nationalists, moved into the mountainous area of Shansi Province in September 1937 and began conducting large-scale anti-Japanese guerrilla warfare in northern China.

These Communist guerrilla forces regularly launched raids against weak and dispersed Japanese forces, located in combat outposts and logistical convoys. The guerrillas also sabotaged railways, roads, and communication cables. These tactics were particularly effective because the majority of Japanese forces responsible for conducting stability operations were thinly deployed in small units stationed in remote villages. The raids became more effective as the Japanese troops became even more dispersed.

The Communists, while vigorously fighting against the Japanese, were eager and assiduous in expanding their sphere of influence whenever they saw exploitable opportunities. A typical example occurred during and immediately after the Xuzhou campaign in May 1938, when the North China Army concentrated considerable forces to launch an offensive operation, which reduced the number of troops available for internal security. The Eighth Route Army took advantage of this opportunity to expand its influence in north China, establishing what it called "liberated zones" in the areas devoid of Japanese troops.

At approximately this time, Mao Tse Tung, in his work "On Protracted War," outlined the three phases of his grand strategy in fighting a war

---

[38] Li, *The Japanese Army in North China*, p. 24.

against Japan: the first phase, a period that allowed the Japanese offensives to occupy the Canton–Wuhan–Lanchow areas; the second phase, when such offensives culminated as Japanese forces lost momentum; and the third phase, when Communist forces could launch a counteroffensive operation to recover the territories occupied by the Japanese. Mao argued that the Chinese guerrilla forces could wear out Japanese troops through the first and second phases, which would establish the conditions for a successful conventional offensive in the third phase.[39]

ORGANIZATION AND TRAINING FOR COUNTERGUERRILLA OPERATIONS

The Wuhan Campaign had begun in June 1938, but it stalled two months later without imposing decisive damage on the main body of the Chinese regular forces. Military planners in Japan decided to prepare for a protracted war by redeploying their forces into a strategic-defensive posture. During this period, a number of independent combined brigades, an organizational structure specifically designed for defensive operations within occupied territories, were activated and sent to north China. Although lacking firepower and the ability to maneuver, such brigades, with their 5,000-man strength, were suitable for small-scale, independent operations in relatively wide areas because of their enhanced command and control capabilities and five subordinate battalions.[40] Similar attempts to organize for counterinsurgency warfare occurred at the division level as the Imperial Army activated divisions specifically designed for stability operations rather than conventional field operations. In total, six such divisions and 14 independent, combined brigades had deployed to north China by 1939.[41]

However, the quality of these units remained in question. Most in the army regarded these divisions and brigades as second-class units because of the nature of operations in which they found themselves. Light infantry combat operations, including counterguerrilla operations, were not considered primary missions for the Japanese Army. First-class units were still expected to fight in high-intensity combat against the regular forces of the Soviet Union, the Chinese Nationalists, and later the United States.

---

[39] Mao Tse Tung, "On Protracted War," in Jay Mallin, ed., *Strategy for Conquest: Communist Documents on Guerrilla Warfare* (Coral Gables, FL, 1970), pp. 71–74.
[40] Japan Defense Agency, *Hokushi no Chian-sen*, vol. 1, pp. 59–60.
[41] Japan Defense Agency, *Shina Jihen Rikugun Sakusen*, vol. 2, pp. 299–300.

Accordingly, the quality of the officers and enlisted personnel assigned to such counterinsurgency units was not high. Nevertheless, operations against unconventional forces were complex and required tactical sophistication and initiative from front-line leaders, particularly given their independent nature. Consequently, the army should have aimed at having the most outstanding officers and noncommissioned officers in these units.[42]

In contrast, there was an attempt to create an elite unit specialized in counterinsurgency operations in the final phase of the war. In September 1943, the north China special security force was organized with intelligence, counterintelligence, and combat capabilities. It was specifically designed to deal with the Communists, whose influence kept growing, particularly in the latter half of the war. The core of this organization was the main body of the military police corps in north China, which had been exceptionally effective in gathering information on the underground operations of the Communists.

Nevertheless, military police units lacked the necessary combat capabilities to destroy the underground bases of the Communists they detected. To remedy this defect, some 1,600 members out of 2,600 in the military police corps in north China, who specialized in political affairs, were transferred to the new organization under a two-star, military-police general.[43] With additional augmentation from combat units, the security force initially consisted of five security battalions and other special units with roughly 5,800 troops and 5,600 civilians. The unit also had capabilities for scientific investigation as well as for analyzing Communist political activities. With such capabilities, the new organization was fairly successful in arresting Communist organizers and seizing arms caches, as well as killing guerrillas in combat. Nevertheless, the effectiveness of the new organization was somewhat questionable for a number of reasons. Although it was good at operations in urban areas, it was not effective in rural areas, where the Communists positioned their major bases. Moreover, most of the leaders with military-police backgrounds did not have experience in commanding combat operations. As a result of their harsh attitude toward suspects, the unit personnel did as much political damage as they enjoyed military success.

As for army training in general, the Japanese Imperial Army placed little emphasis on stability operations because of its preoccupation with

---

[42] Japan Defense Agency, *Hokushi no Chian-sen*, vol. 1, pp. 597–598.
[43] Japan Defense Agency, *Hokushi no Chian-sen*, vol. 2, pp. 431–438.

the Soviet threat. Troops stationed in China were no exception. A report on an inspection of the Tientsin garrison's training in May 1937 almost entirely ignored the readiness of troops to conduct operations against Communist guerrillas. The report stated, "It is appropriate for the garrison to train its troops primarily for anti-Soviet operations and secondarily for anti-China operations." The latter referred to combat operations against lightly armed regular forces. Despite the serious concern about Communist guerrillas in northern China expressed by military planners, there was little evidence that Japanese troops were prepared for unconventional warfare. According to an operations officer of one battalion of the 2nd Independent Brigade, even in 1938, the second year of the conflict, army units deployed to north China for counterguerrilla tasks in many cases began training for such operations only after deployment.[44] The brigade provided five days of education to the operations officers of its subordinate battalions and then five days of irregular warfare training that was totally new to the officers.[45] They then returned to their respective units and trained their troops on irregular warfare at the same time their units initiated actual operations.

JAPANESE TACTICS FOR COUNTERGUERRILLA OPERATIONS

The most serious concern for Japanese troops in counterguerrilla operations had to do with finding and catching the enemy units before they retreated. Because guerrillas were good at hiding among the population, this was extremely difficult. Provided they were not detected, guerrilla forces always enjoyed freedom in choosing the time and place to fight. Retreat was nothing less than a tactic for guerrillas. Because of poor roads and mountainous terrain, where the majority of anti-guerrilla operations were conducted in north China, the mobility of Japanese troops and Chinese guerrillas was basically the same in many cases. Both guerrillas and counterguerrilla soldiers were primarily foot soldiers. Two key factors in counterguerrilla operations were intelligence and tactical mobility: intelligence and counterintelligence capabilities both to detect enemy activities and to secure friendly activities, and the capability to maneuver tactically to maintain contact with guerrillas, which involved the prior deployment of counterinsurgency troops and coordination among attacking forces as well as the physical speed of maneuver forces.

[44] Japan Defense Agency, *Hokushi no Chian-sen*, vol. 1, pp. 65–66.
[45] Ibid.

During April and May 1939, the I Corps of the North China Army, which was in charge of the northeast part of the army's area of responsibility, conducted an offensive operation in the Utai Mountains. When the corps initiated the operations with the 109th Division, the 36th Division, and the 3rd Independent Combined Brigade, it had fairly limited information on the disposition of the guerrillas. Although the corps planned to develop its operations by launching an attack to gain contact with the enemy, the attacking troops failed to make major contact, perhaps because the corps' intention had been detected by the enemy prior to the operation.

Despite having operated with the three major components of the corps for nearly two months, Japanese soldiers saw only empty villages throughout the operation. This failure was apparently caused by lack of information on the enemy and an inability to shield friendly activities from detection. Tactical mobility was also a problem. A divisional staff officer who participated in this operation noted "Japanese troops were too heavily equipped to keep up with nimble Communist guerrillas."[46]

In contrast, in June 1939, counterguerrilla operations conducted by the XII Army Corps, mainly its 5th Division, displayed a successful pattern of tactical maneuver to capture and destroy guerrilla forces. One of the most effective approaches was the centripetal maneuver, which was especially useful when the attacking troops were able to use multiple avenues of approach to close with the enemy and when these movements were well coordinated. The maneuvers of all participating elements were highly synchronized and well exploited to encircle the enemy early in the operation. Later, such maneuvers were directed to pursue and press the guerrillas toward the coast so that the corps could destroy them. During such operations, small aircraft were useful in coordinating the movements of attacking forces and in providing continuous aerial observation to keep the ground forces informed as to the enemy's most recent movements.[47]

CONCLUSION

Lessons learned from the Japanese experience in China illustrate a series of key themes for hybrid warfare. Although historians have already widely studied many of these lessons in other venues, most are still relevant today and are worthy of close examination.

[46] Ibid., pp. 154–161.
[47] Ibid.

A number of historians have argued that Japan fought the Second Sino-Japanese War without clear and consistent strategic objectives. Shinobu Oye, one of the most prominent historians of the postwar Japan, has argued that Japan attempted to achieve unrestricted goals with limited resources. According to his work *Nihon no Sanbohonbu (Japan's General Staff)*, Japanese leaders set an unlimited goal of totally eliminating the Nationalist government.[48] The resources available were obviously limited, mainly because the military establishment wished to leave sufficient assets to deal with its main enemies, the Soviet Union for the army and the United States for the navy.

On 16 January 1938, after the conquest of Nanjing, Prime Minister Fumimaro Konoye declared that "Japan would not negotiate with the Chang Kai-shek administration." Two days later, the government explained that the statement meant that Japan would obliterate the Chinese Nationalist government.[49] This represented an unrestricted goal requiring total war. Meanwhile, the military establishment consistently limited its allocation of resources for the war against China. If there were a consensus among military planners, it would have been the hope for an early termination of the conflict.

There was, however, a sharp division within the Japanese government and the military concerning the ways to realize such a termination of hostilities. On the one hand, Major General Kanji Ishihara, the director of the operations department of the general staff when the war began in 1937, initially insisted that Japanese forces should remain as limited as possible and withdraw from north China to the northern border with Manchukuo so that the government could negotiate with the Chinese Nationalists. On the other hand, there were those who insisted that it was absolutely necessary to inflict severe damage on the Chinese regular forces so that the Chinese would have to negotiate.[50] A major mistake shared by both approaches was that they underestimated the will and the determination of the Chinese to continue the war against Japan.

Behind the inconsistency and indecisiveness of Japan's strategy, there was a serious problem with decision making at the highest level. Kazuo Horiba, a former staff officer assigned to the general staff under Ishihara, pointed out in his work *Shina Jihen Senso Shido-shi (A History of Waging War During the China Incident)* that the center for Japan's decision

---

[48] Oye, *Nihon no Sanbohonbu*, pp. 183–184.
[49] Ibid., p. 175.
[50] Japan Defense Agency, *Shina Jihen Rikugun Sakusen*, vol. 2, p. 202.

making on the China Incident shifted twice within the Japanese government and its military establishment. According to Horiba, the general staff took a leading role at the beginning of the war simply because no other competent element was available or willing to do so.

Among the leading planners within the general staff there were at least two distinct schools of thought, namely the circumspect group and the expansionary group. Key decisions were more often than not the result of compromises between the two. Even Ishihara, representing the limited-war school, failed to argue forcefully for his position in the decision-making processes. For example, when the general staff made the final decision on whether Tokyo should substantially reinforce the Tientsin garrison in mid-July 1937, he refused to argue forcefully against such a strategic approach.[51]

Whereas such military planners engaged in intensive debates over critical issues involving the nation's fate, other elements in the government had neither the influence nor the interest to do more than exploit the possible fruits of the war.[52] From 1939 until the outbreak of the war in the Pacific in 1941, army commands in China took the lead for planning, mainly because many of the original planners of the war on the general staff in Tokyo had transferred to China, while those in charge of planning in Tokyo were newcomers to war planning and less knowledgeable than the commanders and staff officers assigned to China.

When Japan entered World War II in December 1941, China became a secondary theater for the planners in Tokyo, while army commands in China gradually lost their hope for a termination of hostilities. The center for decision making on the war in China shifted back to Tokyo, where military and civilian policy makers took charge of events. In short, the Imperial Japanese Army fought the eight-year war against China with vague and inconsistent strategic goals under fragile leadership, which finally drew Japan into World War II. Horiba noted that Japan resembled an army corps forced to engage the enemy fully because a platoon leader at the front led the whole corps with his passionate aggressiveness.[53] The government's weak political control over military affairs and interservice rivalry between the army and the navy only served to exacerbate this dismal situation.

---

[51] Kumao Imoto, *Shina Jihen Sakusen Nisshi* (*Daily Record of Operations During the China Incident*) (Tokyo, 1998), pp. 88–93.

[52] Kazuo Horiba, *Shina Jihen Senso Shido-shi* (*A History of Waging War During the China Incident*) (Tokyo, 1962), p. 41.

[53] Ibid., p. 31.

Japanese forces in China attempted to win the hearts and minds of the population, but this goal proved elusive. Nevertheless, the correlation between security and economic development is worth mentioning. As a staff officer deeply involved in military planning during the Sino-Japanese War, Kazuo Horiba noted:

> Promotion of local security and improvement of people's lives have a [reciprocal] cause-and-effect relationship. As an area becomes safer step by step, the life of local population can be improved. Only under a situation where local security is achieved can inhabitants have jobs that will build their economy. If their life is improved and stable, nobody would want to become the vermin of the community except for determined insurgents who are a deviant minority among the people.[54]

In other words, military and other aspects of counterinsurgency warfare go hand in hand.

One can find a typical example of this relationship in the recent experience of Japanese troops deployed in Iraq from 2004 to 2006. Japanese Self Defense Forces in Iraq were strictly restricted from using force and were mandated to conduct only reconstruction missions. Without rules of engagement that allowed for security operations, Japanese troops had to rely on other military forces for security and protection. The only means for Japanese troops to improve the security around their area was to maximize the positive correlations between economic development and local security. While providing the local communities with engineering and medical support as well as water purification, staff officers were dispatched to adjacent villages and towns to locate possible reconstruction projects. With assistance from the ministry of foreign affairs, contingents from Self Defense Forces initiated a number of reconstruction projects with Official Development Assistance funds. Such projects varied from small ones, such as repairing school buildings or providing local hospitals with medical equipment, to larger ones, such as building a thermal power plant. Those projects created jobs for local villagers adjacent to the Japanese camp and made such communities support the presence of the troops.

Nevertheless, the initial stage of stability operations should focus on security to build a basis for a positive movement. Security requires the use of military forces and, in most cases, a danger exists of antagonizing the hearts and minds of the local people. Japanese forces in China had a notoriously bad reputation in this context – a reputation that today still causes

[54] Ibid., pp. 576–577.

An Unexpected Encounter with Hybrid Warfare 253

political problems between the two nations. Exemplifying the negative impact of this reputation is the north China special security force, a unit organized in 1943 to operate specifically against Communist guerrillas. Its harsh and cruel treatment of insurgent suspects resulted in severe blowback among the Chinese people. As Lieutenant General Sajiro Okido, chief of staff of the North China Army, stated, "The military police went too far in many cases with their tendency to arrest suspects based on small doubt, and they were not seen as protectors of the population."[55] A staff officer of the North China Army later noted that such a security force with its extremely combative edge frequently destroyed the livelihood of the local population and that a small number of such errors in judgment negated everything positive that had been achieved.[56]

A final point of crucial importance is the ideological aspect of hybrid war, which may need a study all to itself. Japanese military forces never controlled the vast majority of the occupied territory in north China. Japanese military control extended to points (e.g., villages and urban areas) and lines (e.g., roads and railroads) but not to wider areas (*Ten*, *Sen*, and *Men*, respectively, in Japanese). The term *Men* should not be understood just in physical terms, for it includes psychological aspects as well. Because one of the key themes for stability operations is to win the hearts and minds of the population, the ideological dimension of war is also essential. In this context, Lincoln Li has pointed out that the Japanese in north China had no credible ideology to offer:

> The kinds of ideological explanations put forward [by the Japanese] to justify their military actions in China were not expressions of firmly held convictions; they were rather, ad hoc rationalization. The Japanese, themselves, did not believe in the cause of Greater East Asia and East Asian Coprosperity, and what they practiced exposed their readiness to put Japanese interests above everything else.[57]

Assuming the ideological dimension was important and firm ideology was a powerful weapon in the unconventional portions of the Second Sino-Japanese War, one can say that the Japanese Army fought without arms against the ideals articulated by Mao Tse Tung.

---

[55] Japan Defense Agency, *Shina Jihen Rikugun Sakusen*, vol. 2, pp. 475–477.
[56] Ibid.
[57] Li, *The Japanese Army in North China*, p. 117.

10

Hybrid War in Vietnam

Karl Lowe

The war in Vietnam was multilayered, like a Russian babushka doll. It was a civil war within South Vietnam between the communists and other parties. It was a civil war between North and South Vietnam – the artificially divided parts of a single nation. It was an Asian regional war in which North Vietnam, South Vietnam, Laos, Cambodia, Thailand, the Philippines, Australia, New Zealand, China, and the Republic of Korea all played military roles. It nested in the context of a broader East–West war of ideas, in which the United States and the Soviet Union were the chief protagonists. With that layering, the war in Vietnam was inherently a hybrid conflict in which state-of-the-art conventional arms and tactics commingled with the tools and techniques of guerrilla and counterinsurgency warfare.

The term "hybrid warfare" has little meaning to a soldier, airman, marine, or sailor in the thick of a fight. Troops on both sides simply did what they had to do to accomplish their assigned missions and in the hope of emerging from the war alive. The demands of hybrid warfare, however, had clear relevance at higher echelons of authority. In fact, those demands forced political and military leaders to make choices among competing conceptions of what the war was all about, and thereby to determine how best to prosecute it.

Four American presidents, regardless of party, had to deal with Vietnam and its near neighbors in the broader context of the protracted struggle against international communism, itself a higher form of hybrid warfare. On the broader world stage, they had to wage a Cold War that occasionally exploded into direct confrontation in places as diverse as the Taiwan Straits, Berlin, and Cuba, while Korea remained an unsettled and volatile confrontation. For each of those flashpoints, and for lesser crises as well, presidents found themselves pressed by the various influencers of public opinion, to include Congress, academia, and the media; by interest groups that bankrolled both the parties and their opposition; by dissonant voices from inside and outside the government; by fretful overseas friends and allies; and by the Soviets, the Chinese, and their various allies and clients. No president could allow his country to be pushed too hard or too far without stirring political opposition at home and risking the collapse of tenuous alliances overseas. Similarly, no president could afford to become so ensnared in a regional conflict that domestic priorities and other international commitments went begging for resources and attention.

Against that backdrop, Indochina was a distraction but one that American leaders could not ignore. If Laos or Vietnam fell, there were widely held fears that larger and more important nations might follow suit, undermining American credibility as a reliable protector and unraveling a fractious and increasingly shaky global network of regional alliances. With the 1964 election looming, President Lyndon Johnson confronted a replay of the "who lost China" debate, with his opponents' strident calls for a more robust response to democracy's enemies haunting the Democratic Party. Answering that call to action ultimately cost Johnson the presidency.

For Secretary of Defense Robert McNamara, Vietnam represented a management challenge – a need to balance the resource demands of competing security challenges. McNamara's Department of Defense faced the challenge of simultaneously maintaining the strategic nuclear triad on land, sea, and air; preparing forces to fight on a possible tactical nuclear battlefield; preparing for possible conventional wars against large, well-equipped armies in Europe, Korea, and the Middle East; and concurrently dealing with smaller but worrisome insurgencies flaring in Africa, Asia, and South America. For McNamara, with a legacy of success at managing complex industrial operations through quantitative analysis, Vietnam was just another analytical challenge: follow the numbers and a path to success would inevitably emerge. Invisible to McNamara and the analysts who served him was the bloody human dynamic lying behind the sterile data.

The service chiefs faced similar challenges. It had been evident since the late 1950s that counterinsurgency required different doctrine, different equipment, and different individual and collective skills, but there was little room to adapt. The services still had to organize, train, and equip their forces to man the nation's deterrent arsenal, to fight and survive on a potential nuclear battlefield, and to fight possible conventional wars against the Soviets or their proxies. U.S. military forces could not abandon training for a tactical nuclear battlefield and preparations to defeat larger, well-armed opponents in conventional combat in diverse environments to concentrate instead on training to protect a threatened population amid an indigenous insurgency. Stretching to meet those various demands dissipated resources and left no mission adequately addressed. Although the marine corps was not as stretched, it too had global missions that exerted a radically different pull than the war in Vietnam.

The operational level of hybrid war created a different but no less problematic tension in administration councils. While the United States and its allies might have forced North Vietnam to stop aiding the insurgency by threatening its homeland and its principal infiltration corridor through Laos, conditions in South Vietnam dominated discussions. Johnson pressed General William Westmoreland, commander of Military Assistance Command-Vietnam, to provide a plan of action immediately after his assumption of command in 1964. Westmoreland sized up the situation narrowly.[1] He saw his first responsibility as dealing with "the wolf nearest the sled" – an increasingly successful Viet Cong (VC) insurgency closing in on Saigon, while two North Vietnamese Army (NVA) divisions sat poised to invade the Central Highlands from eastern Cambodia. He asked for troops to deal with those concerns first and then asked for more to push the enemy back to the borders, a quest that would elude him for four years because he could not simultaneously separate the VC from the South Vietnamese people.

By summer 1968, when Westmoreland departed, there was no discernible plan for victory, losses were heavy, and war weariness had set in at home. In that environment, General Creighton Abrams, Westmoreland's successor, lacked the freedom of action to choose a radically different path. At best, he could change emphasis to concentrate on protecting the population, but he could not abandon the pursuit of larger enemy formations without placing the population at risk. When given authority to enter Cambodia in 1970, he found himself limited to a distance of 21.7 miles. By the time he received authority to cut the Ho Chi Minh Trail in Laos the following year, the Cooper-Church Amendment excluded U.S. ground forces from operations outside the borders of South Vietnam.

At the tactical level in Vietnam, hybrid warfare posed unrelenting tension. Against an insurgency that might otherwise sweep away South

---

[1] Andrew F. Krepinevich, Jr., *The Army and Vietnam* (Baltimore, MD, 1986), p. 138.

Vietnam's institutions, it was necessary to disperse forces throughout populated areas to root out insurgents; deny their tax collectors access to the population; and protect officials, teachers, and the general public from intimidation or assassination. Concurrently, commanders had to deal with the enemy's ability to mass. Although the VC lived among the people and usually operated in units of fewer than 300 men, all were elements of broader organizations that could assemble into larger units as the situation dictated.

The ability of the NVA to attack from cross-border sanctuaries in three countries increased the complexity of the problem. In some areas, particularly those within a day's march from the borders of Cambodia and Laos, U.S. and allied battalions could not safely disperse to create smaller outposts in contested areas because the VC and NVA could and often did mass to launch major attacks. In heavily populated areas nearer the coast, dispersal and small unit partnerships enjoyed better prospects. When the enemy appeared in mass, fighting tended to be more conventional, involving indirect artillery bombardments by both sides and intense close combat that would have been familiar to units in the Pacific or Italy during World War II. The competing challenge of having to disperse against the guerrilla threat and mass to counter large units remained a major problem for U.S. commanders throughout the war.

HISTORICAL CONTEXT

When the Geneva Convention of 1954 divided Vietnam at the 17th parallel, Ho Chi Minh felt cheated, as did many of his countrymen, whose desire for a unified country the settlement brokered by the great powers had frustrated. While the Communist regime took advantage of the treaty to solidify its hold on the north, there was never a doubt in Hanoi about the ultimate objective – unification under the red banner. North Vietnam infiltrated Communist cadres south to foment rebellion as early as 1955 and began sending the VC material and direct military assistance via Laos in May 1959.[2] Concurrently, North Vietnamese troops drove Laotian forces out of that country's eastern provinces. In response, President Dwight D. Eisenhower dispatched special forces teams to Laos to train royalist forces, but they were too few and too late. In 1961, President

---

[2] Route 559, the Ho Chi Minh Trail, carries the designation of the unit that operated it. Its number is derived from May 1959, the month North Vietnam began sending cadres and supplies into South Vietnam through Laos.

John F. Kennedy intensified the pressure by dispatching an aircraft carrier battle group to the South China Sea and sending U.S. ground forces to exercise with the Thai military. The gambit worked, or so it seemed when the Communists agreed to negotiations.

In 1962, the 14 parties, following talks in Geneva, agreed to the withdrawal of all foreign forces from Laos. It soon became clear, however, the North Vietnamese viewed the accord as no more than a tool for removing the Americans, while continuing their own illicit activities. Bui Tin, former North Vietnam officer and journalist, characterized Averill Harriman, who signed the Geneva Accord on behalf of the Kennedy administration, as gullible and careless, foreclosing a U.S. ground interdiction option that could have had a serious effect on North Vietnam's ability to support the insurgency.[3]

When the United States withdrew its Military Assistance and Advisory Group and special forces teams from Laos, the North Vietnamese, Chinese, and Soviets seized the opportunity to increase their activities. Chinese military engineers built roads by which to funnel supplies to the Pathet Lao. The Soviets brazenly flew military aid directly into Laos, while North Vietnam sent troops into the Plain of Jars in an attempt to drive royalist forces out of the center of the country.

The situation in Cambodia was no less troubling. While Cambodia claimed neutrality, Cambodia's ruler, Prince Norodom Sihanouk, turned a blind eye to VC camps on his territory and permitted Soviet and Chinese arms to flow to the VC via the port of Sihanoukville. By giving the Communists a free hand, Sihanouk sought to counterbalance Thailand and South Vietnam, which he feared as potential invaders. He was walking a tightrope with no safety net.

Moreover, under Achmed Sukarno, Indonesia was well on the way to becoming a Communist state. U.S. friends and allies in the area were increasingly nervous. A persistent Communist insurgency plagued the Philippines, while Thailand and Malaysia worried about potential isolation. Few countries in the region could claim full control of their territory. In Washington, pundits were enthralled with the domino theory, which held that the fall of one weak regime would in turn precipitate the fall of its neighbors, collapsing all of Southeast Asia like a string of dominos. Others, then isolated, would act out of self-preservation to reach an accord with China, destroying America's security perimeter in Asia.

---

[3] Andrew Wiest, *Rolling Thunder in a Gentle Land* (London, 2006), pp. 70–71.

With more pressing problems at hand in Berlin and Cuba, Kennedy was disinclined to send U.S. ground troops to Vietnam. "No more land wars in Asia" had been a steady refrain in Washington since the Korean War, when China sent more than a million "volunteers" to rescue a fellow communist regime on its border. That war had lasted three years, cost 38,000 U.S. lives, and strained U.S. military credibility. To limit political opposition, Kennedy adopted half-measures that put American credibility on the line in hopes of turning the tide in Southeast Asia. He sent aviation units and several thousand advisors to bolster South Vietnam's counterinsurgency effort. In Laos, he authorized the CIA to step up its recruiting, training, and support of anti-Vietnamese tribes in a clandestine war that would continue for the next 12 years and the consequences of which still reverberate among those whom the United States eventually abandoned.

MISREADING THE SIGNALS – 1964

In 2005, the National Intelligence Council published a declassified collection of 174 estimative products on Vietnam produced between 1948 and 1975 by the council itself and its predecessor, the Office of National Estimates.[4] Of particular importance in that collection is a May 1964 Special National Intelligence Estimate (SNIE), which postulated probable regional responses to U.S. options for Laos and Vietnam.[5] Although other intelligence reaches the president's desk daily, SNIEs are coordinated community documents that reflect the shared perspectives of the CIA and the intelligence organs of the Departments of Defense, State, and other cabinet agencies. They include dissenting views and carry weight and authority that other estimates do not. Although presidents can ignore a SNIE, they potentially incur political risks by doing so because the number of cleared people who see the documents is in the hundreds – including the staffs of powerful, independent-minded congressional committees. With an election looming, Johnson was more worried about possible domestic fallout than foreign-policy risks. Given that atmosphere, the May 1964 SNIE holds unique importance.

Explicit in the estimate was the assumption that North Vietnam would minimize its risks and pull back when confronted, while remaining

---

[4] *Estimative Products on Vietnam 1948–1975* (National Intelligence Council, 2005).
[5] SNIE 50-2-64, *Probable Consequences of Certain U.S. Actions with Respect to Vietnam and Laos*, 25 May 1964.

faithful to its goal of national unification. It would resume military activity to achieve that end when American attention shifted elsewhere. Hanoi's apparent eagerness to negotiate in response to the U.S. reaction to events in Laos in 1961 may have motivated the SNIE's assertion that "North Vietnam has pulled back whenever it appeared that its tactics might provoke a major U.S. response." Because it was well understood that the North Vietnamese were violating the 1962 Geneva Accord, the rationale for that estimate is puzzling. North Vietnam never "pulled back" at all; instead, it used negotiations to gain greater freedom of action. Only the United States had pulled back, allowing diplomacy to limit its options.

In November 1964, emboldened by Johnson's campaign pledge that he would not send ground troops to Vietnam, Hanoi sent four infantry regiments, an artillery regiment, and a separate infantry battalion to the Central Highlands in South Vietnam. The last of those units arrived in early January 1965. They and their supplies moved unimpeded via the expanded Ho Chi Minh Trail through Laos and eastern Cambodia.

Another passage in the SNIE estimated how much punishment North Vietnam would be willing to accept from U.S. aerial bombing:

> We have many indications that the Hanoi leadership is acutely and nervously aware of the extent to which North Vietnam's transportation system and industrial plant is vulnerable to attack. On the other hand, North Vietnam's economy is overwhelmingly agricultural and, to a large extent, decentralized in a myriad of more or less economically self-sufficient villages. Interdiction of imports and extensive destruction of transportation facilities and industrial plants would cripple DRV [North Vietnamese] industry. These actions would seriously restrict DRV military capabilities, and would degrade, though to a lesser extent, Hanoi's capabilities to support guerrilla warfare in South Vietnam and Laos.... It is reasonable to infer that the DRV leaders have a psychological investment in the work of reconstruction they have accomplished over the last decade. Nevertheless, they would probably be willing to suffer some damage to the country in a contest of wills with the U.S. over the course of events in South Vietnam.[6]

Thus, the SNIE sent a mixed message, asserting that North Vietnam's leadership was nervous about its vulnerabilities but willing to suffer damage. Some of the president's closest advisors, particularly McNamara, viewed that assessment as an indication that a carefully calculated bombing campaign might bring Hanoi to its senses and buy time for South Vietnam to get its political and military house in order. But North Vietnam

[6] Ibid.

had no intention of giving South Vietnam or the United States an opportunity to thwart its aim of unifying Vietnam under Hanoi's rule.

Ambiguities in the May 1964 SNIE raised hopes that a well-metered bombing campaign might counter North Vietnamese aspirations. Thus, some believed that bombing of military targets in nonstrategic places and perhaps some force posturing around the region might force North Vietnam to back off. The SNIE never addressed how much time such measures would take to produce results, and no one seems to have asked the Joint Chiefs that question. As a result, American leaders had little idea how long they would have to sustain a bombing campaign or how much bombing would be necessary to achieve the desired effect.

Here, one can see the beginnings of hybrid war in Vietnam, one waged with modern high-performance aircraft, countered by similarly modern fighters and a dense array of anti-aircraft weapons, including state-of-the-art surface-to-air missiles, over North Vietnam. Meanwhile, in the south the war continued, for the time being mainly a low-technology effort to counter hit-and-run attacks and acts of sabotage, intimidation, assassination, and other forms of terrorism aimed at dissuading the South Vietnamese people from supporting their government (Figure 9). When the communists thought they could score a major victory, they gathered regiments – on at least two occasions, they concentrated a full division of combat power – waging conventional battles that included the employment of massed field artillery.[7]

INITIAL U.S. GROUND FORCE DEPLOYMENTS – 1965

The Gulf of Tonkin incident in August 1964, followed by a car bombing of the Brinks Hotel and the U.S. officers' quarters in Saigon on Christmas Eve, and a ground attack on the U.S. Army helicopter base at Pleiku in February 1965, ended the debate concerning the commitment of U.S. combat forces to Vietnam. Repeatedly challenged, President Johnson felt compelled to act, spurred by expressions of outrage in Congress and the media. He ordered the immediate bombing of North Vietnam, but only against military targets south of the 20th parallel. That restriction reflected worries about China's possible reaction and hopes the North Vietnamese would see the danger and back off. China did not respond to the bombing, but North Vietnam stepped up its flow of troops and

---

[7] These occasions were at Binh Gia in December 1964 and Song Be in May 1965.

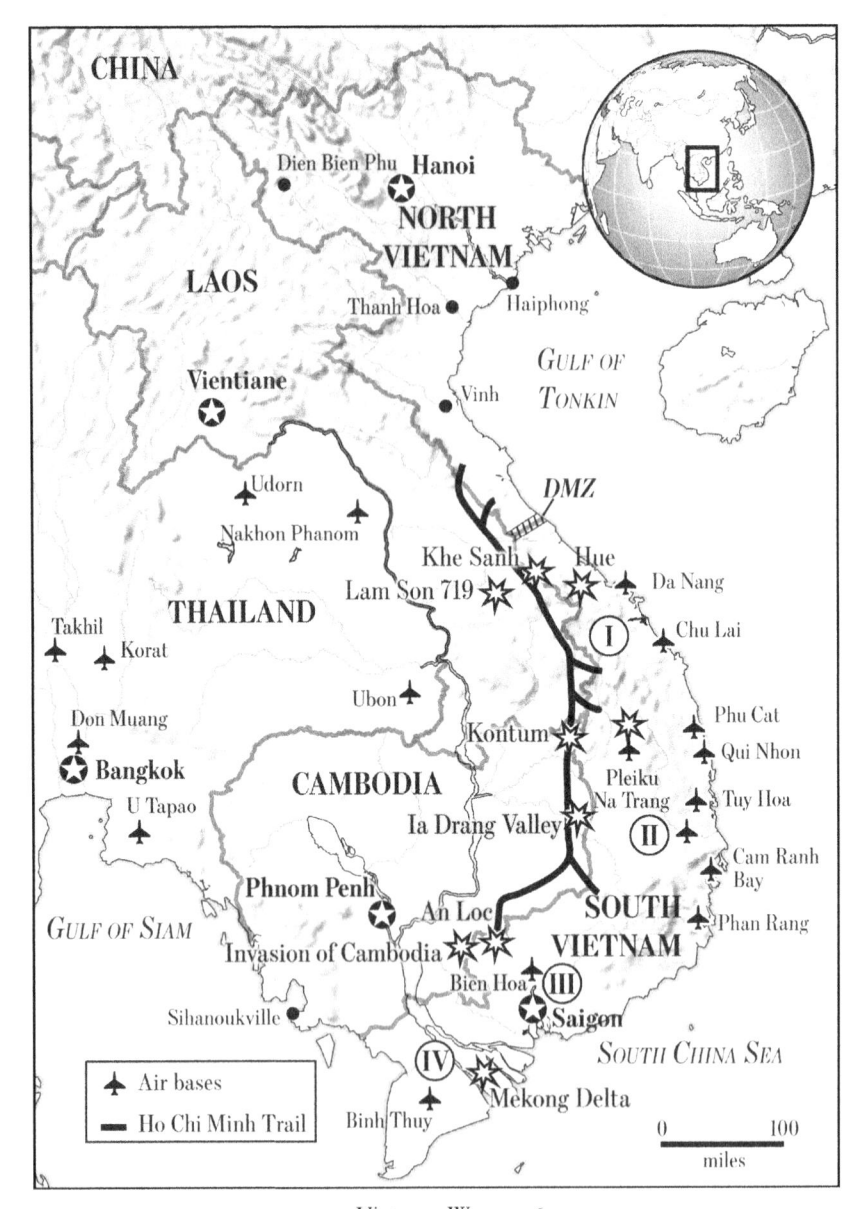

FIGURE 9. Vietnam War, 1965–1973.

supplies to the south, sending three more regiments into the Central Highlands. Limited aerial bombardment was not going to change the minds of North Vietnam's leaders, but that realization would take years to seep through the bureaucracy in Washington.

In March 1965, two battalions of U.S. Marines landed at Da Nang, a few hours' drive from the North Vietnamese border. A month later, a U.S. airborne brigade landed at Bien Hoa Air Base near Saigon and an Australian infantry battalion task force debarked at the nearby port of Vung Tau. In July, two additional U.S. brigades arrived in South Vietnam. A division from the Republic of Korea (ROK) began arriving in central Vietnam in September. By October, three U.S. divisions and two separate brigades had reached South Vietnam. Three more divisions, another ROK infantry division, and a ROK marine brigade were all preparing for possible deployment.[8]

In November 1965, a U.S. brigade fought a three-day battle with a division of North Vietnamese regulars in the Ia Drang Valley of the Central Highlands, a battle in which nearly an entire battalion of the 1st Cavalry Division was destroyed. Studying how the Americans fought, the North Vietnamese were both surprised and pleased that U.S. troops did not pursue the battered NVA units back into Cambodia. The United States and its allies were now going to have to fight both VC guerrillas and a conventional army, whose armament and tactics enabled it to fight a hybrid form of warfare.

THE CHINA FACTOR

Throughout the war, fear of China intruded into every course of action American policy makers considered for pressuring North Vietnam. In 1964 and 1965, when the strategy that would determine the war's course was being formulated, the effect was crippling. Fear of China proscribed any possible path to victory and, amplified by domestic politics, led the Johnson administration to adopt a strategy of painstakingly metered gradualism. The North Vietnamese consistently had time to adjust to the measured changes in U.S. military pressure.

A number of the arguments of that period are instructive. There was fear that U.S. bombing of the Hanoi–Haiphong area might induce

---

[8] The 3rd Marine Division, 1st Infantry Division, 1st Cavalry Division (Airmobile), 1st Brigade 101st Airborne Division, and 173rd Airborne Brigade had all deployed to Vietnam by October 1965. The 4th and 25th Infantry Divisions and 1st Marine Division were at their home stations in the United States being readied for possible deployment. All three deployed to Vietnam the following year, as did the U.S. 196th Infantry Brigade, the ROK 9th Division, and the remainder of the 1st Australian–New Zealand Brigade Task Force. Details of where and when units were deployed can be found in Shelby Stanton, *Vietnam Order of Battle* (New York, 1981).

North Vietnam to ask for Chinese air cover and raise the specter of having to either back off or strike Chinese bases to neutralize the threat. The May 1964 SNIE mentions such strikes as a possible trigger to China's entry into the ground war.[9] Policy makers in Washington feared that killing Chinese air defense personnel in the Hanoi–Haiphong area or sinking Chinese ships in Haiphong harbor would have the same effect. Most feared of all was the risk associated with sending U.S. ground troops into North Vietnam or Laos. Entering Laos was particularly worrying to the State Department because the United States had signed an accord proscribing a U.S. military presence in that country. However, diplomacy only has value if it has credibility. Just as China had intervened when United States forces invaded North Korea, U.S. leaders assumed it would surely do so again if the United States invaded Laos or North Vietnam. Or would it?

The view through enemy eyes suggests otherwise. A series of passages in Andrew Wiest's *Rolling Thunder in a Gentle Land* illuminate the perspectives of senior North Vietnamese officers:

> General Vo Nguyen Giap, the architect of North Vietnam's victory over the French, exhorted his subordinates to press American troops in the South but 'avoid their launching a ground war in North Vietnam, no matter how limited.' Giap knew from conversations with the Chinese that North Vietnam must fight alone, so he worried that the Americans might reverse the military situation and force him onto the defensive. Such a reversal could cost North Vietnam the gains it had made in the South and risk its territorial integrity. China would send air defense, engineer, and medical units, keeping them all north of the Red River near Hanoi and Haiphong, but Mao Tse Tung was not willing to enter [into] another ground war with the U.S.[10]

CHOICES AND VOICES

Against that backdrop of multi-tiered hybrid warfare, one can examine the more direct choices in Vietnam and their implications. Such examination can now draw on the perspectives of former opponents to illuminate what worked and what went wrong. Every contest of wills has at least

---

[9] "Communist China almost certainly would not wish to become involved in hostilities with U.S. forces. It would accordingly proceed with caution, though it would make various threatening gestures. There would probably not be high risk of Chinese Communist ground intervention unless major U.S./GVN ground units had moved well into the DRV or communist-held areas of northern Laos, or possibly, the Chinese had committed their air and had subsequently suffered attack on CCF bases in China." SNIE 50-2-64, p. 3.

[10] Wiest, *Rolling Thunder in a Gentle Land*, pp. 66–68.

two sides, each offering a unique perspective on what was at stake, how the opponents saw the other's strengths and weaknesses, and why they responded as they did with a particular approach to strategy and tactics.

For the Vietnam War, the view from the other side is just becoming visible through efforts such as Texas Tech's Vietnam Project and the translated writings of senior North Vietnamese participants. That body of work, still in its infancy, builds on a rich legacy of similar research from other conflicts, notable examples of which are Basil H. Liddell Hart's *The German Generals Talk* of the post–World War II era and a more recent body of work on the perspectives of Saddam Hussein's regime, led by Kevin Woods of the Institute for Defense Analyses.[11]

A sample of the North Vietnamese view of the war is elaborated in the prolific writings of Bui Tin, a former North Vietnamese officer and senior journalist.[12] Tin was in a unique position to both view and experience the war's evolution during his 37 years as an insurgent and soldier and 8 years as a leading North Vietnamese journalist. As a soldier, he fought against France, the United States, South Vietnam, and the Khmer Rouge, which had provided him broad experience in conventional and irregular warfare on both sides of that murky divide. After his departure from the army as a colonel, Bui Tin worked with North Vietnam's top political and military figures as the defense and foreign affairs editor of *Nhan Dan*, North Vietnam's official newspaper. In that role, he was North Vietnam's chief propagandist, but he was also an idealist whose vision of what postwar Vietnam should become ultimately diverged from that of the regime he served. Troubled by the contradictions he saw, he went into exile in Paris in 1990.

Bui Tin reports that in mid-1964, China unilaterally canceled its military agreement with North Vietnam. Although unstated, there was an implicit "who's in charge" issue – evidenced by North Vietnam's disinclination to include observers from China or the Soviet Union in its councils of war. North Vietnam would not subordinate its forces to a Chinese commander or allow China to dictate its strategy. Likewise, why should China be willing to place its forces under the command of a small former vassal state that was pleading for help? In a January 1965 interview

---

[11] See B. H. Liddell Hart's *The German Generals Talk* (New York, 1948) and Kevin Woods, et al., *The Iraqi Perspectives Report* (Annapolis, MD, 2006).

[12] His perspectives, and those of the North Vietnamese leaders with whom he interacted, are highlighted in *Rolling Thunder in a Gentle Land*. See also Bui Tin, *From Enemy to Friend: A North Vietnamese Perspective on the War* (London, 2002) and *Following Ho Chi Minh: The Memoirs of a North Vietnamese Colonel* (Honolulu, HI, 1995).

with Edgar Snow, an exiled American journalist, Mao said that China's armies would not fight beyond its borders and remarked that the Vietnamese could cope with their own situation.[13] In a compromise, China did send military road builders, hospital staff, and air defenders to North Vietnam, replacing tens of thousands of North Vietnamese in those roles, so they could go south to fight.

The reasons behind Mao's restraint are obvious. Prolonged economic stagnation had steadily worsened China's standard of living, stirring social unrest and challenging Mao's authority. To purge China of real and potential internal opposition, Mao set the "cultural revolution" in motion in 1966, leaving no one able to trust even members of their own family. Although the time might have seemed ripe to divert people's attention by going to war, China's strategic posture argued otherwise. A ground war with the United States would have sapped China's resources, consumed the best of its military forces, risked a U.S. nuclear attack, and left the country dangerously exposed to its other enemies. It would also have elevated the public profile of Marshal Peng Te-Huai, Mao's chief political opponent.

Despite its size, China's military was stretched thin and its weapons were decades older than those of India and the Soviet Union, which had become too close for comfort. In 1962, China had fought a brief, inconclusive border war with India, forcing it to keep forces tied to the Sino-Indian frontier. Another large force remained tied to China's long coastline for fear the Chinese Nationalists might try to exploit the country's social unrest. An even larger force deployed along the borders of Mongolia and the Soviet Union, where Soviet forces sat poised like a dagger pointing at China's heart. As tensions escalated, China and the Soviet Union were to fight a brief, costly war along the Amur and Ussuri Rivers in 1969.

EARLY ALTERNATIVES – 1965

Had a succession of presidents and the policy advisors and intelligence services that served them not missed or misread the signals emanating from Asia in the early 1960s, the United States might have avoided the subsequent agonies that beset it and the region. Johnson's advisors believed it necessary to help Saigon buy time to stabilize South Vietnam, but they failed to appreciate that the American military could accomplish this

---

[13] Mark Moyar, *Triumph Forsaken: The Vietnam War, 1954–1965* (Cambridge, 2006), p. 360.

goal only by putting North Vietnam under more pressure than it could withstand.

Among the major mistakes of the war was the American assumption that the actions of North Vietnam and the VC represented those of separate political entities. Hanoi created that fiction by forming a nominally separate communist party and separate military command structures in the south, but there was never a question regarding who directed the war. Instead of trying to fight an air war in the north and a ground war in the south, the United States should have recognized that the government in Saigon would ultimately have to defeat its own insurgency and could only do so if it reined in the corruption and incompetence that fed recruits to the VC. Accomplishing this objective would take time and a civilian advisory effort that gave greater emphasis to the country's political and economic development.

Because the intelligence community had determined that North Vietnamese industry was not fueling the war effort, an air campaign could only influence support to the insurgency by severing the roads, rails, and bridges that brought Soviet and Chinese aid south. General Dong Sy Nguyen, who commanded the unit responsible for building, maintaining, and operating the Ho Chi Minh Trail, feared that American infantry might cut the trail. "Transportation would have been interrupted, and we have no idea what we would have done to recover. This would have enormously impacted the battlefield in the South." Because communications arteries were hard to destroy and could be repaired quickly, the tempo of bombing required exceeded the available resources and capabilities. Unimpressed with the U.S. air effort, Hanoi increased its flow of troops and supplies to the south. By summer 1965, there was abundant evidence that something bolder would be required to deter Hanoi from its objectives, but the United States lacked a clear path to victory and its ad hoc efforts offered little reason for optimism.

Ironically, initial restraint in the use of air power might have given airpower enthusiasts, including McNamara, hope that a little more bombing might turn the tide. The Secretary of Defense persuaded the president that a more intensive bombing campaign, properly ratcheted and metered to gauge its effect, might compel Ho Chi Minh to stop supporting the war in South Vietnam. Six years later, Hanoi's war weariness gave Linebacker II such a chance, but the odds of having high-intensity bombing achieve that effect in 1965 were remote.

However, in 1965, the United States might have knocked the North Vietnamese off balance by putting its territory at risk and its armed forces on the defensive. Such an evolution would have radically reduced the flow of support to the VC and probably stopped the flow of NVA troops to South Vietnam. The Cambodian port of Sihanoukville lacked the capacity to compensate for the loss of overland infiltration. An offensive would have played to U.S. strengths, signaling and, if necessary, waging a conventional offensive for which U.S. forces were better organized, trained, and equipped – a conventional attack into North Vietnam with concerted operations by air, land, and sea.

When American troops entered Vietnam in 1965, they were instead dissipated to support a mostly static Army of the Republic of Vietnam (ARVN). Tying highly mobile U.S. forces down to static division and brigade sectors and battalion-size fire support bases ceded the initiative to the enemy and radically increased the number of U.S. troops needed to make a difference. This force deployment gave the VC and NVA the opportunity to size up U.S. strengths and vulnerabilities and deploy their own forces accordingly. Moreover, the VC and NVA could choose to fight where and when they might gain an advantage. This operational concept caused the Americans to fight a war on terms they could not easily influence with forces that had to remain organized, trained, and equipped for other missions around the globe – most of which had nothing to do with counterinsurgency. With six division equivalents in Europe and two in Korea facing larger armies, the U.S. Army was hardly in a position to reorganize and refocus its training on counterinsurgency. Trying to do both at once sapped its energy for the next eight years, leaving its forces inadequately prepared to fight on either battlefield. That refrain echoes again today.

To be sure, the defending forces in Saigon and the Central Highlands were shaky in summer and fall 1965, but the imminence of losing them was less clear. There had been riots in the northern coastal cities, a revolt by Montagnard tribesmen against their Vietnamese Special Forces commanders in the Central Highlands, and demonstrations by Buddhist monks in major cities. Given the environment, the main reason for dispersing U.S. troops across the country was the hope of stabilizing South Vietnam's political situation by discouraging further military coups and bolstering the morale of ARVN units. An intelligence estimate released in fall 1964 reinforces that view and may have catalyzed the decision to deploy conventional forces to stem defeat.[14]

---

[14] SNIE 53-2-64, *The Situation in South Vietnam*, 1 October 1964. "A coup by disgruntled South Vietnamese military figures could occur at any time. In any case, we believe that the conditions favor a further decay of GVN will and effectiveness. The likely pattern of

Whatever the intent, U.S. deployments did not cause the North Vietnamese to change either their objective or methods, and they arrived too late to dissuade another coup. General Nguyen Khanh was deposed in February 1965 by a group of generals headed by General Nguyen Van Thieu and Air Vice-Marshal Nguyen Cao Ky, who alternately retained power for the next decade. In light of that development and the popularity of Thieu and Ky with the younger officers in the South Vietnamese military, it seems reasonable to have done something different with the U.S. troops deploying to Vietnam, but plans were hard to change after senior leaders had bought into an operational concept and the logistics were in motion. Units deploying from March through July went where they could do the most good, but there was ample time to refocus the rest on the central objective – stopping North Vietnam's flow of troops and supplies to the south.

Nevertheless, there were alternatives if initial U.S. deployments had placed all three divisions near the 17th parallel, where they would have placed the North Vietnamese in a quandary. Without crossing a single international border, they would have threatened an invasion of southern North Vietnam that would effectively cut the Ho Chi Minh Trail in Laos. To counter that threat, North Vietnam would have had to move more divisions toward the areas where an invasion would have been most likely, including Vinh and Thanh Hoa, farther up the coast. Given the mixed readiness of divisions then in the North, the threat of invasion would likely have required recalling NVA units from South Vietnam. The Central Highlands and the Ho Chi Minh Trail would have mattered less to North Vietnam if its homeland were put at risk.

THE OPERATIONAL ENVIRONMENT

When those who never went to Vietnam think of that country and its war, the image they have is from news footage of the time – tropical jungles and rice paddies, Hamburger Hill, Saigon, and Hue. However, the war had a distinctly different character in each of South Vietnam's four corps tactical zones. A soldier who served in one part of the country would scarcely recognize the Vietnam described by one who served in another – not

> this decay will be increasing defeatism, paralysis of leadership, friction with Americans, exploration of possible lines of political accommodation with the other side, and a general petering out of the war effort.... We do not believe that the Viet Cong will make any early effort to seize power by force of arms; indeed we doubt they have the capability for such a takeover."

just because of differences in geography but also the variations in the people, their religion, and the enemy. Consequently, there was no "one size fits all" solution to either the insurgency or the more conventional threat posed by the NVA.

The ARVN I Corps, headquartered at Hue, was responsible for South Vietnam's five northernmost provinces. There, the North Vietnamese were the dominant foe, although VC were more prominent from Da Nang southward. Along the misnamed "demilitarized zone" (DMZ), the NVA clashed frequently with U.S. Marine patrols, while their artillery routinely shelled U.S. outposts.[15] Just to the west, NVA troops and supply columns crossed Route 9 along the Laotian border with impunity. At points farther south, NVA forces crossed a densely forested mountain range into South Vietnam. From there, trails led down the A Shau and Que Son valleys toward Da Nang and Chu Lai on the coast.

When U.S. air power and infantry combined to make that passage too costly, the NVA dragged anti-aircraft guns onto the ridges – .51 caliber, 14.5 mm, twin 23 mm, 37 mm, and 57 mm Soviet-made guns that turned the air into metal curtains. Soldiers who fought farther south never saw an enemy weapon larger than a 14.5-mm machine gun, never experienced bombardment by anything larger than a mortar or rocket, and never saw an enemy tank until the Easter Offensive of 1972. The people in the I Corps' area are mostly ethnic Vietnamese, a mix of Catholics and Buddhists. They are Trung Viet (Central Vietnamese), whose ancestors once ruled all of Vietnam. They speak a dialect different from that of their brethren in Tonkin to the north and Cochin China to the south. The predominant land form in I Corps is clay hills with patchy vegetation, giving way to arable lowlands near the coast and denser forests and steeper terrain near the borders.

II Corps, headquartered at Pleiku, was responsible for the Central Highlands and a narrow band of coastal lowlands. The NVA was most prominent in the sparsely inhabited highlands, whereas VC were more prominent along the coast. In the highlands, Montagnards were generally hostile to all Vietnamese as a result of centuries of subjugation and condescension. Most were eager allies of the United States – armed, trained, and led by U.S. Special Forces. North Vietnamese regulars staging out of

---

[15] These included Gio Linh, Con Tien, Cam Lo, Camp Carroll, the Rockpile, Dong Ha, Ca Lu, and Khe Sanh, outposts of various sizes from which artillery counterfire could be delivered into the DMZ and from which infiltration corridors could be watched and interdicted.

camps in Cambodia periodically attacked Special Forces camps to deny observation of their infiltration routes and to divert attention from the movement of troops and materiel toward the coast to collect the rice harvest. In division strength, the NVA clashed with the U.S. 1st Cavalry Division (Airmobile) around the Chu Pong Massif on the Cambodian border in November 1965. After nearly destroying two U.S. battalions and suffering severe losses in the process, the NVA, then referred to as the People's Army of Vietnam, withdrew to their base area in Cambodia. Their commander was shocked that the Americans, having gained the advantage, did not pursue his battered regiments – a valuable lesson. Other battles in the highlands made headlines as meat grinders – Dak To, "Hamburger Hill," and Kontum. In 1975, the NVA launched Campaign 275 and, to their shock, swept easily across the center of the country. What Americans had feared most in 1965 came to pass a decade later. The reasons were predictable – incompetent ARVN generals and the absence of the U.S. firepower, logistics, and aviation on which ARVN units had come to depend.

III Corps, headquartered at Bien Hoa, was responsible for the ring of provinces surrounding Saigon and a second arc of provinces to the north and west. There, the foe was mainly VC until the fall of 1968, when North Vietnamese regulars began replacing the losses the VC suffered during the Tet offensive. Soldiers who fought in the III Corps Tactical Zone fought in several entirely different environments. South of Saigon is Long An Province, the beginning of the flat, fertile, and heavily populated Mekong Delta, giving way to the uninhabited Plain of Reeds along the Cambodian border and the Rung Sat, a huge mangrove swamp dipping between Long An and the coast.

In Long An and nearby Tay Ninh, the population is heavily Cao Dai – fiercely independent ethnic Vietnamese, whose religion counts Victor Hugo, Julius Caesar, and Joan of Arc among its saints. Saigon is a sprawling metropolis once called the Paris of the Orient because its architecture blends oriental and French influences in a tropical setting. Its largest suburb is Cho Lon, inhabited mainly by ethnic Chinese. In 1968, Cho Lon was taken twice by the VC and suffered heavily while being retaken by U.S. troops. West of Saigon are sprawling pineapple plantations and scattered settlements of industrious Catholic refugees from the North.

To the northwest is a belt of rubber plantations developed by the French, and still farther northwest are triple-canopy jungles in what came to be called War Zones C and D. There, the VC formed two divisions of their own – organized, trained, and equipped much like NVA units and able to fight as guerrillas or as conventional infantry, as the situation warranted. To the northeast, the jungles ride up the spines of the southern highlands. To the east, rice fields, jungles, and tea plantations blend near Xoan Loc and Nui Dat. At various times in the war, elements of five U.S. divisions, three separate brigades, and an armored cavalry regiment fought in this zone alongside five Vietnamese divisions (including the marine and airborne divisions), a Thai division, the Australian–New Zealand Brigade Task Force, and the Philippine Civic Action Group.

Farthest south was IV Corps, headquartered at Can Tho in the Mekong Delta. The area is laced with rivers, streams, and canals, and fishing is a major industry. Although mainly a fertile region of small farms, the Mekong Delta also includes extensive coastal and inland swamps, particularly in the west and south. It is South Vietnam's bread basket or, more aptly, its rice basket. Here, three ARVN divisions predominated, complemented by elements of the U.S. 9th Infantry Division and the U.S. and South Vietnamese brown-water navies, which plied the waterways between the South China Sea and the Cambodian border. Except during the Tet offensive of 1968, battles in the delta tended to be inconclusive. The Highway 4 corridor was the scene of bloody fighting from 1967 to 1969, as both sides sought control of the main road connecting the delta to Saigon. There, mines and booby traps, interspersed with occasional battles of battalion and sometimes regimental scale, were persistent killers.

THE AMERICAN WAY OF WAR

For the Americans, a war of attrition in Vietnam against an indigenous insurgent foe was not one they were organized for and trained to fight. With their abundant, liberally applied firepower, they were a sledgehammer in search of a gnat. Because Americans were fighting amid the people they were sent to protect, the South Vietnamese suffered grave losses, particularly when the VC chose to fight in a hamlet, village, town, or city. It was hard to win people's hearts and minds and distance them spiritually from the insurgency when their own government was victimizing them and U.S. forces were inflicting more damage on them than any enemy had over the past 100 years. American strategy could not have been less sensible.

Strategy was only part of the problem. There was not just one American way of war in Vietnam. U.S. Marines in I Corps fought three distinctly different wars – a conventional area defense against a conventional foe along the DMZ; a local security war against the VC and NVA in hamlets surrounding coastal cities; and sometimes a conventional urban war, as in Hue in 1968. Later in the war, pitched battles often flared, involving tanks, artillery, and infantry from both sides. In Hue, marines fought house to house, just as their predecessors had fought in Seoul 15 years earlier. Unlike the army, the marines had few helicopters and moved mostly by foot or truck. Although trained and organized as a mobile amphibious force that could have posed a threat to North Vietnam's long exposed coast, the marines were not used that way. Neither were they paired with the navy's riverine forces in the Mekong Delta, incongruously leaving that role to the army, because Westmoreland did not want the marines close to Saigon where they would get ready attention from the media.

The marines' preferred way of war, as reflected in their *Small Wars Manual*, was to live among the people they were sent to protect. They broke selected rifle companies into Combined Action Platoons, reinforced squads that lived among the people in rural hamlets, and worked with local militia platoons. That approach to counterinsurgency left the sparsely populated highlands to the enemy but better protected the populace in the coastal lowlands. The VC nevertheless continued to mine roads, ambush convoys, and engage marine patrols in company and battalion strength. They also continued to covertly reconnoiter, collect taxes, and recruit in the major cities.

The marines' approach did not set well with the army. Westmoreland and other army generals were frustrated with Lieutenant General Lewis Walt, who, with two robust divisions, would not leave his coastal enclave to find and fight the NVA.[16] When offered the opportunity to work with the navy's riverine force in the Mekong Delta, Walt declined, preferring to keep his divisions together under a corps-level marine headquarters in the north. In essence, the marines became another allied army, fighting the war in their own way.

Competing command-and-control structures exacerbated the doctrinal disconnect between the army and the marine corps. By 1968, there were three corps-level headquarters in the I Corps Tactical Zone – the ARVN I Corps, the U.S. III Marine Amphibious Force, and the U.S. Army's XXIV Corps. Although army and marine units sometimes served under

[16] Krepinevich, *The Army and Vietnam*, p. 175.

each other's command, those exceptions were rare.[17] Joint and combined operations worked, but if they became the rule, someone's corps-level headquarters would become superfluous. While tactical necessity compelled cooperation, neither service trusted that the other would use its forces properly. The practice and its costs endure.

Wherever the army fought, helicopters were its dominant form of mobility and a reliable source of resupply, medical evacuation, and aerial firepower. Thanks to senior advocates of air mobility, the army had devoted considerable energy in the early 1960s to pioneering air assault concepts and acquiring a sizeable helicopter fleet. Major General Harry O. Kinnard, who became convinced of air mobility's necessity while serving with the 101st Airborne Division during preparations for a possible invasion of Cuba, led the army's air mobility experiment. He refined the concept in a series of brigade- and division-scale operational tests between 1963 and 1965 in Georgia and South Carolina.

At Fort Stewart in a major exercise before the commitment of large U.S. units to Vietnam, Special Forces-trained aggressors acted as a guerrilla force in dense forests and swamps similar to parts of Vietnam. Clad in civilian clothes, the "guerrillas" lived among the people in surrounding towns, sanctuaries into which the division could not go. They infiltrated the post on foot to establish field-expedient communications sites, caches of food and equipment, and hide sites for their teams. They watched the division's operating patterns and dispositions until given the freedom to strike.

Opportunistically, they then attacked the refuel–rearm sites of aviation units, struck command centers, ambushed convoys, and evaded air cavalry and infantry searching for their hide sites in the swamps. The surrogate guerrillas proved surprisingly hard to find, just by staying under the canopies of trees and moving in the shadows. The exercise revealed the ease with which even inexperienced guerrillas could find and attack the vulnerabilities of a technology-centric army and further underlined the need for responsive intelligence at every level of command to fully exploit the speed of aviation. All of those lessons still apply.

---

[17] In retaking Hue in 1968, a brigade of the Army's 1st Cavalry Division served under the 1st Marine Division. When a marine regiment at Khe Sanh became surrounded and came under sustained artillery bombardment from inside the DMZ, the relationship was reversed. The U.S. Army's 1st Cavalry Division came to the rescue, breaking the siege with the 1st Marine Regiment and an ARVN Airborne Brigade attached. John Prados and Ray Stubbe, *Valley of Decision: The Siege of Ke Sanh* (Annapolis, MD, 1991), p. 419.

To the detriment of the United States, the army largely ignored them in Vietnam.

THE HOST NATION AND ITS MILITARY ESTABLISHMENT – 1965

The environment in Vietnam in 1965 was chaotic. Aside from the political wreckage wrought by a succession of military coups, South Vietnam's army was a disaster. As a result of losses and desertion, most ARVN units were shadows of real companies, battalions, regiments, and divisions. Despite the assistance of nearly 16,000 U.S. and Australian advisors in Vietnam at the time, the pace of change in ARVN capabilities was glacial. With the background of a rural peasantry, the average recruit had little experience with mechanical things and did poorly at maintaining vehicles and helicopters. Like the VC, ARVN units were initially equipped with American weapons from the World War II era, whereas NVA units were armed with newer, lighter Russian and Chinese automatic weapons that outgunned their ARVN counterparts. American officers and noncommissioned officers, comfortable with U.S. training programs, created a copy of them for their allies, but Vietnamese recruits saw little relevance in the training because it bore little resemblance to the war they fought.

In a 3 March 1967 interview in *Time*, General Cao Van Vien, the ARVN chief of staff, summed up the situation, which had changed little in the past 13 years since the army's formation. Corrupt commanders carried "ghost soldiers" on their rolls and further pocketed the pay of dead soldiers while widows and orphans received nothing. ARVN soldiers received little pay, and corrupt company commanders sometimes garnished portions of their meager salaries. Desertion was rampant, and punishable by being forced to live in a cardboard shack with one's family amid the tactical wire and minefields surrounding an ARVN base. If a deserter were lucky, he could escape to join the VC.

Although Vietnam produced field rations for its troops, supply officers in Saigon sold them on the black market and they often ended up in VC hands. With no other way to feed themselves, ARVN troops stole food from the populace – hardly a way to win hearts and minds. That approach to supply represented an unsanctioned tax to compensate troops for their ill-paid service. The result, seen through the eyes of a South Vietnamese village chief, handed the VC an advantage: "when the VC took a meal, it was not like our soldiers way; burst in, demand food, sit around while they were waiting for it to be fixed, eat, and finally grab a couple of chickens and run off. Instead, the VC would go into the kitchen, clean the rice, and while they were waiting for it to cook, they would sweep the house and set the table. When the meal was over they would clean up and then thank everyone politely."[18]

Because of the ineptness and inattention of many of Vietnam's politically appointed senior officers, junior officers were demoralized and often abusive, exacerbating the army's high desertion rates. Desertion was most severe among the three divisions arrayed around Saigon. General Cao Van Vien characterized his 25th Division, stationed south and west of Saigon, as the worst in his army and perhaps the worst division in any army anywhere.[19] On the civil side, the situation was even worse. The people had long ago lost faith in their government and had no reason to hope that things would change for the better.

A look at the situation in one well-documented and critically important province, Long An, provides a sample of what was happening throughout South Vietnam. Under Ngo Dinh Diem, corruption had permeated every level of government. The nuances of what caused people to reject their government and to tolerate, aid, or join the enemy were lost in the careful language of U.S. intelligence estimates, masking the realities faced by ordinary Vietnamese.[20] Jeffrey Race's study of Long An suggests U.S. intelligence was wide of the mark. The southern areas were not "relatively unaffected" and the "slippage in morale and programs" ascribed to the central provinces had gone well beyond "slippage" in the south. By 1965, the government had simply lost people's trust in Long An. Its most serious mistake was reversing the Viet Minh's widely welcomed and economically beneficial redistribution of land by canceling deeds and returning the land to Vietnam's ruling elite. That grievance was exacerbated by the Cong An, a spy network established by the government to keep an eye on those who had returned from military service with the Viet Minh in the war against the French. Cong An operatives routinely used threats and torture to extort payments of bribes, leaving former Viet Minh with

---

[18] Jeffrey Race, *War Comes to Long An* (Berkeley, CA, 1972), p. 73.

[19] Soon after reading Cao Van Vien's interview at the Military Assistance Command Replacement Center in Saigon, I received orders to Advisory Team 99, advising a battalion of the ARVN 25th Division. Not fully comprehending the implications of his characterization of the division or the realities of the situation in Long An Province, I looked forward to the challenge.

[20] "The near paralysis of government initiative in Saigon appears to be spreading rapidly to outlying areas. Although the southern areas appear relatively unaffected... government authority has declined seriously in the northern coastal provinces... A slippage in morale and in programs among provincial administrations, at least in the central provinces, has already begun." SNIE 53-2-64, *The Situation in South Vietnam*, 1 October 1964.

no good choices. Some were idealists who had fought for Vietnam's independence and had no particular interest in taking up arms again, but the Cong An's behavior and government indifference to the population's grievances drove them into the VC's arms. District chiefs received a share of the Cong An's extortion money and therefore turned a blind eye to its activities.

Diem's government rigged elections, making the democratic process a sham and tainting every official with the stain of corruption before he ever took office. His appointment of a military man from Hue to serve as province chief in Long An further exacerbated the situation. He was out of touch with those he governed and cared little about their welfare. People had stopped expecting anything helpful from their government and saw its agents as corrupt, disinterested in their plight, and a danger to their safety. Moreover, the ARVN 25th Division, which garrisoned the province with two of its regiments, was from Central Vietnam. Its predominantly Trung Viet troops spoke a different dialect and had little regard for the populace among whom they served.

Booby traps were planted in fields by locals who seemed to vanish before ARVN and U.S. units arrived. Armored vehicles were an especially favored target. The VC observed where armored personnel carriers could cross streams and then mined the crossings beneath the mud. There, a pressure plate was nearly impossible to find, but a 12-ton armored personnel carrier would be sure to activate it, typically detonating enough explosive to split the vehicle open. In Vietnam, many of the improvised mines were 250-lb and 500-lb bombs dropped by the U.S. Air Force or 105-mm and 155-mm howitzer rounds fired by U.S. or ARVN artillery. The VC recovered many that failed to detonate, moved them onto roads by sled and ox cart, and rigged them with new detonators to serve as mines. Other popular devices were hand grenades, hidden in the vegetation along a trail and set off with trip wires. Little has changed since then, except the detonators have become more sophisticated and these roadside bombs are now called improvised explosive devices.

In March 1967, the VC overran a U.S. rifle company at night only three kilometers from its battalion base camp at Rach Kien. The VC executed the wounded and carried off radios, machine guns, rifles, grenade launchers, and night-vision devices, along with batteries and ammunition. Two months later, the VC overran the headquarters of a nearby ARVN battalion and killed three of its four American advisors, along with more than 30 ARVN soldiers and officers. Asking civilians about the VC typically produced disingenuous answers. Sons, brothers, cousins, and husbands were always "away on business" or "visiting a relative" in some distant town. Who had a workable plan in these circumstances? Who stayed long enough to see a plan through? A battalion advisor's typical tour of duty was six months with the battalion and six months on the regiment, division, or corps staff. District and province advisors remained in their positions for a full year and few volunteered to stay longer.

One battalion's experience, however, suggests that partnerships between U.S. and ARVN units could quickly elevate the capabilities, morale, and confidence of South Vietnamese units. The exemplar ARVN battalion in Long An had had seven U.S. senior advisors since 1965, all captains with no previous combat experience. Its performance had been lackluster at best. Its commander, a major commissioned by the French 15 years earlier, was simply going through the motions, playing it safe and staying clear of his superiors and the VC. Seeing an opportunity, an American lieutenant colonel commanding a nearby infantry battalion took on the role of mentor, role model, and principal advisor to his ARVN counterpart. They met regularly over meals, planned operations together, and paired their rifle companies on operations.

Within three months, the U.S. and ARVN battalions became the most active and successful units in their respective divisions. In collaboration with local district chiefs, the two battalions undertook joint civic-action projects, refurbishing marketplaces, restoring foot bridges on trails to markets, and establishing and equipping medical treatment facilities on the main trails. In each case, the Americans took pains to see to it that the Vietnamese accomplished every project. Americans provided the material, but the Vietnamese provided the ideas and labor – their soldiers working side by side with local civilians. The relationship kindled mutual respect and ensured that locals had a stake in protecting their infrastructure.

Some U.S. commanders discovered through close association with the Vietnamese how to separate the VC from the people, but the process took time and consistency. Where feasible, they spread their companies across contested territory, taking up continuous residence in or adjacent to hamlets and villages. Their troops worked with locals and patrolled by day with district or provincial militias, ARVN units, and navy riverine units. Each night, they set out ambushes along expected infiltration routes to hinder the enemy's ability to move among the populace, to exert political control, to recruit new members, or to collect taxes. After a while, U.S. and ARVN losses to mines and booby traps fell, information on enemy activity increased, numbers of insurgents declined, and people began to harvest and sell crops and carry on commerce. The partnership bolstered

ARVN capabilities and self-confidence. When enemy forces then sought to mass, they could do so only in unpopulated areas, where they were often detected by daylight patrols or "eagle flights," a series of airmobile insertions in which U.S. and ARVN platoons hopped continuously from place to place, seeking signs of enemy activity.

When they found an enemy unit, one company became a fixing force while artillery and tactical aviation pounded likely escape routes and more U.S. and ARVN companies flew into the area to form a steadily constricting cordon. Although cordons were never air tight, the tactic kept the enemy under pressure and inflicted sufficiently severe punishment to disrupt their operations. Had that approach been in wider use by 1967, it would have been harder for the VC to infiltrate such large numbers of troops and weapons into Vietnam's cities, but it could not have prevented it altogether.

The aforementioned description of counterinsurgency operations became the rule after 1968, when General Abrams replaced General Westmoreland as the Military Assistance Command-Vietnam commander, but it misses a fundamental point that Abrams himself recognized. The conflict was not America's war to win; it ultimately had to be settled by the Vietnamese themselves. There were not enough Americans in uniform worldwide to cover all of South Vietnam with the kind of tactics just described, and few U.S. battalion commanders had the requisite instincts to implement such partnerships. ARVN troops and local militias, no matter how thinly spread, could not cover it all either. Approximately a third of Long An Province's populated areas remained VC controlled. Counterinsurgency operations worked, as far as they went, but without an offensive conventional strategy to deprive the enemy of his sanctuaries and to put him on the defensive, military operations could do no more than buy time – the hard, expensive way. Such operations are like medicine that treats the symptom but leaves the disease uncured. The disease that gave the insurgency its recruits was a corrupt, unresponsive, and unelected South Vietnamese political administration. It would have taken decades to remedy the rot that permeated South Vietnam's ruling class. America typically does not have that much political patience.

By 1970, Long An Province was a different place than it had been three years earlier.[21] In contested areas where there had been brown, fallow fields and widespread destruction in 1967, repaired villages were

---

[21] In January 1970, the author returned to Long An as a rifle company commander in the U.S. 9th Infantry Division. The observations reflected here are from that experience.

surrounded by green, well-tended fields. Bomb craters had become fish ponds and watering holes for buffalo. Once impassable secondary roads had been graded and carried traffic of all kinds. Gone from the roads were the huge craters left by mines. The bridge across the Vam Co Dong, blown by VC sappers in 1967, had been fully restored and carried a steady flow of two-way traffic on National Highway 4 – the "rice road" to the Mekong Delta. The ferry site on Provincial Highway 5 had also been rebuilt, opening a second corridor between Saigon and the delta, and it too carried substantial traffic. ARVN troops, ill equipped in 1967, were now equipped with new American weapons, radios, and vehicles and exhibited a refreshing cockiness. Was this metamorphosis the result of better counterinsurgency tactics or the VC's decimation during their ill-considered "general uprising" of 1968? It was some of both, but experience suggests the latter was the more important cause.

In the Plain of Reeds, however, things were much the same as they had been in 1967. There, U.S. troops were compelled to watch their enemy violate every rule Americans were obliged to follow. It was not uncommon to see long convoys of trucks with their lights on, entering the Ba Thu transit camp on the Cambodian side of the border.[22] The Joint Chiefs' 1965 assessment of the futility of a bombing campaign against the Ho Chi Minh Trail was on the mark.[23] Six years of bombing had not diminished the flow of supplies to the south. Instead, infiltration increased even as the bombing intensified.[24] Enemy bases in eastern Cambodia were alive with activity and the Cambodian port of Sihanoukville was still receiving Soviet-bloc arms shipments.

Ba Thu was the southern terminus of the Ho Chi Minh Trail. From there, enemy supplies and troops dispersed, moving by night on slim, flat-bottomed boats, traversing canals and streams to cross the Plain of Reeds and the Vam Co Tay, and Vam Co Dong (Oriental and Occidental Rivers) to reach areas to the south and east. Americans were not allowed to fire on enemy troops and supply convoys staging on the Cambodian side of the border and were not permitted to operate inside a

---

[22] Ba Thu was referred to in captured enemy documents as Base Area 367, the last rest station on a long journey from North Vietnam.
[23] SNIE 14-3-69, *Capabilities of the Vietnamese Communists for Fighting in South Vietnam*, 17 July 1969, para. IIIG.
[24] Seen through enemy eyes, the bombing of the Ho Chi Minh Trail was a failure: "According to our statistics, out of every 100 bombs that were dropped, only 0.23 percent hit the road, which means the Americans needed to drop a thousand bombs to get two of them on the road. Our repairs were quick. We used the exploded dirt and rock to repave the Trail." Bui Tin in Wiest, *Rolling Thunder in a Gentle Land*, p. 70.

kilometer-wide buffer zone along the border. NVA infiltrators generally crossed in platoon or company-size groups, led by VC pathfinders and scout dogs to find and avoid U.S. ambushes.

THE GAME CHANGES – 1970 TO 1975

In early May 1970, U.S. forces invaded Cambodia, following an earlier ARVN assault south of the Saigon–Pnom Penh Highway. In *A Better War*, Lewis Sorley cites Abrams' eagerness to conduct incursions into the sanctuaries. Abrams recognized that he needed to buy time for the South Vietnamese and security for America's withdrawal, and he could do so only by disrupting the enemy's base areas along the border. He also knew that goal could not be achieved with a bombing campaign alone. U.S. Ambassador Ellsworth Bunker was of like mind.[25]

Abruptly, the war changed. Americans were on the offensive, sweeping into base areas across the border, finding hastily abandoned VC and NVA billeting areas, command centers, well-stocked supply dumps, and hospitals, all cleverly concealed amid what had once been a string of Cambodian hamlets. The NVA fought a series of stubborn rearguard actions from the border westward to screen the withdrawal of their higher commands, but in each fight they grew weaker, reflecting both their losses and the collapse of their supply system. As the pursuit gathered momentum, President Richard Nixon ordered a halt to all U.S. operations deeper than 30 kilometers inside Cambodia.

Although the politics might have made sense in Washington (given the tragedy unfolding at Kent State), the stop line made no sense on the battlefield. The NVA could not fight a successful round-the-clock rear guard action against highly mobile U.S. forces supported by aerial reconnaissance and air- and ground-based fires. They could not hope to recover or soon replace the supplies they were losing and could not stop long enough to establish a new base area where they could replace losses, rest, rearm, and refit. The only military course of action that made sense to U.S. commanders was to continue pushing the enemy hard and fast, giving them no chance to regroup. Unfortunately, America's political condition gave enemy forces the respite they needed. NVA and VC forces that were left to regroup beyond the stop line helped capture Saigon five years later.

---

[25] "I think we should have gone into the sanctuaries before we did, because having the sanctuaries gave the enemy the opportunity to raise or lower the level of combat at will. They could retreat to the sanctuaries, reinforce, re-equip, come back and attack. And we couldn't do anything about it." Ellsworth Bunker in Samuel Lipsman and Edward Doyle, *Fighting for Time* (Boston, 1983), p. 149.

It is useful to add that in this hybrid war, the NVA were often poor guerrillas. They were Bac Viets (northerners from Tonkin) trying to blend into a Nam Viet (Cochin China) culture. Although generally disciplined and brave, they were often ill at ease when amalgamated into VC units as fillers. They did not know the land, they spoke with a dialect that southerners mocked, they were homesick, they were sometimes resented by the VC, and they had less resistance than southerners to diseases endemic to the south. They had trained as conventional infantry in North Vietnam, so playing guerrilla amid a semi-alien culture did not come naturally. They remained, however, solid conventional infantry and, when used that way, were a formidable foe.

The following February, the ARVN launched Operation Lam Son 719 to punch down the Route 9 corridor toward Tchepone in Laos. The operation was not intended to permanently occupy the narrow corridor it would establish, advancing only far enough and long enough to destroy two base areas containing supplies stockpiled for a future NVA offensive. The invasion force was to withdraw before the monsoon season began in May. U.S. Army helicopters and U.S. Air Force fighters and bombers supported the operation; the Cooper-Church amendment, passed two months earlier, had prohibited U.S. ground troops, including advisors, from entering Laos. ARVN troops would go it alone on the ground, relying on their own forward observers and air liaison teams to coordinate U.S. fire support. The plan was American in conception, hatched in Washington, and refined at U.S. XXIV Corps headquarters in Vietnam. Participating ARVN units were not told of the operation or their intended role in it until days before the assault was launched. Command arrangements were confused and logistical arrangements had to be cobbled together at the last moment.

South Vietnam's best units, the 1st Division, the Airborne and Marine Divisions, rangers, and armor drove swiftly into Laos and dug in atop ridges overlooking Route 9. If successful, the operation would have cut the Ho Chi Minh Trail at the point Giap had feared in 1964, but by 1971 the area was defended by seasoned combat troops and bypass routes had been prepared to the west of Lam Son 719's stop line.[26] The NVA had positioned 20,000 troops, supported by artillery, armor, and dense

---

[26] "In 1971, when U.S. and ARVN forces launched the *Lam Son* campaign, attacking the Ho Chi Minh trail in southern Laos, it was already too late. The trail had by then branched into numerous byways, circuits, and shortcuts. The invasion created no noticeable decrease in the tonnage transported." Wiest, *Rolling Thunder in a Gentle Land*, p. 70.

concentrations of anti-aircraft guns, around likely landing zones north of Route 9. Another force of roughly 16,000 troops waited to attack from the south. Unlike Cambodia, NVA troops in Laos were close to home, well supplied, and fully prepared. The result was a disaster for the South Vietnamese. Their best troops were routed, and doubt and apprehension replaced the self-confidence that had accompanied the Cambodian incursion ten months earlier. Tragically, Lieutenant General Do Cao Tri, one of the ARVN's ablest generals and the hero of the Cambodian incursion, died when his helicopter crashed en route to assume command in Laos.

If Lam Son 719 had been launched a year earlier when American troops went into Cambodia, there would have been no Cooper-Church amendment and the additional weight of U.S. XXIV Corps, coupled with the ARVN's best units, could have given the invasion force numerical superiority and sufficient resilience to withstand NVA counterattacks. If the Ho Chi Minh Trail had been cut and the Cambodian sanctuary destroyed, the NVA would have lost its best troops and their supplies, painstakingly built up over the previous decade. The enemy would have taken some years to recover, buying Saigon time to get its political act together.

Allowing the ARVN to be defeated in a fight with the NVA was a strategic blunder. ARVN self-confidence mattered to the war's subsequent course, but now it was shattered. In contrast, North Vietnam emerged with its self-confidence restored, now convinced it could defeat the ARVN's best units in conventional combat, an option made all the more appealing by the imminent U.S. departure. Soldiers could be clear-eyed about the implications, but they did not have the president's responsibilities or share his burdens. The president had to answer to many constituencies, international and domestic, and had to balance accounts that were well outside a soldier's perspective – but a strategic blunder was still a strategic blunder. The loss of 58,000 American lives, a divided society, and the loss of self-confidence would influence every U.S. foreign policy decision for decades.

By 1972, the Communists had regained their strength in the south, repopulating or replacing VC main force units with NVA troops. They brought tanks and artillery into I, II, and III Corps zones and launched their Ngyuen Hue Offensive in April 1972. This was no guerrilla-centric general offensive, as the Tet Offensive of 1968 had mostly been. It was an outright conventional invasion involving three full NVA corps, totaling 12 conventionally organized divisions, including tanks, howitzers, long-range field guns, sappers, and mobile anti-aircraft weapons. Nguyen Hue's objectives were less ambitious than the Tet Offensive of 1968. Its three widely separated offensives aimed at grabbing territory and destroying ARVN units. The operation revealed NVA weaknesses. The NVA were not yet able to coordinate tanks and infantry, causing their armor to suffer serious losses. Resolute ARVN infantry halted the NVA at An Loc and Kontum, although it is unclear whether the outcome would have been the same without U.S. air and advisory support. By year's end, the last U.S. and allied combat troops were gone and South Vietnam was on its own. The communist offensive of 1975, intended to be another series of short land grabs, collapsed the ARVN defenses in the Central Highlands and led to the general collapse of the Saigon regime.

It is not clear that the war's outcome could have been different in the end, given the depth of corruption and dysfunction in South Vietnam's government and military command, but there were unquestionably able, patriotic, and motivated people who performed well despite unfavorable odds. Lieutenant General Do Cao Tri, killed in a helicopter crash in 1971, and Lieutenant General Ngo Quang Truong, who commanded the ARVN 1st Division at Hue in 1968 and I Corps in 1972 after the sacking of his predecessor, were able commanders who could have excelled in any army. Younger officers, particularly graduates of the ARVN military academy at Dalat, were among Vietnam's best and brightest and generally led with courage and skill. As in any army, ARVN soldiers, when resolutely and capably led, fought with the same skill, courage, and determination as their foe.

A final view "through enemy eyes" is worth considering:

> In my opinion as a former officer in the People's Army, the idea that America could not have won the Vietnam War is only half right. It is true that the United States could not have won this war totally. But the Americans could have avoided the great losses they incurred, both for themselves and the Saigon regime. If the United States had not over-estimated the potential response of the Chinese, if they had not so gullibly signed the peace accord with Laos in 1962, if they had sent their infantry to occupy the panhandle south of the Gianh River, if they had occupied a small segment of the Ho Chi Minh Trail... the outcome would have been very different.
>
> Take a look, for example, at that period when we incurred the greatest losses in South Vietnam and could no longer replenish our forces without sending troops from the North. I am referring to the time immediately following the Tet offensive, when our bases in the cities and countryside had been exposed and destroyed. This period, lasting from the Tet offensive until the middle of 1971, coincided precisely with the time when the

> Americans were precipitously pulling out their troops and reducing their firepower.... The Americans thereby gave us a great escape route and a quick way to regain our force and position.[27]

That view, penned by an officer of the NVA who served throughout his country's long wars with France, the United States, South Vietnam, and Cambodia, provides useful food for thought regarding the realities of hybrid warfare. Sound tactics and doctrine certainly matter and can achieve much, but only a clear-eyed strategy based on understanding and exploiting the enemy's pressure points offers any chance for success.

Over the years that followed the war in Vietnam, Americans have had time for sober reflection on what happened and why. One value in understanding history is to apply its lessons to contemporary warfare. Although no two wars are alike and the lessons from one are not fully transferable to another, lessons learned from Vietnam remain relevant today. Americans ignore them to their detriment, as they already have in Afghanistan and Iraq.

LESSONS

There are six lessons from hybrid warfare in Vietnam that also apply to varying degrees in Iraq, Afghanistan, and elsewhere today.

1. Because conventional warfare and counterinsurgency require different organizations, training, equipment, and doctrine, it is difficult for any nation to address both. Unable to make a wholesale shift, the United States applies predominantly conventional forces to counterinsurgency roles, and it has suffered frustration amid the resulting drain of blood and treasure.
2. In hybrid wars, tactical commanders confront the difficulty of keeping troops among the population to deny insurgents freedom of action, while simultaneously attempting to pressure large, conventional enemy forces. Seeking to do both has resulted in trying to be impossibly strong everywhere.
3. When an insurgency receives support from across international boundaries, the United States can best apply its considerable conventional military capabilities against the offending country or countries by driving the enemy out of his sanctuaries, an approach that plays to U.S. military strengths while buying time for those it

---

[27] Bui Tin quoted in Wiest, *Rolling Thunder in a Gentle Land*, pp. 70–71.

supports. Although no political administration wants a wider war, the consequences of allowing sanctuaries to exist are a protracted war and diminished credibility.

4. Against an insurgency, the application of major U.S. conventional forces normally has had a lower payoff and more adverse societal consequences than other, lower-cost options such as the provision of governance support, corruption-shielded economic aid, and military training and equipment focused on counterguerrilla operations. Host-nation forces know the land and the people, and if provided proper leadership, training, and equipment, they can better identify and deal with insurgents. Outside powers can better deal with the enemy's larger conventional formations, operating from unpopulated areas or across international borders.

5. Helping a threatened government to defeat an insurgency and develop the strength to deter hostile neighbors requires a willingness to learn and remain long enough to see things through. Such knowledge and endurance requires a relatively small cadre of dedicated, long-serving, and well-supported individuals with wide latitude, as well as the ear and confidence of both the American president and the local host-nation leadership. When large civil bureaucracies and large conventional forces enter the picture, unity of command blurs amid competition among agencies, responsiveness mires in bureaucracy, and Americans come to see the local government as an impediment to U.S. progress rather than the essential target of American help.

6. Intelligence estimates rarely provide the necessary historical depth or nuanced understanding of the interaction of political, social, economic, and military dynamics, or the regional relationships in a conflict. U.S. analyses tend to be stove-piped by bureaucratic boundaries and field reports filtered through the bureaucracy. Thus, they become increasingly blurred by consensus building and Washington's conventional wisdom.

In light of Vietnam's lessons, it is worth considering some of the implications for warfare in the twenty-first century. Americans will not shrink from a fight, but they expect their side to win. If a war drags on for years with no path to victory in sight, they lose patience and withdraw their support, as they did in Vietnam. The same reality is operative today.

If the government of the host country is riddled with corruption, it will take decades to root out the rot and it can only be done by the country's own people – their way, with their institutions, and on their own initiative. The few examples in history of a country's being able to do that under the pressure of war waged on its soil are exceptions to the rule.

If the host government is unable to satisfy its people's demands for social justice but the opposition satisfies that need, the insurgency will persist regardless of military pressure. When the Vietnamese government overturned the popular and productive land reforms instituted by the Viet Minh, it engendered distrust that affected every aspect of governance. Inequitable distribution of oil revenues in Iraq and land grabs by malign power brokers in Afghanistan might represent contemporary equivalents.

To achieve victory in hybrid war, enemy sanctuaries must be destroyed. In Vietnam, the enemy enjoyed sanctuaries in Laos, Cambodia, and North Vietnam, with only brief intercessions. Bombing can irritate, reduce, and impede, but it cannot root out opposition or stop an enemy from pursuing his aims.

When American forces depart a country, Congress and the American public will not continue to defer domestic priorities to bankroll the sustained defense of an ally. In Korea, where U.S. forces remained, U.S. security support continued because it was necessary to protect American forces, and South Korea prospered. In Vietnam, U.S. forces departed, U.S. security support evaporated, and South Vietnam collapsed.

If the U.S. trains the armed forces of a host country to fight in the manner that U.S. forces fight, with all the associated bureaucracy, logistics, technical intelligence, and air power, the host country's forces risk collapse when U.S. forces depart. If the logistics system, intelligence capabilities, and air support of the host nation remain rudimentary, the dependencies its forces developed on the American enablers will leave them unprepared to cope upon the departure of U.S. forces from the theater. Cultivating and educating capable civilian administrators and a public-service-oriented officer corps can make a bigger difference than decades of material aid.

Tour lengths of U.S. military personnel and civilian advisors must be differentiated according to function. America learned too late in Vietnam to adjust senior advisor tour lengths to 18 months, with a break for family leave every 6 months. Gaining a host-nation counterpart's trust and cultivating mutual respect takes time and once gained, it is a precious commodity that must be nurtured. Expecting an ally to constantly adapt to a steady flow of "advisors" on short tours of duty is expecting too much of any human being. The British were able to sustain their influence abroad through a civil service and officer corps that remained on extended hardship tours for many years at a time. They developed a sense of what was needed, what was possible, and how to get things done. In the process, they developed consistent relations with locals who could cope with their shortcomings and learn from their strengths. In contrast, Americans and their allies rotate through Iraq and Afghanistan on brief stints of duty that are often counterproductive.

A defensive war against a hybrid opponent has a low prospect of success. Unless the opponent's source of sustenance can be placed under direct pressure, no battle can be conclusive and victory will remain elusive. Interdicting the sources of an insurgency's funding requires more than military pressure. The flow of money and arms from Iran and extremists from Syria and elsewhere to aid Iraqi insurgents and the flow of money from outside religious radicals and the drug trade to Afghan insurgents are contemporary examples.

Hybrid warfare influences every level of authority differently, creating tensions in training and doctrine, in the allocation of human and material resources, and in strategic and political choices.

Finally, history matters. Knowing a country's history, its heroes, its cultural milestones, its cultural fissures, and its motivations makes its behavior more understandable, predictable, and more readily anticipated and exploited.

11

Conclusion

What the Past Suggests

Williamson Murray

In 2006, the Israeli Defense Forces (IDF) invaded Lebanon with the express aim of destroying the Shi'a militia, Hezbollah, and ending its annoying habit of firing rockets into northern Israel and conducting raids on Israeli garrisons along the Lebanese border. The Israeli military venture was a failure. Despite overwhelming conventional military power, complete air superiority, precision-guided munitions, and considerable conceptualization about how technology might change war in the present and future, the Israelis ran into an opponent who surprised them on a number of levels.

Ironically, to a considerable extent, the IDF's difficulties resulted from its considerable buy-in to the technophilia that had marked the American enthusiasm in the 1990s and early 2000s for what many termed "the revolution in military affairs." The stunning success of the coalition in the Gulf War of January to February 1991 suggested to some Pentagon analysts that the U.S. military had created capabilities that would revolutionize war, at least for those who held the technological high ground. The advocates of the revolution in military affairs argued that technological advances in precision weapons, surveillance capabilities, computers, information systems, and sensors would allow the American military in future wars to see, grasp, and destroy enemy forces before they could effectively respond.[1] Despite the best efforts of the Office of the Secretary

---

[1] For an examination of the actual role of military revolutions and revolutions in military affairs throughout history, see the first and last chapters of MacGregor Knox and Williamson Murray, eds., *The Dynamics of Military Revolutions, 1300–2050* (Cambridge, 2000).

of Defense's Office of Net Assessment to underline that such revolutions in the past were largely conceptual rather than technological, the pursuit of a technological nirvana came to dominate the thinking of much of the American military.

In part influenced by American thinking, the IDF rolled into Lebanon with the expectation that its technological and conventional military superiority would allow it to destroy its opponents in short order. That was not the case. At the tactical level, Hezbollah fought a war that mixed conventional military action with guerrilla and terrorist strikes, all the while firing a large number of missiles at northern Galilee. Deeply entrenched in foxholes, bunkers, and fortified positions and utilizing ambushes and hit-and-run attacks, Hezbollah's infantry inflicted heavy casualties on the attackers. Although in no sense did the Shi'a militia come close to defeating the Israelis, their performance was good enough to enable Hezbollah to claim at least a stalemate, which was as good as a victory to an Arab world long used to defeat at the hands of the IDF. Moreover, if the Israelis did not suffer an outright military defeat, they certainly suffered a political defeat of considerable proportions.

Hezbollah's performance also caught the attention of defense experts and pundits in Washington, a city inhabited by a large body of defense cognoscenti who regard history as a tiresome exercise, certainly not one for the "real experts" in defense matters. To many of these analysts, the combination by Shi'a militia of conventional military tactics with guerrilla and terrorist activities appeared to represent a novel approach to war that would revolutionize conflict in the twenty-first century. Conferences and articles on this supposedly new form of conflict sprouted like mushrooms in the basements of dismal castles. Few, if any, of these exercises in thinking about the future examined history to see if the past might offer context and evidence to understand this phenomena of political entities mixing conventional military operations with the activities of insurgents and terrorists. Given what passes for serious intellectual discourse in Washington, this response to the challenge of hybrid war is not surprising.

Despite the surprise that the events in Lebanon elicited in the American defense community, the historical record suggests that hybrid warfare in one form or another may well be the norm for human conflict rather than the exception. Moreover, history also suggests that such conflicts may well be the most difficult conflicts to win. If that is so, then that wonderful comment by the great American philosopher Yogi Berra – it's "déjà vu all over again" – reverberates as a warning that much of the present only represents an echo of the past. But then, Thucydides had already noted in that greatest of all historical examinations of war that he had written his work because "it will be enough for me... if these words of mine are judged useful by those who want to understand clearly the events which happened in the past and which (human nature being what it is) will, at some time or other and in much the same ways, be repeated in the future."[2]

Ironically, during the 2003 destruction of Saddam Hussein's murderous regime by U.S. and coalition military forces, for a short period that conflict resembled in many of its manifestations hybrid warfare at its most ferocious. Despite warnings from a number of his advisors during the run-up to the invasion, Saddam refused to recognize the nature of the looming American threat: large-scale conventional operations.[3] Instead, given Saddam's perception that it was doubtful the Americans would dare to invade his country, Iraq's substantial paramilitary and conventional forces focused on internal security in the belief that the more likely danger would be, as in March 1991, an internal uprising by the Shi'a. When the invasion came, Saddam, contemptuous of American technology and fighting ability, committed both his conventional and irregular forces to a stand-up fight. The result was that substantial portions of Saddam's paramilitary Ba'ath forces, such as the Fedayeen Saddam, made the mistake of attacking the 3rd Infantry Division in the desert as it moved north along the Euphrates River. There, caught in the open, the Abrams and Bradleys of the American military slaughtered them.

Nevertheless, the ferocity of the paramilitary attacks caught the attention of the Americans, especially the V Corps commander, Lieutenant General William "Scott" Wallace. In an interview with reporters from the *New York Times* and the *Washington Post* on 27 March, Wallace commented that "The enemy we're fighting is a bit different than the one we war-gamed against, because of the paramilitary forces. We knew they were here, but we did not know how they would fight."[4] That remark,

---

[2] Thucydides, *History of the Peloponnesian War*, trans. Rex Warner (London, 1954), p. 48.

[3] For an examination based on the massive haul of Iraqi documents captured by coalition forces in April and May 2003, see Kevin M. Woods with Michael R. Pease, Mark E. Stout, Williamson Murray, and James G. Lacey, *The Iraqi Perspectives Report, Saddam's Senior Leadership on Operation Iraqi Freedom from the Official U.S. Joint Forces Command Report* (Annapolis, MD, 2006).

[4] Michael R. Gordon and General Bernard E. Trainor, *Cobra II, The Inside Story of the Invasion and Occupation of Iraq* (New York, 2006), p. 311.

which almost got Wallace fired by two of the most arrogant and incompetent senior officials in American military history, was spot on.[5]

In fact, luckily for the Americans, Saddam had refused the advice of his most competent general. Lieutenant General Raad Hamdani had urged the dictator to hide his conventional military units in Iraq's cities, where in combination with the Fedayeen they could execute what in retrospect would have looked quite similar to the military operations Hezbollah was to carry out in Lebanon in 2006.[6] But Saddam dismissed the American military and its lethal technological capabilities. Thus, the Iraqi Army stood and fought along the Euphrates, where a combination of U.S. air and ground power destroyed it in short order. Had the Iraqis followed a strategy of burrowing their conventional military forces in the cities and then used the fanatical Fedayeen to attack the Americans within that urban terrain, the invaders of Iraq, especially considering the presence of Al Jazeera and Western journalists, would have faced the problem of digging the Iraqi fighters out amidst millions of civilians, a picture that would not have played well on the world's media stage. As it was, the last battles within Baghdad against a broken and almost leaderless combination of weak conventional forces and Fedayeen turned into a nasty enough experience for the U.S. 3rd Infantry Division.[7]

THE LOGIC OF NUMBERS AND COMMITMENT

In one of his more ironic comments, Clausewitz notes that "no one starts a war – or rather, no one in his senses ought to do so – without first being clear in his mind what he intends to achieve by that war and how he intends to conduct it."[8] Of course, the irony lies in the fact that although most statesmen and military leaders have some conception of what they hope to accomplish in embarking on war, in fact, the connection between the ends and the means they plan to employ is often tenuous at best.[9]

---

[5] The two individuals are obviously the U.S. Secretary of Defense, Donald Rumsfeld, and the U.S. CENTCOM commander, General Tommy Franks.
[6] See Woods et al., *The Iraqi Perspectives Report*, pp. 25–32.
[7] In this respect, see Jim Lacey, *Take Down, The 3rd Infantry Division's Twenty-One Day Assault on Baghdad* (Annapolis, MD, 2007), pp. 208–247.
[8] Carl von Clausewitz, *On War*, ed. and trans. Michael Howard and Peter Paret (Princeton, NJ, 1975), p. 579.
[9] In fact, in some cases, political leaders have had no clear idea of what they hope their war will achieve. The author of this chapter has been involved in a project using Iraqi documents and transcripts of meetings to examine the planning and conduct of the war

Making the historical picture even more depressing is the fact that rarely do those who embark on war possess a realistic understanding of the "other." In the centuries before the birth of Christ, the Chinese military philosopher Sun Tzu commented that one should "know [your] enemy and know yourself; in a hundred battles you will never be in peril" – the most basic principle of war and strategy but one to which few political and military leaders have paid attention.[10]

The problem with not understanding the other, his culture, what he values, and his approach to war is that the enemy will in all such cases fight within a framework that fits his rather than our understanding of war. To fail to understand not only the strategic framework but also the tactical and operational framework within which an enemy will fight is a guaranteed recipe for disaster. Such understanding is basic to any strategy, whether at the grand or theater level. Again, we confront one of Clausewitz's most basic paradoxes: "Everything in war is very simple, but the simplest thing is difficult."[11] Yet, the catalogue of military failures that litter the historical landscape would make it appear that achieving such understanding is nearly impossible for humans.

The basic issue in hybrid warfare has been the consistent ability of those defending their state or political entity to pose a twofold threat to their opponents. By possessing conventional forces that can at the right time and place concentrate sufficient military power to destroy portions of the attacking forces, a defending force presents the attacker with the need to keep his forces concentrated. Yet, the possession of other forces that control the countryside by ambushing messengers, disrupting supply convoys, and attacking isolated units presents the attacker with a quandary: Deal with the enemy's irregular forces by dispersing one's own forces, which in turn makes the dispersed units vulnerable to the enemy's conventional forces, or keep one's forces concentrated and cede control of the countryside to the enemy. Moreover, the employment of large conventional forces, no matter how successful they might be against the dispersed forces of the enemy, may exacerbate the natural hostility of the population against the interlopers, who have disturbed their well-being. And that in turn can only serve to increase the support for unconventional,

---

against Iran that Saddam waged from 1980 to 1988. What is clear in the documents from 1980 is that Saddam and his advisors had no clear idea of what he believed military operations could achieve against the Iranians.

[10] Sun Tzu, *The Art of War*, trans. Samuel B. Griffith (Oxford, 1963), p. 84.
[11] Clausewitz, *On War*, p. 119.

guerrilla forces. The quandary is obvious; yet, those military organizations that have confronted opponents who have relied on hybrid warfare to defend themselves have had a spotty record.

THOUGHTS ON HISTORY AND HYBRID WARS

It would seem on the basis of the chapters in this study that success in such cases has rested on several crucial factors. The first and perhaps the most important lesson is that overwhelming superiority in resources and manpower can be but is not always decisive in such conflicts. Equally important is the will power to expend those resources over substantial periods of time because the historical cases suggest that there are no "silver bullet" solutions in these conflicts. In other words, *blitzkrieg* is not in the vocabulary of hybrid war.

The Roman Empire clearly possessed the resources and the ruthlessness to win a hybrid war against the German tribes. Yet, given the lack of an agricultural base in Germany – and there would not be one until the invention of the moldboard plow in the seventh century AD – did it make sense strategically to fight and win such a hugely expensive war, when it would be exceedingly difficult to sustain Rome's legions logistically on the Elbe? Considering the enormous success of Roman arms and diplomacy following the disaster suffered by Varus and his legions, it would seem that the Romans made the decision not to fight a war to conquer Germania and its fractious tribes on the basis of sound strategic decision making.[12]

Thus, the aims of the great Roman invasions of Drusus and Tiberius that came in the aftermath of the Teutoburg Wald disaster aimed at breaking the German threat to Roman territory, specifically Gaul, rather than at re-creating the province that had slipped away in the darkness of the German forests. The will was no longer there to support such an effort, although most probably for reasons other than Roman unwillingness to bear the costs of such a war. Instead, having tramped through the gloomy forests of Germany, they saw no strategic or political reasons to conquer such worthless lands, at least for the present. A century and a half later, Marcus Aurelius may have aimed at expanding the Empire to the borders of the upper Oder, but our sources simply are not sufficiently clear to

---

[12] Since Edward Luttwak's *The Grand Strategy of the Roman Empire: From the First Century A.D. to the Third* (Baltimore, MD, 1976), the question of Roman grand strategy has attracted considerable interest from ancient historians, many of whom today have come to the bizarre conclusion that because the Romans did not have a term for grand strategy, they could not have had one.

understand what exactly the aims of his wars in the 170s might have been.

Equally important, those who desire to wage hybrid war must possess the means, either from their own sources or from foreign aid, to maintain a creditable conventional capability, one sufficient to prevent their opponents from being able to concentrate on controlling the countryside and the population. The Irish rebels against Elizabethan English rule failed to cross the boundary from partisan-insurgent warfare to conventional war for a sufficient length of time to wage a truly effective hybrid war. Nor were their Spanish allies able to provide sufficient arms and conventional troops to make up for what the Irish lacked, a conventional military capability that would enable the insurgents to win in a conventional, European-style battle. The Irish have always been extraordinarily brave warriors, but they lacked the resources and knowledge to put an effective conventional army in the field. In contrast, the Spanish could never quite see the advantages to their strategic position of supporting the Irish with sufficient conventional forces to provide a real chance for victory over the English. In the end, the determination of history's course is always a matter of the context within which events occur, and from the Spanish perspective, what really mattered was the suppression of the revolt in the Netherlands, not what happened in the cold, wet bogs of Ireland.

The problems presented by hybrid war in the American Revolution and in the American Civil War present a number of interesting contrasts in addition to quite marked similarities. In both cases, the power confronting hybrid warfare should have possessed a deep understanding of its opponent. Yet, as far as British understanding of their colonial opponents went, they might as well have been conducting a campaign on the moon for all the understanding they displayed. That ignorance, of course, stood in the face of the fact that British armed forces had engaged in major campaigns in North America during Queen Anne's War, the War of Austrian Succession, and what the colonists termed the French and Indian War.

Moreover, British military forces spoke the same language as their opponents, derived their attitudes and beliefs from a common culture with the colonists, and had deployed substantial military forces in the colonies over the past three decades. One can, of course, understand the ignorance displayed by the policy makers in London, few of whom had spent a day on the other side of the Atlantic. Nevertheless, that does not explain the apparent ignorance of those who had spent time in the colonies. Thus, the almost complete obliviousness to both the nature of the terrain over which British would wage their campaigns as well as of the colonists they would fight led to a variety of avoidable military defeats. The expedition to Lexington and Concord came close to disaster. Bunker Hill represented the most egregious sort of underestimation of the colonial opponent, which led to a Pyrrhic victory. Only the steadfastness of the British soldiers redeemed the inexcusable stupidity of their generals.

Still, the revolution came close to collapse in the attempt of the colonial militia to stand out in the open and take on British regulars in the battles around New York in late summer and fall 1776. But the British efforts to hold the Jersies with a cordon strategy foundered on the small conventional forces that Washington put in the field in the harsh weather of December 1776 to January 1777. The defeats that his small conventional force administered to the British at Trenton and Princeton were sufficient to keep the flame of rebellion alive. The Americans quickly won back the Jersies, the population of which the conduct of British and Hessian troops had already done much to drive back into the revolutionary camp. But the worst of the British defeats came at Saratoga, where clouds of colonial militia morphed into an effective representation of a conventional military force – at least when operating in the terrain of the semi-wilderness lying to the north of Albany. That defeat extinguished the notion that the British could crush the colonial rebellion even before the French entered the war and confronted the British with the possibility that they might lose not only the colonies but the rest of their empire as well.

The intriguing question, then, is whether the British might have been able to defeat the colonists by another strategic approach, even given their underestimation of their opponent. Some historians and analysts have suggested that had Howe supported Burgoyne's move from Canada by driving up the Hudson to meet at Albany, the British could have sundered New England from the remainder of the rebellious colonies. They would then have been in a position to win the war. However, as Alexander Hamilton commented (see the aforementioned essay on hybrid warfare and the American Revolution), to be effective such a strategy would have depended on a considerably larger army than the British possessed, not only to garrison a number of points along the Hudson River and to patrol between them but to forage as well into Connecticut and Massachusetts.

Such expeditions would have required raiding parties far larger than that launched by Gage against Lexington and Concord or Burgoyne against Bennington, both of which met with disaster. Similarly, the garrisons scattered along the Hudson would have had to be larger than those that Washington picked off along the Delaware at the end of 1776. Thus, to accomplish such a strategy of dividing the colonies, the British would have required a much larger army and enough time to wear the colonists down. Neither resource was available to the British in 1777, especially because the French were awaiting the first favorable moment to enter the conflict. In the end, Howe probably recognized this reality. Thus, he moved against Philadelphia in the hopes of gaining a decisive victory over the colonists by destroying Washington's army and capturing the newly proclaimed colonial capital. Howe's army did capture Philadelphia and gave the revolutionary army a proper pounding at Brandywine, but he failed in the larger strategic aim of causing the collapse of the revolution.

That brings us to the American Civil War, the best example of a conflict in which those conducting hybrid warfare went down to catastrophic defeat. It is therefore worth examining in considerable detail, both for how the North won the war and the unintended costs that victory brought in its wake. As with the British in the Revolutionary War, the North substantially underestimated the commitment and staying power of the Confederacy. But it did possess the resources and the will to fight and destroy an opponent who had recourse to hybrid warfare.

Northern military forces managed to split the Confederacy into two parts with the capture of Vicksburg and Grand Gulf in the summer of 1863. The second great drive in the west from northwestern Tennessee through the center of the state to Chattanooga in 1863 had as decisive an impact on the course of the war as the Mississippi campaign. In both cases, Union forces ran into hybrid warfare in its most virulent form. Large raiding parties of Confederate cavalry, insurgents, and guerrillas all gave the Bluecoats fits. All of these irregular forces presented a constant threat, often realized, to cut Union supply lines that were constantly lengthening as Union forces drove ever deeper into the Confederate heartland. At the same time, Union armies faced major Confederate conventional armies: Grant's Army of the Tennessee confronted Pemberton's army, while Rosecrans' Army of the Cumberland faced the Army of Tennessee under Braxton Bragg.

In December 1862, Grant began an ambitious offensive against Vicksburg from his forward logistics base at Holly Springs in northern Mississippi. However, a cavalry raid led by Major General Earl Van Dorn maneuvered behind Grant's army and entirely destroyed the laboriously stockpiled caches of ammunition and food stored there. Forced to withdraw because of his logistical shortfalls, Grant discovered that he was able to feed his army from what the local farms and plantations along his path of retreat produced. When the locals complained about Union foraging, Grant had a forthright reply: "We had endeavored to feed ourselves from our own northern resources while visiting them; but their friends in gray had been uncivil enough to destroy what we had brought along, and it could not be expected that, men with arms in their hands, would starve in the midst of plenty."[13]

That was a lesson that Grant did not forget. In his fast-moving campaign against Vicksburg in spring 1863, the Army of the Tennessee crossed the Mississippi south of Vicksburg, cut its supply lines to the north, swung northeast to smash Mississippi's capital, and then swung back west to shut up Pemberton's army in Vicksburg. Moreover, Grant moved so fast that the Confederates were unable to concentrate against him or his foraging parties, while Grant's troops possessed sufficient local superiority to ensure that his foragers could strip the countryside clean. With no lines of supply to attack, guerrilla activities were irrelevant. Once Grant closed in on Vicksburg, his army was able to reestablish secure supply lines to the north up the Mississippi River.

The situation in Tennessee, however, was much less amenable to solution. There, a full-scale version of hybrid warfare occurred throughout 1862 and 1863. In fact, so bad was the situation at the end of 1862 that Rosecrans had to deploy almost as many troops to guard his supply lines on the railroads in north and central Tennessee leading to Nashville and along the Tennessee River as he was able to employ in his advance to Stone's River against Braxton Bragg's Army of Tennessee. The situation hardly improved over the course of the remainder of 1863, with raiders such as Nathan Bedford Forrest and local guerrillas making the support of Union armies in the drive to Chattanooga both expensive and difficult.

After Grant wrecked Bragg's Army of Tennessee in November 1863, he and Sherman confronted the problem of how to secure their lines of communication for the campaign that would begin in spring 1864 to take and hold Atlanta. Widespread depredations of Confederate cavalry raids, partisans, and guerrillas would make life difficult for any sustained advance into Georgia. At the same time, Union forces would face Joe Johnston's Army of Tennessee in what promised to be a major struggle between major conventional armies.[14]

---

[13] Ulysses S. Grant, *Personal Memoirs of U.S. Grant*, ed. E. B. Long (New York, 1982), p. 227.
[14] Grant would not assume overall command of Union forces until March 1864. Up to that point, he was the overall commander of the Division of the Mississippi, which encompassed all Union forces between the Mississippi River and the Appalachian Mountains.

Grant, in command in the west until promoted to command all Union armies in March 1864, and Sherman hit on a two-pronged approach to solve their dilemma. The first of these prongs involved a massive program of bolstering the railroad infrastructure that ran across Tennessee to Chattanooga and that was vulnerable to Confederate raiders, guerrillas, and partisans. These railroads, along with the railroad Union troops would reconstruct to supply the movement forward from Chattanooga to Atlanta, would prove the essential component in Sherman's eventual success. The effort to ensure the uninterrupted flow of supplies involved (1) the rebuilding and strengthening of the road beds of the Tennessee railroads; (2) the construction of block houses and defensive positions to protect key bridges from partisans and raiders; (3) the establishment of a large number of caches of ties, rails, telegraph wiring, and other construction materials to enable the rapid repair of any damage the Confederate irregulars managed to achieve; (4) the purchase of an excess number of locomotives and railroad cars to replace those damaged or destroyed as needed; and (5) the establishment of repair teams throughout the system to move rapidly to repair breaks in the line.[15]

Despite Confederate attacks, the logistical system functioned successfully throughout the campaign. As Sherman noted in his memoirs, "The Atlanta campaign would simply have been impossible without the use of the railroads from Louisville to Nashville – one hundred and eighty-five miles – from Nashville to Chattanooga – one hundred and fifty-one miles – and from Chattanooga to Atlanta – one hundred and thirty-seven miles."[16]

The second prong was an approach to the war that aimed at breaking the will of the South's civilian population.[17] Grant had seen this coming as early as the aftermath of Shiloh, but Sherman placed the conduct of the war by the Union best in a series of letters to various civilian authorities in northern Alabama and Georgia who complained about the depredations of his troops at the beginning of 1864:

> The government of the United States has in North Alabama any and all rights which they chose to enforce in war, to take their lives, their houses,

[15] For this effort, see Thomas Weber, *The Northern Railroads in the Civil War, 1861–1861* (Bloomington, IN, 1952), pp. 199–208.
[16] William Tecumseh Sherman, *Memoirs of General W. T. Sherman* (New York, 1990), p. 889.
[17] For an outstanding discussion about what might best be termed the "hard war," see Mark Grimsley, *The Hard Hand of War, Union Military Policy Toward Southern Civilians, 1861–1865* (Cambridge, 1995).

their land, their everything, because they cannot deny that war exists there, and war is simply power unconstrained by constitution or compact. If they want eternal warfare, well and good. We will accept the issue and [dispossess] them and put our friends in possession. To those who submit, to the rightful law and authority all gentleness and forbearance, but to the petulant and persistent secessionist, why, death is mercy and the quicker he or she is disposed of the better. Satan and the rebellious saint[s] of heaven were allowed a continuance of existence in hell merely to swell their just punishment.[18]

That attitude was certainly evident in Sherman's march through Georgia, and to an even greater extent when his troops reached South Carolina, which they regarded quite correctly as the heartland of the secessionist movement. A Union officer, born in Alabama and serving with Sherman's army, noted the following about the march:

I am bound to say, while I deplore this necessity daily [of laying waste to the countryside of Georgia] and cannot bear to see the soldiers swarm. Through fields and yards, – I do believe it is a necessity. Nothing *can* end this war but some demonstration of their helplessness, and the miserable ability of J.D. [Jefferson Davis] to protect them... But war is war, and a horrible necessity at best; yet when forced on us as this war is, there is no help but to make it so terrible that when peace comes it will last.[19]

Indeed, the "Chimneyvilles" created by Sherman's troops in their march through Georgia and especially South Carolina resembled Bomber Command's "dehousing" of the German population in the Second World War, except in this case the Union soldiers allowed the Confederates to exit their houses and barns before destroying them.

While Sherman was wrecking the Deep South, Grant made explicit his intentions of destroying the Shenandoah, that nest of irregulars as well as a well-used Confederate route to invade the North. In a note to Union chief of staff Henry Halleck, Grant made clear that he wanted Union armies to "eat out [the Shenandoah] clean and clear as far as they go, so that crows flying over it for the balance of this season will have to carry their own provender with them."[20] By April 1865, Union troops had wrecked not only Georgia, South Carolina, and North Carolina but also James

---

[18] Quoted in Walter Lynwood Fleming, *Civil War and Reconstruction in Alabama* (Montgomery, AL, 1905), p. 76.
[19] Mark A. Dewolfe Howe, ed., *Marching with Sherman: Passages from the Letters and Campaign Diaries of Henry Hitchcock* (New Haven, CT, 1927), pp. 82, 93.
[20] Shelby Foote, *The Civil War, A Narrative History*, vol. 3, *Red River to Appomattox* (New York, 1974), p. 540.

Wilson's massive cavalry raid that month swamped Nathan Forrest's raiders and destroyed what was left of central and southern Alabama.

As to that bizarre suggestion that a number of armchair Civil War historians have suggested – namely, that Southerners were not fully committed to the cause because they did not continue guerrilla warfare after the defeat of their regular military forces – one might note the comment of a Southern woman in the aftermath of the Confederate catastrophe:

> We never yielded in the struggle until we were bound hand & foot & the heel of the despot was on our throats. Bankrupt in men, in money, & in provisions, the wail of the bereaved & the cry of hunger rising over the land, our cities burned with fire and our pleasant things laid waste, the best & bravest of our sons in captivity, and the entire resources of our country exhausted – what else could we do but give up.[21]

There was, moreover, a warning embedded in Sherman's note to Southerners quoted earlier: If they refused to quit the war, then the North would carry out the extreme measures of dispossessing them of their land and their lives. The war never reached that level, undoubtedly because most Confederates, having seen the extent to which Union destructiveness had reached by 1865, were not willing to engage at a continued throw of the iron dice for an uncertain future.

Union grand strategy and military power certainly suggest that victory is possible in hybrid warfare. But it is also worth noting that, in this case, as in other examples such as Ireland, success came at a price: not only the obvious cost in lives and treasure but also in the deep resentment throughout the South at the results of the conflict that echoed well into the next century. That anger would lead not only to continued Southern hostility but also to the dark cancer of racism that shackled much of America's African American population and which spread from the South to much of the North in the decades after the Civil War. Only in the 1960s did the Civil Rights movement force the United States to recognize the level of national mendacity in how it had been treating a substantial body of its citizens.

There are, of course, ripples in the events surrounding wars that last well beyond the termination of conflicts.[22] However, in many ways, these

---

[21] Quoted in Gary W. Gallagher, "Blueprint for Victory, Northern Strategy and Military Policy," in James M. McPherson and William J. Cooper, Jr., eds., *Writing the Civil War, The Quest to Understand* (Columbia, SC, 1998), p. 18.

[22] For a discussion of the ripples in history, see Victor Davis Hanson, *Ripples of Battle: How Wars in the Past Still Determine How We Fight, How We Live, and How We Think* (New York, 2003).

ripples seem most virulent and destructive in the case of hybrid conflicts. Such wars appear to be the most bitter because they involve the military and society so deeply. If that is the case with the American Civil War, then it is also true in the case of the Franco-Prussian War. On the surface, that conflict seems closer to the cabinet wars of the eighteenth century than to the wars of the people set in motion by the French Revolution. Certainly, the swiftness of the initial victories of Prusso-German forces at Metz and Sedan broke the military power of Napoleon III's bedraggled empire. Given the fact that the Battle of Königgrätz in 1866 had almost immediately led to peace between Austria and Prussia, Moltke and Bismarck had every expectation that the same pattern would emerge from the great victories their armies had won over the French in the opening months of the war. They were wrong.

In fact, the French turned to a levée en masse as they had in 1792. Thus, while the Prusso-German forces besieged Paris, they also confronted attacks on the siege lines from the periphery as well as wide-ranging guerrilla attacks on their lines of communications. After the defeat of the main French armies, the ensuing conflict became a fierce form of hybrid warfare. Two things saved the Prusso-German forces from disaster. The first was the fact that the disappearance of virtually the entire regular army of the French Empire into prisoner-of-war camps meant that there were no cadres on which to rebuild a new army, as had been the case in 1793.

Equally disastrous was the appearance of revolution, the Commune, in Paris, which split French nationalism into two camps, the more conservative of which was willing to deal with the Prusso-Germans to crush the specter of communist revolution. Nevertheless, for nearly half a year from the fall of Napoleon III's empire to the conclusion of an armistice, the Prusso-Germans confronted the problems involved in conducting the siege of Paris deep in France, while their lines of communications and foraging efforts were the targets of *franc tireurs* and more conventional French units attacking from the French countryside, which Moltke never had sufficient strength to hold.

In the long run, the German memory of the Franco-Prussian War, as well as the impact of the deep quarrels between Moltke and Bismarck, led to the development of two extraordinarily dangerous trends in German military thinking. The first emerged from Moltke's belief that statesmen should step back from conflicts and allow the generals to determine policy and strategy during the actual conduct of military operations. That anti-Clausewitzian belief then led to the even more dangerous belief, which marked the thinking of generals such as Ludendorff, that military concerns should drive policy.

Thus emerged the argument that "military necessity" should rule all decision making – an approach to international relations that led to the development of the disastrous Schlieffen Plan.[23] At the tactical level, in 1914, the Germans believed they were again under attack by partisans – *franc tireurs* – and that the proper response was the path of utmost ruthlessness. Thus, because of "military necessity," namely to end the threat of guerrilla attacks, German troops would shoot some 6,000 French and Belgian civilian hostages because of a series of friendly fire incidents and ambushes by Belgians and the French in an attempt to defend their countries. That ruthlessness in turn would move much of American public opinion against the Central Powers and into the Allied camp, with disastrous strategic consequences for Germany.

HYBRID WAR IN THE MODERN ERA

It might seem strange to begin a discussion of modern hybrid warfare with a discussion of the all-consuming conflict of the Peninsular War. Yet, the war in Spain brought together many of the basic elements that were to characterize such wars in the twentieth century. In 1808, the French with their ideology of "liberty, fraternity, and equality" believed they were bringing a proven recipe of radical reform to a corrupt, inefficient, and grossly unfair ancien régime that, in their view, had completely lost its claim to legitimacy. After all, the Spanish people were obviously suffering under the rule of a church still dominated by the Inquisition, a nobility more interested in robbing the peasant serfs they ruled than in providing any semblance of justice, and a monarchy that had proven incapable of defending Spain and its empire for more than a century.

Certainly, to that child of the revolution, Napoleon Bonaparte, it was obvious that if any nation in Europe needed a reformation of its government, religion, and society, it was Spain. Ergo, in that wonderful logic that Descartes and other philosophers conveyed to French ruling elites, Napoleon believed that his armies, bearing the tide of revolutionary reform, would find themselves greeted as the liberators and creators of a new day. He was wrong. In many ways, Spain turned out to be the worst mistake of his career, even worse than the invasion of Russia in 1812. In

---

[23] In this respect, see the outstanding work by Isabel Hull, *Absolute Destruction: Military Culture and the Practices of War in Imperial Germany* (Ithaca, NY, 2006).

the latter case, Napoleon lost an army but recovered sufficiently to almost defeat the allies in 1813. Had a substantial number of his soldiers not still found themselves involved in fighting in the "Spanish ulcer," matters in central Europe in that year might well have turned out differently.

The nature of the hybrid warfare on the Iberian Peninsula suggests how poorly Napoleon understood the nature of the Spanish people. For that matter, neither did Joseph nor the Emperor's marshals who ran most of the war, with the exception of Napoleon's brief foray in 1808 to restore a situation that was rapidly spinning out of control. Besides their obliviousness to the "other," the French possessed neither a clear strategy nor coherent goals. As usual with Napoleon, the emperor confused military strategy with grand strategy. In effect, the French marched into Spain believing that military victory, if even necessary, would be sufficient in and of itself to place Spain firmly under French control. Through the dismal years that followed French intervention, Napoleon and his marshals pursued the ghost of decisive victory in the belief that it would solve the problems the "Spanish ulcer" posed. In the end, they got a proper thrashing from Wellington, but one that the insurgencies throughout Spain had enabled.

On the other side of the hill it is easy, of course, to identify Wellington's campaigns as providing the conventional military threat that supported and enabled the many different insurgencies to attack French foraging parties, couriers, and lines of communications. Yet, one must also realize that Wellington, the British army, and their Portuguese allies spent much of their time in Portugal far from the insurgents. The fascinating aspect of the conflict is the role Spanish armies played in the hybrid struggle. Unwilling to cooperate with each other or, for that matter, with the British, ill equipped and ill trained, and consistently beaten in battle by the French armies, they remained in the field – a nuisance perhaps, but always nipping at the heels of the French. A modern war? Perhaps not, and yet the contrast between French ideals and their ignorance of Spain is striking. When the ideals proved to have little allure to the Spanish population, the French turned to seeking military victory, confusing that with political victory. Without a realistic strategic or political framework, they had no chance of achieving a successful outcome.

Throughout their imperial history, the British consistently confronted hybrid warfare in one form or another. Whereas the war to subdue the American colonists was an abject failure, the British record throughout the nineteenth century was much better. There were, of course, disasters, such as the catastrophe in Afghanistan in 1841, but for the most part technological superiority was sufficient to crush conventional enemies in Africa and Asia, while politically astute agents and policies maintained peace and kept insurgencies from exploding within the borders of Britain's various colonies and dependencies. The Boer War, however, suggested that there were going to be troubles ahead in the twentieth century. It took a massive effort by the entire Empire, at least the white portions of it, to subdue the Dutch farmers, first in the conflict's conventional phase and then to crush the Boer commandos waging guerrilla warfare. Moreover, the British received considerable help in their efforts from the gross incompetence of the Boer leaders. In the end, a combination of ruthlessness (to include the introduction of concentration camps to the lexicon of human evil), overwhelming force, and staying power ended the conflict. But, in fact, the Boers were to be the real winners politically, at least until the collapse of the apartheid system in the 1990s.

Beyond the two great world wars, on which much of historical interest and research has focused and that witnessed their own subwars that resembled hybrid war, the twentieth century was to be dominated by hybrid warfare. In some cases, those states with superior technology and resources were able to win. The British were able to crush the hybrid war in Mesopotamia in 1920 with their huge technological advantage, but the cost of that conflict convinced them that they should allow the Iraqis a modicum of independence, which set that unhappy state on its way to eventual catastrophe.

The Second Sino-Japanese War is the most difficult to explain except in terms of the grossest forms of incompetence. The lack of moral courage on the part of Japan's political and military leaders led to a conflict that, as with the attack on Pearl Harbor, was unwinnable from the moment the Japanese fired the first shot. Here, only those drunk on their own superiority could have believed that Japan might actually be in a position to control all of China both militarily and politically. The resulting hybrid war stretched Japan to the breaking point militarily, politically, economically, and psychologically. Yet, the bizarre system of Japanese governance persisted almost to the end in confusing the narrow interests of the Kwantung Army with those of the Japanese nation. In this world where serious strategic analysis did not exist, the Japanese military system consistently confused hope and the army's martial prowess with reality and a general lack of resources.

The French fought three major hybrid wars in the twentieth century: the first against Moroccan rebels in the 1920s; the second against one of the great revolutionaries in history, Ho Chi Minh[24]; and the third against the Algerian FLN (National Liberation Front).[25] In the first case, the French, given their immense superiority in technology and resources, were able to win. The war in Indochina, in contrast, was an unmitigated disaster in military as well as political terms. Three major factors explain the French defeat. The first was the fact that France, devastated by defeat and German occupation, was simply incapable of winning a war against the Vietminh in the late 1940s. Second, the Chinese Communists were able to provide substantial aid to the Vietminh. But the third factor, the Vietminh leadership, was the most crucial. Not only was Ho Chi Minh a political genius, but the revolutionaries possessed in Vo Nguyén Giáp military genius as well. The conduct of the major battles around the Red River Delta and at Dien Bien Phu reflected the highest form of military competence, abilities that Giáp was to display again in the hybrid war he would fight against the Americans and South Vietnamese in the 1960s and 1970s.

Having suffered a humiliating defeat in Vietnam, the French then found themselves involved in a disastrous war against Algerian insurgents. In that hybrid war, the French won militarily by defeating the FLN's conventional forces and sending them reeling back across Algeria's frontiers with Morocco and Tunisia, crushing what forces were left in the back country and then winnowing out the terrorist network in the cities – all with the utmost ruthlessness. But, in the end, the army's victory went for naught because the very means that it had used to win the war militarily undermined the political consensus necessary to maintain Algeria as a part of metropolitan France.

CONCLUSION

A brief perusal of history would suggest that statesmen and military leaders should always regard war as a last resort because its cost in lives and treasure is rarely commensurate with its gains. World War II was undoubtedly a necessary war for the allied powers, but only the

---

[24] Ho Chi Minh participated in five major communist movements: He was a major participant in the founding of the French Communist Party, the Malayan Communist Party, and the Vietnamese Communist Party, and he was a major figure in both the Soviet Comintern and the Chinese Communist Party.
[25] The great movie *The Battle of Algiers* gives the impression that the Algerian fight for independence centered around the cities, but in fact it involved major conventional operations throughout the countryside.

United States came out of that conflict with its territory largely unscathed. Even then, the number of American military dead, 416,800, represented a terrible burden, although it was low in comparison to the losses of the other major powers. But of all the grisly forms that war takes, hybrid conflicts would appear to be the nastiest. There are no easy roads to victory in such conflicts. Moreover, in nearly every case in the past where the defender has used hybrid means, will has become a factor in the ultimate outcome as the conflict extended in time and space. Victory would seem to be a matter largely of a willingness to spend lives and resources in what one can only describe as a profligate fashion. The North clearly was willing to pay that price in fighting the Civil War, but it is worth noting that the terrible casualties the Army of the Potomac suffered in the spring 1864 campaign against Lee's Army of Northern Virginia came close to collapsing Northern morale and thus losing the war.

The major strategic lesson would seem to be obvious: Do not fight a hybrid war unless the most fundamental interests of the state are at stake. That calculation must rest on an ability to weigh the strategic calculus of means and ends, as well as a thorough understanding of one's opponent: his ideology, his commitment, his history, and his culture. The capacity of the American people to stay what will always be an extraordinarily difficult course is also a critical factor. Moreover, one must understand that there are inherently contradictory tendencies between the demands of conventional war to smash up the physical and human landscape and the demands of counterinsurgency warfare to protect the population and gain their trust and confidence. Given the watchful eyes of 24/7 news coverage and the proclivities of the American people, the strategy of creating a desert and calling it peace is no longer an option for American policy makers. Like it or not, they will have to find other ways to combat hybrid adversaries. In this endeavor, understanding the history of such conflicts would be a good place to start.

Index

Abd el-Qadir, 208
Abdullah Hassan, Mohammed, 219
Abercromby, Sir Ralph, 76, 78
Abrams, General Creighton, 256, 279, 281
Afghanistan, 10–11, 16, 104–105, 209–210, 214, 286–288, 304
Afrancesados, 110, 121, 129
Africa, 201, 208, 214
Agrippina, 38–39
Ahenobarbus, Lucius Domitius, 33
Alba de Tormes, Battle of, 124–125
Albuera, Battle of, 127
Alexander I of Russia, 111n13
Algeria, 8–9, 208, 214
Ali, Hyder, 204
Allenby, General Edmund, 6–7
Almaraz, Battle of, 132
Almonacid, Battle of, 130
Alsace-Lorraine, 178, 182–183
Al Jazeera, 292
al Qaeda, 10–11
American Civil War
  community security and, 152, 155
  Confederate government policy and, 157–158
  Confederate guerrilla activity in
    Alabama and, 163, 165, 299–300
    Arkansas and, 161
    Georgia and, 163, 300
    Kansas and, 167
    Kentucky and, 152, 162, 165, 167
    Louisiana and, 160, 164
    Maryland and, 151–152
    Mississippi and, 160–164, 168, 297–299
    Missouri and, 151–152, 154, 156–157, 166
    South Carolina and, 300
    Tennessee and, 154, 159, 162–164, 167–168, 297
    Virginia and, 151, 154
  consequences of, 301
  counterguerrilla warfare. *See* Union counterguerrilla war
  independence of action and, 158–159, 169
  Massachussetts, 6th Infantry Regiment and, 151
  Quantrill's Raid and, 167
American Revolution, 3, 16, 72–73, 206, 214
  Campaign of 1777 and, 92–100
  British assumptions and, 79–81, 86, 89, 101
  colonial militias
    effectiveness of, 82, 84–85, 88–89, 91–93, 97–101
    population and resource control and, 87–88, 91
  Continental Army and, 85–86, 89, 91–93, 98–101, 206
  control of countryside and, 81, 86n39, 91, 100–102
  French and Indian War veterans and, 84–85, 97

309

American Revolution (*cont.*)
  German mercenaries and, 88–91, 96–97, 99, 296
  Hudson River strategy and, 87, 92–94, 99, 102, 296–297
  Indian forces and, 94–95
  leadership and, 99n70
  logistics and, 80–81, 93, 98
  military systems of discipline and, 75–76
  New England campaigns and, 82–86, 296
  New Jersey conquest and, 89–92, 296
  New York campaign of 1776 and, 86–92, 296
  Philadelphia campaign of 1777 and, 92–93, 95, 100–101, 297
  southern campaign and, 100–102
  strategic and political framework of, 79–82, 86, 92–94, 296
  Tory support and, 86–91, 93, 95–96, 100–102, 206
Amherst, Jeffrey, 6
Andalusia, Spanish community of, 121, 126, 130, 134
An Loc, Battle of, 284
Aragon, 121–122, 127, 134–135
Arminius, 18–22, 36–37, 39, 42
Army of the Republic of Vietnam (ARVN), 268
  condition of, 275, 280
  Corps Tactical Zones and, 269–273
  corruption and, 275
  leadership of, 271, 275, 278–279, 284
  Operation Lam Son 719 and, 282–283
Arnold, General Benedict, 98–99, 101
Assaye, Battle of, 204
Athens, 3–4
Aurelius, Marcus, 294–295
Australia, 254, 263, 272
Austria, 174, 302
Austro-Prussian War of 1866, 172
Augustus, Emperor, 21–24, 28–35, 37
Awadh, 210–213

Bac Viets, 282
Badajoz, Siege of, 127, 131–132
Baghdad, 11, 292
Bailén, Battle of, 121
Baird, General Sir David, 122
Ballesteros, General Francisco, 131, 133–134

Baltimore riot of 1861, 151
Bao Dai, Emperor, 8
Ba Thu, 280
Barbarossa, Operation, 4
Barcelona, 137
Bartlett, Robert, 53
Bates, Edward, 152
Bates, Julian, 152
Baum, Colonel Friedrich, 96–97
Baynard, Captain John, 60
Bayonne, Battle of, 117
Bazeilles, Battle of, 189–190
Beare, Donal Cam O'Sullivan, 68
Beijing, 228, 232–233, 237
Bein Hoa Air Base, 263, 271
Benjamin, Judah P., 158
Bennington, Battle of, 96–98, 296
Beresford, General William, 115, 124, 138, 145
Berlin, 254, 259
Betsy Town, 164
Bezaine, Marshal Francois, 180
bin Laden, Osama, 11
Bismarck, Otto von, 180, 182–183, 186, 191, 194, 302
Blake, General Joaquín, 122
Blanes, Juan, 128
Blount, Charles. *See* Lord Mountjoy
Boer War, 14, 213–218, 222–223
Bonaparte, Joseph-Napoleon, 109–110, 112–113, 120–121, 123, 126, 128–129, 131–133, 135–136, 142–144, 147–148, 304
Bonaparte, Napoleon, 109–113, 116, 120–123, 131, 134, 136–137, 139, 141–142, 144–145, 147–149, 227, 303–304
Boston, 82, 86, 91
Bourbon dynasty, 110, 120, 138
Braddock, General Edward, 78, 205
Bragg, General Braxton, 297–298
Breed's Hill, 85
Breymann, Colonel Heinrich, 97
Brinks Hotel, 261
British Empire
  Afghanistan, and, 209–210
  air power and, 219, 221
  American colonies and, 202, 206
  Anglo-Ashanti Wars and, 207, 209
  Anglo-Burmese War and, 207
  Anglo-Egyptian War and, 207

Anglo-Sikh Wars and, 205
Boer War and, 213–218, 222–223, 305
China and, 207
Free Officers Movement, 220
French and Indian War and, 205
hybrid warfare and, 199–200, 205–206, 213, 221–224, 304–305
Indian subcontinent and, 203–205, 210–213
Imperial Armies. *See* British Imperial Armies
industrialized warfare and, 207–208, 222
Iraq and, 219, 222
mobilization and, 202, 213, 222
naval superiority and, 208
Northwest Frontier and, 210
Peninsular War and, 222
political framework of, 201–202, 205–206, 208–210, 224, 305
revolutions and, 220
Somalia and, 219
strategic framework of, 200–202, 210, 223
Sufi Muslims and, 208
technology and, 207–208, 219
War of 1812 and, 206–207
British Expeditionary Force, 222
British Imperial Armies
adaptation and, 200, 222
Amerindians and, 205–207
Black Week and, 216
Bengal Army and, 210–212
Bombay Army and, 210
combined arms and, 215
components of, 201
conventional warfare and, 206, 213, 220, 222
counterinsurgency and, 206, 211, 213–214, 217, 220–222
guerrilla warfare and, 208–210, 222
Gurkhas and, 211
logisitics and, 204, 217
Madras Army and, 210–211
Mahratta Horse and, 204
noncombatants and, 211, 217, 219
operational framework of, 201, 216, 221
Pashtuns and, 211
recalibration of, 201, 206, 217, 220–223

regimental system and, 202
sepoys and, 203, 210–213, 222
Sikhs and, 211
strategy and, 216, 221–222
tactics and, 207–208, 216, 222
Brooke, Field Marshal Alan, 79n18
Brouncker, Captain Henry, 60
Buell, General Don Carlos, 162
Bui Tin, Colonel, 258, 265–266
Buller, General Sir Redvers, 216
Bunker, Ellsworth, 281
Bunker Hill, Battle of, 84–86, 296
Burbridge, General Stephen, 167
Burgoyne, General John, 92–99, 296
Burrard, General Sir Harry, 121n38
Bush, George H. W., 12
Bush, George W., 11
Bussaco, Battle of, 126
Byng, Marshal John, 116

Cadencies, 21n9
Cadiz, Siege of, 117, 126
Caesar, Julius, 23, 29–30
Cahir Castle, 64
Cambodia, 254, 256–258, 260, 263, 268, 271, 280
Camden, Battle of, 101
Campbell, General Colin, 116
Campoverde, Conde de, 129
Canada, 74, 92–94, 101–102, 206
Canal Zone, 202
Canning, George, 115
Cao Dai, 271
Carew, George, 52, 65–69
Carleton, General Guy, 93–94
Carlos III of Spain, 109
Carlos IV, of Spain, 109–111, 120
Castaños, General Francisco, 122, 131
Cast Lead, Operation, 15–16
Castile, Spanish communities of León and La Mancha, 124, 128–130
Catalonia, Spanish community of, 121, 127–129, 134, 137, 143
Central Highlands (Vietnam), 256, 260, 262–263, 268–270, 284
Central Intelligence Agency (CIA), 10, 259
Champlain, Lake, 74, 94, 98
Changchiakou, 237
Charleston, Siege of, 101
Châteaudun, Battle of, 190
Chattanooga, 297–299

Chatti, 32
Chechnya, 208
Cherusci, 33–34
Chiang Kai-shek, 5, 220, 229, 245
Chichester, Arthur, 65–66
China, 5
    Marco Polo Bridge Incident, 225
    Nationalist government and, 233
    provisional governments and, 233
    Vietnam War and, 254, 258, 261, 263–266, 284
Chinese Civil War, 5, 7
Chinese Communist Army, 243
Chinese Communist guerrillas, 227, 229, 240–241, 243–246, 248–249, 253
China Incident, 225, 251
Chinese Nationalist Army, 225–227, 229, 243, 245–246
Churchill, Winston, 4–5
Cintra Convention, 115, 121n38, 124
Clausewitz, Carl von, 1, 73, 104–105, 137, 196, 292
Clinton, General Henry, 74, 90, 93, 100
Cold War, 11–12, 254
Concord, Battle of, 82, 84, 296
Continental system, 111
Cooper-Church Amendment, 256, 282–283
Cornwallis, Lord Charles, 101
Cortes (Cadiz), 133, 135, 138, 147
Corunna, Battle of, 117, 123
Cowpens, Battle of, 3
Craufurd, General Robert, 116
Crimean War, 172
Cuba, 254, 259
Cuesta, General Gregorio, 124–125
Cumberland River, 164
Curtis, General Samuel R., 161

Dak To, Battle of, 271
Dalrymple, General Sir Hew, 121n38
Da Nang, 263, 270
Danish War of 1864, 172
Dartmouth, Lord, 80
Davis, Jefferson, 158, 169, 300
Dawtrey, Captain Nicholas, 60–61
Dehli, Siege of, 210, 212–213
Delaborde, General Henri, 121
De Lattre Line, 7–8
Democratic Republic of Vietnam (DRV). *See* North Vietnam

Denmark, 113
Devereux, Robert. *See* Earl of Essex
Diem, Ngo Dinh, 276–277
Dien Bien Phu, Battle of, 8, 102, 306
Diest, Wilhelm, 191
Dill, Sir John, 79n18
Dio, Cassius, 22n12, 27, 32, 35, 36n55, 42
Docwra, Captain Henry, 61, 64–66
Dodge, General Grenville, 162
Donaldsville, 164
Dos de Mayo Uprising, 120–121
Drusus, 31–32, 42, 294
Drusus Canal, 31
Duncan-Jones, Richard, 28
Dupont, General Pierre, 121
Duquesne, Fort, 75n7

Ebro River, 121
Egypt, 208
Eisenhower, Dwight, 257–258
Elizabeth I of England, 47–48, 57, 59, 60, 62, 64
El Salvador, 12
Emmaus, 35
England, 45–48, 50–57, 67, 70
Enlightenment, 109
Essex, Earl of, 52, 57, 60, 62–64
European military systems and, 200, 203, 207

Faulkner, Colonel William C., 160
Fedayeen Saddam, 291–292
Ferdinand VII of Spain, 120, 137–138, 147
Field Manual 3-24, 13
Fitch, Lieutenant Le Roy, 164
Fitzmaurice, James, 47
Fitzpiers, James, 63
Florus, 35
Flower, Captain, 63
Fontainebleau, Treaty of, 111, 113, 120
Forrest, General Nathan Bedford, 298, 300–301
Forester, C. S., 118
Formosa (Taiwan), 5
Förster, Stig, 198
Fort Stewart exercises, 274
France, 100, 178, 195–198, 205, 305–306
    Algerian insurgency and, 8–9, 220, 306
    Corps Législatif and, 183
    French Navy and, 184

Government of National Defense and, 183–185
Imperial Army and, 184, 302
Indochina and, 7–9, 82, 220, 306
Franco-Prussian War, 171
consequences of, 172, 195–198, 302
conventional forces and, 187–188, 302
decisive maneuver warfare and, 176–177, 187, 194
Ems dispatch and, 179n19
franc tireurs and, 173, 185–186, 188, 302–303
French Third Republic and, 182–184
German General Staff and, 173, 177–178, 183, 186
German officer leadership and, 190–198
German unification and, 172, 174, 178
hybrid nature of, 172–174
insurgency and, 173, 185–191, 194
Kabinettskriege and, 172, 175–176, 180, 193
mobilization and, 173, 182, 186
nationalism and, 174, 188, 191–192, 194, 302
noncombatants and, 173, 187–191, 195
North German Confederation and, 179
operational framework of, 179–180, 182
political framework of, 174–175, 182–184, 191, 194, 196–197, 302
populism and, 179
prewar planning and, 177–180, 182
strategic framework of, 178–180, 191, 193–194, 302
Volkskrieg and, 173–174, 191, 194, 196
Franks, General Tommy, 292n5
Fraser, Ronald, 113, 144
Fraser, General Simon, 98
Freeman's Farm, Battle of, 98
Fremont, General John, 156–157
French and Indian War, 5–6, 73–78, 84–85, 205, 295
French Foreign Legion, 184
French Revolution, 109–110, 193
Fuller, J. F. C., 141

Gage, General Thomas, 79–80, 82, 84, 296
Galicia, Spanish community of, 121, 127–128, 130, 134, 140, 143, 145
Gambetta, Léon, 183, 185, 191–193
Gates, General Horatio, 98–99, 101

Gaul, 23, 27, 29–31, 294
Gaulle, Charles de, 9
Gaza Strip, 14–16
Geneva Accords (1954), 257, 260, 284
George, Fort, 98
George, Lake, 94–95
George II of Great Britain, 76–77
George III of Great Britain, 82, 89
Germain, Lord George, 74, 79, 81, 92–94
German Empire, 195–198
Germania
geographical challenges of, 29–31
resources and economic strength of, 26–27, 294
strategic framework of, 24, 26
tactics and techniques of, 40–43
Teutoburg Wald, Battle of, and, 18–22, 294
Germanicus, 21, 37–40, 42
Gerona, First and Second Sieges of, 121
Giap, General Vo Nguyen, 7–8, 264, 282, 306
Gibbon, Edward, 23
Giron, General Pedro Agustin, 136
Godoy, Manuel, 109, 111, 113, 120
Goltz, Colmar von der, 193–194
Goya, Francisco, 118
Graham, General Sir Thomas, 136
Granger, General Gordon, 161
Grant, General Ulysses S., 162, 169, 297–300
Great Britain
projection of power and, 73, 102
Great East Asia Affairs Ministry, 238
Greek-Turkish War of 1896–1897, 172
Greene, General Nathanael, 3, 101
Guilford Courthouse, Battle of, 101
Gulf War of 1991, 12–13, 289

Haiphong, 263–264
Haldane, General Sir Aylmer, 222
Halleck, General Henry, 157, 166, 300
Haltern, 20, 32, 42
Hamas, 14–16
Hamburger Hill, Battle of, 271
Hamdani, General Raad, 292
Hamilton, Captain Alexander, 100, 296
Hanoi, 8, 257, 260, 263–264
Harriman, Averill, 258
Helots, 3–4
Henan Province, 229

Henry VIII, King of England, 47, 54
Hérisson, Count Maurice d', 185–186
Herod, King, 35
Hezbollah, 14–16, 289–290, 292
Hill, General Rowland, 133, 136
Hoa Binh, Battle of, 82, 102
Hobkirk's Hill, Battle of, 101
Ho Chi Minh, 7, 257, 267, 306
Holy Alliance of 1815, 174
Hopei Province, 228
Horiba, Kazuo, 250–253
Howe, Admiral Richard, 89
Howe, General Sir William, 79, 86, 88–90, 92–95, 99, 296–297
Hue, 270
Hunter, General David, 157
Hussein bin Ali, 6
Hussein, Saddam, 11, 265, 291–292
hybrid warfare, 139, 144, 149–150, 159–160
  advanced weaponry and, 14–16, 289
  civilian advisors and, 287
  control of countryside and, 293, 295
  conventional force application and, 285, 293, 295, 307
  counterinsurgency roles and, 285, 307
  definition of, 2–3, 86, 171, 199
  doctrine and, 199, 285
  enemy, understanding of, 295–296, 307
  historical context and, 286, 290, 307
  host nation roles and, 286–287
  intelligence and, 286
  leadership and, 17
  lessons in, 285–288
  political will and, 8–9, 286, 294
  population and, 9–10
  propaganda and, 9–10
  resources and, 294–295
  sanctuaries and, 285–287
  strategy and, 285, 293–295, 307
  success, measurement of, and, 146
  tactics and, 290, 293
  terrorist activities and, 290

Ia Drang, Battle of, 263, 271
Iberian Peninsula, 106, 111, 121, 123, 147, 304
  geography and, 107–108
Idistaviso, Battle of, 39
India, 201–204, 210–213, 220
Indochina, 7–9, 102, 255
Industrial Revolution, 174
Iraq War, 10–14, 16, 55, 104–105, 287–288, 291–292
Ireland. *See also* O'Neill's Rebellion
  English interests in, 47–48, 52–56, 67
  Norman Conquest of, 46–47, 54
  sixteenth-century culture of, 46–51, 53–56, 70
  Spanish interests in, 48, 51–52
Ishihara, General Kanji, 227, 250–251
Israeli Defense Forces (IDF), 14–16, 289–290
Italy, 218

Japan, 5
  China Affairs Board and, 234, 236–239
  Japanese Self Defense Forces and, 252
  leadership and, 227, 250–251, 305
  limited conflict and, 225–227, 250
  political goals and, 228, 250, 305
  resources, allocation of, 227–230, 243, 250
  South Manchurian Railway Company and, 234
  theaters of war and, 230–231
Japanese Imperial Army
  administrative affairs and, 231, 237
  conventional offensive operations and, 229–230, 243–245
  counterguerrilla operations and, 228–229, 233, 239–244, 246–249, 252–253
  general staff and, 225–233, 237–238, 250–251
  integration of effort and, 232, 235–236
  internal security and, 229, 235, 238–239, 241–242, 245, 252
  Kwantung Army and, 226, 229–230, 232–234, 305
  lines of communication and, 226–227, 240, 253
  logistics and, 229, 245
  military planning and, 227, 251–252
  modernization of forces and, 226
  nonmilitary operations and, 228, 231–239
  North China Army. *See* North China Army
  pacification corps and, 234–236, 239–240, 243
  paramilitary organizations and, 231

political affairs and, 231–232, 235
propaganda and, 234–235, 240
puppet governments and, 231–233
Tientsin garrison and, 225, 228, 231–232, 234, 243, 248, 251
security operations and, 234–236, 239, 241–242
special security force and, 247, 253
special service groups and, 231–233, 235, 237–239, 242,
stability operations and, 228–231, 239–240, 242, 245, 247, 252–253
strategy and, 225–227, 251, 305
tactics and, 230, 242–243, 245, 248–249
training and, 228, 230, 238, 241, 247–248
Xuzhou campaign and, 240–241
Jehol Province, 234
Jena-Auerstadt, Battle of, 110
Jewish Agency, 220
John VI of Portugal, 138
Johnson, Lyndon, 255–256, 259–261, 263, 266
Johnston, General Joseph E., 169, 298
Joint Chiefs of Staff (U. S.), 261, 280
Junot, General Jean-Andoche, 111, 113–114, 120–121

Kabul, 210
Kabinettskriege, 172, 175–176, 180, 193
K'e-min, Wang, 233
Kennedy, John F., 258–259
Kent State shootings, 281
Khanh, General Nguyen, 269
Khyber Rifles, 201
Kimberley, Siege of, 214
Kinnard, General Harry O., 274
Kinsale, 51–52, 67–69
Kita, General Seiichiro, 232–234, 237
Kitchener, Lord Herbert, 216–218
Knights of the White Camellia, 170
Koch-Breuberg, Friedrich, 189
Königgrätz, Battle of, 177, 302
Konoye, Fumimaro, 236, 250
Kontum, Battle of, 271, 284
Korea, 5, 243, 254, 263–264, 268
Kramer, Stanley, 118
Ku Klux Klan, 170
Kwasny, Mark, 92
Ky, Air Vice-Marshal Nguyen Cao, 269

Laconia, 3–4
Lamb, General Sir Graeme, 55, 137
Laos, 8, 254–260, 264, 269, 282–283
La Romana, General Pedro, 122–123
Lawrence, T. E., 6–7
Lebanon, 14–16, 289–290, 292
Lee, General Robert E., 161, 169
Lee, Captain Thomas, 60–61
Leuctra, Battle of, 4n7
Lexington, Battle of, 82, 84, 102, 296
Li, Lincoln, 253
Liberation, War of, 138
Liddell Hart, Basil H., 265
Lieber, Dr. Francis, 166–167
Lincoln, Abraham, 155, 157
Lincoln, General Benjamin, 101
LINEBACKER II, Operation, 267
Lisbon, 114, 117, 121, 125–126
Little Rock, capture of, 161
Liverpool, Lord Robert, 134–135
Long An Province, 271, 276, 278–280
Long Island, Battle of, 88–89
Lorraine, Operation, 8
Loudoun, Lord John, 75, 77
Lough Foyle, 61, 65–66
Louisbourg, Fortress, 74
Lucknow, Siege of, 210, 212–213
Ludendorff, General Erich, 303

MacDonald, Marshal Jacques, 129
MacFarland, Colonel Sean, 13
MacMahon, Marshal Patrice de, 180
Madrid, 109, 120–123, 128, 132–133
Mafeking, Siege of, 214
Mahratta Confederacy, 204–205, 211, 222–223
Maitland, General Thomas, 116
Maiwand, Battle of, 210
Majuba Hill, Battle of, 216
Malaysia, 258
Manchukuo, 225–226, 228–230, 232, 234, 243, 250
Manchuria, 230, 234
Manchurian Incident, 226, 232, 234, 236
Mao Tse Tung, 5, 208, 245–246, 253, 264, 266
Marion, Francis, 158
Marmont, Marshal Auguste, 128, 131–132
Maori, 209
Marco Polo Bridge Incident, 225, 228, 230–231, 234, 243, 245

Marshall, Sergeant Eugene, 165
Marsi, 38
Marx, Karl, 187
Masséna, Marshal André, 115, 117, 126–127
Mattis, General James, 13
McClellan, General George, 154–156
McCrea, Jane, 95
McMaster, Colonel H. R., 13
McNamara, Robert, 255, 260, 267
Mekong Delta, 271–272, 280
Megiddo, Battle of, 7
Messenia, 3–4
Metis, 209
Metz, 183, 302
Middle East, 201
Military Assistance and Advisory Group, 258
Military Assistance Command-Vietnam (MAC-V), 256, 279
Mina, Espoz y, 119, 128, 134–135, 145
Minden, Battle of, 81
Mississippi River, 164, 298
Moltke, Helmuth von, 172–173, 175, 177–183, 185–186, 188, 191, 194–198, 302
Mongolia, 266
Montagnards, 268, 270
Montague, Captain Charles, 62
Montcalm, Marquis de, 6
Montgomery, General Richard, 76
Montreal, 6, 74
Moore, General Sir John, 115, 122–123
Moore, Thomas O., 160
Morgan, Colonel Daniel, 98
Mosby, Colonel John S., 160–161, 169–170
Mountjoy, Lord, 52, 59–60, 62, 65–66, 68–71
Mughal Empire, 210–211
Munster, 62–63, 65–69
Mysore, Kingdom of, 204, 222

Nam Viet, 282
Nanjing, 233, 250
Napoleon III, 173, 179–180, 182–183, 190, 302
Napier, General Sir William, 124, 143
Na San, Battle of, 8
National Estimates, Office of, 259
National Intelligence Council, 259

Navarre, Spanish community of, 128, 134–135, 140, 143, 146
Navarre, General Henri, 8
Nemoto, Colonel Hiroshi, 233, 237
network-centric warfare, 13
New Orleans, surrender of, 160
New People's Association, 233–235
New Zealand, 209, 254, 272
Ney, Marshal Michel, 122
Nguyen, General Dong Sy, 267
Nguyen Hue Offensive, 283–284
Nigeria, 209
Nine Years' War. *See* O'Neill's Rebellion
Nixon, Richard, 281
Norman Conquest, 45–46, 54
North China Army
    conventional operations and, 230, 243, 249
    counterguerrilla operations and, 239–244, 253
    nonmilitary activities and, 228, 232, 235, 238, 242
    resource allocation and, 229–230, 305
    special service section of, 232–234, 237, 239
    stability operations and, 230–231, 239–240, 242
    training and, 230–231
    mission of, 228–230
Northern Alliance, 10
North German Confederation, 179
North, Lord Frederick, 80, 82
North Missouri Railroad, 156
North Vietnam (Democratic Republic of Vietnam), 254, 256, 258–262, 267
North Vietnamese Army (NVA), 256, 268–269, 271, 281–284
    sanctuaries and, 257, 263
North West Mounted Police, 201

Ocaña, Battle of, 124–125
O'Donnell, Hugh, 52, 61, 68–69
Ohio River, 164
Okamura, General Yasuji, 239
Okido, General Sajiro, 253
Olmert, Ehud, 14
Oman, Sir Charles, 106, 110, 141
O'Neill, Hugh, 45–46, 50, 52, 57, 59, 64–65, 67–70
O'Neill's Rebellion, 45
    commencement of, 57

decapitation strategy and, 53
devastation and famine strategy and, 62, 65–67, 69, 71
population-centric counterinsurgency and, 62
mixed war strategy and, 60–61
Spanish intervention and, 57, 64, 66–69
submission and pardon policy and, 59, 61–66, 70–71
Oñoro, Battle of, 127
On War, 1, 73, 104–105
Oporto, Battle of, 115
Oye, Shinobu, 250

Pakistan, 11
Palafox, General José, 122
Palestine, 6–7, 202, 219–220
Pale, The, 46
Palmyra, 164
Pamplona, 137
Pannonia, 36–37
Partisan Ranger Act, 158
Paterculus, Velleius, 33–35, 37
Pathet Lao, 258
Pea Ridge, Battle of, 161
Peloponnesian War, 3–4
Pemberton, General John, 297–298
Peninsular War
  allied offensive of 1812 and, 128–134
  British Army and, 115–118, 121–125
  consequences of, 137–139
  Constitution of 1812 and, 138
  economic embargo and, 111
  French Army and, 112–113, 134, 136, 140–142, 145
  French invasion and, 120–121
  French retreat 1813–1814, 134–137
  geographical overextension and, 112–113, 124, 136, 141
  hybrid nature of, 139–149, 303–304
  insurgency and, 124, 137, 140, 304
  irregular forces and, 118–119, 124, 128–131, 134, 144–146, 148–149
  leadership and, 116–117, 140–145
  logistics and, 112, 117, 125–126, 136, 141–143, 148
  Napoleon's campaign of 1808, 121–123
  operational framework of, 118, 126, 133–134, 136–137, 141–144, 146, 148–150
  Portuguese Army and, 114–115, 124, 128, 135, 145, 149
  Portuguese frontier 1809–1811 and, 123–128
  provincial militias and, 118, 127–129
  Royal Navy and, 117–118, 149
  sociopolitical framework of, 107–111, 137, 146–148, 303–304
  Spanish Army and, 113–114, 124, 130–131, 134–136, 144–145
  Spanish collapse of 1808, 122–123
  Spanish uprising and, 120–121, 140
  strategic framework of, 116, 125, 136–137, 143–144, 147–149, 303–304
  juntas and, 113, 121–122, 130, 133n67, 142
Pentagon Papers, The, 146
Percy, General Lord Hugh, 82, 84
Petraeus, General David, 13, 55
Philippine Civic Action Group, 272
Philippines, 254, 258
Philip III of Spain, 51, 65
Phu Doan, 82, 102
Picton, General Thomas, 116
Pitt, William, 74, 76–77, 81
Plain of Reeds, 280
Pleiku Air Base, 261, 270
Pope, Major General John, 156
Porter, Rear Admiral David D., 164
Portugal, 107, 110, 138, 146
Price, Major General Sterling, 160
Princeton, Battle of, 91, 296
Protestant Reformation, 47
Prussia, 174, 176, 178, 186, 302
Punjab, 205, 208, 220
Putnam, General Israel, 85
Pylos, 3–4
Pyrenees, 107, 136

Quantrill, William Clarke, 167, 170
Quebec City, 6, 74

Rahman, Abdur, 210
Rall, Colonel Johann, 91
Randolph, George W., 158
Ramadi, 13
Rawdon, Lord Francis, 101
Reade, Captain Thomas, 60
Red Army, 230, 245
Red River Delta, 7–8, 306

Republic of Vietnam. *See* South Vietnam
Res Gestae, 22–23
Richardson, Colonel Robert V., 159–160
Riedesel, Friedrich Alfred Baron von, 96
Roberts, Lord Frederick, 216
Rodrigo, sieges of Ciudad, 126, 131–132
Rogers, Major Robert, 78
Rogers' Rangers, 78, 85
Roman Empire
    economic strength of, 28–29, 34, 44
    operational framework of, 31–40, 43
    strategic framework of, 22–24, 43, 294
    Teutoburg Wald, Battle of, and, 18–22
Roman Republic, 23
Roon, Albrecht von, 186
Rosecrans, General William, 155–156, 297–298
Rovira, Francisco, 129
Royal Navy, 74
Royal Welch Fusiliers, 85
Ruffin, Edmund, 154
Rumsfeld, Donald, 11, 105, 292n5
Russia, 110–112, 131, 174, 195–196, 198, 303
Russian-Turkish War of 1876–1878, 172

Saguntum, Battle of, 124, 127
Saigon, 256, 268, 271
Sakai, General Takashi, 237
Salamanca, Battle of, 132–133, 135
San Sebastian, 137
Sanchez, Don Julian, 128–129, 134
Santocildes, General José, 130–131
Saragossa, sieges of, 118, 121–122
Saratoga, Battle of, 98–100, 296
Schlieffen Plan, 303
Schuyler, General Philip, 87
Second Sino-Japanese War, 5
    Chinese Nationalist Army, 225–227, 229, 243, 245–246
    Chinese Communist guerrillas and, 225, 227, 229, 240–241, 243–246, 248–249, 253
    Eighth Route Army and, 245
    hybrid nature of, 227–228, 253
    Japanese assumptions and, 225–226
    Japanese Imperial Army. *See* Japanese Imperial Army
    lessons learned and, 249–253
    outbreak of, 225
    Soviet deterrence and, 226, 228, 232, 247–248
    strategic framework of, 225–228, 232, 250–251, 305
    warlords and, 244–245
    Wuhan campaign and, 246
    Xuzhou campaign and, 245
Sedan (1870), Battle of, 180–183, 302
Segestes, 36n56
Sepphoris, 35
Seven Years' War. *See* French and Indian War
Seville, 113, 130
Shamyl, Imam, 208
Shansi Province, 241, 245
Sheridan, General Philip Henry, 186
Sherman, General William T., 298–301
Sian Incident, 245
Sidney, Henry, 55–56, 60, 62
Sierra Leone, 209
Sihanouk, Prince Norodom, 258
Sihanoukville, 258, 268, 280
Silveira, General Francisco, 115
Sino-Soviet border conflict of 1969, 266
Sixth Coalition, War of the, 112, 137
Sokoto, 209
Somalia, 209
Souham, General Joseph, 133
Soult, Marshal Nicolas, 115, 122–126, 132–134, 136, 145
South Africa, 214
South China Sea, 258
South Manchurian Railway Company, 234
South Vietnam (Republic of Vietnam), 254, 256, 259–261, 276, 278–279, 284
Soviet Union, 218
    Second Sino-Japanese War and, 225–226, 228, 230, 232, 243, 246, 250
    Vietnam War and, 254, 258, 265–267
Spain, 51, 100, 109, 138, 218, 227
    Elizabeth I and conflict with, 47–48
Sparta, 3–4
Special Forces, U. S., 10–11
Special National Intelligence Estimate (SNIE), 259–261, 264
Special Operations Executive (SOE), 5
Spicheren, Battle of, 180
Spion Kop, Battle of, 217
Stafford, Sir Francis, 63–64
Stark, General John, 78, 85, 96–97

Index

Stockton, Richard, 89
Stokes, Colonel William B., 163
Strasbourg, 183
Stuart, General James E. B., 161, 170
Suchet, Louis Gabriel, 127–128, 132, 136, 139, 144
Sugambri, 31–32
Sukarno, Achmed, 258
Sultan, Tipu, 204
Sumter, Thomas, 158
Sun Tzu, 224,
Sweden, 111, 113
Syme, Ronald, 29, 40
Syria, 35

Tacitus, 21, 26–27, 39–41
Taiwan Straits, 254
Tal Afar, 13
Talavera, Battle of, 124–126, 135
Taliban, 10–11
Tarragona, 127
Tassigny, General Jean de Lattre de, 7
Taylor, General Richard, 160
Te-Huai, Marshal Peng, 266
Tel el Kebir, Battle of, 207
Tet Offensive, 10, 271–272, 284–285
Teutoburg Wald, Battle of, 18–22, 36, 42
Thailand, 258, 272
Thieu, General Nguyen Van, 269
Thirty Years' War, 176
Thucydides, 4, 102–103, 291
Tiberius, Emperor, 22, 28, 32–35, 37, 40, 44, 294
Ticonderoga, Fort, 92, 94–95, 98
Tilsit, Treaty of, 111
Tokyo, 229, 232, 238, 251
Tonkin, Gulf of, 261
Tora Bora, 11
Torres Vedras, Lines of, 125–126
Toulouse, Siege of 1814, 137n78
Trafalgar, Battle of, 109–110, 114
Trenton, Battle of, 91, 296
Tri, General Do Cao, 283, 284
Trochu, General Louis, 183
Trung Viet, 270, 277
Truong, General Ngo Quang, 284
Tyrone's Rebellion. *See* O'Neill's Rebellion

Ugaki, Kazushige, 237
Ulster, 57, 60–62, 65–69, 71

Union counterguerrilla war
 Atlanta campaign and, 299–300
 amnesty and, 169
 Buell Commission and, 162
 Cavalry, 5th Tennessee, and, 163
 code of military conduct and, 166–167
 conventional forces and, 154, 159–162, 168–169
 Lieber Code and, 166–167
 Mississippi Marine Brigade and, 164–165
 noncombatants and, 155–156, 161, 164–168, 170, 299–301
 partisan rangers and, 159–161, 168–169
 psychological stress and, 165–166
 railroads, bridges and telegraph attacks and, 154, 156–157, 162, 165, 299
 rebel irregulars and, 151–152, 154–159, 161–163, 168–170, 297–298
 Reconstruction and, 170
 Richmond, fall of, and, 169
 river guerrillas and, 163–164, 167
 Secessionists and, 155
 special operations and, 162–163
 strategic policy and, 155, 157, 168, 170, 301
 Union Army and, 152, 155, 159, 161–162
 Unionists and, 155, 159–160, 168
 Union Navy and, 164–165
United States, 225, 246, 250
 counterinsurgency and, 11–13, 220
 Department of Defense, 255
 military doctrine and, 11–13, 16, 255–256, 273
 propaganda and, 10
 public opinion and, 255, 281
 resource allocation and, 255
 security challenges and, 255–256
 U. S. Special Forces and, 270–271
United States Army, 230, 263, 274
 Corps,
  XXIV Corps, 273, 282–283
 Divisions,
  1st Cavalry Division, 263, 271
  101st Airborne Division, 274
  9th Infantry Division, 272
  10th Mountain Division, 10
United States Marine Corps, 230, 263, 270, 272–273
 Small Wars Manual and, 273
 III Marine Amphibious Force and, 273

Utai Mountains, 249

Vala, 21n8
Valencia, 121, 132, 136, 143
Van Dorn, General Earl, 160, 297
Varus, Quintilius, 18–22, 27–28, 32, 34–37, 43, 294
Venegas, General Francisco, 130
Vetera, 32
Vicksburg, 99, 297–298
Victor-Perrin, Marshal Claude, 117, 122, 124–125
Vien, General Cao Van, 275–276
Viet Cong (VC), 256, 270, 273, 275–276
   Cambodia, camps in, 258, 281
   force deployment and, 268
   infiltration and, 268, 279
   NVA, integration with, 282
   operations among people and, 257, 272, 278
   recruitment and supply of, 267, 275, 277
   Tet Offensive and, 10, 271
Viet Minh, 7–9, 82, 276, 306
Vietnam, 7–9, 255, 257, 259
Vietnam Project, 265
Vietnam War, 11–12, 104, 146, 220
   air assault concepts and, 274–273
   Army of the Republic of Vietnam. *See* Army of the Republic of Vietnam
   bombing campaign and, 261, 263, 267, 280
   Central Highlands, 256, 260, 262–263, 268–270, 284
   command and control structures and, 273–274
   Communist offensive of 1975 and, 284
   conventional operations and, 257, 268, 270, 273, 279, 283
   Cooper-Church Amendment and, 256, 282–283
   counterinsurgency operations and, 268, 273, 279
   demilitarized zone (DMZ) and, 270, 273
   domino theory and, 258
   Easter Offensive of 1972 and, 270
   historical context of, 257–259
   Ho Chi Minh Trail and, 256, 260, 267, 269, 280, 282–284
   hybrid nature of, 254–257, 260, 263–264
   infiltration and, 256–257, 268, 270n15, 280–281
   intelligence, misreading of, 259–261, 264, 266–268, 276, 284
   interdiction and, 258, 260, 270n15, 288
   lessons learned and, 285–288
   logistics and, 269
   Military Assistance and Advisory Group, 258
   Military Assistance Command-Vietnam (MAC-V), 256
   Nguyen Hue Offensive, 283–284
   noncombatants and, 256–257, 272, 278
   North Vietnamese Army. *See* North Vietnamese Army
   operational level of, 256, 268–272
   riverine forces and, 272–273
   17th parallel and, 257, 269
   sanctuaries and, 257–258, 263, 280–281, 283
   strategic level of, 263–264, 272, 281–283
   tactical level of, 256–257, 268
   unexploded ordnance and, 277
   U. S. ground force deployments, 261–263, 268–269, 281
   U. S. military advisory effort and, 278–279, 287–288
   U. S. military planning and, 256
   Viet Cong insurgency. *See* Viet Cong
Vimeiro, Battle of, 121
Vinicium, Marcus, 33
Vitoria, Battle of, 136–137, 146

Wallace, General William, 291–292
Walt, General Lewis, 273
war
   absolute aims and, 172–173, 176
   annihilation, strategy of, 174, 177, 187
   decisive maneuver warfare and, 176–177, 187, 194
   ends and means and, 187, 292–293, 307
   enemy, knowledge of, 293, 307
   guerrilla warfare and, 208
   hybrid warfare. *See* hybrid warfare
   Kabinettskrieg and, 172, 175–176, 180, 193
   limited war and, 172–173, 176
   mobilization and, 175
   modern warfare and, 173, 303
   nationalism and, 174, 176

noncombatants, 175, 293, 303
nature and conduct of, 172–173,
  192–193
politics and, 175, 196, 307
social complexities of, 173
technology and, 289
total war and, 173–175, 218, 222
Volkskrieg and, 173–175
War of 1859, 172
War of 1812, 206–207
Washington, General George, 78, 85,
  88–89, 93, 296
Waterloo, Battle of, 138
Wehrmacht, 4–5
Weissenburg, Battle of, 180
Wellesley, General Arthur. *See* Wellington,
  Duke of
Wellington, Duke of
  Peninsular War and, 106, 112, 114–117,
    121–128, 130–138, 142–149,
    304
  Second Anglo-Mahratta War and, 204,
    222

West Bank, 15
Westmoreland, General William, 256, 273,
  279
Wilhelm I of Prussia, 187
Willis, Captain Humfrey, 60
Wilson, General James, 300–301
Wittich, Friedrich Wilhelm von, 190
Wolfe, James, 6
Wolseley, Garnet, 202, 207, 209
World War I, 172, 222
  Middle East campaign and, 6–7
World War II, 225, 251, 306–307
  Allied offensives and, 230, 238
  Eastern Front and, 4
  resistance movements and, 5
Wörth, Battle of, 180

Yaginuma, Takeo, 236
Yanagawa, General Heisuke, 237
Yellow Ford, Battle of the, 57
Yorktown, Battle of, 102

Zulus, 209